THE LOVE AFFAIRS OF
MARY QUEEN
OF SCOTS

MARY STUART WHEN SIXTEEN
Painter unknown. Owner, the Duke of Devonshire.
Photo, Hanfstaengl.

THE LOVE AFFAIRS OF
MARY QUEEN
OF SCOTS

A POLITICAL HISTORY

MARTIN HUME

FOREWORD BY
DR. ANNA GROUNDWATER

Racehorse Publishing

CONTENTS

FOREWORD

BY DR. ANNA GROUNDWATER

'ONLY PERSONAL AND PASSING INFATUATION FOR [BOTHWELL] could have blinded so able and ambitious a stateswoman as Mary to the fatal sacrifice she was making in taking him to her arms' (p. 224)

So writes Martin Sharp Hume of Mary's fatal decision in 1567 to marry the forceful earl of Bothwell, a man complicit in the murder of her late husband Darnley. In this, we can see two of Hume's main themes in his enthralling life of Mary, Queen of Scots: her personal attractions, her impressive courage, and her acute political ability set against the greatest flaw that undermined these assets, her proclivity to surrender all sound judgement to sensual passion.

In these pages, Mary is revealed in all her monarchical splendour and human frailty, as Hume paints a rich portrait of a rounded, complex, and compelling personality, whose justifiable ambitions were repeatedly blown apart by falling in love with unsuitable men.

> 'It was almost as if a malison accompanied the matrimonial regards of Mary Stuart. One after the other, her husbands and suitors had died prematurely and unhappily; Francis in early youth, Darnley cruelly murdered, Bothwell a prisoner in exile, Norfolk on the scaffold, and Don John of a broken heart; all dead but Mary...' (p. 302-03)

Mary, he writes, was also unlucky, her political fortunes inextricably intertwined with those of her English counterpart, the wily Elizabeth I, a woman with whom she is inevitably compared:

> 'Mary in most respects possessed a much finer and nobler nature than Elizabeth; she was a woman of higher courage, of greater conviction, more generous, magnanimous, and confiding, and, apart from her incomparably greater beauty and fascination, possessed mental endowments fully equal if not superior to those of the English queen. But whilst the caution and love of mastery of the latter always saved her from her weakness, Mary Stuart possessed no such safeguards, and was periodically swept away, helplessly and irremediably, by the irresistible rush of her purely sexual passion.' (p. 3)

And when it came to the last dangerous diplomatic dance between these two talented queens, Elizabeth, as she almost always did, came off best, Mary kneeling before her executioner at Fotheringhay as the ink dried on Elizabeth's signature of her death warrant.

Hume set out in the early 1900s to write a history of Mary's life that focuses on the political effects of Mary's three doomed marriages, and a multitude of marriage negotiations. He recounts how Mary's first suitor, at the tender age of a few months, was Henry VIII of the 'auld enemy' England on behalf of his infant son, the future Edward VI. Scottish resistance to that proposal triggered the violent Anglo-Scottish wars known as the 'Rough Wooing,' and a series of English invasions only ultimately defeated with French assistance. The 'auld alliance' with France, the country of Mary's mother Marie de Guise, was then further cemented by her daughter Mary's upbringing at the French court, and the proposal of a match with the future French king, Francois II. A glittering future for Mary seemed assured, and duly she became queen of France as well as that of Scotland in 1559. But then the bad luck, that Hume shows dogging Mary throughout her life, brought a swift end to that reign as Francois succumbed to illness in 1560. Mary Queen of Scots was back on the marriage market.

At first it was the Catholic crowned heads of Europe that sought to make their diplomatic best of Mary's widowhood, and the opportunity this gave them to recalibrate the power balance in the confusion of the post-Reformation. But proposals foundered in the face of her ex-mother-in-law Catherine de Medici's refusal to countenance strengthening Mary's position. With no marriage imminent, Mary returned somewhat slowly to her homeland Scotland, and her neglected royal duties there.

At this point Hume shows how her overriding ambition became abundantly clear, and that was the greatest royal prize she hoped to secure, that of the crown of England. Mary's claims to the English succession were through her grandmother Margaret Tudor, Henry VIII's sister. She was, as Home writes, 'ready to plot and plan for carrying out, at any cost of life and suffering, the dream that animated her from her girlhood to her death.' (p. 278) However Elizabeth was equal to this challenge. Whichever marriage scenario Mary considered next was to be shaped by her English ambition, and Elizabeth's attempts to frustrate it since such an acknowledgement would endanger Elizabeth's own throne. From then on, Elizabeth and her counsellor Cecil schemed to control Mary's marital future—and their ploy was to offer her Elizabeth's own favourite, Robert Dudley, earl of Leicester.

Stung by this insult, Mary began to look elsewhere, her eye falling on her cousin, the good-looking Henry, Lord Darnley. On paper he was a good choice, but Mary's infatuation with him blinded her to his obvious deficiencies (this 'tippling young booby of a consort' [p. 186]), something that she would speedily regret. At the same time, Hume notes how Mary's 'natural sensuousness' (p. 92) combined with her courtly flirtations appeared jarring for some in newly Protestant Scotland and left her open to censure. The fall-out of the disastrous Darnley marriage, and a whirlwind of accusation after his murder left Mary tainted and vulnerable, desperately in need of the good judgement she had exercised in the earlier years of her reign.

Unfortunately for her, the 'rough and hirsute, shaggy and stern, the strong man' (p. 184) Bothwell seemed to offer some protection and in unseemly haste she rushed again into marriage. Bothwell's own ambitions then became clear, alienating those nobles who might have supported the couple, and bringing about Mary's downfall, imprisonment, and ultimately her forced abdication. A year on, she had fled, and was at Elizabeth's mercy in England. Nineteen years later, after successive failed plots to marry Mary off to a good Catholic, and to secure a Catholic queen on the Protestant Elizabeth's throne, Mary was dead.

Throughout all Mary's fore-shortened life, Hume demonstrates how her political fortunes were also dominated by the wider picture of a fractured Europe beset by religious differences between Catholics and Protestants, and as France and Spain vied for dominance. France was in the throes of decades of religious wars. Philip II of Spain was attempting to regain control over the crown of England, lost on the death of his wife Mary Tudor. In all this Mary Queen of Scots was but a pawn in a game played by more powerful monarchs.

Hume does this by using his extensive knowledge of primary sources in the archives of England and Spain, and his own background as editor of the *Foreign State Papers relating to Spain* in the time of Elizabeth. He makes enthralling use as well of a plethora of English papers and correspondence, of the canny Cecil, of Mary and Elizabeth's own letters, and those of their enemies. And in his hands, these dusty archives come alive, the dialogues between the protagonists making you feel as if you too were sat at the Spanish ambassador's candle-lit table as he dined with Mary's negotiator William Maitland of Lethington. Hume himself had Spanish connections, inheriting a Spanish fortune that enabled him to focus on research and writing. One of his first and most popular books was on Elizabeth, drawing on similar material that he would use for Mary. And it is this European background that perhaps makes Hume's *Mary* different from many others, offering much more persuasive context for her ultimate failure. That, and his penmanship, as he narrates one of the most controversial and contested lives of a Scottish monarch in all its technicolour glamour and tragedy.

Mary continues to fascinate us, the drama of her life played out again and again in historical fiction and on stage and screen. As I write, in the last year, her life has been the subject of one festival, one dark comedy at the Edinburgh Fringe, one dramatic production, one major feature film, and a Netflix series, *Reign*. Hume's *Mary* gives us the even more dramatic background on which these all draw.

PREFACE

THE SCIENCE OF HISTORICAL WRITING HAS NEVER ENTIRELY shaken itself free from the vices of its origin. The heroic ballad, hyperbolically exalting the central figure whose doughty deeds it sang, was necessarily the work of a whole-souled admirer of its subject: the kingly chronicle that succeeded it was written, either by a court scribe in the pay of the potentate whose reign it recorded, or by a dependant of the victorious rival who had deposed him. The natural result was that the conspicuous personages of history were usually represented as paragons of goodness and wisdom, or as monsters of crime and folly. They were assumed to have created the circumstances by which they were surrounded, and to be swayed in their policy with regard to them, only by their own innate virtue or viciousness. They were, indeed, regarded, not so much as human beings, subject to the ordinary mixed motives and impulses that rule all men, as originating forces, dominated either by beneficent or malefic instincts. When once they were classed, either amongst the sheep or the goats, there was the end of it, and there was no necessity to seek any further to find the mainspring of all the actions of their lives.

Now that the opening of national archives and the extensive reproduction of historical documents have rendered it possible, and indeed necessary, to supplement the old-fashioned history, taking a broad and superficial view of events, by more intimate studies of the real motives and influences of political action, the same tendency is observable. For the sake of convenience the episodical histories, which of late years have multiplied so rapidly, have usually assumed a biographical form; a series of events being grouped around the prominent figures, in order that the human interest of the historical narrative may be increased. The result, in many cases, is excellent, though it sometimes happens that the author is tempted to shut out from his purview all political factors other than his own subject; but the great drawback to the grouping of historical incidents around a prominent actor in the events related is, that the more interesting the personality the more centralised in his character the history becomes, whilst the events themselves and the concurrent influences upon them are proportionately dwarfed and thrown out of perspective. Studies dealing with events, written round such fascinating individualities, in a great number of cases, indeed, become passionate attacks upon, or vindications of, the characters of the principal persons, and it is assumed that if the latter can be proved either to have been very good or very bad, the influence they exerted upon their times needs no further explanation.

The only excuse that can be advanced for the production of a new book on Mary Stuart is that her supremely interesting personality has so frequently led her historians into the by-path of inquiry as to her virtue or vice, as to have obscured, to some extent, the reasons for her disastrous political failure; which, as it seems to me, did not spring from her goodness or badness as a woman, but from certain human weaknesses of character, quite compatible with general goodness and wisdom or with the reverse, but which fatally handicapped her as against antagonists who are less subject to such weakness.

It is a curious consideration that the sixteenth century was sharply divided into two well-marked periods, the virile first half, when Charles V, Henry VIII, and Francis I—three *men* if ever such existed—made circumstances and originated policies; and the feminine latter half, when Elizabeth Tudor, Mary Stuart, Catharine de Medici, and the cautious, timid, narrow, almost womanish Philip II had to deal, as best they could, according to their lights, with the circumstances and problems that had been set for them by others. The whole of the policy of these four most prominent personages of their time was consistently feminine, if not feline. The chicane of political courtship and marriage proceeded without interruption for many years as a main branch of European diplomacy. If a rival was becoming too strong, his neighbours did not attempt to beat him in the field, but developed a languishing desire to marry another rival, who was dropped as soon as the object of the wooing was served. With bewildering mutations in the persons of her suitors, Elizabeth managed to keep the ball rolling until she could snap her aged fingers at the world, and boasted that, after all, she died a virgin; whilst Catharine practically ruled France for twenty years by her dexterous manipulation of the matrimonial affairs of her children.

It was Mary Stuart's misfortune, as it was many years later that of her unhappy niece Arabella, that she thought she was capable of playing Elizabeth's cunning game without Elizabeth's peculiar advantages; and the disaster that fell upon her cause was the direct result of this mistake. An attempt is made in this book to tell, at length, the story of the marriage intrigues by which Mary Stuart hoped to compass her great ambition. The question of how good, or how bad, she was as a woman, has been kept as much as possible in the background. It is specially as a politician that I have wished to regard her, for she represented in her own person the principle which, if she had succeeded, would have destroyed the Reformation, and established the supremacy of Spanish Catholicism in Europe. However wicked she might have been personally, that would not have altered the result, if the ends she sought in her marriages had been attained. Murder was at the time almost as legitimate an instrument of policy as matrimony, and a generation that revered Catharine de Medici after St. Bartholomew, that applauded Philip II. for the execution of Montigny, and lauded Alba to the skies; a generation that regarded with approval the religious martyrdoms under Mary Tudor and Elizabeth, would not have turned against Mary Stuart, if her diplomacy had been successful. Every one in Scotland and out of it knew that the men who persecuted her were much more guilty of the murder of Darnley than she was; and yet they were exalted and honoured until their political enemies wrought vengeance upon them.

The recent publication in full of the *Scottish State Papers* relating to Mary in Mr. Bain's *Calendars*; the *Hatfield Papers*, printed by the Historical Manuscripts Commission; and the textual translations of the *Spanish State*

Papers of the period, produced by His Majesty's Government under my own editorship, have enabled me to supplement other known sources of information with many details and extracts from documents which have not hitherto been quoted at length. In a book such as this, abounding in controversial points, many of my conclusions will doubtless be challenged; but I would wish to assure my readers, that though I have nothing extenuated, I have nought set down in malice, my one object being to elucidate the influence exercised, in the most critical period of modern history, by the management of her Love Affairs by the most pathetically interesting woman in the annals of our country.

MARTIN HUME.

LONDON, *September* 1903.

LIST OF ILLUSTRATIONS

I

INTRODUCTORY

New problems created by the Reformation—Readjustment of European power—Personal influence in politics—Personal characteristics of Mary Stuart—Their effect upon her political actions—Her complicity in Darnley's murder of secondary importance politically—The struggle between England and France to control Scottish policy—Death of James V—Birth of Mary, 8th December 1542—Attempts of Henry VIII to obtain possession of the infant—Her proposed marriage with Edward, Prince of Wales—Arran and England—Sadlier's description of the infant Mary—Falsity of Mary of Guise and Arran—The treaty between England and Scotland for Mary's marriage—Mary crowned—Henry VIII betrayed—Lennox sides with England—Treaty signed between Scotland and France—Mary to marry the Dauphin Francis—England at war with Scotland—Intrigues to capture Mary—She is sent to France, August 1548.

WHEN IN THE GREAT HALL AT WORMS, ON THAT EVER-MEMORABLE April day in 1521, before the panic-stricken princes, Luther insolently flung at the Emperor his defiance of the mediæval Church, the crash, though all unheard by the ears of men, shook to their base the rotting foundations upon which for hundreds of years the institutions of Europe had rested. The sixteenth century thenceforward was a period of disintegration and reconstruction, in which fresh lines of cleavage between old political associates were opened, new affinities were formed, and the international balance readjusted. Hopes, aims, and fears before unknown; ambition, greed, envy, and defiance were to mingle and divide in the bubbling cauldron of change, with infinite perturbation and distress, for many a year, before the atoms cooled and coalesced into the form which modern Europe took. This process of transformation from mediævalism to the systems which have developed into our own gives to the study of sixteenth-century history a fascination and importance possessed by that of no other modern period; and justifies the minute consideration of every influence which left its mark upon the events of the time.

Although I am not inclined to exaggerate the power exercised over the development of peoples by the mere personality of the prominent actors in the great drama of national progress, it would be idle to deny that the peculiar characters of the high personages who directed policies in the sixteenth century had a very considerable bearing upon the final result of the long struggle. The cold-blooded, cautious suspicion which dictated the system of Philip II hampered his action and fatally handicapped his cause. Whilst he was pondering and seeking compromising pledges, binding everybody but himself, others were taking the inevitable risks and acting. It is almost platitudinous to say, that if Philip had not been so desperately anxious to 'mak siccar' before he moved, the civilisation of Europe would have developed upon lines quite different from those now followed. Again, if Catharine de Medici had possessed a tithe of her Spanish son-in-law's conscientious steadfastness, or any religious conviction at all; had Charles IX and Henry III been decent persons, or the Guise ambition less unscrupulous, France might have been spared its devastating civil wars, and religious liberty have been established as a principle in a country emancipated from Rome. Or if Elizabeth Tudor had not been from the circumstances of her birth inextricably bound up with the antipapal party in Europe, England would probably have reverted to Catholicism. More than once Elizabeth was within an ace of making terms with the enemy at her gates, and entering the inner ring of old royalties, whom she alternately flattered and defied, and always envied. But the peculiarity of her parents' position, her own imperious hatred of submission, and the maritime enterprise of her people, always held her on the brink, and she never took the plunge. Elsewhere I have attempted to describe how Elizabeth's personal vanity and love of domination, counteracting each other, kept her for a lifetime in the matrimonial balance, and how her loudly trumpeted celibacy, combined with avidity for male admiration, were dexterously utilised for the national advantage by the Queen and her sagacious minister, though with frequent misgivings and apprehension at treading so slippery a declivity. But if Elizabeth by her long marriage juggle, and by the fortuitous adjustment of her qualities, contributed powerfully to keep England Protestant and France wavering; secured for the critical years the inactivity of Spain, the resistance of Protestant Holland, and the freedom of English navigation, her rival Mary Stuart was a hardly less powerful factor in the triumph of England, by reason of certain defects in her character, the consequences of which will be dealt with at length in this book.

Mary in most respects possessed a much finer and nobler nature than Elizabeth; she was a woman of higher courage, of greater conviction, more generous, magnanimous, and confiding, and, apart from her incomparably greater beauty and fascination, possessed mental endowments fully equal if not superior to those of the English queen. But whilst the caution and love of mastery of the latter always at the critical moment saved her from her weakness, Mary Stuart possessed no such safeguards, and was periodically swept away, helplessly and irremediably, by the irresistible rush of her purely sexual passion.

Nearly every writer who has dealt at length with the career of the most beautiful and unhappy of queens has been drawn into the vortex of controversy as to the genuineness or otherwise of the Casket Letters: and other perhaps more important points of Mary's life have been to some extent neglected or overshadowed by this interesting problem. Probably everything that can be said has been said on this point, usually with a partisan violence on both sides which has done much to obscure the real issue. Mr. Andrew Lang has recently summed up with great acumen and impartiality the whole evidence for and against the Queen, on a close examination of the text of the letters themselves; and the fact of the subject having been treated so fairly and dispassionately by him from his own point of view, clears the ground somewhat for an equally impartial consideration of the general aspect of Mary Stuart's character and actions, especially with regard to the influence exercised upon the latter by her lack of control in her various love affairs. We shall see that the deplorable errors and follies that led her downward from freedom to lifelong imprisonment, from happiness to misery, from a throne to a scaffold; that warped her goodness, made her a helpless plaything for her cunning enemies, and ruined the religious cause she loved better than her life, were the outcome, not of deliberate wickedness, or even of habitual political unwisdom, but of fits of undisciplined sexual passion, amounting in certain instances to temporary mania, combined with the unquenchable ambition inherited from her mother's house. Beauty and other feminine perfections she must needs have possessed—a lovely hand, a sweet voice, caressing grace and ready tears, amongst others—for, after allowing for all the courtly flattery of a generation that compared Elizabeth's painted mask at sixty to the face of an angel, Ronsard's tender lays and Brantome's enthusiastic praise of the Scottish queen convince us, if we had no other proof, as we have hundreds, that many men upon whom she looked were dazzled and blinded by her peculiar personality. But, withal, a contemplation of her known authentic portraits, even those taken in the best years of her youth and happiness, does not carry conviction that her physical beauty alone can have been the cause of the extraordinary influence she exercised over the men who came within the sphere of her attraction. The subtle quality we vaguely call fascination must have been hers to an extraordinary degree to reinforce the charms of the long, fair, oval face, the narrow, side-glancing eyes, and the straight, lengthy Greek nose; the fascination must have been there, though the painters merely hint it, that sets men's hearts aflame, and sends the hot blood surging up to blind the judgment. And fascination such as this, and all men know it, let them feign ignorance as they may, is but the involuntary natural manifestation of the character within, transcending speech and leaping over barriers, appealing alone to hearts attuned, and gathering potency itself from the answer flashed back unwittingly by those who respond to its sensuous message.

As was the case with those of Elizabeth, what we call, for want of a better name, the love affairs of Mary Stuart were in most cases purely political,

and intended by those who promoted them to serve interests apart from the happiness of the persons principally concerned. It is intended in the present book to give a brief review of the various proposals made for marriage with the Queen of Scots, in order to explain their bearing upon the great political issues of the time, and to show how in certain cases where Mary's imagination was stirred her political judgment, conspicuous in the other cases, deserted her, and her temporary weakness led her and her cause to ruin, and powerfully aided the policy of Elizabeth.

It was a game so skilfully played by those who took the leading part in it, the broad issues were so tremendous, the stakes of the players themselves so important to them personally, that no points could be lost with impunity; and we shall be able to observe that Mary Stuart failed because she made more mistakes than her adversaries, mistakes, it is true, often arising out of her superior magnanimity and her stronger trust in the honour and honesty of others. This was of itself a weakness at a time when the falsity of politicians had been elevated to a fine art; and her own early lessons must have taught her that dissimulation was the favourite weapon of contemporary statesmen, and more especially of the school to which her instructors belonged. But when to this weakness was added the belief on her part that she could use matrimonial intrigue to forward her ends in the same way that Elizabeth did, notwithstanding the great difference in their characters, the inevitability of her ruinous failure was manifest.

Whether she was actually privy to the murder of Darnley or not does not vitally affect the main issue. Unless we are content to believe that the whole of the contents of the Casket were forged, which I most emphatically am not, however much certain of the papers may have been doctored, we must come to the conclusion that her infatuation for the person of Bothwell began before her husband's death, as we know it continued after it, notwithstanding the euphemistic explanations at a subsequent period, when the glamour had worn off her temporary obsession; and in that case her actual complicity or otherwise in the murder of her consort would probably have made no great difference in the march of events. Darnley, with his weakness, his vices, and his follies, surrounded by nobles who hated and were jealous of him, at issue with his wife whom he had disgusted, and scorned by a people whom he had offended by his presumption, was condemned in any case to disappear, as Murray, Lennox, and Morton subsequently disappeared, with much less reason against them than he had. It was not so much Darnley's death and the assumed complicity of his wife in his murder that led Mary along the first steps on the *via dolorosa* of Carbery, Loch Leven, Carlisle, and Fotheringay, as the anger of her envious, discontented nobles, and the indignation of Murray, that the Queen should endure, even if she did not seek, the adulterous embraces of a Scotsman of no better rank than their own. The timely murder of Darnley was only an added opprobrium and ignominy to the main fact. The value of human life, as against the assumed welfare of the State or the sovereign, was so small in the sixteenth century, in comparison with that which we attach to it to-day, that Mary might well have been willing to wink at the sacrifice of her troublesome consort without incurring the penalty of being regarded as a monster of wickedness, as she would be according to the ethics of our own times. The violent removal of obnoxious personages was a recognised political instrument of the sixteenth century, and the act was easily condoned for the sake of the result. Philip II regarded himself, and was regarded by his people, as a saint, notwithstanding the sacrifice of Montigny, the Prince of Orange, and many other human obstacles in the path of his policy. Catharine de Medici lived revered, and died in the odour of sanctity, in spite of St. Bartholomew and poisonings innumerable. The death of Amy Robsart of Throckmorton, and a host of other suspected victims, did not suffice to make Leicester unpopular; and the monk Clement was hailed by the clerical party throughout Europe as a hero for killing Henry III, just as the latter was welcomed with open arms by the Huguenots after he had gloated over the murder of Guise. Nay, Mary Stuart herself, when Murray fell before Hamilton's harquebus, had nothing but sweet words and rewards for the assassin of her brother, and not one thought the worse of her for that. It is therefore easy to overrate the political importance of Mary's guilt or innocence in Darnley's murder, and the question has concentrated the attention of investigators, not really so much on account of its influence upon historical events, which was purposely exaggerated at the time and since, as because it decides to a large extent whether the Queen of Scots is to be regarded personally as a saint cruelly sacrificed or as a sinner rightly punished; and provides a ground whereupon sentimental polemics of opposite views may disport and attack each other's creeds.

An attempt will therefore be made in this book to trace the influence aimed at or exercised upon the great events of the century of the Reformation by the various matrimonial affairs of Mary Stuart, and by her personal idiosyncrasy in connection with them, whilst avoiding the religious or romantic bias that has so often led the Queen's biographers to tell only that part of the story that supports their particular views regarding her goodness or badness as a woman according to the code of the present century; an aspect of her life which is quite secondary in real historical importance, however attractive it may be as a subject for abstract speculation.

In the secular struggle of the house of Aragon and its successor the Emperor Charles V with France for the domination of Italy, the only effectual guarantee against the danger of England's actively throwing in her lot with her traditional friend the possessor of Spain and Flanders and attacking the northern coasts of France whilst the latter power had its forces occupied in the south, was for the King of France to keep a tight hold of his alliance with Scotland, and so to control the policy of the Scots as to enable him at any time to produce a diversion on the Border that should keep England too busy to trouble her southern neighbour, or interfere in favour of the Emperor when he was at war with his rival. The existence of the Scottish 'back door' to England, with an ever-probable enemy on the other side of it, had thus for centuries been a check on English influence and power, and a humiliation to English kings in their antagonism with their nearest Continental neighbour. But with the spread of Lutheranism in Germany, and Henry VIII's defiance of the papacy, the Catholic powers, drawn together by an instinctive movement of self-preservation in face of a common danger, found a fresh bond of union in their orthodoxy, which, to some extent, superseded their old antagonistic ambitions. In these circumstances the policy of English statesmen, which aimed at the control of Scottish foreign relations to the exclusion of French influence, became, not as it had been for centuries, simply a desirable object to be patiently striven for in season and out of season, but an imperative need, in order to preserve

England's independence; for if Henry lost the power of balancing one of the great Catholic sovereigns against the other, he had no longer the means of shutting the Scottish back door, and might at any time be attacked, front and rear, to his inevitable destruction.

A series of royal minorities and consequent regencies had weakened the power of the sovereign in Scotland almost to extinction, and the lawless, jealous, semi-independent nobles practically monopolised the armed force of the country. Their poverty and greed made them particularly susceptible to such influence as Henry VIII could wield, and from the early days of his defection from Rome *divide et impera* became the active policy of the English king in his nephew's realm. By that course alone could he hope for safety for his own country. At a time when (1542) the rival ambitions of Francis and the Emperor in Italy still caused their mundane antagonism to be stronger than their religious affinity, and both had need of England, the opportunity for Henry to prevail in Scotland came. He had chosen to side with Charles in the coming war, but before openly showing his hand he set about disabling the Scots for harm whilst Francis was too busy to defend them. A pretext for war was always easy to find by the wolf against the lamb, and on the plea that James V was mustering his forces on the Border, the strife began. James was surrounded by traitors, for English money and religious dissension had profoundly divided the Scottish gentry. Cardinal Beaton, the King's principal adviser, was intensely unpopular, the powerful Douglas family was disaffected or exiled, and the forces with which James rashly attempted to raid the western English marches, though large, were wild and undisciplined. The disgraceful rout of the Scots at Solway Moss (24th November 1542) was a natural result, and sent James, heartbroken, flying to Tantallon; thence to Edinburgh to meet his divided Council, and then across the Forth to Falkland to die.

Only four years and a half before this Mary of Guise, a worthy daughter of that branch of the house of Lorraine that had settled in France, had married James as his second wife. Two sons had been born to them and had died in infancy. The gossips were agog for weeks before the battle with premature news of the birth of another child; and whilst the Scottish king lay sick unto death, there came to him tidings that, on the 8th December 1542, at Linlithgow, a girl-child had been born to him, an heiress to his ancient crown and to the troubles that had overwhelmed her father. The babe was said to be premature, a very weak child and not like to live,'[1] but in any case her coming brought no solace to James. He had been a gallant lover and faithless; Mary of Lorraine had been but a passing fancy, and was already supplanted in his heart; a child by her, and especially a girl, touched him less than one by his mistress at Tantallon would have done; and he heard the news with his prophetic presage of evil which has passed into common speech. 'The devil go with it. It will end as it began: it came with a woman and it will end in a woman';[2] a prediction not fulfilled by facts. The King spoke little afterwards, as Pitscottie tells us, but turned his back to the lords, and his face to the wall'; and when his hour had come, looked up and beheld all his nobles about him, and gave a little smile of laughter, then kissed his hand,' and so passed; leaving the week-old Mary Stuart queen of the troubled realm. When James's strength and speech were ebbing, the Cardinal held to his dying eyes a scrap of paper for his assent. It purported to be a will leaving Beaton regent, jointly with other nobles of his choice—Arran, Murray, Argyle, and Huntly—but was afterwards asserted by Arran to be a forgery, and the arrangement was upset after a few days' trial and a violent scene between the Cardinal and Arran, who, as head of the Hamiltons, claimed to be next heir to the crown.

In the meanwhile Henry of England was busy. Some of the principal nobles and gentlemen of Scotland had been taken prisoners at the Solway fight, and carried south in Henry's power. They were plied with arguments to show how patriotic and beneficial it would be to seize the opportunity of uniting England and Scotland by a marriage between the Prince of Wales and the baby Queen. They agreed with alacrity, and together with Bothwell and Angus, both English partisans in exile, signed a request to Henry, 'to take into his hands the young daughter of Scotland and the whole realm, with promise to serve him to that intent.'[3] But besides this undertaking, ten of the prisoners,[4] stalwarts for England all of them or enemies of Arran, signed a secret pact binding themselves to recognise Henry as King of Scotland in case of the Queen's death, to the exclusion of the Hamiltons. On this undertaking the whole of the prisoners went north, to carry out the policy, but before they could enter Scotland news came that Arran had been made sole protector, and that a marriage was already being discussed in Edinburgh between his son and heir and Mary Stuart, 'whom they now call princess.' This was rightly looked upon as a blow at the English plans. It was obvious that if the news was true the prisoners could not openly advocate their policy at Arran's court until they knew how the land lay, and proposals were discussed for the violent seizure of Mary and the fortresses, for the removal of Beaton and Arran, and for the assumption of power by the English faction. These desperate counsels were overruled, and the returning prisoners undertook to compass Henry's design by more peaceful means, though with but small intention apparently of fulfilling their pledges. Already divisions were occurring in Scotland itself. Arran was at issue with the Cardinal, and suspicious of the French relatives of the Queen-Mother, the Duke of Guise, her father, being reported to be on the point of sailing for the purpose of seizing Dunbar and other strongholds. So even Arran began to chant to the English tune. He was reported to Henry as being 'a great favourer of the Scriptures, and a man of very good conscience'; 'a sober man, coveting no great things of the world,' and so on. Arran himself wrote to Lord Lisle (Dudley) that he 'intended to reform the state of the Kirk.' The returning Anglophil exile, Sir George Douglas, was received by him with effusion; and in spite of Beaton's protest, Douglas and his brother, the Earl of Angus, were restored to their lands and station (January 1543).

The effect of the Douglas influence was soon seen. Before the end of January Arran told Sir George, that if he were only sure of peace with England he would lay hands on the Cardinal, and reform the Church of Scotland, as Henry had done in England.[5] The very next day (27th January) the Cardinal was arrested in the Council Chamber, and borne off amidst the shrieks of the Queen-Dowager, who had risen from her sick-bed at Linlithgow to attend the council. It was a strong measure, but Arran was not a strong man, and stood aghast at the effect of his own action. No priest in Edinburgh would say Mass, nor christen children, nor bury the dead. Argyle, Murray, Huntly, and the Catholic lords demanded the prelate's liberation, and threatened violence if their demand was not complied with.

All this drove the overweighted Arran more and more into the arms of the Douglases and England. He busily promoted the circulation of the Scriptures in English, professed to fall into the English plans for the marriage of Mary, arranged a three months' truce to afford time for diplomatic action, and summoned a parliament at Edinburgh which should set the seal on the Anglicisation of Scotland and formally restore the lands of the Douglases. But Henry VIII, impatient and imperious though he was, was not allowed to have all his own way. The Scottish returning nobles, now that they were in their own country and no longer prisoners, were less compliant than before; and French intrigue was busy, for Francis I could not afford to let Scotland go without a struggle before Henry declared war against him. Hollow negotiations for the marriage of Princess Mary Tudor and the Duke of Orleans were kept up acrimoniously in England, but they deceived nobody; and though Guise himself still lingered in France, Henry was in a fever of apprehension when he heard that a French councillor, Cheman, was being sent to direct the Scottish Council pending the arrival of the Duke, and that Captain L'Orges (Montgomerie) was to accompany him 'in case of a ruffle.' Worst of all news came that the young Earl of Lennox, a Gallicised Scotsman, handsome and popular, and heir to the Scottish crown failing Arran, whom the French regarded as illegitimate, was also on his way to Scotland to marry the Queen-Mother and assert his heirship.[6]

Henry's great anxiety was to obtain possession of the baby Queen Mary at once, in accordance with the promises made by the Scottish prisoners before they left England; and to counteract Scottish opposition and French influence, Sir Ralph Sadlier was sent to Scotland. He was a graphic letter-writer as well as a skilled diplomatist, and has left us precious material for history, but he was handicapped by finding on his arrival at Edinburgh that the parliament had been prorogued the day before, after having adopted a resolution authorising ambassadors to proceed to England, but stipulating that Mary Stuart should remain in Scotland until she had completed her tenth year. It was, they said, 'an ryte hie and ryte grete inconvenient to the realme of Scotland to grant thareto (*i.e.* to Henry's demand for the immediate surrender of Mary) for sic reasons and causis as the imbassadours hes hard declarit by the Counsale of Scotland, and as they can schew particular-lie themselves,' and they decided that, 'as for the keping of our said soverane ladyis personne within the realme . . . that her personne be kepit and nuirst principallie be hir moder, and four lordis of the realme that or lest suspect and chosen thereto."[7] At the same time a rival parliament of Beaton's friends had met at Perth, demanding the Cardinal's release, the suppression of the New Testament in the vernacular, and the appointment of the persons to proceed to England as ambassadors; but on Arran's summons the lords who had adopted this course afterwards attended the Edinburgh parliament and agreed to its decisions.[8]

Sadlier was made much of by Arran, but the latter, watched by jealous rivals, dared not modify the resolution to keep Mary in Scotland. Sir George Douglas and his brother Angus (Henry's brother-in-law) did their best: the former said that he had not slept three hours any night for six weeks, but even he repudiated any positive promise to deliver Mary to the English at once, 'and they that made such promises are not able to perform them. For surely, quoth he, the noblemen will not agree to have her out of the realm, because she is their mistress.' Douglas, indeed, was rather indignant that Henry should expect so much at once. Had he not, he asked Sadlier, already worked wonders in the time, worming himself into Arran's confidence, causing the seizure of the Cardinal, and turning all Scotland away from France and towards England? But, he said, affairs must not be pushed too hastily, or all would be spoilt. Give him time, he pleaded, and the King of England should govern Scotland; but if it were tried now, 'there is not so little a boy but he will hurl stones against it, and the wives will handle their distaffs, and the commons universally will rather die in it: yea, and many noblemen and all the clergy be fully against it.' Sadlier and his master were far from contented with this, and urged the forcible abduction of Mary; but this again and again was declared to be impossible of execution, such were the precautions taken for her protection.

On the 22nd March (1543) Sadlier had his first interview at Linlithgow with Mary of Guise, the Queen-Mother, who on this occasion showed herself as subtle and false as behoved to be a daughter of her house. There was nothing she desired more, she professed, than the union of England and Scotland by her child's marriage with Edward, and she would be guided by Henry alone in all things. But privately she warned Sadlier against Arran.

He had himself told her that his arrangements with Henry were all pretence, and that they would keep Mary in Scotland until Henry died, when they could 'so handle matters that the contract should serve no purpose.' Arran, she knew, meant to marry the child to his own son, and the only way was for some plan to be devised by which Mary might be carried to England. 'If your Majesty stand not fast on that point the marriage will never take place.' She said that she herself was in danger if Arran learnt that she had told this secret to Sadlier, and she would still continue to feign opposition to the English marriage. But she rather incautiously showed her hand by suggesting that the Cardinal, if he were released, would side with England. This was too much for Sadlier, who gruffly rejoined that 'the Cardinal would do more hurt than good, for he had no affection towards England.' She indignantly denied the current rumours that she was to marry the Earl of Lennox. She had been a king's wife, she said, and her heart was too high to look any lower. Her hatred and fear of Arran blazed out again and again. Would that her child were in Henry's hands, or anywhere, rather than at the mercy of the next heir to her throne. 'And he (Arran) said, quoth she, that the child was not like to live, but you shall see whether he saith true or not, and therewith she caused me to go with her to the chamber where the child was, and shewed her unto me, and also caused the nurse to unwrap her out of her clothes that I might see her naked. I assure your Majesty, it is as goodly a child as I have seen of her age, and as like to live, with the Grace of God.' And so, at the age of four months, Mary Stuart made her first conquest.

Hardly was Sadlier out of earshot when Mary of Guise tearfully prayed Sir George Douglas to help her in preventing her child from being carried to England. Well might Sadlier write to his King, as he did on the next day, that there was 'some jugglery here,' which he would try to fathom. Arran, when sounded, vehemently protested his faithfulness towards England, and his approval of the marriage. He cared, he said, nothing for France, so long as he had Henry's friendship, and the Cardinal was in safe keeping.[9] Besides, he protested, if he had been so minded he might easily have passed in parliament a resolution to marry Mary to his son. No man would have said him nay, and he was aggrieved that Henry should doubt him, for he had had 'mickle cumber among the Kirk men for his sake.' Even Sadlier

believed that Arran would if he were able adopt the reformed doctrines officially in Scotland. But for all his efforts the English agent could make no way
with Scots, even with Angus and his brother Douglas, towards the abduction and delivery of Mary to the keeping of her great-uncle Henry, who
thereupon began to threaten an attack by arms, unless the promises of the
Scottish nobles were kept. Henry, indeed, with less than his usual foresight,
was inclined to believe the Queen-Mother's professions rather than those
of his own friends the Douglases; and the practical release of Beaton, and
Huntly's suggestion to remove Mary and her mother to Stirling, aroused his
ire against Arran to the highest pitch, notwithstanding the Regent's canting
professions of Protestantism and demands for Testaments.

Arran swore most solemnly to Sadlier that the Queen-Mother was a
true Frenchwoman, and that she had belied him in her attempt to injure
him in Henry's eyes. If he had desired to marry Mary to his son, he said,
not a nobleman in Scotland would have opposed him. Indeed, at one time
he had had such an idea, but the return of the prisoners from England with
the offer of the marriage with Edward had caused him to change his mind.
Some days afterwards the Queen-Dowager had her turn with Sadlier, and
declaimed just as loudly against the falsity of Arran as the latter had against
her. He had told her, she said, that he would rather die than deliver Mary to
the English. He was just fooling the King of England for his own ends, and
she it was who alone desired the marriage and upbringing of her child in
England. 'And greatly she feared the surety of the child (in Scotland), for she
heard so many tales that the governor would convey her to a strong house
of his own, where she should be altogether in his hands.' 'So that I perceive,'
continues Sadlier, 'she is in fear of her destruction, and I therefore wished
her in England, which the Queen also wished for her part, saying that she
would then be in her friends' hands out of all danger.'

Nothing can be more certain than that it was furthest from the Queen-
Mother's design to hand her child over to England. She was an astute
stateswoman, and in constant communication with her father, uncle, and
brothers, whose interests were largely concerned in the maintenance of
French influence and Catholicism in Scotland; and the education of Mary
in the schismatical court of Henry would have been a deathblow to their

hopes in that respect. It is clear to see that her attempts to draw Henry into a pointblank demand for the immediate surrender of Mary, which she knew that Arran and the lords dared not grant, in the face of the Church, the Catholic nobles, and the people, were intended to precipitate a rupture which should give a pretext for French intervention, and perhaps prevent Henry from aiding the Emperor in the coming campaign. On the other hand, Henry's best friends, such as the Douglases, Glencairn, Maxwell, and others, could only counsel prudence and patience. The Regent Arran, they said, feared that if Mary were sent to England 'she would never die,' or rather that if she did another child would be substituted for her, so that, in any case, Henry might be master of Scotland. If, said Maxwell, Henry was not content to let Mary remain in Scotland for the present, then he must come and take her by force. 'By God's body,' quoth he, 'if his Majesty will prosecute it, there is no doubt but that he shall obtain it, for the realm is not able to withstand his power.' In vain Sadlier reproached the Scottish ex-prisoners for their failure to keep their promise. They could not, they said, go against all the realm; and their countrymen were determined not to let their Queen go. In the meanwhile the Cardinal was set free, and Lennox had without opposition landed in Scotland, with gold and Frenchmen, and held his strong castle of Dumbarton. Rumours came that they, with their Scottish sympathisers, would attempt the seizure of the infant, and it was clear that if Arran adhered to their party the English cause in Scotland was lost. Henry urged the removal of the child to Edinburgh Castle, but that was too near England to suit Arran, and he found excuses for non-compliance.

It will be seen here that many cross-currents were influencing events, over and above the main stream of policy which tended to the winning of Scotland from the French and Catholic connection to that of England and Protestantism. There were the innumerable family feuds which divided the Scottish nobles, the ambition of the Guise family, the pretensions respectively of Arran and Lennox to the heirship of the crown, the impatient character of Henry, and the zeal of religionists on both sides; but for the moment the crucial point at issue was the possession of the six-months-old bairn, now jealously guarded in Linlithgow Palace by her mother and the nobles appointed by parliament. The figure in the turmoil which excites most sympathy, in view of the documents now before us, is that of Arran. There was a general tendency at the time and since to regard him as a poor, simple, shifty creature, as he certainly became later, but a consideration of the difficulties of his position at this time, and the manner in which he faced them, should do something to rehabilitate his memory. His part was a hard one. He knew that Scotland was too weak to withstand the force of England, whilst he also saw that with Mary in Henry's hands his own chance of the heirship was gone. The Cardinal, the Queen-Mother, and the Catholics were strong in the country, and so were the Douglases and the 'English' lords. The domination of the former would have meant at that time the triumph of Lennox, and the ruin of Arran and the Hamilton interest, whilst the complete victory of Henry would have been equally disastrous to them. So Arran temporised as well as he might, even in the face of the great bribe held out to him of little Elizabeth Tudor's hand for his son.

The Scottish ambassadors in England found Henry still wrathfully insistent upon the immediate delivery of the child-queen who was to marry his son, and the complete abandonment of the French connection by Scotland. Arran dared not consent, and summoned the nobles to Edinburgh. Even Lennox attended, and was nominally reconciled to his deadly foe Angus; and the whole assembly adopted a new set of propositions to be submitted to Glencairn and Sir George Douglas, both English partisans. After infinite bickering, and suspicions, a treaty for the marriage of Mary Stuart and Edward Tudor, with peace between the two realms, was signed at Greenwich on the 1st July 1543, by which the bride was to be delivered to the English at the age of ten years, and married to the prince when she was twelve, hostages in the meanwhile being given to England for the fulfilment of the treaty. But still Henry was uneasy. Lennox refused to deliver Dumbarton, and Stirling was held against the Regent by Erskine; the Cardinal was still at liberty to plot against Protestantism, and Arran, as usual, was endeavouring to hunt with the hounds and run with the hare.

News came to Henry, even, that Sir George Douglas and his brother Angus would rally to the Cardinal at the persuasion of Argyle; there were rumours on the Border that the Humes and Scotts were mustering to raid the English marches, and worst of all, the Cardinal, with Huntly and his friends, were preparing forces to seize Mary at Linlithgow. But once more a hollow reconciliation was patched up, and a meeting of nobles summoned to ratify the English treaty. Henry was still shrewdly suspicious that an attempt would be made to convey Mary out of the country, and assembled his forces on the Border, in order to invade Scotland at the first moment that the Catholic party seemed aggressive.[10] Mary of Guise, who was really in the thick of the plot, sought again to reassure the English ambassador. Sadlier saw her at Stirling on the 20th August 1543, and she assured him that she was as faithful as ever to the English connection. She was the more confident now that her daughter had been released by the convention of lords from the power of Arran, and placed in the safe custody of the nobles appointed by the parliament to guard her. Arran, she continued to assert, was the real villain of the piece, and she alone was the friend of England, desiring nothing better for her daughter than her conveyance to England, and her marriage with Edward. When Sadlier spoke slightingly of the Catholic lords, however, she stood up for them stoutly, and said that they opposed Arran only in the interest of the safety of their sovereign lady. Her daughter, she said, 'grew apace, and would soon be a woman, if she took after her mother,' Mary of Guise herself being very tall; and she showed Sadlier the child, 'who is right fair and goodly for her age.'[11]

And thus the intrigue grew. Arran himself went to St. Andrews ostensibly to reconcile the Cardinal to the ratification of the treaty. The Churchman sulked and refused to meet him, and was at once proclaimed a traitor by Arran. Both sides flew to arms, but the Cardinal's party had the start, and Arran could only pray for aid, which Henry was too suspicious of him to grant. But in the meantime the war between France and England at sea had actually commenced, and relations became more bitter every day. The Scots treaty with England had been confirmed at Holyrood on the 25th August, and the Laird of Fyvie was sent to England to obtain Henry's ratification; but Scottish opinion was now strongly suspicious of Arran's subservience to England. Scottish ships under French convoy had been captured at sea, and the whole country was straining in the leash to preserve its independence. Arran at length, beset by Henry's haughty demands on the one hand and the Cardinal's defiance on the other, bent his head before the storm and betrayed his paymaster. On the 3rd September he fled from Edinburgh and joined the Cardinal at Falkirk, near Stirling, where a general reconciliation took place with Huntly, Lennox, Murray, Argyle, and Bothwell. There, in the ancient castle on the rock, he bent his knee before the Churchman. He had been forced to act as he had done, he said, by the King of England, who had urged him to despoil the Church and sack the monasteries. In humble contrition he undertook to deliver all the strong places to the Cardinal, but the solemn ban of the Church was pronounced upon him for his past impiety. The next day, Saturday, Arran did penance for his sins before the friars of Stirling, promising never to offend again. Then taking the sacrament he was formally absolved, and delivered all effective power to the triumphant Cardinal Beaton.[12]

On the morning of Sunday, 11th September 1543, Mary was crowned Queen of Scotland in the chapel of Stirling Castle, 'with such solemnity as they do use in this country, which is not very costly.' Arran bore the crown before the infant, his rival Lennox the sceptre, and Argyle the sword of state. Thus Mary of Guise had so far won the day, for she knew now that her child would never marry an English prince. Henry was furious at the trick that had been played upon him. Let Douglas and his friends seize the Queen by force, he urged; but, above all, let them watch that she was not spirited away to France, and another babe put in her place. 'The falsehood of the world is such, and the compasses such of that Cardinal and the Queen-Dowager, as if things be not specially foreseen and provided for in time, they will grow to further inconvenience.'[13] But Stirling was strong, and with the doubtful exception of the Douglases, Scotsmen were determined that their Queen should remain where she was, and the Dowager rarely lost sight of her child for an hour.

Affairs went from bad to worse. French ships, with men, arms, and money came to Lennox at Dumbarton; legates brought powers to raise ecclesiastical subsidies in Scotland, and the Pope's blessing to the Cardinal; and notwithstanding the studied moderation of the latter towards England, it was made quite clear to Henry that he did not intend to hold by the treaty of marriage and alliance. The only remedy that Henry could readily suggest was the forcible seizure of the Cardinal himself, which in the circumstances was quite impracticable. The presence of the French ambassador La Brosse, and of the papal legate Grimani, was particularly disconcerting to the English party. Grimani was nearly kidnapped by Angus, at Glasgow, and escaped to Stirling in disguise before dawn one morning, warned just in time by a messenger from Mary of Guise. The treaty with England was obviously crumbling, and the two countries rapidly drifting into war. All Scotland, but a few Douglas adherents, were in favour of friendship with France; and Sadlier himself was in hourly danger, though hidden away in the strong Angus castle of Tantallon.

But for no great length of time was it possible for Lennox and Arran to be on the same side. The King of England had much to offer, and though Lennox had come to Scotland with the French influence at his back, he was willing to throw his weight on to the other scale if the English king would give him his niece, Lady Margaret Douglas, daughter of Angus and Margaret Tudor, Queen-Dowager of Scotland, for his wife, and grant him a revenue similar to that which he would lose in France.[14] Whilst this intrigue was still in progress, the Cardinal's parliament met in Edinburgh (11th December 1543) and declared that as Henry had not ratified the treaty within the stipulated time, the agreement made with England was at an end. Nor was this all. Jacques de la Brosse and Jacques de Mesnaige, councillor of the parliament of Rouen, were welcomed by the assembled nobles as representatives sent by Francis I to request a renewal of the ancient alliance between France and Scotland; Cardinal Beaton and his friends being authorised by the parliament to conclude an agreement with them. On the 15th December 1543 the new treaty with France was signed, and Scotland once again threw in her lot with her old friend and defied her ancestral enemy.

Notwithstanding the attempts of the Scots still to temporise with Henry by suggesting that Mary's marriage with the Prince of Wales might after all take place when the children grew to fit age;[15] and the French suggestions to the Emperor that they were prepared, and able, to divert Henry from his alliance with Charles, by causing Mary and her mother to be conveyed to England with the support of Guise,[16] it was quite obvious to the English king that he would have to crush Scotland by force before he could safely send his troops across the sea to join his ally in conquering France.

Hertford's sanguinary invasion of Scotland by sea was therefore effected in the spring. Arran and the Cardinal, taken by surprise, were beaten and put to flight between Leith and Edinburgh early in May.[17] The Scottish capital made such terms as it might with the conqueror, but was pillaged and ravaged, as was Leith; and all the country round was wasted by fire and sword. The two principal Scottish ships of war were captured in harbour, and then Hertford and his army, leaving Scotland bleeding and powerless for harm, but wellnigh united now in indignation against England, returned home, ready to lend to the Emperor their aid in overrunning France. Lennox, almost alone of the Scottish nobles, now sided with England; for even George Douglas was said to be 'thick with the Cardinal'; and the young earl was betrothed to Lady Margaret Douglas, Henry's niece, in June, binding himself thenceforward to hold his person and his castles at Henry's orders. But he undertook something more important still: namely, that he would 'travail to the uttermost of his wit and power to get her (Mary's) person into his own keeping, and so deliver her forthwith into his Highness' hands with all diligence possible, to be nourished and educated at his Majesty's order.'[18] The child herself had been conveyed to Dunkeld when Hertford and his troops had approached Stirling, and there, under the watchful care of her mother, she grew and throve, whilst Scotland, nominally at war with England and the Emperor, could only look on at the contest and pray for the victory of her friends the French.

Whilst Henry was still at war (January 1545) news came to him that the Governor (Arran), the Cardinal, and the other lords, had agreed to give their Queen to the French king to marry, and had signed and sealed a bond to send both queens into France next spring,[19] and Henry retaliated by constant forays across the Border. More than once Arran sent to the Emperor to beg for the inclusion of Scotland in his peace with France, and to Francis pleading for aid to withstand English attacks, or the Scots would after all be obliged to come to terms with England.[20] Montgomerie (M. de L'Orges) was sent from France to Dumbarton with a small force; but Francis had his hands full,[21] and could not effectually protect his ally, Hertford's destructive raids in Scotland continuing unchecked throughout the autumn, with the assistance of the foreign mercenaries recruited for the purpose.

In these circumstances Arran and many of the Scots lords began to waver again. 'There is no talk of a great war between the English and the Scots: on the contrary it looks as if there was some sort of connivance between them. The Scots will not move unless money from France causes them to do so, for they much prefer to receive French aid in money rather than men';[22] and fresh hints were thrown out of a marriage between Mary and Arran's heir. 'In good truth it appears to be the most probable arrangement, for the Scots love to be ruled by their own countrymen rather than by a foreigner. Besides which, such a marriage would probably avoid the danger that the son referred to might at some future time raise opposition to the princess, he being a very near heir to the crown. However, as the girl is an infant, matters may change.'[23] They did change, and promptly. Cardinal Beaton was murdered at St. Andrews at the end of May 1546, whilst yet the peace negotiations between Henry and Francis were in progress; and Arran, to his secret satisfaction, found himself relieved of the burden of a coadjutor more powerful than himself, whilst Henry could hardly be expected to look with disapproval upon an act which had removed from his path the strongest Scotsman who favoured France and the papacy.

But the murder of the Cardinal also banished any lingering hope that might be entertained by Arran of securing the hand of Mary for his own son, because with the disappearance of the only man who could present Scotland with a united front to speak for herself, the disposal of the young Queen in marriage became a pawn to be used in the diplomatic contest between England and France. There had been a talk of marrying Prince Edward to a niece of the Emperor; and to counteract any such idea Francis undertook, as a part of the peace stipulations with Henry, to promote the marriage of the Prince of Wales with Mary Stuart. That he ever intended to do so is in the highest degree improbable. When, indeed, Henry became too pressing about it, saying that the stipulation was in fact an agreement that the marriage should take place, Francis replied that he did not look upon it in that light, as the child was too young yet to speak for herself; and French emissaries were sent to Scotland to consult Arran, and obtain from him a confirmation of the French view. To the annoyance of Francis, Arran and his Council replied that they submitted the matter entirely to him. 'He had expected another answer, but in the face of it he could not avoid making a promise that when the Princess of Scotland reached a proper age he would do his best to incline her to such a marriage. The people here (Paris), Sire, insist that these promises do not bind them to anything, but even they confess that the King of England will endeavour to hold them to the condition.'[24] So uneasy was Francis at the situation into which he had been forced, that he obtained for Mary of Guise assurance from Rome that any pledge she might be obliged to take in the name of her infant daughter for the marriage of the latter with the English prince could be subsequently nullified.

With infinite humiliation on the part of the Scots, Henry, almost on his deathbed, granted to them their nominal inclusion in the peace treaty with France; but aggression never ceased on the Border, and the distrust of Arran's hobnobbing with France increased. The murderers of Beaton still held the castle of St. Andrews against the Regent Arran; and, whether Henry was an accomplice of the crime or not, he powerfully aided the criminals with means to defy Arran. The latter had his reasons to rejoice at the disappearance of Beaton, but his own heir was held by the murderers in St. Andrews, and their contempt of his authority with English connivance, together with the violent reproaches of Mary of Guise, spurred him into an attempt to capture the place by siege.

On Henry's death Somerset was as anxious as the King had been to secure Mary for his nephew Edward; and knowing that a great French force was being sent by sea to Scotland, he, too, mustered his army with a large number of foreign mercenaries to enforce the treaty for Mary's marriage. Before he took the field the French army had landed, captured St. Andrews, and levelled the fortress to the ground (August 1547), and once more England and France joined issue on Scottish ground for the possession of their exhausted quarry.

Somerset's inept three weeks' rush into Scotland, and his chance victory at Musselburgh (Pinkey), which he failed to follow up effectively, only drew the Scots and French closer together. Young Mary was hurried away to safety at beautiful Inchmahome, in the middle of September, a few days after Pinkey was fought;[25] but intrigue was still resorted to for the purpose of capturing her, since it was seen to be impossible by English force alone.

The Scottish lords, with Sir George Douglas at their head, were ready, one after the other, to hold their itching palms for English bribes, to haggle for maintenance and high marriages in England, and to suggest plans for the seizure of their Queen; but those who were not false in their offers were unable to fulfil them. Whilst the five-year-old child was planting her gardens and plying her needle, all unconscious of the plotting for her dainty little body, Mary of Guise was striving her utmost to turn to the advantage of the French connection the present hatred of the Scots against England arising out of Somerset's invasion.

Early in November, only seven weeks after the battle of Pinkey, a meeting of nobles in Stirling discussed the desirability of sending Mary to France; and in January 1548 Arran finally burnt his boats and embraced the French cause. He bound himself to summon a parliament which should consent to the marriage of Mary with the infant Dauphin Francis, to send the bride at once to France to be brought up, and to surrender to the French king the Scottish fortresses to hold in gage. For this Arran was to be protected and favoured, and to be made a French duke. The Queen-Mother still worked hard in winning nobles to her cause, and when the parliament was assembled early in July at a nunnery outside Haddington, in the midst of the besieging French army under Marshal D'Essé, there was no dissentient voice raised to the French demands for the marriage and custody of the little Queen. Mary was at the time safe in Dumbarton Castle, and no time was lost in making preparations for her deportation. Whilst the French fleet from the Forth was cleverly evading Somerset's cruisers by sailing round the north of Scotland to Dumbarton, Mary of Guise travelled from Haddington to bid farewell to her child. As she left the besieging camp she stood for a moment at the back of the nunnery to gaze upon the town, when the English gunners getting their range, a tempest of cannon-shot fell upon her party, killing many of her courtiers by her side.[26] Swooning with emotion and sorrow, she pursued her way to the west.

With such state and splendour as Scotland could afford Mary was surrounded during the last days she was to spend as a child in her own realm. The two lords who had hitherto protected her so well, Erskine and Livingstone, were still with her and Lady Fleming her step-aunt, who had cared for her education so far. Many girls and boys of about her own age, daughters and sons of Scottish nobles, formed her juvenile court, and especially four young Maries, Fleming, Livingstone, Seton, and Beaton, were her maids and constant companions. Two at least of her bastard half-brothers accompanied her on her voyage: Robert Stuart, Abbot of Holyrood, and his younger brother the Prior of Coldingham; but the eldest James Stuart, Prior of St. Andrews, who so profoundly influenced her afterlife, remained with another brother for a time longer in Scotland.[27]

In the splendidly appointed galley of the King of France, thus gaily attended, tiny Mary Stuart, with her dazzling fair skin and her shining yellow hair, sweet and demure, we are told, in her baby grace, sailed out of the Clyde in the first days of August 1548, the betrothed bride of the heir of France. She was not yet six years old, but already she had been thrice disposed of in marriage: to Edward Tudor, to James Hamilton, and to Francis de Valois, in addition to the several less formal suggestions that had been brought forward for her hand.[28] Her realm, it was even thus early seen, was to be the poise whose shifting or standing should decide the final balance of European power, disturbed by the Reformation. The disposal of the little Queen by one or the other of the rivals was regarded, according to the ideas of the time, as to a great extent the disposal of the nation whose nominal head she was. What some of the wisest of contemporary statesmen failed as yet to see, was that in the proportion that free religious inquiry upon which the Reformation rested became stronger, the power of the sovereign to dispose of the thoughts and lives of subjects dwindled. France seemed when Mary Stuart sailed in the King's galley to have won the game, and to hold Scotland thenceforward in the hollow of her hand, because Mary was to be Catholic and French. But with John Knox thundering for freedom from the Roman harlot, and with English gold encouraging Scottish religious emancipation and impatience of restraint, the symbol remained in the hand of France, but the reality slipped away.

II

MARY'S EARLY YEARS IN FRANCE

Mary and her grandmother—Her education—Mary as a factor in French politics—Mary as a child—Cardinal Lorraine's care of her—His influence on her character—Her Latin letters—A separate household given her—Diane de Poictiers and Catharine de Medici— Suggested marriage with Courtnay—Brantome's description of Mary at fifteen years—Ronsard's and Du Bellay's poems—Description of the Dauphin Francis—His love for Mary—The tone of the French court—Mary's betrayal of Scotland at her marriage—Description of the wedding—Progress of affairs in Scotland—Catholic alliance between France and Spain.

THE FOOT OF MARY STUART FIRST TOUCHED THE SOIL OF FRANCE on the 14th August, at the little port of Roscoff, in Brittany.[29] Escorted by a body of the famous Scots guard of the kings of France, the little Queen slowly travelled from château to château, by Morlaix and Nantes, to Saint Germain-en-Laye, being met on the way thither by her grandmother, Antoinette de Bourbon, Duchess of Guise, whom Henry II had requested to organise the household and education of the little stranger. The letters of the staid old Duchess to her daughter, Mary of Guise, on the occasion, sound a human note that rings true across the centuries, and tells us more than reams of diplomatic correspondence would do. The Duchess writes on the 3rd September 1548: 'I was more glad than I can say to learn of the

25

arrival of our little Queen in as good health as you could wish her to have. I pity the sorrow that I think you must have felt during her voyage, and I hope you had news of her safe arrival, and also the pain that her departure must have caused you. You have had so little joy in the world, and pain and trouble have been so often your lot, that methinks you hardly know now what pleasure means. But still you must hope that this absence and loss of your child will at least mean rest and repose for the little creature, with honour and greater welfare than ever before, please God. I hope to see you yet sometimes before I die. . . . But believe me, in the meanwhile I will take care that our little Queen shall be treated as well as you can desire for her. I am starting this week, God willing, to meet her and conduct her to St. Germain, with the Dauphin. I shall stay with her there for a few days to arrange her little affairs, and until she grows somewhat used to the Dauphin and his sisters.[30] Lady Fleming,' the Duchess continues, 'will, if the King allows it, remain with the child, as she knows her ways; and Mademoiselle Curel will take charge of her French education. Two gentlemen and other attendants are to be appointed to wait upon the little Queen, and her dress and appointments shall be fitting to her rank.'

Mary arrived in France at a favourable time for female education. The new learning for ladies, that had become fashionable throughout Europe, found its noblest centre in the court of Francis I and Henry II; and the great movement that gave to England such erudite ladies as Queen Elizabeth, Lady Jane Grey, Lady Bacon, and Lady Cecil, gave to France the elder Princess Margaret de Valois, Renée of France, Duchess of Ferrara, Jeanne D'Albret, Mary Stuart, and her fellow-pupils the Princesses Elizabeth and Claude. It is certain that the most scrupulous care was exercised to educate Mary worthily. She was surrounded in the convent where she and her fellow-princesses were taught, for the first few months of her life in France, by gentle and wise influences alone; and later, when she lived with the other royal children in Henry's court, no laxity of conduct or coarseness of speech was allowed before her. That the tone of French society at the time was as licentious as well could be, and that the influence of the Queen, Catharine de Medici, where it could be exerted, was likely to be a bad one, is unquestionable; but Catharine was powerless for harm until after her husband's death, and at least an appearance of propriety and devotion was kept up at court until that event happened.[31] Mary's great ally and protectress, Diane de Poictiers, Henry's powerful mistress, even, was outwardly most jealous in preserving her dignity; and though Mary may have learnt her crooked political and diplomatic methods from her uncles Guise and Cardinal Lorraine, and their great rival Catharine, it is most unlikely that any moral influences but those of almost stilted propriety were allowed to touch her in her most impressionable years.

The Duchess of Guise thus writes to Mary's mother a few months after the little Queen had arrived in France: 'It is impossible for her to be more honoured than she is. She and the King's eldest daughter, Elizabeth, live together, and I think that this is a great good thing, for they are thus brought up to love each other as sisters. It is not enough to say that they do not trouble each other in the least, for she (Mary) never works at night or sleeps in the daytime, and is very playful and pretty, and the two children are as fond as they can be of each other's company. They are always well accompanied, and are often in the Queen's chamber, so that nothing could be desired better for her than she has. Do not believe people who write falsely to you to the contrary, for they often complain without reason, and would prefer to have separate habitations, so that they might live as they pleased, which certainly would not be to the advantage of the little Queen, your daughter.'

That Mary's literary education, even in these early years, was carefully conducted, is evident from the accomplishments she possessed. Brantome says that she knew Latin well, and at the age of thirteen declaimed an essay in Latin before the King and Queen, advocating the higher education of women. Her French, says the same authority, was more elegant than if she had been born in France. She played well on the cither, the harp, and the harpsichord. Her dancing and grace of movement were eulogised, as well as her horsemanship;[32] and after allowing for all the exaggeration of courtiers and poets, it is undoubted that Mary was well taught, and an apt pupil. Her hardest lessons were probably those which schooled her to the trade of royalty: to control the demonstration of emotion, to recite by rote grave commonplaces to ambassadors and visitors, and to listen patiently to addresses beyond the comprehension of a child.[33] The fact of their superiority and power was for ever kept before the eyes of infant royalties, and such a system usually succeeded in crushing out of the unhappy little creatures all youthful spontaneity long before they reached adolescence. That it did not result in making the woman Mary Stuart a prig, as it did most other great ladies of the day, including to some extent her companion, Elizabeth de Valois, is a proof of her strong natural character and marked individuality, but it certainly encouraged her hereditary pride, and the over-weening sense of sacredness of sovereignty which contributed largely to the causes of her ultimate ruin.

Scotland for centuries had been a piece in the hands of France to check-mate England when needful, and to prevent a hostile coalition between the latter power and the rulers of Spain or Flanders; but, with the spread of the newer ideas of religion in France, the latter country itself developed divisions, and Scotland became for a time not only the sliding makeweight on the international balance, but an active factor in the internal politics of France. The house of Lorraine had, from the birth of the anti-papal move-ment in Europe, been foremost in their championship of the traditional claims of the Church; and the French branch of the house represented by Duke Claude, and afterwards by the Dukes Francis and Henry and their brothers, naturally espoused the same side, which, in Paris at least, was also the popular one. The appearance of the Guises as French princes, allied by marriage with the royal house and claiming their privileges to the full, nat-urally aroused resentment in the house of Bourbon, princes of the blood, whose claim had previously been unrivalled; whilst their ostentatious push-ing of the papal cause, with obviously ambitious aims of their own, was also displeasing both to those great nobles who had for so long been paramount in the state, the Montmorencis, and their kinsmen the Chatillons, and to the not inconsiderable number who had imbibed some sympathy for the new ideas of religious reform. The devout and decorous concubine, Diane de Poictiers, sided with the Guises; and naturally the neglected Queen Catharine de Medici favoured the opposite party, biding her time when she might deal a blow at the Guise and pro-Catholic faction, whose aggrandise-ment she knew meant her own enfeeblement. The marriage of the King of Scots to Mary of Guise had been a great stroke of policy for the bride's family, and the aid subsequently sent to Scotland by France had been opposed bitterly, and minimised as much as possible by the parties at court who were jealous of the rise of Guisan influence. The betrothal of the infant Mary to the Dauphin, and her deportation, had been similarly combated; but Diane de Poictiers was all-powerful with Henry II, and she and the Guises had their way in spite of Catharine and the Montmorencis.

It will be seen, therefore, that whilst Mary was still a child she was the centre of a great intrigue in French home politics, as well as being a precious international pledge; and the visit of her mother to France in September 1550, for a year, was avowedly for the purpose of obtaining support for her claim to the Scottish regency, still nominally held by Arran (Duke of Chatelherault), with the object of carrying out more firmly than before the policy most conducive to the Guisan objects in France. By bribes and address she had won over a large party of the Scottish nobles to her views, and with ceaseless persistence pursued her aim until (in 1554) she was successful. That her openly French policy in Scotland was for a time accepted without protest, and the opponents in France itself of the Guise domination silenced, was owing greatly to the accession of the half-Spanish Mary Tudor to the throne of England, and her marriage with Philip; such an alliance being, as usual, a signal for the close drawing together of France and Scotland on the old national lines that had existed before the opening of the Reformation. This was, however, but a passing phase, which disappeared when Elizabeth succeeded and pledged England to an anti-papal and nationally independent policy. This short digression has been necessary in order to show how many warring interests surrounded Mary, even in her childhood, and caused her future to be of greater importance to Christendom than that of any other woman of her time except Elizabeth Tudor.

They were not all friends, therefore, in France that approached the young Queen in her years of innocence. In 1551 a plot was discovered to poison her by a Scotsman of her own name, whom some historians have without adequate proof sought to identify with an anonymous Scot, presumably a spy, who was sent to Mason, the English ambassador in France, by Edward's Council;[34] but it does not appear probable, in the absence of positive evidence, that Somerset's government would at this period have run the risk of entering into such a murder-plot, by which, for some time at least, no great advantage could be gained by England. On the other hand, the interest of the Hamiltons in the early disappearance of Mary is obvious. In the meanwhile the child grew in beauty and precocity. The staid, dignified little letter written to her mother in 1552[35] shows her direct initiative at several points. Her mother had charged her with secrecy upon certain matters, to which she replies: '*Je vous puis assurer, madame, que rien qui viendra de vous ne sera sceu par moy*'; and with all seriousness she discusses the affairs submitted to her, though with many dutiful protestations of her humble obedience to the more mature judgment of her elders. It is evident, too, that her advisers in France were the Duke of Guise and Charles, Cardinal Lorraine, her uncles. She writes in this connection: 'I have shown the letters to my uncle Guise, as I thought you would wish me to do so; although in view of the orders you send me I should not have shown them to any one, only I was afraid that I should not be able to understand them without his help. . . . I would have written to you in cipher, but my secretary tells me it is not necessary yet.' She begs in the same letter that her servants may be better paid, and, evidently in obedience to the request of her mother, encloses two letters written separately with her own hand: 'so that you may be able to show that to my master without any one knowing that you have written to me about it.'

This for a child of ten shows a precocious development, which, given natural ability, would be a likely result of the kind of training to which she was submitted. The astute Cardinal Lorraine (the younger) evidently took pride in the progress of so apt a pupil as his niece. This is how he describes her in letters to her mother early in 1553, he having just accompanied the King to Amboise on a visit to the royal children: 'She has grown so much, and grows daily in size, goodness, beauty, and virtue,[36] that she has become the most perfect and accomplished person in all honest and virtuous things that it is possible to imagine, either in gentle or simple rank. I can assure you that the King is so delighted with her that he passes much time talking with her, and for an hour together she amuses him with wise and witty discourse as if she were a woman of twenty-five.' The whole family were to come to St. Germain, and young Francis was to be furnished with a separate household. In giving this news to his sister, Cardinal Lorraine shows the cloven hoof, and allows us to see his enmity towards the Queen Catharine de Medici. The latter, he says, will not allow her two elder daughters to have any separate household, but has decided to keep them close to her under her own control, 'determined that whilst she lives, or they remain single, no one shall have any authority over them but herself.' The Cardinal then urges his sister to act in the same way towards Mary, namely, to appoint her household and governors for her, or in other words to withdraw her from the influence of Catharine. 'I pray you act strongly in this respect, and you will thus always have the more power over her'; and he sends to his sister a complete list of the persons he proposes to form Mary's household. 'Believe me, madame, she already possesses so high and noble a spirit that she shows great annoyance at seeing herself so poorly treated, and she is anxious to be free from this tutorship and to live in a dignified fashion.'[37]

It may well be supposed that with such a preceptor as Cardinal Lorraine to influence Mary's natural pride, and to mould her a fit instrument for the Guise ends, there would be but little love between Catharine and the niece of her enemies. As we have seen, the two daughters of France who were Mary's schoolfellows were kept in close tutelage under the watchful eye of their mother, whilst Mary was in the enjoyment of a separate household paid by Scotland, and was surrounded by Scottish nobles and gentlemen. Thus attended, and with Cardinal Lorraine ever watchful, it was evident that Mary was protected at all points from the political influence of the Queen. If Conæus is to be believed, Mary, who with the rest of the royal family spent some hours every afternoon in the Queen's presence-chamber, used to watch Catharine's every movement, and treasure up every word that fell from her lips, presumably in her precocious desire to learn and imitate how a queen should carry herself. Catharine asked her once why she preferred her company to that of her young companions, and Mary's courtly answer could not have deceived the wily Italian, who hated the child she knew was waiting under the tutelage of her foes to play the part of Queen of France as soon as Providence might decree. It was gall and wormwood for Catharine de Medici, but she took her vengeance to the full when her opportunity came.

The pedantic, artificial, little Latin letters or exercises which at the age of about twelve years Mary addressed daily to Princess Elizabeth[38] show how constantly the child's thoughts dwelt upon the splendour of her destiny. The faulty construction and self-conscious tone of these curious documents add to their value, as showing that they were the genuine unaided production of Mary herself. Quoting Plutarch, who she says is a philosopher worthy of teaching a prince, she writes: 'He who counterfeits a prince's coin is punished: how much more severely should he be punished who corrupts a prince's mind: for, as Plato tells us, the people of a State are apt to take after their princes.' Again: 'The true grandeur of a prince, my dear sister, is not in splendour, nor in gold or fine purple, or rich gems and other pomps, but in prudence and wisdom: and just as a prince is different from his subjects in his dress and manner of living, so should he differ from them in their foolish and vulgar ideas.' The next day Mary pursued the same line of thought. 'The prince ought not to boast principally of the blazonry and signs of nobility he receives from his parents, but should seek first of all to imitate their virtues. That is the first thing; the second is that a prince should be well taught in arts and sciences, and third and least is the painted blazonry of his ancestors.' Amidst all this mass of prunes and prisms the natural little girl occasionally pushes through to the surface. Princess Claude had been naughty one day, insisting upon drinking excessively just before going to bed. The tutor had asked the elder sister Elizabeth to reprove her for it, but Elizabeth had frankly replied that she too wanted to drink before she went to bed. Mary Stuart, in her Latin theme at all events, was quite shocked at this. 'We should be examples to the people,' she wrote. 'How can we reprove others unless we ourselves are faultless? A good prince must live in such sort that great and small may take example by his virtues.' Unfortunately for this high-sounding precept, Cardinal Lorraine, writing to his sister a few months previously, lets us see that Mary Stuart, even at twelve years old, was still human, notwithstanding her priggish copybook. 'It was good to see your daughter, who is in excellent health, better than ever. I am astonished that people should write to you that she is sickly. They must be ill-natured people, indeed, to say such a thing, for she was never better in her life, and the physicians say that, to judge from her constitution, she may, with God's blessing, live as long as any of her relatives. It is true that she has experienced at times some faintness, but this is only caused by her forgetting herself and eating too much. She has always a very good appetite, and if she had her way and ate as much as she liked, her stomach would often suffer for it. But I am having more care than ever taken of her way of life, and hope that we shall so well carry out the trust you have confided to us that her line shall be well continued. I scrupulously go through every apartment once a month myself, and inquire minutely into everything that is done; and I take care to order that no stranger whatever is to be allowed to enter or frequent any of the offices; and that all the officers carry out their duties properly.'[39]

Mary thenceforward was nominally her own mistress, but really under the guardianship of the Cardinal; and although possessing a separate household, still accompanied the royal family in their daily life. Her correspondence with her mother at this period, whilst frequently showing the guiding hand of Lorraine, contains increasing signs of independent action on the part of Mary herself. The Earl of Huntly, to whom she and her house owed much, had asked for the reversion of some benefice or office, his petition apparently having been endorsed by the Queen-Regent Mary of Guise. Mary thereupon wrote to her mother: 'Please pardon me, and do not take in ill part if in the government of my realm I take example from the King (of France), who never grants a benefice to any one until the possessor thereof is dead.'[40] She begins also at this time to ask favours for her servants, and to show liking for some and repugnance to others. With her governess, Madame de Paroys, indeed, she seems to have had quite a serious quarrel about the distribution of her wardrobe, in which the governess thought she was not fairly treated; and by numerous indications in the course of her correspondence it is evident that at the age of about thirteen or fourteen the result of Mary's training as a child-monarch had been to stamp indelibly upon her character the impression of her sovereign privileges and exalted destiny.

She was now of an age, too, for the Guise interest to make capital out of her by using her authority to increase the French control over her country. Arran and the Scots nobles had been bribed wellnigh to their hearts' content, and meekly accepted the decision of the French parliament that Scotland should in future be governed in Mary's own name; and in 1554 her decree making her mother Regent during her absence was confirmed in Edinburgh, whilst Knox and the growing party of reformers looked sourly on, knowing that with Catholic Mary Tudor on the English throne no help could come to them from that quarter. The Guises, indeed, were triumphing all along the line, and, as events turned out, their attempts to garner the harvest of their success too fast caused the downfall of their hopes. With her uncles and Diane de Poictiers Mary was upon terms of the closest friendship: 'And as for my uncle the Cardinal I say nothing (with regard to his kindness), for I am sure you already know. . . . It is incredible how careful they all are for me.'[41] Belonging thus, as she did, to the party of her kinsmen and the concubine, Mary must necessarily have been on terms of more or less polite antagonism with Catharine de Medici, although court etiquette brought them frequently together; and it is not unlikely that at this period it was that the ill feeling between the two queens led to the taunt said to have been uttered by Mary to her prospective mother-in-law, that the latter was 'a merchant's daughter and would never be anything else.'[42] If it had been possible for the Queen with the Bourbons, the Montmorencis, and the Chatillons to upset the marriage treaty, which aided so much the glorification of the Guises, they would have done so; and there is no lack of evidence that they tried. In April 1556 Cardinal Lorraine writes to his sister praising more than ever the good conduct of his niece, 'who is so good and virtuous that she could not behave better if she had a dozen governesses' (instead of none); 'and . . . the King told me that he thought of having her married this winter, which no doubt he will do if you come, but I think not otherwise.'[43] Cardinal Lorraine told the Venetian ambassador somewhat later that the King was desirous of having the marriage hastened in order to put a stop to the proposals which on every opportunity were brought forward for marrying Mary elsewhere, and it may well be believed that between the rival intrigues of the Montmorencis and the Guises the weak Henry was often perplexed. At one juncture (1556) the former family seemed likely to win the game. Francis de Montmorenci, son of the Constable, Henry's old and dearest friend, married the King's legitimated daughter, and the marriage of Mary Stuart and the Dauphin then trembled in the balance. A proposal was at once started to marry her to young Courtnay, who had been the native

pretender for the hand of his cousin Mary Tudor previous to her marriage with Philip. The French pretext for the proposal was a plausible one, namely, that the efforts of Philip II to marry Princess Elizabeth Tudor to a nominee of his own threatened the permanent domination of England by the Spanish interest to the prejudice of France, and that the establishment of Courtnay as King-Consort of Scotland under French auspices would effectually put a stop to that danger.

The promotion by the Guises of the new war in league with the Pope against Philip, both in Italy and Flanders, again cast the Montmorenci influence into the background; and the crushing defeat and capture of the Constable at St. Quentin (August 1557), followed by Guise's brilliant campaigns in Italy, and afterwards in Picardy, raised the uncles of Mary Stuart to the highest pitch of power and favour. The Bishop of Ross tells us that the decision to hurry forward Mary's marriage was the direct result of the defeat of St. Quentin, as it was feared that in the event of France being badly beaten by Philip and the English, the Scottish parliament might withdraw their consent to the marriage. Another reason is given by the Venetian ambassador. He says that the completion of the marriage would enable France to make use of Scottish forces as a diversion against England in the following year's campaign.[44] In either case it is evident that the marriage of Mary at the particular period when it was effected was a move promoted by the Guises, in the first place to forward their own political aims, and, to a smaller extent, to serve what they considered French national interests.

Mary Stuart was now over fifteen years of age, at a time when the fascination of her budding womanhood first began to cast its spell over men. Brantome says: 'Her great beauty and virtue grew in such sort, that when she was about fifteen years old her loveliness began to shine in its bright noonday, and to shame the sun itself with its brilliance, so beautiful was she. . . . It was good to hear her talk, both to the great and the humblest. Whilst she stayed in France she always devoted two hours each day to study and reading: and there was no science upon which she could not discourse well. Above all, she loved poetry and poets, especially M. de Ronsard, M. du Bellay, and M. de Maisonfleur, who all wrote beautiful poems for her, which I have often seen her read in France and in Scotland with tears in her eyes and sorrow in her heart. . . . Whenever she addressed any one she had a very sweet, fascinating, and pretty, yet dignified, way of speaking, and with a discreet and modest sort of familiarity and gentle gracefulness. . . . She had, too, this special perfection to enchant the world. She sang sweetly, accompanying herself on the lute with lovely hands, so finely fashioned that those of Aurora herself could not surpass them.'[45]

The courtly poets, Ronsard especially, piled up their adjectives in her praise, to an extent, that if half they said of her was true, her place was amongst the angels rather than amongst the daughters of men. Her fair skin, her bright eyes, her lovely hand, and inimitable grace are sung in verses innumerable. Amongst them all, Du Bellay appears best to catch the secret of her charm, which must have lain in her general sympathetic attractiveness rather than in perfect beauty of particular features.

> 'The tongue of Hercules, so fables tell,
> All people drew by triple chains of steel.
> Her simple glance where'er its magic fell,
> Made men her slaves, though none the shackles feel.'

The boy Francis de Valois, to whom this wondrous young paragon was affianced, was but fourteen. A poor, bilious, degenerate weakling, stunted of figure and unprepossessing of face, but, young as he was, already devoted to the beautiful girl whom from his earliest years he had been taught to regard as his future wife. Throughout the correspondence of the time we find traces of his frequent illnesses, usually fevers and agues, which left the lad weak and exhausted after his recovery. He was shy and timid, as his father had been at a similar age, though less inclined to, or indeed capable of, manly exercises than he. He was as yet too young to have engaged actively in the vices of the outwardly brilliant and devout, but intensely immoral, court, but he appears to have been, nevertheless, fully alive to the desirability of his bride.[46]

What were Mary's feelings towards him at first it would be more difficult to say.[47] Familiarity with the idea of life-union with him, one of the two greatest marriageable princes in Europe of the time, must have accustomed her to any shortcomings in his appearance, whilst her pride cannot fail to have been flattered at the deference with which the Dauphin was surrounded, and the splendour of the destiny apparently reserved for him. She was now, moreover, at an age when, precocious as we have seen her to be, she could appreciate much of what was passing at court before her eyes, and of necessity must have regarded gallantry with lenient curiosity, if not with anticipation. The King, of whose virtues she heard so much, was living in unconcealed adultery with Mary's special patroness, a devout dame of high lineage, whose daughter's hand was sought by some of the proudest nobles in the land; laxity of conduct, in such a court as that described by Brantome, must have been treated more as a joke than otherwise. Mary must have understood by this time that her aunt and governess was also the King's mistress, and that even her admired uncle the Cardinal, great Churchman and prince though he might be, was a sensual profligate, who spared neither innocence nor virtue in the pursuit of his pleasures.[48] Such influences as these, acting upon an already precocious mind, had probably quite reconciled Mary to the idea of an early marriage, even with so undesirable a husband in appearance as the Dauphin Francis, apart from the promptings of ambition, and the direction of her uncles, whose guidance she had been schooled to accept from early childhood.

In the late autumn of 1557 the Scots parliament were summoned by the Queen-Regent to receive the demand of the French king that the marriage, so long ago before agreed upon, should be effected; and although, as Buchanan says, the Scottish reformers well knew that closer relations with France meant a menace to their liberties, they were powerless to resist; and a bribed nobility appointed eight ambassadors to proceed to France and conclude the espousals. They were instructed to obtain a pledge from Mary and her husband to preserve intact the laws and privileges of Scotland; and, on their arrival after a voyage of great danger, a formal promise to that effect was given to them (15th and 30th April)—Mary by letters-patent having previously authorised them,[49] in conjunction with her grandmother, Antoinette Duchess of Guise, to settle the terms of the marriage contract.

This was on the 16th March 1558, but whilst the public treaty was being solemnly discussed, Cardinal Lorraine was urging his niece towards one of the greatest acts of treachery ever committed by a sovereign against his people. How far Mary herself was conscious of the shameful character of the documents she signed has been a favourite subject for discussion between her partisans and her detractors, but great as may be the responsibility of the Guises in the matter it is impossible to acquit Mary Stuart of blame. She was young, it is true, and had always looked towards her uncles for guidance. Scotland was, moreover, for her now little more than a name. It was spoken of before her as savage, uncouth, and rough, and its population was regarded as semi-barbarians for the most part whose only culture came from France. Doubtless Mary had been brought to believe that such a country, poor and isolated, must necessarily fall a prey to England and lose its Catholicism unless it became an integral part of the realm of France. But after making all allowances it must be recollected that Mary had already shown in many letters still extant that she understood perfectly her sovereign position and privileges, she was clever and clear sighted, and it is impossible to avoid the conclusion that the interests of the Guises and of France were her first care, whatever became of Scotland. Cardinal Lorraine had everything his own way. There were none to gainsay him, for the Constable Montmorenci was a prisoner of war, and Henry II was of course delighted to endorse a policy so flattering to his hopes as that of making Scotland a French dependency. As usual, the Guises grasped more than they could hold, and with such a nation as the Scots the undertakings signed by Mary would have been in any case impossible of fulfilment. But this fact does not render Mary the less guilty of levity in thus, so far as she could do it, bartering away her birthright, without even the smallest mess of pottage in return. On the 4th April she signed at Fontainebleau the three documents which made Scotland a fief of France.[50] In consideration of the protection always given by the kings of France to her realm, and the care that had been taken of her (Mary) by Henry II, she declares that if she should die without heirs of her body, 'she gives in pure and free donation to the kings of France, present and to come, all her realm of Scotland, and all her rights and claims to the crown of England,' and the king through Cardinal Lorraine accepts the gift, 'to the profit of the crown of France.' As if this were insufficient, Mary next undertook that Scotland and its entire revenue should remain thenceforward pledged in gage to France until the whole sum of a million (crowns) in gold was paid as a return for the expenses that had been incurred by the King in the defence of the country; and to crown the iniquity, Mary affixed her signature to yet another document, by which she divested herself of the power of ever retracting or annulling the free donation she had made of Scotland to France, in default of heirs of her body.

It is obvious that the terms of these documents were not communicated to the Scottish emissaries, who, however humble they might be, would not have dared to confirm this betrayal of Scotland, and injustice to the Hamiltons; but the matter can hardly have been kept so secret that James Stuart, Mary's base brother, had no inkling that something was being done underhand. He was now twenty-six years of age, and was known to lean to the side of the reformers, as against France, and as one of the emissaries was actively engaged in settling the public treaty in which the interests of Scotland were duly safeguarded.[51] His suspicions may have been strong, but he was as yet powerless to act. The lesson was not lost upon him, though all went smoothly on the surface, except for some distrust when the Scottish ambassadors replied in answer to the French demands that they had not brought authority to crown Francis as their Queen's consort.

Splendid as had been some of the French courtly ceremonies under Francis I, they were all thrown in the shade by the blaze of magnificence that accompanied the first marriage of Mary Stuart. It was an age of ostentatious sumptuousness, when men and women in their garb and mien sought to realise the dreams of the poets, and like all periods of moral decadence it was characterised by the emulation of people of all ranks to outshine their fellows in richness of attire. For weeks before the ceremony, we are told, all the shops and ateliers of Paris, the jewellers, the embroiderers, the habit-makers, and mercers were crowded with purchasers. Within the palace of the Louvre naught was heard but the clamour of workmen erecting stands and theatres for the coming festivals, and every gallant and fine lady, every poet, wit, or artificer, contributed something to the attractiveness of the spectacle.[52]

The first betrothal or hand-fasting took place on the 19th April in the great hall of the Louvre, when Mary in all her radiance glittering in white satin and gems was led up to Cardinal Lorraine by Henry II, whilst the young bridegroom, barely fourteen years and three months old, was conducted by the first prince of the blood, Anthony of Bourbon, titular King-Consort of Navarre, gay and debonnaire, light and vain as ever, though the triumph of the Guises must have been a bitter pill to him. After the young pair had joined hands, and pledged their troth before the Cardinal, a grand banquet and ball followed, of which several accounts exist. In the midst of the dancing the King of Navarre whispered ruefully to the Venetian ambassador as he passed that the unforeseen had happened.[53] At the public ceremony a few days afterwards mercurial Paris went crazy with joy. For over two hundred years no Dauphin had been wedded on French soil, and for motives of policy it suited the Guises to show by the splendour of the feast how completely they had brought Scotland under French tutelage. So whilst the festival lasted all went well. Opposite the great west door of Notre Dame a vast amphitheatre was erected, and a sumptuous gallery hung with blue velvet sown with golden lilies traversed the great space from the bishop's palace, and so up to the high altar of the cathedral itself. Before the door stood the Pope's legate, the Cardinal, Archbishop du Bellay, and the prelates of France, whilst lines of halberdiers kept the space open and bands of music beguiled the time of waiting.

It was the crowning day of the Guise triumph, and when the brilliant Duke Francis came to give a last glance at the preparations before the other principal actors came, he showed by one act in what quarter he looked for support in his soaring ambition. Bowing low to the prelates and nobles who clustered round the staging, he saw that the view of the route was blocked from the vast crowd on the amphitheatre and in the streets by the knots of courtiers who thronged the space. To humiliate the aristocracy and curry favour with the Paris mob was always the Guise policy, and the Duke with an imperious gesture made the nobles stand aside that the crowd might see the show unimpeded. Then the marriage procession swept round from the bishop's palace. Heralded by music, preceded by hundreds of courtiers in gay apparel, there came the princes of the blood and the great Churchmen of the royal house, Cardinal de Bourbon (himself long afterwards a puppet-king of France) and the two Cardinals Lorraine—the wicked old John, already tottering to an execrated grave, and Charles of Guise the real hero of the day. With soaring gold cross before him marched the Pope's nuncio, bearer of the special blessing of the Pontiff on the wedded pair; and then, glittering and handsome, the titular King-Consort of Navarre leading by the hand the shrinking little bridegroom, abashed by the thunderous cheers that greeted him. Henry II himself conducted the beautiful young bride, tall and slender, with a perfect grace prematurely adorning her sixteen springs. She was clad in a blue velvet robe covered with silver lilies and piled with flashing gems, and bore upon her fair young brow a diamond coronet worth half a million crowns. 'She looked,' says Brantome, 'a hundred times more lovely than a goddess from heaven, as she went to her wedding on that morning full of brave majesty; and so she did as she danced at the ball in the afternoon, and still more when as evening fell she bent her modest steps in disdainful indifference to consummate her vow to Hymen's altar. And every voice in the court and in the great city outside resounded with her praise, saying that blessed a hundred times was the prince who was yoked to such a princess. If Scotland was worth much, its Queen was more precious still; and even if she had possessed no crown or sceptre, the divine beauty of her person alone was worth a kingdom; but being a queen she brought a double fortune to her happy husband.'[54]

As the silver trumpets brayed the message that the Church had set its seal on the union, great cries of 'largesse' went up from the throats of the multitude; and gold and silver coin was flung broadcast, in the names of the King and Queen of Scotland, to a mob which tore and fought for it like savage beasts to their own destruction. After high mass inside the cathedral and the offering of homage to the Dauphin as King-Consort of Scotland, dinner was served in state in the Archbishop's palace hard by, the heavy gold crown of Scotland being suspended over Mary's head the while. And then, amidst enthusiasm indescribable, the procession slowly made its way through the thronged streets to the old palace of the Tournelles, Mary riding in the same litter with Catharine de Medici, Queen of France, who nursed her hate and smiled upon her defeat. At the great ball after supper Mary led out first her friend and comrade, Elizabeth, the King's eldest daughter, to dance a stately pavane. The young Queen's train, we are told, was six ells long, and had to be carried behind her by a courtier as she trod the measure. Not even in Paris had ever such splendour been seen as this; and the triumphs and devices—tedious and trite as they seem to us now—were regarded by the spectators as the acme of ingenuity and magnificence. 'Out of the gilded chamber,' we are told, 'there marched the seven planets, garbed as the poets have described them to us.' These were beautiful girls, who sang an epithalamium as they advanced through the hall. Then came five-and-twenty hobby-horses caparisoned in gold, each ridden by a feigned young prince in shining garments; white ponies drew triumphal cars with heathen deities, muses, angels, and the like; and so, for two full hours, the show of beauty and voluptuousness went on. The crowning act was the entrance of six brave galleons with swelling sails of gold, upon the decks of which two seats were placed—one occupied by a young prince, masked, and the other still vacant. As the vessels swept past the marble table at which the princesses sat, each prince in turn sprang out and captured the lady of his choice, the young bridegroom of the day bearing off in triumph his own Mary Stuart.

It was a brave show, and it was meant to be so, for it signified much more than the rejoicing over the marriage of a boy and girl, however highborn. It seemed to be, so far as men could see, the final triumph of the Guise and papal party in France, and the deathblow to English Protestant hopes of redressing the possible union of the Catholic powers against the Reformation, by ranging Scotland permanently on the side of the anti-papal party. Mary Tudor was known now to be fading away childless, and her death must certainly bring to the surface the strong Protestant elements in her country. With Scotland inimical and Catholic they might be crushed, and the Reformation in Europe defeated; and the Guises thought that surely now they held Scotland in their grasp, to be used in their own behoof when the time for action should come.

Mary Stuart had been their puppet, for they had reared her from her infancy to play the part; but in the later stages of her maidenhood, and during her short married life, she must have been a willing one, consciously partaking of the Guise aims and sacrificing everything to serve them.[55] Without evidence it would be unfair to suggest that on this occasion she allowed her eagerness for an early marriage with Francis to influence her to the surrender of Scotland to France for the sake of bringing it about. She probably believed in all sincerity that the adoption of any other course than that she took would mean the domination of her country by its 'ancient and inveterate enemy, England,' and its eventual abandonment of the faith which she had been taught to believe offered the only road to human happiness and eternal salvation.

Thenceforward the 'King Dauphin' and the 'Queen Dauphiness' acted together in the government of Scotland, under the watchful direction of the Guise brothers. As we have seen, the demand that Francis should immediately be crowned King after his marriage had been indignantly refused by the Scottish commissioners.[56] Four of them—Cassilis, Rothes, Fleming, and the Bishop of Orkney—in all probability fell victims to their temerity in standing athwart the path of Guisan ambition. Not Knox alone, but others less prejudiced than he, assert that they were poisoned 'with Italian posset or French fegges'; and Buchanan also says that James Stuart (afterwards Earl of Murray) took the same dose and was saved only by his youth and strength of constitution, though he suffered the evil effects of the poison for the rest of his life. The uncompromising Catholic, Leslie, also speaks of the commissioners suffering from 'evill drogges'; and there can be but little doubt that the four commissioners were murdered for their patriotism.[57] Mary, in writing to her mother on the subject, says no word of regret,[58] although in the letter she gave to the commissioners on their return to Scotland she expresses her satisfaction with their conduct in France. The survivors, according to the promise they had given to Guise, supported on their return to Scotland the demand made by the French ambassador to the Scottish parliament that the crown matrimonial should be conferred upon Francis, and that his name should figure with that of Mary upon all patents, seals, and coins issued by the Scottish crown.

The Queen-Dowager in Scotland had, in the meanwhile, carried to the verge of prudence, and beyond, the policy initiated by her brothers in France. Surrounded by French ministers and advisers, civil and military, subordinating all Scottish interests to those of her native country, Mary of Guise had already aroused the jealousy of a powerful faction of nobles against the intruders. The ex-Regent Arran (Duke of Chatelherault), and even the Earl of Huntly, protested against their country being dragged by France into the war against England and the Spanish power; and the growing party of Scottish reformers resented bitterly the persecution to which they were exposed without disguise by the Queen-Dowager.

The long-foreseen death of Mary Tudor, Queen of England (November 1558), radically changed the aspect of affairs, and the arrival of Knox in Scotland almost simultaneously with the insolent attempt of the Regent to suppress by force all religious rites but those of her own Church (May 1559) was a signal for open resistance to her authority; and the sacking of the monasteries by the 'rascal multitude' then made the Regent understand that the forces arrayed against her were not only those of greedy nobles and sober ministers, but a considerable body of the hitherto condemned and disregarded common people, who understood neither political intrigue nor merely verbal protest. Though civil war was averted for a time by hollow treaties, the union of Protestant lords, thenceforward the 'Lords of the Congregation,' became an active power in the state, looking yearningly towards the new anti-papal Queen of England for help and support, and forming a permanent party opposed to the French and Catholic domination of Scotland. The Guises had bent their bow to snapping point, and it had broken in their hands. A purely French and Catholic Scotland, such as they aimed at making it, would have been incompatible with the existence of an independent Protestant England, now that the daughter of Anne Boleyn sat on the throne, and could make no binding pact with the papacy, which regarded her as a bastard, or with Philip, the champion of Catholic orthodoxy.

In the meanwhile, Mary Stuart passed the first few months of her short married life apparently in full contentment with her young husband. In August, four months after her wedding, she speaks in a letter to her mother of 'the honour which the King and Queen, and the King, my husband, continually pay to me.'[59] Francis accompanied his father to the campaign in Picardy in the following month, and his wife speaks of writing to him there; and many small indications tend to prove that Mary was as much in love with Francis now as he was with her. He was intellectually infinitely inferior to her, but she appears to have exercised all her powers of fascination to please him, partaking of his outdoor sports, and lavishing attentions upon him, in return for which he became her abject slave, to be manoeuvred by her as the guiding brain of Cardinal Lorraine might direct.

The growing power and boldness of the Protestants in France, and above all, the countenance given to the Calvinist assemblies by the princes of the house of Bourbon and the anti-Guisan nobles, persuaded Henry II's present advisers and Philip II that this was no time for the champions of Catholicism to be fighting each other; and when the death of Mary Tudor was imminent, a firm peace and union was negotiated between France and Spain, with a secret agreement to the effect that both powers were in future to join forces to extirpate utterly all manifestations of heresy throughout Europe. Mary Stuart's friend and sister-in-law, Elizabeth, still almost a child, was to be married to stern Philip—instead of to his son, to whom she had been promised—France was to be allowed a free hand to make Scotland Catholic by force, as a counterbalance to a potentially heretic England, subsequently to be crushed; and in return, France was to refrain from disturbance on the Flanders frontier, whilst Philip branded his doubtful Dutch and Flemish subjects with the withering sear of Spanish orthodoxy.

It was a pretty plan on paper; but, as events turned out, it was stultified, because its framers left out of account, or underestimated, the strength of certain factors which had to be reckoned with: the envy of the French and Scottish nobles; the ability and facility of conscience of Elizabeth Tudor and Catharine de Medici; the distrust and hidebound stolidity of Spanish Philip; the natural strength and attractiveness of the principle of religious liberty; and, finally, the lack of moral control, which, with all her devotion, handed Mary Stuart thralled into the hands of the enemies of her cause.

III

MARRIED LIFE AND WIDOWHOOD

IN FRANCE

*The new influence introduced by Elizabeth into European pol-
itics—Mary's claim to the English crown—Throckmorton in
France—Condition of affairs in Scotland (1559)—Death of Henry
II and accession of Francis II—Rise of the Guises—Mary's influence
in France—Married life of Mary and Francis—War in Scotland
and death of Mary of Guise—The Treaty of Edinburgh (1560)—
Dissensions in France—Death of Francis II—Grief of Mary, as
indicative of her character—Projects for her re-marriage—The young
King's love for his sister-in-law—Arran a suitor—Various other
proposals—Don Carlos—Bedford's mission to France—Interviews
with Mary and Navarre—Mary at Rheims—Scottish missions
to her—James Stuart and Leslie—Mary's secret hopes based on a
Spanish marriage—Refuses to ratify the Treaty of Edinburgh—
Preparations for her departure from France.*

THE RENEWED PEACE NEGOTIATIONS THAT FOLLOWED THE ACCES-
sion of Elizabeth to the throne of England demonstrated that a fresh force
had been introduced into European diplomacy. The consummate statesmanship with which Elizabeth and her advisers parried the attempts, both
of the Guise party and their opponents in France, to inveigle England into

secret peace negotiations which might embroil her with Spain, was the first proof given to the world that the daughter of the great Harry had inherited his spirit, and in future meant to use the difficulties of other powers to serve the ends of England, but not to be made an instrument herself, as her sister had been. Calais had to go, it is true, for Philip would not spend a ducat to recover it for a heretic, and Elizabeth well knew that, as yet, she could not fight France alone for its recovery; but when the peace treaty of Cateau Cambresis was eventually signed (2nd April 1559), it left both France and Spain, notwithstanding their secret agreement against all heretics, elbowing each other to be first to make Elizabeth's friendship, and if possible to secure the nomination of her future husband.[60] One of the principal arguments hinted at by the Spanish party to force Elizabeth's hand was the probability that France would endeavour to establish the claim of Mary Stuart to the throne of England as the next Catholic heir, in consequence of Elizabeth's heresy.[61] The Spanish ambassador wrote that she 'raved' at the mere idea of such claim, and threatened the French with all manner of dire punishment for it, much to the delight of the Spaniard, who assiduously salted the wound that he had opened.[62] But for the irritation caused by these continual malicious suggestions, and the Guisan zeal of the Queen-Regent of Scotland to crush the Protestants in her daughter's realm, it is probable that the so-called claim of Mary Stuart to the throne of England would have remained a mere theoretical one, to be used when need arose by French diplomatists to forward their own ends;[63] but the hint of it was enough to draw the Scottish reformers and Elizabeth together for the purpose of embarrassing the Guise influence, and it caused the agents of England in France to watch Mary's words and actions with a jealous suspicion, of itself almost sufficient to provoke reprisals.

The first letter written by Mary and her husband, Francis, to Elizabeth on the conclusion of the treaty of peace (21st April 1559), certainly gives no hint of any unfriendly intention on their part. In the letter, which was carried by Lethington (William Maitland) on his way from France to Scotland with the ratification of the treaties of peace, Elizabeth is addressed, naturally, in her full title of Queen of England, and is assured of the desire on the part of Mary and her consort to 'demourer perpetuellement bons frères et *sœur, et entiers amys'*; but the evil seed of suspicion had already been sown, and English statesmen were sourly looking upon the young Queen of Scots as the enemy of their country. The first note of this feeling is seen in a letter from Sir John Mason, one of the peace commissioners, who reports to Sir William Cecil that the 'Queen of Scots is very sick, and these men (*i.e.* the French) fear that she will not long continue. *God take her to Him as soon as may please Him.*'[64] Mary, in good truth, appears to have been in very delicate health at the time. She had suffered frequently from various illnesses before her marriage, but the heart weakness, probably arising from indigestion, which we have seen troubled her even as a child, seriously threatened her life during her short period of wedlock in France. When Sir Nicholas Throckmorton went to France for the ratification of the peace treaty, and to remain afterwards as Elizabeth's resident ambassador, he considered it necessary to ask Elizabeth how he should bear himself towards Mary and the Guises, and was told, practically, there was no need for him to have anything to do with them at all officially; but, 'as for your dooings with the familye of Guise, it shal be mete to show good countenance towards them; and if ye shal find any friendshipp in them, to entertayne it with as good. If otherwise, ye maye dissemble the same, as ye shall see meetest; for it is best to knowe them without knowledge. If any harme be meant it is to be learned thence; and therein may ye have best help of Scottes.'[65]

Before Throckmorton had proceeded beyond Boulogne, he was able to send to Cecil two specimens of the painted scutcheons to be used for decoration during the peace and marriage festivities. They represented the arms of Scotland and France borne by Mary and her husband, and quartered with them those of England; and, although by themselves they might have been innocent enough, the suspicions engendered by the Spaniards, coupled with Cardinal Lorraine's imprudent eagerness, gave to them an importance which led to disastrous results.[66]

At their first interview with the French royal family Throckmorton and his colleagues did not see Mary Stuart; 'for that, as it is said, they (*i.e.* Mary and the Princess Margaret, afterwards Duchess of Savoy) be somewhat sickly'; and this fact is also mentioned by Howard in his letter to the Queen. Mary, however, was well enough to receive the Englishmen on the same day. They found her seated with her husband by her side, and they first addressed Francis with the usual diplomatic compliments. Montmorenci was close to the lad's side, and whispered to him what he had to say in reply; to the effect that he was glad there was peace, and that he would do all he could to preserve it. The letter jointly to Mary and him was then delivered, and read aloud by a secretary. 'Whereupon the Queen herself made answer, in effect, that for the better observation of the treaty she and her husband had sent the ratification to your highness . . . and they would omit nothing that might tend to the conservation of the same: and that, for her part, she had the more cause to do so, for the near parentage which is betwixt your two Majesties.' It is evident that, for the moment at least, the Montmorencis were again to the fore, and doubtless the Constable was glad to get the interview over so well, without the Guise interference; for he hurried the ambassadors away on the plea of Mary's 'weaknesse.' Throckmorton reported at the same interview that, 'in myne opinion she looketh very ill, very pale and grene, and therewith all short breathed: and it is whispered here amongst them that she cannot long live.'[67]

A week later Howard saw her again, for the purpose of witnessing her oath to the peace treaty with Scotland. On this occasion she conspicuously took the lead, 'to speake more than her husband'; and said that, being Elizabeth's good-sister and cousin, she was rejoiced at the peace that had been concluded. She was indeed, so far as words went, most emphatic in her professions of a desire to live on good terms with England. Henry II also, now that Montmorenci, his old friend and mentor, was by his side, excelled himself in polite attentions to Elizabeth's representatives; but Cardinal Lorraine, ever fertile in expedients, cleverly arranged for the King to proceed in June on a series of visits to houses belonging to the Montmorencis and Diane de Poictiers, thus securing a free hand for himself in Paris, at least for several weeks.

The effect of this manoeuvre soon became apparent. Mary Stuart was ill at the time: swooned once in church, and repeatedly after eating, and was reported by the Spaniards to be suffering from an incurable malady; but still the activity of her friends was unabated. Apart from other causes, there were sufficient in the news she received from Scotland to aggravate her constitutional weakness. The Queen-Dowager had found the reformers and discontented nobles too hard a nut for her to crack. She had broken faith with them more than once, and at last attempted to capture their leaders by treachery and to suppress Scottish religious liberty with French pikes. This was too much; and the Lords of the Congregation raised the standard of Protestantism, driving the Queen-Regent into Dunbar; and then through the larger towns of the south and east of Scotland a gust of fury against the Mass and the priests had swept, sparing nothing, however beautiful, that seemed to savour of idolatry. That the reform party should look to Elizabeth for support was natural, and just as natural was it that the Queen-Regent should send, as she did, swift couriers to her brothers, craving the aid of French arms to cram papacy down the throats of the obstinate Scots. Throckmorton therefore watched suspiciously and jealously the proceedings of Mary and the Guises in Paris whilst the King was away. They were winning English Catholics by bribes and pensions to join their party; they were inquiring as to the number of ships at Elizabeth's disposal; they were busy preparing a strong French force for Scotland, under their brother the Marquis d'Elbœuf; and already (7th June 1559) the English ambassador was persuaded that Mary Stuart and her uncles intended at the earliest opportunity to attack Elizabeth, simultaneously on the side of Scotland and in the Channel. Doubts even were whispered as to the stability of Montmorenci. 'The Dolphin (reported Throckmorton) is counted to be the head of all those doings in Scotland; and it is discoursed that in case the Constable be brought to grant to war with us, that it is for feare of displeasing the King Dolphin.'[68]

With such news as this speeding to Elizabeth by every courier, it is not surprising that she should on her side encourage the Scottish rivals of the house of Guise.[69] We have seen in an earlier page how the Hamiltons had been ousted from their pre-eminent position by French Guisan intrigue. They were, it is true, poor creatures, both father and son, but their right was undoubted, and they were good enough tools for the Queen of England whilst she wanted them. The eldest son of the ex-Regent Duke of Chatelherault, the Earl of Arran, was in France, where he had been reared; and secret messengers, Randolph, Killigrew, and other trusty diplomatists, skilled in Scottish affairs, were sent backwards and forwards from Elizabeth to him, and to Throckmorton in Paris, to urge him to action. This was the time, said they, with half Scotland in arms against the French and priestly tyranny, for him by a bold stroke to seize power as a native prince; and, with the aid of England, to assert his exalted birthright. A more splendid bait even than this was held out to him. The Queen of England herself was unmarried. What if he became a favoured suitor, and ruled over England and Scotland jointly with her. He was nearly idiotic, but the suggestion was too tempting to be foregone, and he forsook the French for the English. But his interviews with English agents, secret though they were, did not escape the vigilance of the Guise spies, and he was peremptorily summoned to the French court to answer for himself. With infinite cunning, and through dire danger for both, Killigrew managed to smuggle him out of France across the Swiss frontier, and afterwards to England, though proclamations ordered his capture, dead or alive; and whilst it suited English interests he was used and befooled, and so passes for a space out of this history.[70]

It will thus be seen that in June and July 1559 the insatiable ambition and unstatesmanlike rashness of the Guises and their niece had dragged England and Scotland once more to the brink of inevitable war before the signatures of the peace treaty were well dry. The escutcheon business, puerile as it was, whilst useless as an assertion of Mary's claim to England, could not fail to irritate Elizabeth; and Throckmorton was ordered to remonstrate with the King and the Constable to the effect that 'Whatsoever the heraulds or paynters shall vaynely devise, no such things shall be set forth or published to the world.' Signs multiplied that the Guise party intended to force a conflict before Elizabeth's throne was secure.[71]

In the course of some feigned suggestions of theirs to marry the Duke de Nemours (Jacques of Savoy) to the Queen of England, their agent told Throckmorton that when the suitor asked for Montmorenci's support, which the latter would not promise, the Constable had said: 'What! do you not know that the Queen Dolphin hath right and title to England?'[72] and every day by some such insidious whisper as this the breach was made wider.

The preparations for the ratification of the peace between France and Spain, which was to be accompanied by the betrothals of the King's eldest daughter Elizabeth to the King of Spain, and his sister Margaret to the Duke of Savoy, kept Paris in a fever of excitement whilst these troubles grew. Rehearsals of the martial sports to be exhibited at the ceremony furnished interesting preliminary shows to the courtiers; receptions of great person-ages deputed to take part in the betrothals kept the royal family and the greater nobles busy; and Mary Stuart and her young husband were active figures in all the splendid turmoil, rejoicing probably more than any at the thought that the close bonds now to be forged between France and Spain would secure to the Catholic party a free hand in their efforts to dominate Scotland, with ulterior views upon England, in favour of Mary Stuart.

The splendid rejoicings that accompanied the espousals of the princesses on the 26th and 27th June do not nearly concern our subject; but at the great tournament that took place on the 27th under the shadow of Bastille, hard by St. Antoine, it was noted that, as Mary Stuart was carried through the press in her litter to witness the encounter from the royal tribune, her servants cleared the way with shouts of 'Place! place for the Queen of England!' and when the Dauphin's band of knights began the joust, they were preceded by two 'Scottish heralds: faire set out with the King Dolphin's and the Queen Dolphin's arms, with a scutcheon of England set forth to the show, as all the world might easily perceive, the same being embroidered upon purple velvet, and set on with armoury upon their breastes, backes and sleaves.'

Almost hourly the distrust deepened in sight of such indications as these. On all hands the rumour spread that, now that the dreaded King of Spain was Henry's son-in-law, and no longer to be feared, a great French force would be sent to re-establish the authority of the Queen-Regent and the clergy in Scotland, and afterwards to deal with heresy in England. With a heavy heart, if not a frowning face, it must have been, that Throckmorton sat in his gallery on the 30th June to witness the last and most pompous of the tourna-ments that celebrated the coalition against the faith of which his Queen was champion; and the triumph, so far as men could see, of the Catholic union formed to crush Protestantism throughout the world. Henry II himself, gal-lant and handsome, proud of his pre-eminence on the tilting-ground, rode a big bay war-horse, decked, like its rider, with the black and white device of the widowed Diane de Poictiers. Foreign soldiers, princes of the blood, and the nobles of France, crowded the lists in glittering raiment; and all sought to win the approval of the fair spectators by their dexterity and grace. It was Henry's dominant passion to excel in this exercise. He was a fine horseman, and a bold tilter, and, as is usual in the case of princes, his performances lost nothing from lack of appreciation. On this occasion he appeared to be more than usually determined to distinguish himself. The encounter was nearly over, for the light was waning, and the King, so far, had vanquished all comers; but he lusted still for fresh honours, and challenged the Franco-Scotsman, Montgomerie, Sieur de L'Orge, to run against him. The Scotsman at first refused point-blank to tilt against his King, and, when pressed, urged many excuses. Henry, annoyed at this, insisted upon the challenge, now in the form of a command. Catharine de Medici, in the meanwhile, desirous of ending the dangerous sport, sent a messenger from her tribune to pray her husband to tilt no more for that day, but to come and receive from her and the ladies the praise due for his past prowess. The King had his way in spite of all. At the first shock of the combatants Montgomerie's lance carried away the King's visor, but was broken with the force of the impact; 'and, so with the rest of the staff, hitting the King upon the face, gave him such a counterbuff as he drove the splint right over his eye on his right side, the force of which stroke was so vehement, and the pain he had, withal, so great, as he was much astonished, and had great ado, with reeling to and fro, to keep himself on horseback.' The King was at once succoured and disarmed, and the wound, not being outwardly large, was thought at first not to be dangerous, although 'Marry,' says Throckmorton, 'I saw a splint taken out of a good bigness, and nothing else was done to him on the field; but I noted him to be very weake, and to have the sens of all his lymmes almost benommed, for, being carried away as he lay along, nothing covered but his face, he moved neither hand nor fote, but laye as one amased.' Rapidly bearing him across the river to the palace of the Tournelles, his officers shut the doors against all comers but the two brothers Guise and the Constable.

Gloom fell upon the gaudy merrymakers, and each man, by his looks, dumbly asked his neighbour what the calamity might portend. The accession of a King and Queen, still not much more than children, known to be as ductile clay in the hands of the Guises and the extreme papal party, meant almost certainly the fall of Montmorenci and the moderates, and the unchecked and unsparing persecution of the religious reformers in France: it meant, sooner or later as it seemed, a great national war of conquest against England, which, if successful, would result in the triumph of the papacy throughout Christendom; and, well as such a programme might suit the personal ambition of the Guises, it filled with dismay the purely French princes and nobles who had seen with delight successive Kings of France break or weaken, one by one, the bonds that held their national Church in subservience to Rome.

Whilst the King lay dying at the Tournelles, on the third day after his hurt, Cardinal Lorraine with his brother and friends summoned a council, and urged that rigid means should at once be taken to crush the Protestants in Scotland. Mary's bastard brother James, who had survived the 'evil drogges' at Dieppe, was to be captured and killed, as were the Earl of Argyle, Erskine of Dun, and all their friends and followers; and, but for the timely warning sent by Throckmorton, the iniquitous plan would have been carried out. Nor was this the only step taken thus hurriedly by the Guises whilst yet the King, with a splinter through his brain, lingered in agony. Five thousand soldiers were despatched to the coast for embarkation on the warships, the galleys were ordered from the Mediterranean to the Channel, and all was made ready for the domination of Scotland, as a first step towards the subjection of religious thought to the papacy, and of Great Britain to France. The plan, as has already been pointed out, failed because, amongst other shortcomings, it overrated the power of religious affinities to obliterate traditional national aims and policies.

On the 10th June 1559 Henry II breathed his last, and the old Constable, with bitterness in his heart, watched ceaselessly until its sepulture by the corpse of the King who had loved him better than he had loved his own father, and with better reason. Swift horses had gone racing to the south of France to summon the first prince of the blood, Anthony de Bourbon, King of Navarre, whose right it was to share the councils of the new King. But Montmorenci knew that Anthony was a weak reed to lean upon, and that nothing now would withstand the masterful Cardinal and his splendid brother, Francis of Guise. Too late, the dying King himself had seen the danger, and had with his last breath begged Catharine de Medici to insist upon exercising a share in the government. But she had to settle her long account now, and her first care was to barter with the Guises for the disgrace of their patroness and her rival, Diane de Poictiers, in return for which she was content for a time to stand aside whilst the Cardinal did as he listed with Francis II and Mary, King and Queen of France and Scotland.

Though all they did must have been tinged with the influence of their mentor, neither Mary nor her husband was quite a cipher. Francis appears to have been a lad of eager ambition, stirred to vivacity by the spirit of his wife. He was lying sick when the brothers Guise and the Cardinal, with the Duke of Nemours, entered his chamber, and kneeling, greeted him as King. Francis sprang up in almost joyful excitement, protesting that he was now well, and ready to accompany them to the Louvre to receive the homage of the corporations. Followed by his weeping mother and his wife, young Francis proceeded triumphantly to perform his first ceremonial act as King of France; but when anything beyond ceremony was demanded of him he still turned instinctively to stronger spirits than his own. 'The House of Guise now ruleth,' reported Throckmorton only a few days after Henry died, and a fortnight later he says: 'the Queen-Mother hath, though not in name, yet in deed and effect, the authority of Regent . . .; the state being governed by Cardinal Lorraine and the Duke of Guise.' 'And, seeing how the House of Guise ruleth, with whom I am in very small grace, and that the Queen of Scotland, who is a great doer here and taketh all upon her, hath so small an opinion of me, I shall be able to do small service with her.'

These extracts, and many others to a similar effect that could be quoted, demonstrate the positions held by the various *dramatis personæ* at this juncture. Francis, uxorious, ambitious, and eager, but weak and submissive; Mary, keenly alive and responsive to the far-reaching policy of her uncles, and, like them, determined to do her part with a masterful hand; and finally, Catharine, Queen-Dowager, for a time making common cause with the Guises as the strongest party, and dissembling her dislike to them, in payment for the persecution of Diane de Poictiers.

Harmony seems to have existed for a time, even, between Mary and her mother-in-law. The former, we are told by Throckmorton (13th July), was ungrateful enough to demand immediately after the King's death that

Diane de Poictiers should 'make accompt of the French King's cabinet, and of all his jewels'; and she in her letters goes so far as to speak sympathetically of Catharine's sorrow in her bereavement. 'She is so much troubled still at the illness and death of the late King, that I fear she will fall seriously sick of grief—I think that, were it not that the King her son is so obedient that he will do nothing but what she wishes, she would soon die, which would be the worst thing that could happen to this poor country, and to all of us.'[73] To judge, indeed, from Mary's own correspondence and the observation of contemporary writers, they seemed to have been an exceedingly united family for the few months after Henry's death. Mary never fails to praise her husband for his goodness; and it is evident that he, for his part, was more *éperdument épris*' of her than ever.

That Mary had gained entire power over her husband, and knew it, is shown by a letter she wrote to her mother in the early spring of 1560. The cause of the papal party had been going badly in Scotland. The expedition of the Marquis d'Elbœuf to aid his sister Mary of Guise had been dispersed by storm, and the Queen of England's army and navy, supporting the Lords of the Congregation headed by Chatelherault and his son, had driven the French soldiers of the Queen-Regent into their fortress of Leith. Mary of Guise herself had been formally deposed from the Regency by the lords, and both the English and Scottish Protestants had assumed the authority of Mary to abolish the government of foreigners by force in Scotland. Cunning William Maitland of Lethington, the brain of the revolt, fiery Knox the tongue of it, and Kirkaldy of Grange the strong arm, with the ambitious Stuart bastard, had together contrived to weld into a solid force Scottish impatience of religious dictation, and patriotic repugnance to armed foreign government; England was now openly in the field on the side of the Scots as against France—a fit return for the pretensions of Francis and Mary to the crown of England.

The inevitable reaction against the Guises had, moreover, taken place in France. The Bourbon princes, and some of the most powerful nobles, smiled upon the growing power of the Huguenots, and the conspiracy discovered against the Guises at Amboise, and the bad blood caused by the subsequent executions (March 1560), had put the Guises on the defensive; and to all the prayers of their despairing and beleaguered sister in Scotland they were forced to send but a faltering answer. At this juncture it was that Mary wrote comforting her mother, now closely beset by enemies in Edinburgh Castle. 'I can assure you,' she writes, 'that the King has so much care to succour you that you cannot fail to be content with him. He has promised me to do so, and I will not let him forget it, nor the Queen either, who has honoured us by weeping at your troubles. I have urged her so, that I am sure that she will not fail to send you all the help she can.'[74]

Francis in the meanwhile had grown very rapidly, and was now sixteen, but his health was still delicate, as was that of Mary herself. Vicomte de Noailles, dining with Throckmorton in the autumn of 1559, told him that her weakness was increasing to such an extent that she could not live long, and the Spanish ambassador was eager to carry the news to him, that 'she looked very evil' at dinner; 'and was so weake, as even before all the presence that was there, she fell on swooning, and was in very dangerous case, as she always is after a meale. When she was with aqua composita and other things revived . . . she retired.' The royal couple, however, notwithstanding their poor health, continued for the great part of the autumn and spring in progresses through Central and Eastern France. The coronation at Rheims was followed by a series of journeys in which, contrary to previous custom, the houses of the great nobles were avoided, the stopping-places usually being either royal palaces or those belonging to the house of Lorraine.[75] Mary Stuart's jointure of sixty thousand livres was to be drawn from Touraine, and it was to this part of France that she affected particular attachment. The beautiful young Queen therefore received such a welcome, with her husband, at their entry into Tours, and subsequently at Chenonceau, as to have inspired poets and chroniclers to record in glowing language this, the brief bright summer of Mary's life.[76]

But behind all the extravagant rejoicing and eulogy of the 'divine Francis,' there lurked a grisly spectre that refused to be conjured away. No effective aid could be sent to Scotland; for three-quarters of the French nobles shrank away from the Guises, and even Navarre, the first prince of the blood, was meeting the English ambassador, disguised and at night, in order to express his adhesion to the Queen of England and her party, as against

Mary and her uncles. The French troops were in hopeless case shut up in Leith, and beleaguered by land and sea; and the rash and foolish assertion of Mary's claim to be Queen of England without sufficient power available to force the claim, had already placed her in dire danger of losing the crown of Scotland itself. Young Francis, too, who had overgrown his scanty strength, began to develop symptoms of a disease that might have been expected to appear in the grandson of Francis I. As his mother and Cardinal Lorraine carried him from one place to another in search of health for him, the ene-mies of the Guises spread a hideous rumour that the premature decay from which he suffered could only be remedied by the administration of baths consisting of the blood of newly killed infants. As the poor lad was carried through his realm, the people turned in horror from him, and children were hidden until the royal train had passed far on its way. Mary consoled him as best she might, stricken, as she herself was, with the deadly fear for her own mother, pining away in far Scotland amidst those who hated her faith and her house; but the defection of his people struck Francis to the heart, and he grew more feeble and unhappy as the evil consequences of the Guise policy became increasingly apparent.

In February 1560 even Cardinal Lorraine himself began to get fright-ened at the strength of his opponents,[77] and he entered into negotiations with Elizabeth of England, but for a long time without success. Philip II was almost equally anxious to arrange matters, and urged both the English and French to come to terms.[78] He had just entered into the Catholic league with France, but there was nothing that suited him less than that Mary Stuart, practically a French princess, should establish a claim to the crown of England. His aim was to disarm Elizabeth as soon as possible by her marriage to some husband favourable to him, and that the birth of heirs to her crown should effectually shut out the French from England. Notwithstanding Mary's own smiling assurance to Throckmorton that her 'good sister' Elizabeth should find her 'a better neighbour than the rebels,' Elizabeth would not, and did not, slacken for a moment the siege of Leith; and the unfortunate Queen-Dowager in Edinburgh Castle slowly broke her heart at the failure of her brothers to jus-tify by sufficient force the aggressive policy they had imposed upon her. Mary loved her mother dearly—indeed, her affections were intense wherever they were placed—and when she heard in April that the Dowager's life was in grave danger she was inconsolable. She refused comfort, even from her husband, and finally herself took to her bed, ill with grief. At length, worn out with trouble and responsibility, Mary of Guise died in Edinburgh Castle at midnight on the 10th June 1560.[79] For many days after the news came none dared tell it to her daughter, and when finally Mary heard of her mother's death, 'she passed from one agony to another,'[80] until her own life was despaired of. With this bitter blow, the declining health of the young King, and the consolidation of the anti-papal party in France under the Bourbon princes, the Guises were perforce obliged to confess themselves beaten and subscribe to Elizabeth's hard conditions.[81]

On the 6th July 1560 the Treaty of Edinburgh was signed, by which the French troops were to be immediately withdrawn from Scotland, except a few at Dunbar and the Inch, and in the future no foreign soldiers were to be sent to Scotland without the consent of the Scottish parliament,[82] which assembly, or rather the Congregation, was in future to be supreme, the government being thus made more absolutely a constitutional monarchy than even England was at the time. The right of Elizabeth to the crown of England was unreservedly acknowledged in the treaty. To this pass had the unstatesmanlike disregard to opposing forces on the part of Cardinal Lorraine led the interests of the cause he was supposed to serve. The triumph of Mary Stuart's marriage with Francis was more than neutralised by the hurry of the Guises to reap advantage from the union. Mary Stuart's first 'love affair,' if her marriage with Francis can be so called, was the foundation of all the calamities that subsequently befell her. It may be contended that, in any case, as Queen-Consort of France and Queen-Regnant of Scotland, under a Guise tutelage, a conflict with Elizabeth and the Protestants would have been inevitable sooner or later, but it must be recollected that, without the forces of France behind them, even the Guises would have been powerless, and but for Mary Stuart's fascination and dominion over her youthful husband, the resources of his realm—or even the threat of employing them against the Scottish Protestants—would not have been at the unchecked disposal of Cardinal Lorraine. The most powerful nobles in France, the Bourbons, the Chatillons, and the Montmorencis were opposed to the coercion of Scotland and the irritation of England by French arms. Catharine de Medici, with no religious conviction, and jealously distrustful of Guise influence, would have been only too glad, as events afterwards proved, to hold a middle course and keep friendly with Elizabeth; and against all these elements Cardinal Lorraine and his brothers would have been powerless but for the essential fact that their niece exerted absolute dominion over her enamoured boy-husband, whose will, however swayed, none in France might dare to withstand.

The clouds darkened over France during the autumn of 1560. The terms of the Treaty of Edinburgh were hard for Frenchmen to stomach, but the proceedings of the Scottish parliament in August made things even more difficult than before. The papal jurisdiction in Scotland was abolished, a complete Presbyterian organisation was established, and the celebration or hearing of mass was made punishable by heavy penalties and even by death. It is certain that, as the Venetian ambassador writes, no King of France could ratify a treaty that produced such results as these, except with a rope round his neck.[83] It is quite evident, moreover, from the letters of the French pleni-potentiaries at Edinburgh, that notwithstanding the full powers granted to them by Francis and Mary, there was no real intention from the first to rat-ify the treaty thus forced upon them.[84] Mary herself made no secret of her anger in her interview with Throckmorton on the subject.[85] The existence of the treaty, nevertheless, and the urgency of Elizabeth to obtain a due rat-ification of it, intensified the opposition of the French nobles to the Guises, Cardinal Lorraine especially being profoundly hated as the principal author of such a humiliation. The Bourbon Prince of Condé, Anthony of Navarre's brother, had been treacherously cast into prison on a charge of complicity in the Huguenot plot at Amboise, and the first war of religion in France was now hurrying towards its commencement. Catharine the Queen-Mother was already taking a more prominent share in the government, seated by the side and even taking precedence of Mary Stuart; for the growing weak-ness of Francis foreshadowed her own supremacy, and her keen intellect was busily engaged in conciliating or dominating various interests, in prepa-ration for the great change that she knew was imminent.

The royal family were moving from one palace to the other in Central

France, and on the 18th November were to proceed from Orleans to Chenonceau. On the 17th, however, Catharine, alarmed at her son's condition, insisted upon his taking to his bed. The illness was nothing, said the courtiers, anxious to curry favour with Lorraine. A mother's fears had exaggerated the gravity of it, they insisted; others asserted that it was a mere device of the Guises to keep the King from being worried by petitions on his way. But on the next day, and the next, faces grew graver at Orleans. The lad, reduced by frequent low fevers,[86] and enfeebled, as Throckmorton says, by 'his too timely and inordinate exercise now in his youth,' the natural result of too early a marriage, was unable to withstand the inflammatory disease that had attacked him in one of his ears and his brain. Mary was unceasing in her devotion to her husband,[87] she, Catharine de Medici, and the three Guise brothers being alone admitted to his presence. Mary Stuart and her uncles, indeed, were the only persons in the world who had reason to dread the King's death. Cardinal Lorraine for some time previously had been plotting a murderous blow at the Huguenots, and exacting pledges of orthodoxy from all those about the court; and there was hardly a man in France or Scotland so dull as not to know that upon the ebbing days of the youthful monarch there depended the lives or liberties of thousands, perhaps the fate of the religious freedom of the world.

When at length, on the 5th December 1560, Francis II breathed his last, after a disastrous reign of sixteen months, there was no one to weep for him but his young widow. Catharine leapt at one bound to the supreme power as Regent for the new King Charles IX; the Bourbons, the Montmorencis, the Chatillons, and the great reform party in France, England, and Scotland, found themselves freed, as if from a dread nightmare,[88] for the most unpopular man in France, Cardinal Lorraine, was no longer supreme master, and the fascinations of his niece had lost their potency to command the resources of a great nation and serve the policy of her mother's house. Catharine made but small pretence of mourning her son, who had been more amenable to his wife than to her,[89] though the loose accusations against her of having hastened his death by poison are absurd, seeing that the cause of his death was undoubted. Still less credible is the assertion said to have been made by Leslie, Bishop of Ross, many years afterwards, that Mary had poisoned her first husband.[90] She, as we have seen, was the principal, if not the only sufferer by his death, and, malicious innuendo apart, every piece of evidence goes to prove that she was overwhelmed with grief at his death. Throckmorton, writing to Elizabeth on the 6th December, says she was 'as heavy and dolorous a wife as of right she had good cause to be, who by long watching with him during his sickness, and painful diligence about him, and specially by the issue thereof, is not in the best tune of her body'; and the testimony of the Venetian ambassador fully confirms this view. 'So, by degrees, every one will forget the death of the King, except the young Queen his widow, who being no less noble-minded than beautiful and graceful in appearance, the thoughts of widowhood at so early an age, and the loss of a consort . . . who so dearly loved her, and also that she is dispossessed of the crown of France, with little hope of recovering that of Scotland, which is her sole patrimony and dower, so affect her that she will not receive any consolation, but brooding over her disasters, with constant tears and passionate and doleful lamentations, she universally inspires great pity.'[91]

This was written only three days after the death of Francis; but for weeks later Mary remained isolated and shut out from the light of day, seeing no men but the new King, a boy of nine, his younger brother, the King of Navarre, Constable Montmorenci, and her uncles.[92] Brantome's testimony as to Mary's intense sorrow for her loss is very valuable. He says that, whilst he knew her, she never recovered from the pallor which her grief produced on her face. It is a somewhat curious reflection that has not, I think, yet been made, that the oft-quoted poem, written by Mary herself on her bereavement, tender as it is, gives us a key to the real state of her feelings, and to the apparently contradictory contemporary statements with regard to them.[93] Throughout the poem it is her own condition that she pities. Not a word of sorrow for the premature cutting-off of the life of young Francis, or grief at the suffering he had borne.

> 'Qui en mon doux printems,
> Et fleur de ma jeunesse,
> Toutes les peines sens
> D'une extreme tristesse:
> Et en rien n'ay plaisir
> Qu'en regret et desir.'

Her own loss of pleasure, the waste of her beauty and youth, the absence of something that ministered to her individual wellbeing, the occurrence of a misfortune that condemns her to

> 'En soupirs cuisants
> Passer mes meilleurs ans,'

are the main burden of her railings against fate. There is no reason whatever to doubt her sincerity in this respect; and the discontented pity she felt for herself, at having her life and ambitions thus early dislocated, was quite compatible with a keen watchfulness through her tears for another chance that might restore to her a position as advantageous as that which she held before her husband's death. We shall have other opportunities of observing that this note of essential selfishness is present in all the pathetic lamentations in which Mary indulged for her many subsequent afflictions. She always bids for pity for her own sufferings or disasters, and bewails her own hard fate, without a thought, apparently, for those who suffered for her cause. In her writings, as in her acts, we see the passionate woman avid for enjoyment, and resentful of anything that deprived her of the sensuous delight of life. The plaintive beauty who appeals to the pity of men, in sorrow and distress, wields the most powerful weapon in the feminine armoury; and when her claim is only that youth and loveliness should be happy, her fascination is irresistible. The weeping widow, disfigured and faded with grief, thinking nothing of herself, but only of the one that has gone, appeals to no one, and attracts no one, except from a broad charity for human suffering; but she who only bemoans her own sad state instinctively asks for sympathy and consolation, by which the happiness she yearns for may be restored, and pity, love, and hope are inspired in the hearts of men by her complaints. This appears to have been the case with Mary, and doubtless contributed not a little to the extraordinary sympathy she always excited in her distress.

On the very day of the King's death Throckmorton sounded the alarm as to Mary's possible second marriage. Everything was in confusion at Orleans. The Guises, thought Throckmorton, would not surrender their supremacy without an armed struggle; and 'if things be slept till the house of Guise (if they have the government and disposing of the new King and this realm as they had) find the means to marry their niece to the said new King . . . things will remain in the same state they are now in.'[94] Brantome, like a good Guisan as he was, says that King Charles was afterwards madly in love with his sister-in-law, and would have married her if he had had his own way;[95] and the English ambassador probably read Mary's character aright when he said that, as far as he could learn, she would have no objection to such a match, as 'she more esteemeth the continuation of her honour, and to marry one that may uphold her to be great, than she passeth to please her fancy by taking one that is accompanied with such small benefit or alliance as thereby her estimation and fame is not increased.' Almost with vehemence, therefore, Throckmorton urged his mistress to seize the opportunity of approaching the Queen-Mother and Anthony of Navarre with messages of sympathy, and thus to strengthen their hands against the Guises and the papal party. Elizabeth lost no time in acting upon the advice; but before the Earl of Bedford could be despatched upon the mission all Europe was planning marriages for Mary Stuart.

Chamberlain, the English ambassador in Madrid, saw the Duke of Alba soon after the news of the death of Francis arrived there (22nd December), and the conversation naturally drifted to the subject. Did the Duke think that the French would allow Mary to return to Scotland? tentatively asked Chamberlain. 'No: they probably would not,' replied Alba; 'but rather that they would seek to have the disposing of her again. God had diverted the French intents this time,' continued he, 'but Elizabeth had better be well prepared, for their intents were evil enough, and would have burst out within less than three months.'[96] 'The discourse of this court,' says Chamberlain, 'upon the Scottish Queen-widow are diverse: some think with dispensation the French will seek to match her with the new King; others with one of the uncles, the Prior of St John; some talk of the Prince of Spain. . . . Others remember the King of Denmark, and the new King of Sweden.' Randolph, the English agent in Scotland, reported that the Scots were talking of a match with the King of Denmark (27th December). The King of Navarre was anxious that the Earl of Arran should be the happy man;[97] whilst the Guises, promptly recognising that Catharine would never let her little son Charles, however lovelorn he might be, fall into the net of Mary and her uncles as his brother had done, strove their utmost to promote a marriage between their niece and Philip's only son,[98] Don Carlos. Philip feigned to entertain the idea, for it was a powerful lever by which he might move Elizabeth to his ends; and Chantonnay, the Spanish ambassador, and Don Juan Manriquez, who travelled from Madrid ostensibly to condole with Catharine for the death of her eldest son, both paid exaggerated court for a time to Mary Stuart and Cardinal Lorraine.[99] The retort to this on the part of England was an equal show of cordiality by Elizabeth to Catharine, Navarre, and the Huguenots;[1] whilst at the same time she opened negotiations with the Spanish ambassador in London, Bishop Quadra, for her own marriage with Robert Dudley under Spanish auspices, and the reconciliation of England with the papacy by means of a Council of Trent.[100]

Bedford left for France at the end of January, nominally to condole with Catharine and Charles on the death of Francis, but really to checkmate the Guise plans for Mary Stuart's marriage. He was to demand the ratification of the Treaty of Edinburgh, and to reproach Cardinal Lorraine for past proceedings, whilst professing a desire for amity with Mary in future. Mary herself was to be addressed in similar terms, and to be urged to banish distrust of the English intervention and the civil and religious changes in her realm. But above all Bedford was to keep in close touch with Navarre and his party, and with the Protestant Duchess of Ferrara (Renée of France). Bedford and Throckmorton were to 'explore the likelihood of the marriage of the Scottish Queen; wherein they shall employ their devices to procure it to be either in her own country, or in such place as may least augment her strength; and if they shall see any disposition in the house of Guise to seek marriage with Spain or Austria, they shall solicit the King of Navarre' (and also the Duchess of Ferrara), 'in secret manner, to impeach it, as a thing that shall tend to his great detriment.'[101]

Bedford and Throckmorton, in consequence of the illness of the latter, were not received by Catharine until the 16th February at Fontainebleau, where splendid preparations had been made for their entertainment. After their formal condolences to Charles IX and his mother, the ambassadors were conducted by the Duke of Guise (Cardinal Lorraine having already retired defeated to Rheims) to Mary Stuart's chamber. She was very 'sorrowful of look and speech,' and replied to Elizabeth's condolences somewhat tartly that 'as the Queen *now* shows the part of a good sister, whereof she has great need, she will endeavour to be equal with her in goodwill.' At subsequent interviews with Catharine they found her full of cordiality and desire to be friendly with Elizabeth, but not by any means inclined to play with her cards on the table, and to pronounce wholly in favour of the Huguenot party, as Navarre and his brother Condé had done. Mary Stuart was even more cautious, and, when asked to ratify the Treaty of Edinburgh, replied that, Cardinal Lorraine being absent, she had been unable to take counsel on the subject, as Elizabeth recommended her to do, but would give an answer later. When at a subsequent interview she was again pressed to ratify the treaty, she replied that she must consult the Scottish nobles first. It was not until the eve of Bedford's departure that he and Throckmorton spoke to Navarre about Mary's marriage. In reply to their approaches the titular King assured them that the match in hand was not with Don Carlos, but with the Duke of Austria, about which match the Emperor's ambassador had recently been closeted with Cardinal Lorraine.[102] 'How can you prevent it?' asked Anthony, in reply to Bedford's exclamation of dissent. 'Well,' replied Throckmorton, 'whilst she remains in court, at least, nothing of the sort could be settled without our knowing it; but if she went, as was intended, to Joinville, on the skirts of Lorraine, and not far from Germany, it might be secretly carried through.' Navarre promised to do his best to prevent Mary's journey to Joinville, but added, turning to Throckmorton, 'But, Master Ambassador, I told you a remedy against this mischief, whereunto you make me none answer: you know what I mean.'[103]

The efforts of Navarre were effectual in delaying but for a short time Mary's projected journey to Lorraine. She left Fontainebleau a month later, and after a day in Paris, occupied in choosing fit dresses and adornments from her wardrobe, she proceeded direct to Rheims (20th March). There were assembled all the Guise brothers and their mother, and the air was thick with marriage intrigues. The Prince of Orange's sister, the Duchess of Arschot, was there, which made Throckmorton nervous of a possible marriage in that direction.[104] The King of Denmark's envoy arrived in Paris with an offer of his master's hand for Mary immediately after the latter had left, and he too wended his way eastward to see her. But what was most feared by Elizabeth and her ministers was that Mary's stay at Rheims, Joinville, and Nancy might afford an opportunity for a sudden conclusion of a wedding with one of the Archdukes of Austria, who had been hankering around the bait of the English queen until her astute coquetry and Dudley's manoeuvres had made them despair.

But the Guises were bidding for higher game even than this. The religious divisions in France were rapidly coming to a head. It was evident that the papal party, for the time at least, was in the background; and that the Queen-Regent had no intention of allowing the Guises again to grasp the supreme power. The Guises cared nothing for France, as was proved later, and they doubtless thought it in any case legitimate to counterbalance the Bourbon and Huguenot approaches to England by a close alliance between themselves and Spain; though France might be deluged with blood, and suffer eventual dismemberment as a result. Cardinal Lorraine feigned entire absorption in his religious duties at Rheims, but Catharine disbelieved him, as she had reason to do; and his numerous letters to Spain proposing his niece's marriage with Don Carlos were accompanied by others more numerous still from the Queen-Regent to her daughter Elizabeth, Philip's wife, and to her ambassador, Monluc, imploring them to prevent any such arrangement, which she well knew would destroy the religious balance in France upon which her tenure of power rested. All sorts of hints were thrown out by her to dissuade Philip from such a match. Her own daughter Margaret of France might marry Carlos;[105] she herself would go south and meet Philip to cement with him a strict Catholic alliance; the King of Navarre would submit to Spain and be a good Catholic. These and a host of other clouds were raised by Catharine to cast a shadow upon the Guise plans and prevent what would have been gall and wormwood to her, the elevation of Mary Stuart to a commanding position and the restoration of Cardinal Lorraine to power.[106] Nor was Elizabeth of England idle. She and Dudley once more began to puzzle the old Bishop of Aquila in London with half-uttered assurances that, if Philip would bless their union, England would submit to the

Pope and be good again. The simultaneous effect of all these influences soon shelved for a time the idea of Mary's marriage with Don Carlos, and Cardinal Lorraine had to confess himself checkmated again by two women.

Mary herself stayed quietly in the convent at Rheims, of which her aunt Renée of Guise was abbess, until the middle of April, and then travelled to Joinville to sojourn with her saintly grandmother, the Dowager of Guise. What she herself thought of the marriage question at the time we do not know at first hand. Whilst she yet remained at the French court she had sent four Scottish envoys to Scotland to carry assurances of regard, and promises of forgiveness for past acts, to her people. When these envoys saw Lethington at Craigmillar in February they told him that, 'to show her subjects how she tenders their weal, and the honour of her country, she will not apply her mind to marriage, though already many sue her, as the King of Spain for his son, and the Kings of Sweden and Denmark for themselves, until she be in a place to have the advice of her nobles and the assent of her people.'[107] But, however sincere this promise may have been when it was made, it is certain that the active negotiations above referred to of Cardinal Lorraine with Spain a few weeks later on her behalf cannot have been conducted without her full knowledge and consent.

The antagonistic parties in Scotland were both of them naturally anxious to bid for the Queen's support. The Catholic section, much larger than was openly avowed, was in high hopes that Mary's return would bring the complete suppression of Protestantism; and a secret convention of Catholic nobles and bishops appointed Leslie, afterwards Bishop of Ross, to proceed to France for the purpose of advising the Queen. The parliament held in Edinburgh, according to Mary's request, appointed with a similar object James Stuart, Prior of St. Andrews, her illegitimate brother. The Protestant party was in a fever of apprehension as to the consequences of Mary's arrival in Scotland, and was desirous of delaying it as long as possible, in order that further assurance of English support might be obtained in case of an attempt to destroy religious reform by force. James Stuart tarried a time in England for the purpose of conferring with Cecil; and Leslie managed to obtain audience of Mary before her brother arrived.

The Queen was on her way from Rheims to Lorraine when Leslie met

her at the village of Vitry (14th April 1561). All that the wit of the priest could urge was fervently pressed upon her to cause her to beware of the Protestant and English party, who, without her consent, had weakened almost to extinction her royal prerogative, and had penalised the exercise of the faith in which she was so strenuous a believer. Above all, said Leslie, let her be cautious of the Stuart bastard who had assumed the leadership of the party that aimed at reducing her to the position of a puppet ruler of a heretic realm. Let him be seized in France and rendered powerless for harm, and Mary might land in Huntly's country surrounded by the Catholic nobles, and 'overshadow' the heretics. But Mary knew well that the Catholic party in Scotland was not strong enough without foreign support to crush reform, and without a great marriage foreign support she could not hope for. So, when James Stuart overtook her the following day at St. Dizier, she smiled upon him, and brought to bear all the battery of her fascinations to win him, her brother, to her own side. To this she had been advised by her wisest councillors in France, including her Guise kinsmen, and indeed, as we see it now, it was her only statesmanlike course. Before James's arrival measures had been devised by the Guises to bribe him with a cardinal's hat and other tempting offers; and Throckmorton was afraid that the temptations would be too much for him. Then indeed, he thought, would the Protestant and English party in Scotland be in a parlous case.[108] But Lord James knew where the real strength behind him was; and as he rode with his sister towards Nancy, even her offer to him of the regency of Scotland during her absence could not win from him a pledge to forsake the friendship of Elizabeth of England, or abandon the Protestant faith that he had embraced. But she let him go under the belief that his commission as temporary ruler of Scotland should follow hard upon his heels to Paris, and only after his arrival there and his secret conference with Throckmorton was the news received that the Queen had changed her mind, and had determined, as was said, to look alone to Huntly and the Catholics for support.[109]

Whatever may have been the influence that caused Mary to take this step it was one of the most unfortunate in her life—for it threw down the gauntlet to the Queen of England, to the able and unscrupulous James, and to the growing power of Protestantism which he now led in his sister's realm: the three forces which ultimately vanquished her and her cause. The Duchess-Dowager of Lorraine at the time was that clever Cristina of Denmark, the first cousin of Philip II, and it was she, with her young son the Duke and his child-wife Claude of France, that entertained Mary during her stay. Mary had nothing more to hope from Catharine de Medici, who had already shown her claws to her daughter-in-law, and there was no other power than Spain that could by force impose Catholicism upon Scotland and paralyse the English influence. All the evidence points towards the probability that the further progress made at Nancy with the negotiations for a marriage between Mary and Don Carlos, or his cousin the Archduke Charles, persuaded her that she was now strong enough to defy James Stuart and her Protestant government. This conclusion is confirmed by the fact that her subsequent change of policy, when she first arrived in Scotland, coincided with the cooling of the idea of a Spanish marriage for her, owing to Catharine de Medici's warm approaches towards Philip, and Elizabeth's clever matrimonial juggling with all of Mary's possible suitors.

To the renewed demands of Elizabeth's envoys that she would ratify the Treaty of Edinburgh Mary also thought herself strong enough to return a negative answer whilst at Nancy and afterwards at Rheims. Her arrival in Lorraine had evidently increased in some way both her own firmness of purpose and her importance in the eyes of others. Whilst at Nancy she was entertained splendidly—'beholding pleasant farces and plays, and using all kind of honourable pastimes within the palace'[110] and upon her return to Paris (10th June), after an attack of sickness at Nancy and Joinville, which prevented her from attending the coronation of Charles IX at Rheims, she was met in great state a league from the city by all the princes of the blood and the French nobility, and the King and Queen-Mother awaited her outside her lodging.[111]

There was no longer any hesitation as to her voyage to her own realm. Scotland had been represented to her as a savage and inhospitable land, peopled by rebellious and turbulent folk, and a voyage thither from the France she had learned to look upon as her own country was a dread nightmare to her:[112] but her ambition was great, the splendid chance of a marriage that should link her to Spain, and place in her hand the strength necessary for her purpose and that of her uncles, over-rode all other considerations. If she could, with her personal fascination and authority, gain the permission of her government to marry a Spanish or Austrian prince under Philip's auspices, the highest of her hopes might yet be realised, and she might live to sit on the throne of a Catholic Britain, even if surrounded by Philip's pikemen.

Throckmorton was fully alive to the dangers of the situation. He took the opportunity of Mary's stay in Paris to press upon her again (18th June) the ratification of the treaty with England, and found her, as before, amiably inflexible to all his diplomacy. She would do everything in her power to please his Queen; every Frenchman should leave Scotland, and she hoped that Elizabeth would cease to shelter her rebel subjects, but she proudly said she would not be constrained by her own people in the matter of religion. 'God commanded subjects to be obedient to their princes,' she said: she believed her religion to be the true one, and nothing on earth would make her change it. She would constrain none of her subjects; but she hoped that Elizabeth would not aid them to constrain her. And, for all Throckmorton's religious arguments and dialectical skill, he could not move her from this position. His spies told him that the Spanish marriage was still being dealt with. Philip had said that 'he would be loth to marry his son to a process, but that if her matters were clear, he knew no party that he would more gladly match his son with'; and, *more suo,* the Spanish king advised Mary to dissemble with the Scots upon her first arrival until he was at liberty from the war with the Turk: 'then she may proceed with rigour against those who will persevere in their religion repugnant to hers.'[113]

These were the ideas that the hopes of a Spanish marriage had nourished in the breast of Mary Stuart as the day for her voyage to Scotland approached. She had quite recovered the aplomb which for a time had failed her after her loss, and in view of the flouts of her late mother-in-law. She was striving, as she knew, for a great prize, and there was nothing, as yet, that hampered her in the full exercise of her high natural qualities of statesmanship. She asked for an assurance that Elizabeth's navy would not molest her on her voyage; but when the request was somewhat churlishly refused unless she would ratify the treaty, she expressed her regret that she had asked for what she had no need. It is evident from Cecil's letters[114] that the English and some of the Scottish Protestants believed that, so long as Mary was prevented from going to Scotland and settling matters there, the Spanish match would hang fire; and it is equally probable that this was the very reason that determined Mary to undertake the voyage at all hazards.

Throckmorton saw her at St. Germain on the 20th July, when he found her chatting with M. d'Oisel, who had just arrived from England with Elizabeth's refusal of Mary's request. She rose as the English ambassador entered the chamber, and having heard from him his mistress's message, she gave a truly feline scratch to Elizabeth by bidding those present to retire out of hearing, as 'she knew not well her own infirmity, nor how far with passion she might be transported; but she liked not to have so many witnesses of her passions as his mistress had, when she talked with M. d'Oisel.'[115] Then with exquisite skill she blended, in a long address, innocent surprise at Elizabeth's attitude, indignation at unfriendly acts and unfounded suspicions, and veiled threats that she was not without powerful friends: but as to the ratification not an inch would she budge. All the past acts had been done by her late consort and her uncles: she now stood alone and upon another footing, and would take no steps until her council in Scotland had advised her. When later in the day the English ambassador took leave of her for the purpose of discovering, if he could, when and how she proposed to sail, she told him that she hoped the wind would be so favourable that she need not come to the English coast; 'but if she did then his mistress would have her in her hands to do her will of her; and if she was so hard-hearted as to desire her end, she might then do her pleasure and make sacrifice of her. Peradventure that casualty might be better for me than to live in this matter, quoth she, God's will be done.'[116]

Five days later Mary Stuart rode out of St. Germain with a great train of Scottish and French nobles. Her baggage and household had preceded her, and had gone to Havre, but her own place of embarkation was kept strictly secret, so secret, indeed, that Throckmorton half believed that the whole thing was a feint, and that she would not go at all, but would simply stay at Calais watching events. Slowly she rode through Northern France accompanied by her six Guise uncles, and whilst yet on the way she made another attempt to obtain a safe-conduct from the English queen, this time through the King of Navarre, who sent a special messenger to Elizabeth for the purpose. Mary again sent for Throckmorton when she was at Abbeville, and made a new appeal to him. She repeated her assurance that she only wished for friendship. She had quite abandoned the use of the English arms, which her late husband had assumed. Her Guise uncles would no longer advise her, and she could not possibly ratify the treaty without the counsel of the Scottish nobles. This was obviously only for the purpose of delay, and Throckmorton finally took leave of the Queen on the 8th August, as she rode towards Calais, where her galleys awaited her, keenly spied by English agents, whilst yet another envoy from Mary hurried to make a last request to Elizabeth herself for a safe-conduct.[117]

The ties that bound her to France were weakened by every league that she passed upon her way. Already her thoughts and ambitions lay towards the mighty power of Spain and Flanders, whose morose master at this juncture of her life openly expressed his compassion and sympathy for her, and his indignation at Elizabeth's treatment of her in refusing her a safe- conduct. When at length she entered the town of Calais, with the victorious Guise who had snatched it from the English by her side, the French chapter of her life had ended. Thenceforward she might yearn for the comfort, the splendour, the security, that France had afforded her, she might even receive wordy sympathy and ostentatious tears in her troubles, but she could command no more for her family or religious ends the resources of the French monarchy, because the sovereign who ruled it for years to come was a jealous woman who hated her; with no strong religious convictions, no fixity of policy, no honour, and no conscience; whilst on the English side of the channel Mary was also pitted against another woman similarly endowed; and against two such antagonists her feminine weapons were impotent.

IV

MARY QUEEN REGNANT OF SCOTLAND

The voyage to Scotland—Mary's grief and apprehension at leaving France—Her companions—Bothwell, Chastelard, Brantome—Policy of Lethington and James Stuart—Mary lands at Leith (August 1561)—Her reception—Knox and Mary—Religious discord in Mary's court—Difficulties of James and Lethington—The problems they had to face—Plans for Mary's marriage—Attempts to gain Elizabeth's recognition of Mary as her heir—Lethington's efforts to that end—The only alternative a match with Don Carlos—The Hamiltons' plot—Civil war in France—Elizabeth's action to counteract the Spanish marriage intrigue—Mary's light-heartedness in face of her troubles—The revolt of the Gordons and death of Huntly—Fresh attempts to reconcile Elizabeth to Mary's heirship—Lethington goes to London—Assassination of Guise—Lethington offers Mary to Don Carlos—Negotiations with the Spanish ambassador and with the English Catholics—Elizabeth suggests Robert Dudley or his brother—Her real object in this.

MARY REMAINED SORROWFULLY IN CALAIS FOR SIX DAYS AWAITing the safe-conduct that came not; but at length (14th August), determined to face the risk of capture, she bade farewell to most of the brilliant train that had accompanied her so far, and embarked on one of the two beautiful galleys that rode in the harbour. Brantome's touching description of her heart-broken farewell to her friends and to her beloved France has been quoted until it has become threadbare, and the pathetic picture of the interesting Queen reclining on the stern railing of her vessel as the day faded, straining her streaming eyes to catch a last glimpse of the land she loved, is too well known to be quoted here. That she bitterly regretted the need which forced her to leave France is certain; for was she not leaving security, comfort, elegance, and devotion, to face uncertainty, discomfort, uncouthness, and the distrust of a large section of her people? There was no reason why she should be consumed with love for Scotland. The country was a distant memory to her personally, and since she could remember it had always been in seething revolt against her authority and her faith. Her beloved mother had been sacrificed to its turbulence, and she was full of sad foreboding that the task that had broken down Mary of Guise would claim as a victim her daughter as well. No wonder that the sight of a ship foundering with all hands before her eyes, as she glided out of Calais harbour, wrung from her the heartcry, 'O God! what an omen have we here.'

With her on the galleys were three of her uncles, the Duke d'Aumale, the Grand Prior of St. John, and the Marquis d'Elbœuf. The four maids of honour who had been her companions from infancy, the four Maries, were also near her, and a crowd of French and Scottish noble ladies and gentlemen, who were willing to brave the risks of such a voyage for her sake. Amongst them were two men, who perhaps at the time but little attracted her attention, but who nevertheless were in the dim future to sway her fate and die miserably for love or lust of her. One of them, broad of shoulders, stout of limb, was a young Scotsman of five-and-twenty, whose characteristic was strength rather than beauty. Stubborn red hair, cropped close, covered his massive head, and a great warlike beak of a nose overshadowed a mouth of enormous width and a heavy jaw.[118] But yet James Hepburn, Earl of Bothwell, was no boor. He had been reared at the French court, and was fully conversant with all the graces of his time; his hands and feet were fine and aristocratic, his bearing was gallant; and though violent passion, over-bearing resistance, marred his elegance, the magnetic force of him dominated the love of many women. The other man was cast in different mould. A Frenchman Chastelard, a mere lad, a dangling courtier of the newer school that had become fashionable in the last two years in France; bearing a sword by his side, but oftener toying with his lute; sweet of voice, languishing and lovelorn in demeanour, a pretty fribble to look at as he sighed his verses, but, like the little Abbé of two centuries later, hiding beneath his soft gentleness more profligacy and vice than a dozen rough soldiers might. He was in the train of Montmorenci's son and heir, D'Anville, who also accompanied Mary to Scotland; and Brantome gives a characteristic specimen of his poetic compliments, addressed to Mary even thus early. Seeing the ship's lantern being lighted on her galley, 'il dit ce gentil mot': 'Surely there be no need of that light to guide us over the sea. The sweet eyes of our Queen are bright enough to illumine all the ocean with their dazzling fires, nay, to set it in flames if needs be.'

As the groaning slaves, toiling at their oars, slowly urged Mary's galley through the mirky North Sea towards her own land, the party that had in her absence changed the national religion, monopolised the government of the state, and diminished the prerogative of the sovereign, were in a fever of apprehension as to the consequences of her advent. James Stuart and Lethington, foreseeing their danger, had for some time been striving to bring about an agreement between Elizabeth and Mary, by which they and the Protestant party might be assured of continued power, and Mary conciliated by being acknowledged heir to the throne of England failing Elizabeth and her descendants.[119] But such a solution as this, plausible as it looked, was one that the policy of Elizabeth could never admit, especially to serve other interests than her own; and when the governors of Scotland convinced themselves at last that Elizabeth would play her own game only, and that the coming of their Queen was inevitable, they could but look to their English friends for protection against the destruction which threatened them. Knox himself whimpered to Elizabeth, deprecating the feared attempts of Mary to stir up the anger of the English queen against him on account of his attack on women governors. Lord James, Lethington, and Morton agreed with Cecil in wishing that she (Mary) might be stayed; 'and were it not for obedience sake, some of them care not though they never saw her face. They try to prevent the wicked devices of her mischievous papist ministers. . . . They do what they can for the religion and amity with their neighbours—and need look to themselves, for their hazard is great, as

they see. There is no safety for them but in our Queen's (Elizabeth) favour, for friends abroad they have none, and few trustworthy at home. . . . They are feared with her (Mary's) refusal, and fear her thrusting Englishmen out of the country. . . . Lethington doth all he can to satisfy you of things here—he thinks it best she come not—but if she do, let her know she shall find obedience and service if she embrace Christ and desire peace with her neighbours. . . . Mr. Knox is determined to abide the uttermost, and others will not leave him till God have taken his life and theirs.'[120]

This was written whilst Mary was at Calais, and Lethington followed it by repeated letters of his own to Cecil, full of craven fears. The lukewarm Protestants, he said, would fall away if Mary came, and the 'papists' were already plucking up courage: it would be well for the English to place a strong force at Berwick; 'so long as we stand in doubtful terms; it will discourage the enemy, and make us bolder.' 'I pray you advise me in this dangerous case, whereto my wit is not sufficient, as well in the common cause as in my particular, who am taken to be chief meddeler and principal negotiator of all the practiques with England. Though I be not in greatest place, yet is not my danger least, specially when she shall come home having received at her Majesty's (Elizabeth's) hands so great a discourtesy.'[121]

Mary's tiny fleet, shrouded in mist during part of the voyage, saw nothing of the English forces she had feared. It is more than doubtful, indeed, whether there was any serious intention of waylaying her at sea, though if she had entered an English port, as at one time seemed possible, she might have been detained; and if the little English squadron sent out on pretence of arresting pirates had made a mistake and captured the Scottish galleys instead, there would have been no great grief thereat in the English court, although, doubtless, officially Elizabeth would have been much shocked. But we may be sure that she would have extorted Mary's signature to the Treaty of Edinburgh before she let her go,[122] however much she might have railed at the captors, for such was Elizabeth Tudor's way. On the morning of the 19th August 1561, several days earlier than had been expected, the galleys entered the port of Leith. Little preparation had been made, for people still doubted the Queen's coming. Mary herself saw her country with a sinking heart; and when informed that during the fog she had been in great danger of being lost upon the rocks, she replied that, for her own sake, there was nothing she would have welcomed more than death; though she would have been sorry for Scotland if she had died.

With such mutual dread between the Queen and her government Mary Stuart set foot on her own land. There were no great personages at Leith ready to receive her except her bastard brother Robert Stuart, and she breakfasted at Captain Lamb's house surrounded by those who had come from France with her. Soon, however, the people began to flock in from Edinburgh: first the Duke of Chatelherault; and then, plucking up courage, there came doubtingly those who most feared her advent. It was an ominous beginning, and Mary was in low spirits.[123] For her ride into Edinburgh there attended her a single horse for herself, and for her train a lot of little rough hackneys shabbily caparisoned. The contrast with past splendour was too much for the overstrung nerves of the Queen, and she broke down at the sight of the sorry equipage; bursting into tears, and sobbing out that this was very different from the rich and beautiful cavalcades she had disposed of in France and had enjoyed so long; but since she must change her heaven into a hell, she must eke have patience.[124]

In this gloomy and resentful spirit, a combination of pride and self-pity, Mary first faced her people, as she rode from Leith to Holyrood. The elements of the tragedy were here all complete. A profoundly divided people—dour burgesses, and clansmen looking only to their chiefs—a jealous governing class, who had used the weakness of their sovereigns to render themselves supreme, an administration kept in power by the money and intrigues of a foreign country for the purpose of crushing the religion of the sovereign and of a large section of the people; and on the other hand a proud young Queen, loving pleasure and material comfort above all things; accustomed to splendour, luxury, and deference, such as her own country could not give her; discontented with her fate, wounded at the limits placed by her subjects upon her authority; and above all representing in her own person the extreme papal party in the Christian church, which was the sworn enemy of her nearest neighbour, and of the type of religion adopted by her government and the reformers amongst her own people. Only great sacrifices from one or the other side, with infinite patience and wisdom on

both, could save the situation which began so inauspiciously; and, clever as were the principal parties in the struggle, patience, tolerance, and self-sacrifice were precisely the qualities in which most of them were lacking.

Mary did her best to dissemble her discontent. Her uncles were at her side whispering to her wise advice to smile upon all men, and bide her time. But it must have been a hard task for the proud beauty, for of provocation to anger there was plenty: the noisy welcome of the citizens to their Queen, the psalm-singing, the discordant music under her window, the blazing bonfires that made night hideous, disgusted the fine French courtiers, though Mary herself feigned to enjoy the harmony.[125] But though the townspeople were delighted with her at first sight, and, as Mauvissière says, 'thought themselves extremely happy to have such a Queen, who was the most celebrated beauty of the age,' they had no love to spare for the outlandish papists who accompanied her; and to avenge some fancied affront the mob pursued her French almoner to her very chamber the morning after her arrival, with intent to kill him. She managed in the first few days to persuade the Protestants, and even suspicious James Stuart, that they had nothing to fear from her; but, wrote Randolph, a week after her landing, 'all men persist in the same mind that they were before they saw her—the Protestants stout in God's cause, and the papists nothing encouraged for anything they have found.'[126] Mass was first celebrated in her chapel on Sunday, five days after her arrival, and few but her own household attended it, whilst 'Mr. Knox's sermon' was crammed to overflowing with nobles and burgesses. The next day a compromise was effected with her Council, that the Queen might continue her religious services in her own house without interference. Lord James and Lethington were still her principal advisers, but under the surface the fires of discord glowed: Bothwell had openly quarrelled with Arran, and was fain to quit the court; Huntly and the other Catholic nobles came swaggering in with troops of tousled, armed clansmen at their heels; Mary herself looked sourly upon Randolph the English agent, and asked a bystander what *he* was doing in Scotland; and, above all, Knox, steeled against blandishments and graces, 'thundereth owte of the pulpet, so that I feare nothynge so mych as that one day he will marre all. He ruleth the roste, and of hym all men stonde in feare—woulde God he knew how mych.'[127]

Lethington started for England a few days after his Queen's arrival, the hope of Lord James and himself being that the bait of the English succession for Mary would make her tractable to their ends. Whilst this flattering hope lasted James was all amiability and conciliation to his sister, and the Queen herself, with a similar object, strove her utmost to reassure the English party. The first interview which Randolph had with her as Elizabeth's representative was for the purpose of protesting against the depredations of certain Scottish pirates, and Mary went out of her way to convince him of her earnest desire to live in friendship with her cousin of England. She had reason enough to look askance at Randolph, for she knew full well that he had been the crafty tool by which Elizabeth had worked so successfully upon Scotland. But even with him she was gracious; and, as James told him afterwards, had simply remarked, when his back was turned, that she saw it was intended for Randolph to remain. 'Well! let him stay,' she said, 'but I will have another one there (in England) as crafty as he.'

So long as diplomatists and politicians alone had matters in hand all went smoothly. Elizabeth most graciously gave permission for two of Mary's uncles and young Montmorenci (d'Anville) to pass through England on their way home, the belated passport for Mary herself came, and allayed some of the irritation caused by its first refusal, Mary and her uncle Elbœuf did their best to please the Protestants, and with considerable success;[128] whilst Lord James was equally careful not openly to offend the Catholics. But Knox and the bigots were as constant grit in the wheels and spoilt all. On the occasion of Mary's state entry into Edinburgh (4th September) the emblems that greeted her displayed a lamentable want of gracefulness and good feeling. Up to this time, at all events, there had not been the slightest indication on the part of Mary that she had any notion of coercing her subjects in the matter of religion; yet the first allegorical greeting that met her was a child, who, released from a suspended globe on high, descended as an angel to hand her a Protestant bible and psalter, with the keys of the city; and as she progressed through the streets, on all sides were pageants and inscriptions recalling to her 'the vengeance of God upon idolaters.' They had arranged as a climax the 'burning of a priest at the altar, at the elevation'; but this—either in sham or earnest—was too much for Huntly, and he put his foot down and stopped it. The Duke of Chatelherault and his son Arran had retired from court, and begun to fortify their castle of Dumbarton, as soon as the first mass was celebrated, and Knox surpassed himself in intemperate violence. 'I assure you,' wrote Randolph to Cecil in reply to his recommendation to the Protestants to stand firmly, notwithstanding blandishments, 'I assure you the voice of one man is able in one hour to put more life into us than 500 trumpets continually blustering in our ears.'[129] The 'one man,' Knox, had his famous interview with Mary two days after the state entry. We have seen what she was: a young woman, proud and tenacious of her prerogative, conscious that her place in the coming great struggle between freedom and authority in religion was in the forefront of the ranks of the strictest orthodoxy. Her uncles were the leaders of the cause in France, and it was the only party to which she could look with confidence for the recognition of her claim to the English throne. Temporising at the time, in the hope that an arrangement might yet be made with Elizabeth that would afford her a lever for future action, Mary desired, above all things, to conciliate the various interests that might be inimical to her, and summoned Knox to Holyrood to exercise her fascination upon him. Him also we know as embodying what has since become a recognised type of religious Scotsman. To him the only righteousness, the only salvation, was to be found within the narrow limits of his own view of his own creed. All else was anathema; and with beauty, and sweetness, and mercy, with kindly pity for the erring, with humble recognition of the frailty of human judgment, with tender trust in God's goodness even to the guilty, John Knox would hold no parley.

Thus, arrogant as a swashbuckler, consciously righteous as an archangel might be, and inflexible as a judge upon the bench, he stood before the Queen. With eloquence and skill he justified himself as a good subject in the abstract, and though he had written against woman rule, 'and had been chosen by God to disclose to the realm the vanity of the papistical religion, with the deceit, pride, and tyranny of the Roman anti-Christ,' if Mary would not persecute the true faith he would undertake not to attack her authority. But soon the discussion turned to purely religious points, and both disputants lost their temper. Knox inveighed against Rome and the Mass, and claimed for subjects freedom from all religious dictation from their princes, in defence of which principle subjects might, he said, legally rebel. 'Let kings protect and foster the pure Church of God.' 'But you are not the Church that I will nourish,' replied the Queen. 'I will defend the Church of Rome, which I think the true one'; and her last words were drowned in a flood of tears, in anger rather than sorrow, maliciously suggests Randolph. But Knox was now fairly in the saddle, and tears moved him as little as graces had done before. 'Your *will*, Madam, is not reason; neither does your *thought* make the Roman harlot the true immaculate spouse of Jesus Christ. Wonder not, Madam, that I call Rome a harlot; for that Church is polluted with all kinds of spiritual fornication in doctrine and manners.' Lord James smoothed matters over as well as he might, and the colloquy ended more peacefully, Knox being accorded permission to address the Queen again on religion. But though Protestants affected to believe that their champion could win the Queen to his views, Knox himself from the first interview understood, as well as Mary did, the hopelessness of such a belief. 'The Queen neither is, nor shall be, of our opinion,' wrote he to Cecil; 'and, in very deed, her whole proceedings do declare that the Cardinal's lessons are so deeply printed on her heart, that the substance and quality are like to perish together. . . . In communication with her I find such craft as I have not found in such an age.'[130]

Thus, between two incompatible inflexibilities, matters grew gradually embittered, despite of all the efforts of politicians of both parties. Many of the courtiers who had professed Protestantism were encouraged by the Queen's firmness to smile upon the Mass again. Whilst Mary was on a progress and staying at Stirling[131] (14th September), the discord came to a head. High Mass was being celebrated with full pomp in the Castle chapel, when Lord James and the Earl of Argyle lost control of themselves, and in anger molested the singing men, whereupon a general fight ensued, in which more than one tonsured pate was broken. A few days afterwards, at Perth, the 'pageants' were so offensive to the Queen that she fell ill in the street, and had to be lifted from her horse and carried fainting to her dwelling. Huntly and James had a violent quarrel, almost a fight, because the former said that if the Queen commanded it, he would set up the Mass in three shires; and gradually, in one part of the country and another, the Catholics plucked up boldness to celebrate their services without concealment. Lethington, hurrying home from England, with cold comfort of the arrangement he had hoped to effect, found things in this unsatisfactory state. On all sides people were murmuring against Lord James and him. 'The papists think they favour England, others that they are too affectionate to their own[132] (interests).' Protestants thought them too ready to sacrifice religion for politics, and Knox alternately sneered at and denounced men who wished to 'swim between two streams.' These two men had to bear the brunt of extremists of all parties, and it behoved them to cast about for a remedy before they were swept off their feet and destroyed. Their great plan for conciliating Mary by obtaining her recognition as heiress to the English crown was hanging fire, though no stone was left unturned, either by Mary or her two principal advisers, to persuade Elizabeth to agree thereto.[133] All that submission and soft words could effect was being done, though, notwithstanding the growing hatred of the people to the Mass, the violence of Knox, and the daily quarrels that raged around her, Mary herself never wavered in her own religious observance, or feigned any personal approach to Protestantism.

The only card that remained unplayed in the hands of James and Lethington was Mary's second marriage. If that could be so arranged as to carry with it either the recognition of Mary's right to the English succession, or the power finally to defy Elizabeth, all might still be well; otherwise it was evident that Scotland must become a mere vassal, to be used by the English queen solely for her own ends. It was high time, indeed, that Scotsmen should endeavour to coalesce on a national policy of their own, instead of allowing their family feuds and religious divisions to play into the hands of other nations. Although Mary had only been in Scotland for a few months, affairs had already drifted into a pitiably lawless condition. The Duke of Chatelherault and his son Arran were sulking away from court, refusing to give up the fortress of Dumbarton; Bothwell, always near the Queen, and thus early assuming the position of her personal champion; Lord James and Lethington growing daily more unpopular and distrusted, even amongst the Protestants; and Mary herself an object of bitter attack and denunciation. Brawls in the court were almost of daily occurrence, either between the craftsmen or the nobles; and Mary on more than one occasion was threatened with forcible abduction, the mad and foolish Arran being the instigator, and—until later, as will be related—Bothwell, his sworn enemy, being the champion on the other side.[134]

The position was thus an extremely difficult one for the two men at the head of affairs, desirous as they were to steer a moderate course. Extremists on both sides distrusted them; their endeavours, and those of Mary, to obtain from Elizabeth some consideration for Scottish interests, had hitherto been absolutely fruitless, and it behoved them, as Scotsmen first, who like other politicians of their time looked upon creed as the handmaid of statesmanship, to use the marriage of the Queen as an instrument to rescue Scotland from the position into which it had drifted.

Of pretenders Mary naturally had many. The King of Sweden, persistently snubbed by Elizabeth, was actively pushing his suit to Mary by means of his agents in Scotland.[135] The Pope's special nuncio in France, Cardinal Ferrara, despatched in October the Savoyard agent Moret to England and Scotland with a feigned mission, his real object being to urge Mary again to marry either Guise's henchman Nemours (Jacques de Savoie) or the Duke of Ferrara.[136] But the Guises were now in the background; and Anthony of Navarre, as soon as he heard of the mission, sent an emissary of his own, the Huguenot de Foix, a relative of Jeanne d'Albret, to frustrate the Guisan plans. At the hint of Navarre Elizabeth delayed Moret in London until de Foix had got a fair start on the northern road, and, notwithstanding Moret's subsequent speed, the Huguenot saw Mary at Holyrood a few hours before his rival. De Foix, doubtless, had something positive to say about a marriage, in addition to trying to put a spoke in the Guisan wheel, for it was noticed that Mary blushed more than once during her interview with him, and was very gay and happy.[137] But she and her advisers had bigger game in view than either Moret or de Foix could offer her. After she had seen de Foix she sent for Randolph, and told him how glad she was to have heard of Elizabeth's good health. 'You must bid him (de Foix) welcome to Scotland,' she said; and then the Marquis d'Elbœuf[138] went out of his way to profess his love and devotion to the English queen. When a Guise did this there was always some mischief afoot.

Mary herself had quite recovered her good spirits, and appears to have

enjoyed much better health than in France. Though she preserved her decorum in her council-chamber, her youthful gaiety asserted itself as soon as she had shaken off the trammels of ceremonial, greatly to the scandal of the unco' guid, who considered that the leaping and skipping that went on were not 'comely for honest women.' Music, minstrelsy, card-playing, outdoor sports, and indoor masques, all delighted her. Her own birthday, the marriage of her two brothers Robert and John, the latter of whom was a great dancer and a special favourite of hers, the reception of ambassadors and the like, were all excuses for merrymaking eagerly seized upon. The memorial Mass on the anniversary of poor young Francis's death hardly broke in upon the gay junketings, not a Scottish noble of them all deigning to appear, or put on mourning garb.

The kindest of messages went backward and forward to Elizabeth, there was even a talk of a friendly meeting between them to banish all difficulties, and at the wedding of Lord James (Earl of Mar, soon to be Murray) Mary publicly drank to Elizabeth's health, and handed the golden cup as a token of amity to Randolph.[139] But behind all this gaiety and blandishment the matrimonial intrigue was busy, and both sections of Scottish nobles, the Catholics and the professed Protestants, were endeavouring to outbid each other, with the object, in either case, of forcing the hand of England. In the autumn the Catholics of Scotland and England secretly approached the Countess of Lennox—Lady Margaret Douglas, daughter of Queen Margaret Tudor, Mary's grandmother. Lennox had forfeited his estates in France and Scotland when he married Henry VIII's niece, and had since resided on estates granted to him in the north of England. The countess was fussy and ambitious, sympathising with the Catholic cause. Lennox was weak and vain, and their elder son Henry, Lord Darnley, now nearly sixteen, a spoilt and pampered boy, brought up by his mother in constant contemplation of his royal descent, was, failing Mary, the eventual heir of the crown of England; and it was a clever move of the Catholics to intrigue for a marriage, which, independently of Elizabeth's will, might give to Mary under their auspices the almost assured succession of England, by uniting the claims of the two next heirs. Whether Mary herself was a party to the negotiation at this juncture is not quite certain,[140] though she unquestionably received her aunt's approaches; but Cecil's spies were everywhere, and before the matter had gone beyond the preliminary stages Lady Margaret and her husband were summoned to London and placed under keeping. The countess put a brave face on the matter at first, and admitted to Elizabeth that she had tried to marry her boy to Mary. Why not? There was no harm in that. He was next heir to England after Mary, and the match was a fitting one.[141] Alas! the poor lady did not know the English queen yet so well as she learned to do afterwards by bitter experience. She was humble enough to Elizabeth before she died.

But Mary and her Protestant advisers had a greater marriage than any of these in their eyes, a project so bold and daring, if it could have been effected, as to have successfully checkmated Elizabeth for good. Lethington and James had done their best to gain the help of England. They had abased themselves before Cecil and his mistress, and had received nothing in return; a continuance in the moderate course was clearly becoming impossible in Scotland, and it was almost hopeless to expect any reciprocity from England that should keep Mary on her independent throne in peace, with these two men, Lord James and Lethington, as her ministers. They were Scotsmen, as patriotic as men usually were in their day; their adhesion to England and the Protestant cause had been purely political and selfish, and they seem now to have concluded that a time had come for them to play the great game for the advantage of their own country and themselves, rather than serving as tools for others. They were clever men, especially Lethington, but they were not clever enough for their plan. There were opponents and friends more cunning still, and in any case it was late to hope to remedy by a reversal of policy the effects of twenty years of drifting.

When Moret, the Savoyard envoy, saw Mary in November, he was soon made to understand—although he probably was already aware of it—that neither Nemours nor Ferrara would do for the Queen of Scots. He was a Guisan, and must, of course, have known something of Cardinal Lorraine's bold plan of a year ago to marry her to Don Carlos; so, after his first talk with the Queen, one of the Scottish councillors took him aside and asked him to forward a marriage of the Queen with the heir of Spain. Moret appears to have given a sympathetic answer, and was assured 'that there was not a man,

Catholic or heretic, in the kingdom, except the Earl of Arran, who did not ardently desire such a match; and even the Queen herself was thinking of it and hoping for it.'[142]

When Moret saw Mary again she did not dissemble with him as to her wishes. He asked her what the heretics would think of it. They would be only too glad of it, she told him; 'and even though on religious grounds they might be sorry, there were so many other things dependent upon it that, so long as she did not leave the country, they would not object, or at least until she had children that she could leave as her successors.' Moret found that 'Lord James and the principal people in the country are of the same opinion.'[143] Not a word of this was allowed at the time to reach even the vigilant Randolph; and the Huguenot de Foix went back to France assured that he had been successful in checkmating the Catholic suggestions for Mary's marriage.[144]

Quite a scare took place in London in March when the news came that the King of Sweden's envoy had formally offered his master's hand to Mary. Troops were made ready on the Border, English warships were put into commission, and for a few days affairs looked threatening. But just then Mary's uncle, the Marquis d'Elbœuf, passed through London on his way home, and laughed to scorn the idea of his niece marrying Eric. Elizabeth and Dudley made much of Elbœuf; it was said in order to win him to a marriage between Mary and Arran; the most unlikely match in the world now, as probably Elizabeth knew. Arran doubtless still dreamt of the possibility of it, and his foolish plots to kidnap Mary may probably be explained by his fear that the great Catholic marriage was contemplated which would end his chances for good. The first of these attempts (January 1562) involved the plot to murder Bothwell, with whom Arran was always at feud; and the apparently inexplicable complicity of Bothwell himself in the second plan (March 1562) may probably have been caused by his jealousy at the idea of Mary's marriage with Carlos. After years of bitter enmity Arran and Bothwell suddenly became inseparable 'at preachings, huntings, and elsewhere.' Mary grew suspicious, and had them closely watched. One day they rode together from Edinburgh to the Hamilton castle of Kinneal, and Bothwell opened the matter by saying that he knew Arran was the most hated man in Scotland, both by the Queen and by Lord James (Mar) and Lethington. 'If you will follow my advice,' he said, 'I have an easy way to remedy everything; that is, to put the Queen into your hands, and to take away your chief enemies the Earl of Mar and the Laird of Lethington.' Arran assented at first, and his father the Duke of Chatelherault even more emphatically; but Arran lost nerve, and the next day wrote a full confession to Mary. When his father learned of the delation his rage knew no bounds; and Arran in fear of his life shut himself up in his chamber, and sent a secret message to Mar through Randolph, praying for aid. He then escaped from the window by twisting his sheets into a rope, and walking half clad through the night to the house of Kirkcaldy of Grange in Fifeshire, where the poor creature lost his wits altogether, and babbled of witches and devils and the like. His father Chatelherault had no course now but to give up Dumbarton and humbly protest his innocence and loyalty. Thenceforward not even a pretence could be maintained of Arran's fitness to marry the Queen, either by fair means or foul, and the house of Hamilton recedes into the background. But Bothwell was made of sterner stuff. He too hastened to throw himself at the feet of his sovereign, and plead for the pardon which he did not deserve. Mary was righteously indignant with him, for she had piled favours upon him; and he was confined first at St. Andrews and then in Edinburgh Castle, whence he escaped during the turbulent times five months later, to run his baleful career.

In the meanwhile Elizabeth had gained an inkling of the plan to marry Mary to a Spanish prince, and with her usual agility changed her tack at once. She had other good reasons for doing so at the time. Guise had shortly before let loose the dogs of war in France: the Protestants at Vassy had been massacred, and the Duke had entered Paris in triumph. Elizabeth was preparing to help Condé, but she dared not concentrate the united Catholic interest against her country; and she at once began to be amiable to Mary Stuart. The differences between them could easily be settled, she said. The much-talked-of interview was arranged; great preparations were made for the journey of both sovereigns to the meeting-place in the North of England; and Lethington and James were once more persuaded that the succession of Mary to the throne of England would be recognised, the tranquillity of

Scotland secured, and their own power perpetuated by means of an alliance with Elizabeth.

Lethington himself arrived in London early in June to settle the details of the interview. Elizabeth had an ally now in the matter. It was as important to Catharine de Medici as to her that Mary should not marry a powerful prince, and especially Don Carlos, in order that Spain and the Guises might not become too powerful; and she accordingly sent an envoy of her own (De Croc) to England and Scotland at the same time as Lethington came, to work to the same end as Elizabeth. Lethington explained to Elizabeth that Arran was no use any longer as a decoy-duck, and must be dropped; and suddenly the Darnley proposal was smiled upon both in England and in France. There was no real intention, on the part of Elizabeth at least, to allow it to take place; but it was an excellent means to delude Lethington and Mary into the idea that the coming settlement would include the recognition of the latter as the heiress of England. It puzzled all observers, and above all the Countess of Lennox, who could not follow such rapid transformations. The Spanish ambassador, cunning as he was, thought that Elizabeth was in earnest, and would persuade young Darnley to be a Protestant and her humble servant, as husband of Mary. Dudley expressed himself in favour of the match, the Countess of Lennox wrote secretly to Mary in a hopeful tone, and Lethington went back to Scotland rejoicing that the way seemed clear for reconciliation with England, on the lines that he had always advocated.

Alas! hardly had he reached home than the whole scene was changed. The Huguenots had shown unexpected strength and boldness. The massacre of Vassy had stirred them to action at last, and a great army had been raised to crush the Guises once for all. Condé, Dandelot, and Coligny were for the moment the masters of the situation. Orleans had defied the Catholics; Normandy was in arms for freedom of religion; and the Protestants throughout France were straining their eyes for the help that was to come to them from England. It was evident, then, that there was no present need for Elizabeth to conciliate Mary Stuart. The Guises were at grip with their foes in France, and could spare neither strength nor money to help their niece; and Elizabeth hoped by her usual means to counteract Mary's coquetting with Spain, so long as the Catholics of France were powerless for harm.

So in July 1562 Sir Henry Sidney was sent to Scotland with polite regrets from his mistress that she was reluctantly obliged to defer until next year her longed-for interview with her dear sister the Scottish queen.

In the meanwhile Mary was getting on no better with her subjects, and this rebuff from Elizabeth was as heavy a blow to her as it undoubtedly was to Mar and Lethington. The Queen's gay, light-hearted mode of life offended the Protestants almost as much as her Mass; whilst the Catholics were intensely irritated by the fruitless conciliation of England and the unchecked predominance still exercised by the Protestant party. Huntly, the most powerful noble of the north, had retired in a rage when the interview with Elizabeth had been negotiated. He had other reasons for anger as well. The rich earldom of Murray, of which he had held the revenues for some years, was promised to Lord James (Mar); his second son John Gordon, a handsome young gallant who had lingered round the Queen love-smitten,[145] had got into trouble by his violence in Edinburgh, and had but just fled from the Queen's prison in which he was confined. So when, the interview with Elizabeth being postponed, Mary decided to undertake her arduous progress through the wild north of her realm, it was with no amiable feelings towards the Gordons, whose territories she was to traverse. Going by way of Stirling and Perth, Mary was still further incensed by young Gordon's disobedience to her order that he should surrender himself under arrest; and when she arrived at the Gordon town of Aberdeen, she issued a peremptory command that Huntly should not be accompanied by more than a hundred clansmen when he came to pay homage to her. The fat old chief, however, trooped into the grey city with fifteen hundred broadswords, and still the Queen's resentment grew. Refusing to lodge in Huntly's castle of Strathbogie, which she scornfully passed on her way, she came to Inverness (9th September), of which fortress the Gordons were the hereditary keepers, and she was denied admittance, except with the permission of Huntly's eldest son, Lord Gordon, who at the time was staying at Hamilton with his father-in-law Chatelherault, in hopes, doubtless, of adding the Hamilton faction to his own.

This refusal stung Mary and Murray to the quick, and the cry of treason was raised. The Gordon clansmen were gathering on all sides, and prompt boldness alone could save the Queen. Both Mary and Murray were prompt and brave, and prepared to attack the castle in force. To fight against the sovereign who demanded entrance into her own fortress was a serious matter, and Huntly wavered at home in his own house of Strathbogie, finally ordering the Inverness garrison to surrender their charge to the Queen. Mary was nothing daunted. She promptly hanged the captain, and set his head upon the battlements as a warning; other chiefs were cast into the dungeons, and the rest of the garrison were pardoned. Randolph writes to Cecil: 'In all these garboyls I . . . never saw her merrier, never dismayed, nor never thought that stomach to be in her that I find. She repenteth nothing, but when the lords and others came in the morning from the watch, that she was not a man to know what life it was to lie all night in the fields, or to walk upon the causeway with a jack and knapschall (*i.e.* helmet), a Glasgow buckler, and a broadsword.'[146]

Though Huntly continued to throw the blame upon his sons, the Gordons had gone too far to retreat, and they gathered a large force under John Gordon, some seven hundred clansmen or more, all told, determined to risk everything and capture the Queen by force as she passed across the Spey on her way south.[147] The news was brought to Murray; and again Mary and he were equal to the occasion. The nobles from the south were summoned, and soon the Queen's force was greatly stronger than that of the rebels. In answer to the Queen's summons Huntly could only protest with tears that he was loyal, and that the whole of the fault lay with his unruly sons. Mary laughed at the pretence, and at the claim that the family were being oppressed because they were Catholics.

When, however, Grange went to Strathbogie to arrest Huntly, and bring him to his sovereign, the earl was forced to show his hand. Escaping in his indoor garb by a back gate (9th October), he joined his sons in their rebellion and was publicly proclaimed a traitor. In vain his friends, and many of his relatives, prayed for mercy. His highland foes, Forbeses, Frasers, Grants, Munroes, and the rest of them, flocked to the Queen's standard; and when the forces met at Corrichie Huntly's men wavered and half deserted ere a blow was struck. There was treachery, too, amongst the highlanders in Murray's force; but his boldness and the firmness of his pikemen carried the day. One hundred and twenty Gordon clansmen fell, and a hundred were captured in their flight. Huntly and his two sons, the younger Adam, a boy of seventeen, were made prisoners, the earl himself dying of apoplexy as he sat on his captor's (Andrew Ridpath's) horse. John Gordon, whose vanity and ambition of the Queen's love had been the chief motive of his action, was beheaded, unskilfully, in her own sight, though she saw the execution with tears.

How far Mary may have encouraged his hopes by her attitude to him, it is difficult to say—as it is in regard to the case of Chastelard, of which we shall speak in the next chapter—but there is no doubt, from the observations of Randolph, of Knox, of Buchanan and others, that her behaviour at this time and subsequently struck those who saw her as being somewhat free and light. It was probably nothing worse than the ordinary code of manners in the French court, somewhat accentuated by Mary's natural sensuousness, and the absence of any restraining authority over her; but in the rigid dourness that characterised the Scottish Protestantism of the time, it certainly gave rise to suspicions, for which there is no apparent ground, with regard to her moral conduct at this period.

In the meanwhile, though the result of the Huntly rising had cowed the Scottish Catholics, it was obvious to Murray and Lethington that matters could not be allowed to linger indefinitely without an arrangement that should ensure Mary's tranquillity, either in accord with or in defiance of Elizabeth. The latter was determined to help Condé and the French Protestants to the utmost of her power, and in November 1562 endeavoured to reassure Mary on the subject. Elizabeth was suffering from smallpox when Randolph presented her letter to the Queen of Scots at Aberdeen; and this fact may explain the amiability with which the latter heard of Elizabeth's determination to throw into the scale against the Guises the whole power of England. But it was clear to Lethington that, sooner or later, Scotland must be dragged into the French quarrel, unless the two queens could be conciliated; and whilst Elizabeth was at war with the Catholics, it seemed to him and to Mary a good opportunity for making another attempt to secure the recognition of her right to the English succession. Catharine de Medici was determined to prevent such an agreement if possible, and at once began a diversion by suggesting a marriage between Mary and the child Charles IX. Her agent Villemort swore to Mary that the Council of England had agreed that, if Elizabeth had died in her recent illness, Mary should not succeed; and in a dozen ways Catharine tried to sow discord to Elizabeth's detriment. The object was quite plain to Mary as she let Randolph know. As usual she was willing that Catharine should be checkmated, whilst she did not wish the Guises and Elizabeth to be at open war, which would make a reconciliation between England and Scotland more difficult, besides boding danger to her kinsmen. Lethington, therefore, again went south in February with such a mission as it seemed would in one way or another solve the great question of national alliance and Mary's marriage once for all. The position at the moment was a very favourable one for Scottish interests; since both parties in France were busy, Elizabeth was involved in the quarrel, and either Catholics or Protestants might think it worth while to buy the Scottish alliance at a good price. The ostensible object of Lethington was to intercede between Elizabeth and the Guises, but the real aim was to renew now more forcibly than before the demand for a close understanding between the two queens, on condition that Mary should marry to Elizabeth's satisfaction, and be recognised as heiress presumptive to England. If the English were as hard to deal with as before, he was to hint that he was going to France to negotiate the marriage of his mistress with Charles IX This was, of course, mere make-believe for the purpose of bringing Elizabeth to reason, his real instructions being, if he found he could make no impression upon the English queen, to push forward actively Mary's marriage with Don Carlos, through the Spanish ambassador in London.

Lethington found Elizabeth and Cecil as bland and evasive as ever. The Duke of Guise had just been assassinated before Orleans, and Mary Stuart's main supporter abroad had thus suddenly disappeared. Lethington's negotiation with regard to Mary's intercession therefore fell through, and he was soon convinced that, with affairs as they were, his Queen had now nothing to hope for from Elizabeth. He had done his best for years to secure for Scotland tranquillity and independence, on Protestant lines with an English alliance, and he had failed; for England would take everything and give nothing in return. He therefore took the step that he had contemplated a year before, determining to throw over England and Protestantism by marrying Mary to a nominee of the King of Spain, and defying Elizabeth to do her worst.

Lethington dared not be seen openly conferring with the cunning old bishop who represented Philip in London; but late at night, again and again, his barge was silently brought to the water-gate of old Durham House in the Strand, and there for hours the Scottish statesman, the stern unbending Protestant, conferred with the popish bishop, whose house was the trysting-place for all the enemies of the reformed faith. Lethington had, indeed, quite lost hope in Elizabeth and Cecil. His interviews with them, and their change of tone when the assassination of Guise was announced, had convinced him that both he and Murray had been played with ever since the death of Mary's husband; and in his secret interviews with Bishop Quadra he guardedly showed his resentment at Elizabeth's treatment of him. The crafty old Spaniard was in Elizabeth's black books just then. His house had been raided for the apprehension of persons, other than those belonging to his household, who attended his Mass; and he himself was being treated with marked offensiveness, as he usually was when the Catholic cause in France was in a bad way. But he carefully stored up the memory of every slight offered to him, and took his revenge how and when he might.

To widen a breach between Elizabeth and the man who, above all others, had established the influence of England and Protestantism in Scotland, was an opportunity too good to be lost, and Lethington was courted and made much of in the frowning old mansion which lay between the Strand and the Thames. When the servitors had left the room, and the bishop and his Scottish guest were alone at table after dinner one day in the middle of March, a leading question from the Spaniard opened Lethington's lips, and he told the whole story of his and Murray's disappointment at the way in which Scotland had been treated by the English queen and her minister. It is clear from his statement that Mary had been hoodwinked equally with her ministers. Cecil's verbal hints and half-promises with regard to the English succession and the meeting of the two queens were seen now to have been nothing but feints for the purpose of paralysing any negotiations between Mary and a foreign power, and to drive her into marriage, as Lethington said, either with 'the Earl of Arran or a still meaner suitor.'[148] The Scottish queen had hoped against hope for some time that Elizabeth's embroilment with France might furnish, sooner or later, an opportunity for intervention, which should place Scotland in a position for making a good bargain on its own behalf. But the murder of Guise, and the temporary collapse of the Catholic militant party in France, had at last banished this hope, and also that of obtaining for Mary any alternative support from France itself. When Lethington told Elizabeth that he thought of going to France to negotiate there, she replied that he might go as soon as he liked, a widely different answer from that which she would have given if the Guises had been uppermost at the time; and Lethington acknowledged that the negotiations with which he had been intrusted on behalf of his mistress were now 'ridiculous and contemptible.' When the Scottish minister, out of breath, paused in the long recital of his woes, the Spanish bishop suggested, by way of feeler, that Mary had better make the best of matters, and accept any husband that Elizabeth might appoint for her, in exchange for the recognition of her right of succession to the English crown. Lethington rightly understood this to mean that a more frank declaration of his own views was desired, and at once replied that his Queen would never do that. In the first place, he said she would marry no Protestant, though he were the master of half the world; and in the second, she would not take a husband of any sort at Elizabeth's bidding, even if by doing so she could at once gain recognition of her English claims. She knew full well, he said, that a husband chosen for her by Elizabeth would only be one of her subjects, whom she would rather die than accept; and besides, after she had lowered herself and married thus beneath her, she would have the same difficulty as now in getting her English rights of succession acknowledged; and she would be less able than ever, after a mean marriage, to urge them by force of arms. No, repeated Lethington, the idea of an agreement based upon the submission of Mary to Elizabeth must now be abandoned, and another policy altogether adopted. The Queen-Mother and the French anti-Guisans, moreover, were playing Elizabeth's game for their own ends, and were approving of Arran or his father as a suitor for Mary. Mary was determined to have nothing to say to either of them; 'and, as for Arran, she hated him so much that when she heard that the Queen of France had given him some hope of the match, she complained bitterly that de Foix should have any dealings or secret understandings with her subjects.'

The bishop did not jump too eagerly at Lethington's bait. What do you think of the Archduke Charles as a husband for your Queen? he asked.[149] Lethington was aware that the Emperor had neither money nor power, even if his Protestant princes would have allowed him, to force Mary's claim to the English succession.[150] Such a match, he replied, would never suit his mistress, as the Archduke had nothing to recommend him but his relationship to King Philip; 'and that alone is not sufficient for the aims that the Queen (Mary) and the Scots have in view'; . . . 'if your Majesty (Philip) did not promise great support and effectual aid to the Archduke, he (Lethington) thought that there was no chance of such a match being acceptable.'[151] Then Lethington unmasked his batteries somewhat: the person that these English people were so mortally afraid of, as to give themselves no rest, was Don Carlos, 'as they feel sure that your Majesty will play them a fine trick some day when they least expect it.' The old bishop chuckled at this. The English, he said, in fear of such an eventuality, had up to recently made all manner of attempts to conciliate Spain in the matter of religion; but the fear seemed to have worn off now, as the Huguenots were paramount and at the bidding of Elizabeth, and the Scots were of her religion also. Lethington knew that this was an invitation for him to define the position of his party in Scotland as regarded religion; and he, a leader of the Protestant party and friend of Knox though he was, at once began to minimise the importance of the reformation in his country. Elizabeth, he said truly, cared no more for one religion than for another. 'Our religion in Scotland,' he continued, 'is very different from that of the English, who have only abolished the sacraments, but have retained all the old abuses.' It was simply nonsense to think that the question of religion was really at the bottom of the present state of affairs. The fact is, he continued, that both Elizabeth and Catharine de Medici are in great fear of the marriage of Don Carlos and Mary, and with good reason, because, 'if your Majesty entertained it, not only would you give your son a wife of such excellent qualities as those possessed by his (Lethington's) Queen, who in prudence, chastity, and beauty was equalled by few in the world, but you would also give him a power almost approaching (universal) monarchy by adding to the dominions already possessed by your Majesty two entire islands, this and Ireland; the possession of which by your Majesty would give no trouble whatever, having regard to the attachment which the Catholics bear to this marriage and the union of these two crowns . . . his mistress having no enemies here (in England) but Protestants.'[152]

It will be seen that Lethington was ready to go over, bag and baggage, to the other side, both in religion and politics, if the interests of Mary and Scotland could be served thereby; but the wary old Churchman was anxious to learn whether he spoke for others as well as himself. He objected, therefore, that all Scotsmen were heretics, and hated the idea of subjection to Spain in consequence. Yes, replied Lethington, it was true that most of the Scottish nobles were Protestants, but they were so obedient to their Queen that they would rejoice at her marriage, even to a Catholic, if it was pleasing to her and advantageous to her realm. Besides, he continued, even in the matter of religion it would be easy for them to bring the country into peaceful submission. How, inquired the bishop; but Lethington's reply when he was thus driven into a corner was not quite satisfactory. He was sure, he said, that the Protestants would allow the Catholics to celebrate Mass privately in their own homes without molestation. The Spaniard demurred at this. Why not publicly in churches? he asked. Well, perhaps even that could be arranged, replied Lethington, though he was not quite sure. Still, both he and Murray had great influence with the preachers, and he thought they could manage it easily; and here he slipped in a few words of fear as to the introduction of the Inquisition into Scotland. The talk about the cruelty of that institution was an absurd fable, the Spaniard assured him: only moral suasion was used to secure the uniformity of the faith; but, whatever Catholic husband Mary might choose, Scotland would have to put up with some such methods. This was as far as either party would go at the time in the conversation, and, with warm professions of personal sympathy with the proposed marriage on both sides, the four hours' conference ended, Lethington promising to write to Murray on the subject, and the bishop to obtain Philip's views.

It is clear that Lethington had not adopted this entire change of policy without the full consent of Mary, and probably, also, of Murray. The predominance of the Huguenots and 'politicians' in France had temporarily brought Catharine to the side of Elizabeth in forwarding the idea of a Hamilton marriage for Mary; and such a marriage, as we have seen, would have been distasteful to Mary, ruinous to Murray, and utterly destructive of the political influence of Scotland in any direction. The rallying of Murray and Lethington to the ultra-Catholic side was, therefore, quite in the order of things, though it proved how little either of them cared for the abstract question of creed. The idea of a marriage between Mary and young Charles IX was still kept alive as a diplomatic possibility; but it was understood on all hands now to be nothing more than a feint to divert the Scottish queen from the dreaded Spanish marriage to which events seemed tending.

Lethington wasted no time after his interview in opening communications with the Catholic party in England, previously his bitter enemies. The discontented English nobles of the old stock, who hated Cecil and Leicester, were ready at any time to join a promising coalition with the object of overthrowing the Protestants; and they, one and all, gave Lethington assurances of support in the Spanish marriage of his mistress, and in the fateful changes in England that such a marriage must necessarily bring. Only let her marry Don Carlos, said they, and they would salute her as the rising sun. Lethington was frequently in secret conference now with the Spanish bishop in Durham House, and Cecil's spies must have noted the fact; for a week after the interview just related Elizabeth had her counteracting stratagem ready, and an astounding one it was, throwing the whole of her rivals into confusion.

One day whilst Lethington was chatting with her, doing his best, as usual, to extract some declaration favourable to Mary's claim to the English succession, Elizabeth remarked that, 'if the Queen of Scots would take her advice and wished to marry safely and happily, she (Elizabeth) would give her a husband who would ensure it, and this was Lord Robert (Dudley), in whom nature had implanted so many graces that if she wished to marry she would prefer him to all the princes in the world.' Now for the last three years Dudley's relations with Elizabeth herself had given rise to endless scandal, and it was the general belief that they were married, or in any case ought to have been; and this bold move of the Queen's, offering her own lover as a husband for Mary, took Lethington utterly by surprise. His wits were keen, but he could not follow instantly this sudden shifting of Elizabeth's policy, and it was some moments before he had the courtier's phrase upon his lips as an answer. It was a great proof, indeed, he said, of her love for his mistress, that she was willing to surrender to her a person so dearly prized by herself; but he thought that his Queen, even if she loved Dudley as dearly as Elizabeth did, would not marry him and so deprive the latter of all the joy and solace that his company afforded her. 'Ah!' sighed Elizabeth sentimentally, 'I wish to God the Earl of Warwick his brother had the grace and good looks of Lord Robert; in which case we could each have one.' This was really too much for Lethington, who failed to divine what the Queen was driving at, and in his confusion could only bow. 'The Earl of Warwick is not ugly either,' she went on; 'he is not ungraceful, but his manner is rather rough, and less gentle than that of Lord Robert, though he was worthy of wedding any princess.' The Scottish minister at least understood that the idea of such a match as this, if it were seriously meant, would be scouted by all classes of his countrymen, and most of all by Mary herself; and by way of diversion suggested, as if in joke, that Elizabeth should marry Lord Robert Dudley first, and have children by him, and when she died she could leave Mary as heiress both to her husband and her kingdom; so that in any case Dudley's children would be kings of England. This sally, as was intended, put an end to the subject, but Lethington was so confounded by the new move on the part of the English queen that he was for rushing back to Scotland at once to take counsel; but as his mission to France had still to be effected, though now only for appearance-sake, he left on his journey thither at the earliest possible moment.

Elizabeth must, of course, have been aware that Mary would never consent to such a match as that suggested with Leicester or Warwick, but it was her fixed policy, and doubtless a wise one in the circumstances, to diminish the importance of the Scottish queen as an international factor, and, sure as she was now that the French ruling powers would not raise a finger to support Mary, it was a clever and a safe retort to the ambitious plans for a Spanish match for Elizabeth to embroil Scottish opinion, and ostentatiously to treat Mary as an inferior vassal sovereign, only worthy to accept such a subject husband as the English queen might deign to appoint for her. This suggestion of a marriage with one of the Dudleys was not an isolated fact. It was indeed only made plausible at the time by the success that had attended just previously another and more insidious move in the unscrupulous conspiracy of Elizabeth and Catharine de Medici to discredit the Scottish queen in the eyes of the world, and reduce her power to co-operate, by marriage or otherwise, with the Catholic party in England or on the Continent. This branch of the conspiracy must be related in the next chapter.

V

MARY IN SCOTLAND.

DON CARLOS OR ROBERT DUDLEY?

The Chastelard folly—Probably incited by Catharine and the Huguenots—Mary's imprudent condescension—The Hepburn scandal—Mary's behaviour offends the Puritans—Philip's reply to the marriage proposals—His futile policy of caution—Mary's objection to the Archduke Charles—Her main object to obtain the English throne by a powerful Catholic marriage—Philip's aim—Elizabeth forbids Mary to marry either Carlos or the Archduke—Lethington again confers with the Spanish ambassador—His changed tone caused by Elizabeth's clever diplomacy—Philip's answer reaches England—The Spanish verbal message to Mary—Death of the ambassador interrupts communications—Randolph proposes an English nobleman to Mary—Determination of Mary to persevere in the Spanish negotiations—Mary again receives Randolph—Her policy of delay—Fresh hopes of Don Carlos—He is to be sent to Flanders to marry her—Randolph urges Dudley's suit—Elizabeth's real object in this.

IT HAS ALREADY BEEN RECORDED THAT AMONGST THE TRAIN OF French courtiers that had accompanied Mary to Scotland was a member of the household of Constable Montmorenci's son, a youth named Chastelard. Young Montmorenci himself, M. d'Anville, as he was called, was supposed to cherish an affection for the Queen; but if such was the case it does not appear to have gone beyond the demonstration of a respectfully erotic admiration for a great lady, which was in accordance with the fashion of the times. With Chastelard it was different. He was a gentleman of Dauphiné, a great-nephew on his mother's side of the Chevalier de Bayard, and, like him, of slender, graceful form and gentle mien, which belied his strength, boldness, and dexterity in sports and arms. He was one of the most fashionable of the court poets of the school of Ronsard, writing to highborn dames languishing love-sonnets, which to the taste of the present day would appear outrageously insulting, if not indecent, but which were regarded by their recipients as the inevitable homage to their conspicuous charms. Mary, a poetess herself, and, as we have seen, frank and unrestrained in her demeanour towards men, probably took a fancy to the enamoured gentleman. Brantome, who was the friend of Chastelard, says that 'she was pleased to read his verses, and even answered them, often making him good cheer and entertaining him.' Even thus early, during her voyage to Scotland, Chastelard hinted to Mary, in an Italian sonnet, that his love for her was not platonic. Of what use, he asks, is it to possess widespreading domains, cities, crowns, and bowing people, to be admired, respected, feared, and gazed at, and yet sleep alone in glacial widowhood? Mary loved admiration and her own pleasure. To have one more man in innocuous love with her, and above all one who could tell his love in such pretty verses, doubtless amused her. Chastelard could be treated as a lap-dog, and banished or beaten if he went too far in his worship; and when he accompanied his master back to France with open lamentations at having to leave the object of his love, the Queen would naturally look upon his despair and misery as the poetic exaggeration of an ordinary sentiment permitted by the manners of the time.

Chastelard was a Huguenot, but had been brought up by the Montmorencis, who led the moderate or 'political' party, which sought to reconcile religious factions, and to govern France by a purely national policy. The outbreak of the first war of religion threw into the hands of the Montmorencis the task of reconciling the extremists, which they ultimately did for a time; but in the meanwhile the Huguenots, who were in technical revolt against royal authority at Orleans, had to be dealt with by force of arms. Chastelard, a Protestant, was loth to fight against his co-religionists, and could not join them to fight against his patrons the Montmorencis. He had continued in France to proclaim in verse and speech his hopeless love for the Queen he had left in Scotland, and few people in the court could have been ignorant of his outspoken passion. When therefore he begged Montmorenci's permission to return to Scotland for a time, to avoid his difficulty with regard to taking sides in the religious war, and d'Anville gave him letters of recommendation to Mary, he, in his half-crazy worship of a queen, would appear to be an ideal instrument in the hands of Mary's enemies to compromise her. The Montmorencis were consistently opposed to Mary's marriage in France, and the strengthening of Guisan influence everywhere, but they were not enemies to Mary personally. Their moderate policy favoured a reconciliation between Elizabeth and Mary, on terms which would secure to the latter a recognition of her English claims, whilst disabling her from interfering in the French struggle or helping the Guises. But the aims of Catharine de Medici and the Huguenots went beyond this. Catharine had a personal grudge to serve, as well as a vital political necessity, in preventing the marriage of Mary with a Spanish prince;[153] whilst to the extreme Huguenot party, depending mainly as they did upon England, it would have been fatal for Mary to have established, by means of a Catholic marriage or otherwise, her right to the English succession, unless she was ready to go over entirely to the Protestant party and become the vassal of Elizabeth in all things, which was out of the question.

As we have seen, the discussion of a match between Mary and the Archduke Charles had gone far before the winter of 1562, and the still more dangerous suggestion of a marriage with Don Carlos was in the air and known to be Mary's dearest desire. The vapouring poet's vanity might easily be worked upon by suggestions of Mary's familiarity with him to attempt an act which might discredit her; even if we do not admit that he went to Scotland knowingly with a treacherous political purpose. In any case, when he passed through London in October 1562, he boasted that he was going to Scotland 'to see his lady love';[154] and on his arrival in Scotland he was welcomed more than graciously by the Queen. 'He is well entertained and hath great conference with the Queen,' writes Randolph,[155] 'riding upon

the sorrel gelding that my Lord Robert (Stuart) gave her Grace.' Onlookers
were puzzled as to what his errand might be, and it was noticed that when he
handed to Mary d'Anville's letter 'her countenance signified good liking of
the contents.' The sighs and philandering of the poet promptly began again.
He presented to the Queen in his first audience 'a book of his own makinge
written in metre'; and jealous watchers noted frowningly 'the over-great
familiarity that any such personage (as the Queen) showeth to so unworthy
a creature and abject a varlet.'[156] Whether his head was turned by this familiarity, or he was simply carrying out his instructions, is not clear; but in any
case, on the night of the 12th February, whilst Mary was closeted till past
midnight in her cabinet with Murray and Lethington, giving to the latter
his final instructions for his mission to England, the Frenchman concealed
himself under the Queen's bed, fully armed with sword and dagger. He was
discovered by her ladies before she entered the chamber, and was expelled,
the Queen being kept in ignorance of the fact until next morning. When she
learned it she angrily ordered him out of her sight, though apparently she
was not implacable, for the poet was allowed to follow the court when later
in the day the Queen left Holyrood for St. Andrews. On the 14th Mary slept
at Burntisland, and when her two ladies had undressed her and she was prepared for her bed, Chastelard, who had concealed himself in a private closet,
suddenly appeared and approached the Queen. What followed is variously
related. Randolph, writing the next day, says that 'he setteth upon her with
such force, and in such impudent sort, that the Queen herself was fayne to
crie for helpe, and the matter so manifest that no colour could be found to
hide the shame and dishonour. The Earl of Murray was sent for . . . whom
the Queen incontinently commanded to put his dagger into him, which
had been done if God had not put into his mind to reserve him to be justified according to law.'[157] The news flew abroad instantly. A swift messenger
sped upon the road south, passing Lethington on the way without word to
him, carrying the tidings to Elizabeth with hints to Mary's dishonour. 'The
beginning of a lamentable story, whereof such infamy will arise as I fear,
however well the wound be healed, the scar will for ever remain.' So wrote
Randolph; and in his case the wish was father to the thought; for he was
prompt with his suggestion to open the wound to Mary's good name. 'Your

honour (Cecil) seeth what myschief ensueth of the over great familiarity . . . unto so unworthy a creature and abject a varlet as her Grace ever showed to him. . . . What colour soever can be laid upon it, that it was done for his master's sake; yet I cannot but say it had been too much to have been used to his master's self by any princess alive.'[158]

This is the testimony of the English agent, who was certainly not well affected towards the Queen; and Knox, her self-righteous enemy, was even more outspoken in his innuendoes against her.[159] That she was free in her intercourse with Chastelard and other men to an extent that would have appeared harmless at the French court, but which shocked the more rigid Scottish sense of dignity, may be accepted as a fact; but if Mary had desired an immoral intrigue with the Frenchman we may be perfectly certain that she would have found a way without this open scandal to indulge in it; and the very fact of her alarm and indignation being so great when, as he said to justify himself for his previous trespass, he approached her in her chamber, should be proof that whatever may have been Chastelard's motive in his mad proceedings, the Queen herself was not a party to his presence in her bedroom. He is spoken of as 'a little Frenchman who was always joking with the ladies,' and when he was seized by Mary's guards he attempted to laugh the matter off; but Murray at least was determined to give a lesson in caution to Mary herself, and refused to make light of it. 'The man that takes most sorrow is the Earl of Murray, lest worse be judged of it, and of the familiar usage of such a varlet than was meant by her.'

A week afterwards at St. Andrews Chastelard was executed. The romantic stories of his last moments on the scaffold represent him as sighing still for love of 'his cruel mistress'; but evidently something more compromising than lovelorn sighs and poetic rhapsodies was wrung from him before he left the world. 'He died repentant,' says Randolph, 'confessing privately more than he spoke openly.' What he confessed Randolph was not told, but we get a clue to it in a quarter more likely than any other to be rightly informed. Lethington had found to his distress the court already ringing with the news when he arrived in London, and Mary herself shortly afterwards wrote him a secret letter—as he told the Spanish ambassador—giving him the details. Chastelard, he said, had confessed 'that he had been sent from France by persons of distinguished position, with sufficient means and apparel, in order that he should get a footing in the court and household of the Queen of Scotland, and try to make himself so familiar with her and her ladies that he could seize the opportunity of obtaining some appearance of proof sufficient to sully the honour of the Queen. . . . The persons who sent him on this treacherous errand were, according to Lethington, several, but she who gave him the principal instructions was Madame Curosol. The Queen writes to Lethington that the other names are such that they cannot be entrusted to letters; but I know not whom he suspects.'[160]

Now it is true that this may have been an attempt on the part of Lethington to reassure the Spanish ambassador with regard to any suspicion of the moral conduct of Mary, whom he was so anxious to marry to Don Carlos; but Randolph's remark quoted above gives support to the idea that Chastelard must have made some important avowals before his death, the general drift of which could with advantage be communicated to the Spaniard but not to the Englishman. If such were the case, it could only be something damaging to the Protestant party in France, with which England was in league, and of which Chastelard was an adherent; and it is difficult to avoid the conclusion that the hapless, love-cracked poet had been egged on to his action, in the hope of compromising Mary, by the Queen-Mother and her Huguenot allies of the moment. It is incredible that Chastelard can have believed that he could force Mary in the presence or close neighbourhood of her ladies; but the Queen's enemies in France, for political and personal ends, may well have persuaded him that she was really in love with him, and that boldness on his part would meet with its reward. If once he was made to believe that, Mary might easily be compromised, though what became of the unhappy instrument himself was doubtless a secondary consideration to the intriguers. Probably neither they nor Chastelard ever imagined that the latter would be executed for the liberty he took; and it is indeed evident that Murray deliberately made out the offence to be as heinous as possible, first as a warning to Mary against her lightness of demeanour, and secondly, to convince the father of the great bridegroom they were angling for of the rigidity of her virtue. An example was needed, moreover, for this was not the first case in which Mary had been treated in a way that might give rise to the suspicion that she herself had encouraged indecorousness towards her person. When, in the previous autumn (1562), she was chatting in the garden with Elizabeth's special envoy, Sir Henry Sidney, a certain Captain Hepburn had approached and handed her a paper. Fortunately, being busy, she did not open it in Sidney's presence, but afterwards handed it to Murray (then the Earl of Mar) unopened. To his intense indignation he found the contents to be a grossly indecent set of verses addressed to the Queen, with a still more outrageous drawing at the foot of the missive. Hepburn fled to England when he heard the hue and cry; and Mary fell ill with grief and shame, especially as it might 'give occasion to Sir Harry Sidney and the other gentlemen with him to muse much at his (Hepburn's) boldness, or judge of herself otherwise than occasion is given by her and hers.' The same fear that people might misjudge her again assailed her and made her ill after Chastelard's insult; and thenceforward for a time her old schoolfellow and cousin Mary Fleming slept with her.

There must have been something in the Queen's expression or manner thus to inspire men with sexual passion rather than high-minded devotion or fear of her. Elizabeth, whose moral conduct, according to all known evidence and presumption, was much more reprehensible than that of Mary, never allowed her slaves to assume the slightest liberty or overt familiarity on the strength of her passing fancy for them. They could but sigh and flatter and fawn when she smiled upon them, or pine and weep when she frowned; and Essex, the proudest of them all, found to his undoing that Elizabeth would be master and mistress too, however fervently she might love. But Mary's qualities were widely different from those of her cousin. She was as tenacious of her sovereign privileges as was Elizabeth, and could be as haughty as she; but when she unbent in her exuberant love of life and avidity for pleasure, she drew men to her by sweet feminine wiles, and the unconscious but powerful fascination of an ardent nature. Unlike Elizabeth she did not hector her lovers into a condition of maudlin ecstasy, but inspired them willingly or unwillingly with a passion so strong that it overcame fear and made them bold. She it was, not they, who had to weep; and for her every hour of light-hearted abandonment a bitter retribution of suffering was wrung; for the people who surrounded her could not understand how a woman could be light-hearted and yet not a strumpet: gaiety and vice were in their eyes necessary concomitants; the hard, sour, and ugly alone were good, especially for others.

Mary had dire need of her elasticity of spirits at this time, for blow upon blow fell upon her. The tragic death of her two uncles drew from her 'manie a salte teare'; whilst Randolph and Murray 'laughed at our wills' at the evil tidings. None dared at first break through poor Mary's pastime of 'riding up and down hawking and hunting' to tell her of her younger uncle's sad fate, until Mary Beton, 'hardiest and wisest of them,' gently broke the news. The Queen was disconsolate with grief at the ruin that had fallen upon her kinsmen's cause; but the courtiers slunk away in corners to hide their joy in pretended tears; and, as Randolph reports, 'I never saw merrier hearts with heavier looks since I was born.' Whatever the Queen did was wrong in the sight of those near her. After dwelling upon her intense grief at the murder of her uncle, Randolph in the next paragraph of his letter sneers at her because he and Murray managed with long trying 'to wrynge a laughter or two out of her: and so far as I can see this sorrow will break no man's heart here.'

Early in June Mary received the English agent, who had to present a special letter to her from Elizabeth. The Queen was in bed, as he said, 'rather for ease than for any grief of her body,' and he remained chatting with her in the presence of Murray only for over an hour, whilst she expressed delight at Elizabeth's friendly messages. Randolph gibes ill-naturedly at the Queen's thus receiving him, and at the same time the Scottish courtiers were 'bursting with envy' that 'the Englishman must be brought to the Queen's bedside, she being in bed!' Anything was good enough to be used as an instrument to bring odium upon the unfortunate young woman. Randolph relates with eager glee (13th June) that when the Scottish parliament enacted that adultery should be punished with death: 'That self-same night . . . the Queen's French priest, her ordinary chaplain, was taken with another man's wife in his bed.'

Mary, indeed, was on uncongenial soil.[161] 'Mr. Knox,' writes Randolph, 'is so hard unto us that we have laid aside much of our dancing.' The Queen's Mass priest was cuffed by some of Murray's men one dark night at Dunbar;

and on Christmas day (1562) none of her musicians would sing, either at Mass or Evensong. 'Thus is her poor soul so troubled for the defence of her silly Mass, that she knoweth not where to turn her for the defence of it.'[162] 'Mr. Knox hath no hope (to use his own terms) that she (Mary) will ever come to God, or do good in the commonwealth. He is so full of mistrust in all her doings, words, and sayings, as though he were either of God's privy council that knew how He had determined from the beginning, or that he knew the secrets of her heart so well that neither she did, or could, have for ever one good thought of God or his true religion. . . . On Sunday last he (Knox) inveighed sorely against the Queen's dancing, and little exercise of herself in virtue or godliness. The report being brought to her ears yesterday, she sent for him and talked long with him. Little liking there was between them of one or the other, yet did they so depart as no offence or slander did rise therefrom.'[163]

If Mary had been an angel instead of a fallible young woman, overflowing with ambition, pride, and a desire to enjoy life, it would have been difficult for her to have conquered by diplomacy and conciliation the forces thus arrayed against her. Determined to obtain, by fair means or foul, the recognition of her English claims, and to reassert, in Scotland at least, the supremacy of the Catholic faith,[164] rapidly gaining the conviction that Elizabeth was tricking her, notwithstanding her loving letters, and knowing well that Catharine de Medici would spare no effort to prevent any Guise from becoming dangerously strong by a foreign alliance, it is no wonder that Mary of Scotland should at last have been able to win Lethington,[165] and for a time probably even Murray, to abet her in an attempt to confound all her enemies by a swift and secret marriage with the Spanish prince.

But promptness and boldness, which were the essence of the plan, were impossible where Philip II was the deciding factor. Stolid deliberation, an ingrained determination to bind all his associates with triple bonds, whilst remaining himself uncompromised; the interminable consultations and inquiries, the exaction of precise assurances and guarantees from others in exchange for vague generalities from himself; all the cumbrous machinery necessary to his character and methods, made negotiations with him comparatively easy of frustration by the nimble opponents, whose feminine wit and easy consciences enabled them to use more flexible means than his. It took three months for Philip to answer Lethington's unexpected advances, and the answer, when it came to London at the end of June (1563), was such as Philip loved to indite. His greatest praise was for the prudence with which his ambassador had avoided committing himself in conversation with the Scottish minister; 'and seeing that the bringing about of this marriage may perhaps be the beginning of a reformation of religion in England, I have decided to entertain the negotiation. You will see that it is carried on in the same way that it has been commenced, if you consider that way safe and secret; telling them to inform you of all the engagements and understandings they have in England (*i.e.* with the Catholics); and you, knowing how valuable such information may be to me, will carefully advise me of everything, together with your own opinion upon it. Inform me, step by step, of everything that happens, but without settling anything, except to find out the particulars above referred to. You may assure them (*i.e.* Mary and her ministers) of my intention, but you must urge them, above all, to use the utmost secrecy in all the negotiations, as the benefit to be derived from the affair depends absolutely upon nothing being heard of it until it is an accomplished fact. If it becomes known that such negotiations are afoot, and that I am concerned in them, the French will be greatly alarmed, and will strive their utmost to frustrate them . . . or to counteract any profitable result that may arise. As for the Queen of England and her heretics . . . you may easily guess what they would do if they heard of it . . . , so it is absolutely necessary that you should keep it secret, and urge secrecy upon those with whom you deal, and upon their mistress'[166] (*i.e.* Mary Stuart).

For a long time Cardinal Lorraine had been in close treaty with the Emperor to marry Mary to the Archduke Charles, and the matter was now looked upon by Ferdinand as practically settled. Lethington had fairly stated his mistress's mind when he said that she was strongly opposed to this match, as certainly all classes of Scotsmen were. She herself, in a subsequent document,[167] attributes the failure of the match with Don Carlos to the arrangement made without her consent by Cardinal Lorraine with the Emperor. 'Besides her displeasure at the consequent frustration of the other marriage, she found no use at all to her realm in the match with the Archduke; he being a foreigner, poor and far away, the youngest of his brothers, and unpopular with her subjects,[168] and without any appearance of means or strength to help her in her claims to the English succession.'

This latter consideration was ever uppermost in the minds of Mary and her Catholic friends, whilst the Scottish Protestants dreaded a weak Catholic consort as much as a strong one. The Archduke Charles, therefore, although unable to serve Mary's objects, would have aroused the opposition of England and France almost as strongly as a Spanish marriage would have done. That the Guises should have preferred the Austrian prince is quite comprehensible, and shows that in all their action they thought of their own interests before those of Mary. What they needed at this time was a Catholic Scotland, whose forces should be at the bidding of their party in France. A Spanish domination of England and Scotland would have crushed them in common with other Frenchmen, and strenuous Catholics though they were, they did not relish the idea of a Spanish master. That sacrifice to their ambition came many years later. Philip, when he wrote the characteristic letter above quoted, was well aware of the arrangement with the Emperor; and he told his ambassador in the same letter, that if he thought equal advantage could be gained by a marriage of Mary with the Archduke Charles as with Don Carlos, he would favour the former, 'out of affection for his kinsmen.' But still he was quite ready to play the underhand game and deceive them whilst any probability existed of Mary's marriage with young Charles IX. This attitude of Philip is a testimony to the cleverness of Lethington's and Mary's diplomacy in keeping up the appearance of negotiations with Catharine for the French match, though it must have been evident to them that after Guise's death and the ruin of his cause such a match was impossible. How fearful Philip was of the French marriage is seen in this sentence of his letter: 'I well bear in mind the trouble and anxiety I underwent from King Francis when he was married to this Queen (Mary), and I am sure if he had lived we could not have avoided war ere this, by reason of my protection of the Queen of England, whose country he would have invaded, as he intended to do. To go to war for other people is not at all to my liking . . . and in this case, seeing whom I should be helping, it would be doubly disagreeable.'

Here we see the divergent aims of the various parties. Mary, despairing of obtaining by peaceful diplomacy Elizabeth's recognition of her heirship to the English crown, or of being able without a strong force to secure for her faith supremacy, or even toleration in Scotland, was determined, if possible, to turn the tables upon Elizabeth, the Protestants, and the predominant parties in France by bringing the power of Spain into Great Britain, and changing the secular policy of Scotland, which had always opposed Spain the friend of England, and had clung to France the enemy of both. The Guises, temporarily crushed by the death of their chief and his brother, yet with a strong party still in France, knew that a Spanish domination of England and Scotland, though it would secure Catholic supremacy, would have humbled France and have rendered it impossible for them to use Mary as an instrument for their family or party aggrandisement. They therefore aimed at a match that should make Scotland Catholic and nothing more.[169] Philip was rubbing his hands with glee that Mary had ceased to be French, and that with good fortune he might see Scotland, the back door to England, open to him, and the English Catholic nobles ready to join Mary Stuart under Spanish tutelage to depose Elizabeth. But it is unlikely that he intended to marry Carlos to Mary unless he obtained such pledges from the English and Scottish Catholics as convinced him that they were strong enough to elevate Mary to the joint crowns; and, as usual with Philip, this was the real point upon which the project of Mary's Spanish marriage was wrecked. Elizabeth and Catharine de Medici, for different reasons, were resolved that Mary on no account should marry any prince (and particularly a member of the house of Austria-Burgundy) who could aid her to make Scotland Catholic, or bring her into effective union with the Catholics of England or France. The aim of both queens was therefore to draw Mary into a marriage which should reduce her international importance, and lower her personal prestige with the Catholic party throughout Europe. In addition to this Elizabeth was also on the alert to prevent the possibility of Mary's marriage with a French prince, and hence her own desperate diplomatic flirtations with the juvenile sons of Catharine de Medici.

When Lethington took leave of Elizabeth on his return to Scotland (20th June 1563), she told him that she knew very well that negotiations were in progress to marry his mistress either to Don Carlos or the Archduke Charles; and she would tell her quite plainly that if she married either of them, or any member of their family, she would be her enemy; but that if she married to her (Elizabeth's) satisfaction, she would treat her as a good sister, and make her heir to England. When Lethington recounted this conversation to the Spanish bishop the latter asked him whom Elizabeth wished his mistress to marry. Lethington's reply shows that he had already grown doubtful about Don Carlos. At this time Philip's reply to his proposal had not arrived, and Elizabeth's promise to make Mary her heir if she satisfied her in her marriage probably still weighed heavily with Lethington. At all events, he spoke to the Spaniard in a very different tone from that which he had used three months previously. Very likely, he replied, Elizabeth wished his Queen to marry a private gentleman or some Protestant prince. 'Will your mistress do so?' asked the Spaniard. 'I fear not, but if she wishes to please her subjects and succeed in her affairs, she ought to do so,' said Lethington. 'I do not know,' he continued, 'how we can put up with the Archduke. He is so poor, and we have no money to give him.' Lethington's short-lived sympathy with a thoroughgoing Catholic policy had thus evidently yielded to the diplomacy of Elizabeth and Catharine, and he went back to Scotland, once more, the Queen of England's humble servant.[170]

He had before his eyes in Elizabeth's palace at Greenwich an object-lesson more significant even than the English queen's open threat to his mistress. By the side of Elizabeth, and in high favour, now stood the bewildered Margaret, Countess of Lennox, and the talk of the court was that if Mary dared to marry against Elizabeth's wish, young Darnley and not she would be proclaimed heir of England. A cloud of rumours were flying too, both in England and Scotland, that even the Catholics would prefer that Mary should take her cousin Darnley for a husband, with Elizabeth's blessing and the heirship, than that the poor Archduke should in spite of the English queen be foisted upon them to destroy all hope of the union of the crowns under Mary. At the same time Lethington left himself a loophole to return to the Spanish match, which he knew his mistress preferred, if circumstances rendered such a course desirable. The Archduke he would not hear of, as we have seen, but he still dangled before the Spaniard the fear that Mary might after all wed the French king. His last words to the ambassador gave his irreducible minimum condition for the acceptance of the Archduke (failing Don Carlos, of whom by reason of Philip's long silence he had evidently lost hope). Unless Philip would maintain the Archduke and undertake to provide means for Mary to enforce her English claims by arms, his mistress would make the best of matters, and marry a husband to Elizabeth's liking in return for the heirship to the English throne.

About a month after Lethington left London for Scotland Philip's important letter, already quoted, reached the hands of his ambassador in London. The old bishop was feeble and ill when he received it, and was doubtful of success. Lethington's changed tone, and Elizabeth's firm veto on a Spanish or Austrian marriage, made him think that perhaps negotiations for another husband had gone further than he knew, and he dared not send to Mary or her ministers Philip's approval of her marriage with his son for fear that the whole plan might be divulged to the English, the international relations rendered more bitter than ever, and the fate of the English Catholic nobles still harder. The ambassador saw, moreover, how inadequate Philip's slow methods were to the quickly moving circumstances. 'The remedy is a weak one,' he wrote to the Duke of Alba, 'for so dangerous a malady. When they (the Scots) see that instead of giving them a firm reply, we come only with halting proposals, I know not what they will think. It is useless to ask them to give me information as to the support the Queen of Scots can count upon in England for the information of the king. Lethington knows well that all this has been done long ago, as he told me what he was doing, and of course I could not hide my communications from him. We have been spoken to by the same people about the marriage, and those who have urged me to propose it to his Majesty (Philip) have also pressed Lethington to recommend it to his Queen, and have given him lists of Catholics and others who could raise troops for her service.'[171] In fear and doubt, therefore, the Spanish bishop at last decided to invent an excuse for sending one of his confidential agents to Scotland, with a verbal message to Mary herself, saying that he had very important intelligence to convey to her respecting her marriage, and begging her to send a trustworthy envoy to London to receive it for her. The messenger left London in the middle of July (1563) and saw

Mary during her progress in the Western Highlands. The details of the interview are not known; but it is evident from what followed that the Queen received the message with delight. She had sent back to France two months before, with a procrastinating answer, Cardinal Lorraine's emissary, who had visited her to gain her final consent to a marriage with the Archduke, and in June she had treated Eric of Sweden's new matrimonial approaches with increased coolness. Randolph, moreover, had just been summoned to London by Elizabeth for the purpose of laying new plans for the frustration of the threatened Austrian match, which was the only one that for the moment the English thought probable, thanks to the secrecy and slowness of the Spanish negotiation. Mary's hands were therefore free to grasp the welcome opportunity of renewing the splendid plan which early in the year had been unfolded by Lethington to the Spanish ambassador in London. Luis de Paz, the Spanish agent, hurried back to his master with Mary's verbal reply, but found the old bishop breathing his last at Langley, and the promising negotiations were again interrupted until a new medium of communication had been devised.

In the meanwhile Randolph received from Elizabeth and Cecil his instructions for driving Mary into a marriage which should deprive her of international importance. He was to tell Mary that the plots of Cardinal Lorraine to the detriment of England and to marry Mary to the Archduke were known, and though it was not believed that Mary had any sinister intent, yet such a match 'would hinder our wish to favour by all means that we can to try and determine her right and title, whether she be, or ought to be, by the law of God and man, our next cousin in blood by our father, and succeed us in this crown of England, if we shall depart this life without children.' The old bait, as will be seen, was still considered efficacious. If Mary asked Randolph whom Elizabeth wished her to marry, he was to reply, 'as if of his own accord,' that he believed that 'some person of noble birth within our realm, having conditions and qualities meet for the same,' would best content his mistress: 'yea, perchance, such as she would hardly think we could agree to, might be found out to content her, and therewith be agreeable to us, and to both our nations; and further her interest, if so she should appear that she be our next heir'; and Randolph was again to threaten 'that no mighty marriage must be sought for, if she or her Council regard either amity or favour of this realm.'[172]

By this message Darnley or Leicester is evidently indicated as Elizabeth's candidate; but to those who are versed in her methods and policy, nothing can be more certain than that both the succession bait, and the Darnley inducement if it was suggested, were insincere. Elizabeth never had any intention of declaring either Mary or any one else her heir, and certainly did not desire to unite the two Catholic pretenders to her throne in one inter-est; but the Archduke's match, amongst other possible proposals, had to be defeated, and the course adopted by Elizabeth seemed the most likely to secure the end desired. Cecil, too, wrote a confidential letter to Lethington, vaguely holding out hopes that the long-promised settlement with Mary for the marriage and recognition of the latter would really be effected. The pretence had grown a little threadbare by this time, and Lethington replied somewhat curtly that Cecil's news was 'comfortable,' though he was 'unable to conceive Cecil's full meaning.' But he added significantly, that though it might suit Elizabeth to have her relations with foreign princes 'hanging in suspense,' 'yet well I know that the Quene my maistres' estate is soche as may not long stand in doutfull terms with foreign princes, and therefor must shortly resolve one way or other. . . . I pray God time be taken, while it last, for I fear if the present be not well plyed, the like shall not be offered hereafter.'[173]

After conference and dinner with Murray and Lethington, Elizabeth's agent saw the Queen of Scots at Craigmillar, on the 1st September, to deliver the pregnant message with which he was charged. Mary was excited and voluble, interrupting Randolph in his discourse with so many excla-mations and inquiries that 'scharce in one howre I could utter that which myght have byne spoken in one quarter.' When, at length, he had finished, the Queen requested him to put his message in writing, that she and her councillors might duly consider it; and Randolph, with the uncomfort-able conviction that the currents were not setting entirely in his mistress's favour, wrote to Cecil, that although the Protestants of Edinburgh were as strongly Anglophil as ever, and dreaded much the Catholic match which they believed was 'a makinge'; yet, as for Mary herself, 'I fear she is more Spanish than Imperial, and if my judgment fail me not you shall find it true.'[174]

Now that Mary and her ministers knew from the verbal Spanish message that Philip was willing to treat for her marriage with his only son, it is evident that the vague half-promises of Elizabeth and Cecil had less potency than at any previous time. This is plainly seen in the dignified reply sent by Murray to Cecil, who had written to him in alarmed remonstrance upon receiving Randolph's report. There was, Murray assured the English minister, 'very small handling' of the dreaded match Catholic in Scotland, great as had been the noise made about it elsewhere; and Cecil was, said Murray, worrying himself unnecessarily about it. Mary, he promised, would take no sudden step in the matter, nor would she act 'without long deliberation, and the advice of her loving subjects and most assured friends.' But he continued, 'it is not her Majesty's honour to impede and stop the suit of princes, nor can I advise her highness so to do.' Murray told the bare truth. Very little had been done in Scotland in negotiating either the Spanish or the Austrian match. The latter negotiation had been entirely managed by Cardinal Lorraine, and was at this time, as we have seen, practically rejected by Mary, except on impossible conditions of Spanish support; whilst the marriage with Don Carlos had gone no further than the advances made by Lethington and the English Catholics in London early in the year, and the conveyance to Mary of the vague verbal message by the Spanish agent Luis de Paz, to the effect that the King of Spain was willing to negotiate with her. But the tone of Murray's letter, and the *suggestio falsi* that it contains, fully confirm Knox's suspicions conveyed to Cecil a fortnight later, that not only had the Queen won over most of her councillors and nobles to her plan for the great combination that might enable her to beat Elizabeth at her own blustering game, but that even Murray, 'the man most inward with you and dear unto me,' was not absolutely to be trusted.

Randolph hurried home to England, full of doubts and fears, and carrying from Mary a diplomatic inquiry, intended to delay matters whilst forcing Elizabeth to declare herself more openly. What marriages, she was to be asked, would be, in the opinion of the Queen of England, 'sortable' for her sister of Scotland. Elizabeth, however, had no intention of allowing herself to be drawn prematurely, and Randolph posted back to Scotland with a mere variation of his former message, to the effect that his mistress recommended 'some fit nobleman within the island, well affected to concord; but that no child of France, Spain, or Austria would be acceptable'; and once more Mary was warned that largely upon her choice of a husband the recognition of her right to the English succession would depend.

Mary was ill in bed—with overmuch dancing, said some, with overmuch devotion, said others—when Randolph arrived in Edinburgh, and a few days later (11th December 1563), whilst still in bed, she received him. Elizabeth had sent her by him a splendid ring, which she displayed upon her finger with girlish delight. That, and the bridal ring of her late husband, Francis, must go to the grave with her, she said, 'and willingly should never be out of her sight.' But jewels and fine words were powerless to allay the uneasiness caused by the vague hints and veiled threats with which she knew Randolph was charged. For weeks previously she had been 'divers times in great melancholy, her grief being marvellous secret, and she often weeps when there is little apparent occasion.' But now she grew rapidly worse, until her life was almost despaired of for a week, though she evaded the formal conveyance to her of Elizabeth's second message. Randolph reported the opinion that 'the Queen's sickness is caused by her utterly despairing of the marriage of any of those she looked for; they abroad being neither very hasty, nor her subjects here very willing, or bent those ways. This conceit, say some, has been in her head some five weeks or more.'[175] We can probably make a better guess than Randolph at the real reason for Mary's depression when we call to mind that the death of the Spanish bishop in London, of which she must have heard in September, had dashed for the time her hope of carrying through speedily and secretly the match upon which her heart was set, and which, she knew, Philip was ready to negotiate, and no more. Weeks, perhaps months, might pass before confidential communications could again be established with far-away Spain; and in the meanwhile Elizabeth's arrogant exigency was increasing. Mary did her best to delay matters by remaining in bed, and deferring her critical conferences with Randolph, whilst she endeavoured to get into confidential correspondence with Cardinal de Granvelle in Flanders, and the Duchess of Arschot, who at an earlier stage, as will be recollected, endeavoured to engineer a marriage between Mary and Don Carlos.

It was in the last days of December 1563 that at length the Scottish queen, unable to delay further, listened formally, still in bed at Holyrood, to Elizabeth's message, of which doubtless she knew the purport weeks before. Again she heard that though the Queen of England would mention no name of a suitor she recommended, yet she still harped upon 'some nobleman of her realm, who besides many other good virtues should have special desire to unite the two countries in perpetual concord.' After some fencing Mary told Randolph that she understood more than the words conveyed. She did not know what the world would think of the match hinted at; but, as for Elizabeth's expression with regard to the English succession claim, that was satisfactory to her. Tiring, at last, of long-winded diplomatic phrasemaking on both sides, Mary broke out with: 'Master Randolph! you have something else to say to me. Tell me plainly what is in your mistress' mind, that I may . . . give you a resolute answer.' 'I have delivered my message, Madame,' was the reply, 'but if you will give me leave to say my own opinion, I should advise you to send some trusted adviser to confer with her Majesty, and learn her mind.' Randolph stood aside for a moment, and Mary called Argyle to her. 'Randolph would have me marry in England,' she said to him. 'What!' replied Argyle, 'is the Queen of England become a man?' 'Who is there in England whom you would wish me to marry?' asked Mary with rising pride. Argyle was a strenuous supporter of the English party, and could not, at least in the presence of Randolph, turn his back on Elizabeth's suggestion. 'I wish,' he said, 'that there were so noble a man in England whom her Grace could like.' 'That would not please the Duke.'[176] exclaimed Mary. 'If it please God and be good for Scotland, what reck whom be displeased,' retorted Argyle; but the Queen gave no sign by face or gesture of what she thought of the proposal herself; and for days afterwards she kept her bed, though observers were fain to remark that she did not now seem ill. Nor was she; but delay was vital for the success of her plans.

People in Edinburgh besieged Randolph to know what it all meant. Whom did his mistress wish their Queen to marry? The general idea was that Darnley or the Earl of Warwick (Ambrose Dudley) would be Elizabeth's choice; but Randolph himself apparently thought that Leicester was meant, though he kept his idea secret, except from a very few upon whom he could depend. He believed, however, that Mary herself so understood his vague expressions. He was right at this time (New Year's day, 1564) in his opinion that the Archduke's match, so dearly desired by Cardinal Lorraine, was 'off,' though he was incorrect in thinking that this was the reason for Mary's sadness. In vain he waited for the Queen's answer to Elizabeth's message. For weeks Mary kept him in play, entertaining him often and chatting gaily with him, but never committing herself to a formal conference; for Cardinal Lorraine had heard the news of Elizabeth's project to marry his niece to one of the Dudleys, and was vehemently urging Mary by letters not to 'abase herself' to serve the turn of the heretics. Catharine de Medici also had taken fright at such a possibility, and sought by presents and sweet messages, which Mary deeply distrusted, to wean her daughter-in-law from a match which would deprive France, in any case, of a possible ally against England at need. But, above all, what spurred Mary to continue her clever procrastination, with which Elizabeth was bitterly reproaching poor Randolph, was the fact that at last, at the end of January 1564, she had managed to establish communications with Cardinal de Granvelle, and things began to look hopeful again for the marriage with Don Carlos.[177] Mary's spirits rose as she also saw herself courted and flattered by the French, who suddenly granted all the requests she had long preferred in vain. Her illness, real or assumed, had delayed grave discourse with Randolph through December and January, but in February it was her 'mirth and pastimes' that occupied her to exclusion of business. Such banquets were held as no Scotsman recollected to have seen, except at the marriage of a sovereign; and though Elizabeth's health was drunk deeply and often, no answer was sent to her message.

In the meanwhile Mary's French secretary Raulet and other emissaries were speeding backwards and forwards to Flanders; and the Florentine Angelo with messages from the Duchess of Arschot and de Granvelle came continually to infuse fresh hope and confidence in the Queen of Scots. The latter was doing her best to persuade Cardinal Lorraine also to espouse her idea of a Spanish match, but of success in this she was not too confident.

The Cardinal, after imprisonment and banishment, was in February 1564 suddenly summoned by Catharine to court on his return from the Council of Trent, and, to the stupefaction of most onlookers, was treated with marked cordiality by the Queen-Mother. The reason of Catharine's new-born amiability to him is not far to seek. The coming and going of agents between Mary and Granvelle could not escape the notice of spies: some of the letters, indeed, had been intercepted, and it was soon evident both to Elizabeth and to Catharine that the dreaded union of Spain and Scotland was being planned behind their backs. When, therefore, Cardinal Lorraine was received so kindly, his niece, at all events, was under no misapprehension as to the significance of the fact. *'Je prie a Dieu,'* she writes to Granvelle on the 11th March 1564, *'qu'il sache bien guarder de croire aux belles paroles de ceux que, je m'assure ne le desirent si pres d'eux qu'ils en font semblant. Je lui en ai bien ecrit ma fantasie. . . . Quant à moi, je ne me puis guarder d'en etre en grande peine.'*[178]

To Elizabeth it was even more important than to Catharine that the Spanish-Scottish project should be nipped in the bud at any cost; and, whilst the Queen-Mother's counter-stroke was to draw closer to her son-in-law Philip II and once more cross the scent with her suggestions for a marriage of Elizabeth[179] with the boy Charles IX, and of Mary Stuart with his younger brother Anjou, the Queen of England found herself at length obliged to speak clearly with regard to the name of her candidate for Mary's hand. Randolph had been for some time past growing somewhat fractious at the impossible task imposed upon him. He knew, he said, that Mary's 'noble stomacke can never imbase ytself so lowe as to marrie in place inferiour to herself,' and none of her councillors would advise her to do so. Besides, even the best friends of England were urging upon him the unfairness of forbidding Mary to marry a foreign prince, and yet withholding the name of the nobleman whom Elizabeth wished her to take. But what puzzled Randolph more than anything else, was why Dudley was to be the happy man. Mary, if she chose an Englishman at all, would of course only have the best, namely, Robert Dudley, and he surely could not forsake the refulgent sun in England which he worshipped; and if he did, how could a lover so disloyal and fickle ever be respected by any woman again.[180] Why did not Dudley marry Elizabeth herself, asked Randolph of Cecil. These, and a dozen similar doubts, raised by the Scottish ministers as well as by the English agent himself, cannot have been without influence in deciding Elizabeth to declare herself. Mary and her advisers had used every diplomatic art to draw from Randolph a hint as to the person to be proposed; but as he says he 'styflye stondes,' and kept his own council, saying just enough in a non-committal way to make Murray and Lethington able to guess that Dudley was the man indicated.

The talk with Mary always turned upon wedlock now: the sorrows of widowhood, the comforts and joys of wifehood and motherhood, and the like; but both parties kept on their guard, and would mention no names, though by most people in Scotland, with the exception of Mary, Lethington, Murray, and Argyle, it was believed that Darnley would finally receive Elizabeth's support. Murray and Lethington either believed, or pretended to believe, that there was now no probability of any foreign match being arranged, and unreservedly pledged themselves to favour any suitor recommended by Elizabeth; but it is unquestionable that Mary was at this time (the spring and summer of 1564) in close communication with de Granvelle, and had received assurance that Don Carlos would be sent to Flanders to facilitate an interview with her.

In the meanwhile, amidst a prodigious amount of banqueting, piping, and dancing, and much sour suspicion of intended treachery against the Protestants,[181] Mary played her game with wonderful adroitness. Her answer to Elizabeth, when it was given in March, consisted only of amiable platitudes, and her discourses with Randolph about marriage always left the poor man dazed with doubt. She could not forget her dear Francis yet, she said; she was still young and could wait; and then, in the next breath, she deplored that no suitors courted her. Sometimes she found it incompatible with her modesty to discuss the person of her future husband, but said that if Randolph would consult Murray and Lethington they would tell him her mind. They were just as vague as she, and would not go beyond generalities; and when at last, in March 1564, Elizabeth and Cecil understood that in diplomatic delay they had met their equals, Randolph was instructed to mention several impossible suitors, and wind up his list with the name of Lord Robert Dudley, who was to be specially praised.

Randolph saw Mary at Perth late in the month, and she heard his message with feigned surprise. It was so sudden, she said, and she must have time to consider such a suggestion; but as the Englishman pressed her, she asked him whether he thought it befitted her dignity to marry a subject. Dignity, he replied, was not the only thing to be considered, and surely there could be no greater honour than to marry one who might gain for her such a realm as England. To this Mary answered that she hardly expected that. Elizabeth might marry, and, in any case, would probably live longer than she herself. The point now to be considered, she continued, was to please her friends, 'who would hardly agree that I should abase my state so far as that!' Then she sent her courtiers out of hearing, and said: I did not expect to talk so far upon the matter now, but since we have begun it, 'I will sitte downe and reason homlye with you.' 'Now, tell me, Master R., doth your mestres, in good erneste, wysh me to marrie my Lord Roberte.' Randolph assured her that she did, and that no worthier man than Dudley could be found. And then Mary, in a few trenchant sentences, laid bare the many disadvantages of the proposal, its onesidedness, and the uncertainty of any advantage from it accruing to her, even if she lowered herself to it.

At supper, afterwards, they were all sarcastically merry over it, Murray asking why Randolph did not use his eloquence in persuading Elizabeth to marry, instead of 'troubling our Queen, that yet never had more thought of marriage than she hath of her dinner when she is hongrie.' Lethington was closeted with Mary far into the night, and on the following morning gave Randolph his answer. The Queen, he said, had been taken by surprise, and could not either accept or reject the proposal 'on so shorte advysement.' She wished to learn more of the conditions and guarantees offered by Elizabeth, and begged that a councillor, such as the Earl of Bedford, might be sent to Berwick to confer with a special envoy from Mary. But, in the meanwhile, 'for the person himself she could have no myslykynge of hym, of whome the reporte was so good, and by her good syster was so recommended.'[182]

It is impossible to believe that Elizabeth ever intended to allow her own lover Dudley to marry the Queen of Scots, or that he would have consented to do so whilst he had any hope of wedding Elizabeth herself. There was, however, no other possible person whom the latter could trust to play the part in the comedy she wished, and to renounce the pretence when required. Her one desire, for the moment, was to prevent Mary from marrying a foreign prince, and the only lever she had for the purpose was that of the English succession. This, however, had become somewhat worn and weak by itself, and in future needed to be used in conjunction with a marriage negotiation. There was no one in England but Darnley who was really a suitable match for Mary, and it is highly probable that in certain circumstances, conjoined with the absolute submission of Lady Lennox and her son to Protestantism and the English interest, Elizabeth was prepared to accept Darnley as a suitor for Mary, though, even so, she would never have proclaimed either of them her heir. But Lady Lennox was unwise; she was, moreover, a stanch Catholic, who had an eye on the English succession for herself, as the only serious Catholic claimant; and, much as she desired to propitiate Elizabeth, she would not surrender her position. Dudley, on the other hand, was a perfectly safe instrument. He might be flashed before Mary, jointly with the English succession, until the danger of a foreign match had blown over, with the certainty that at any moment Elizabeth could bring him to her feet again with a smile, or what would be a more probable signal between them, a wink, leaving Mary more discredited than ever, and her chances of making a dangerous match proportionately reduced. Dudley was therefore adopted as the stalking horse, because with him alone Elizabeth was free from risk, and apparently certain of humiliating Mary whilst leaving her without a husband after all. The plan was a clever one, but, except on conditions which she would never have granted, it was too good from Elizabeth's point of view to succeed with Scotsmen so wary as Murray and Lethington, obedient servants though they now were to England. Mary's pride, moreover, would have saved her from the dangerous pitfall dug for her on this occasion, even without her ministers' aid. It was a little later, when her passion over-rode her prudence as well as her pride, that she handed herself bound to her enemies.

VI

DIPLOMACY VERSUS LOVE

*Leicester's suit cools for a time—Elizabeth's change of front—
Betrayal of Mary by Cardinal Lorraine—Catharine's intrigues to
prevent Mary's marriage—Offers a French prince—Castelnau's
mission to Scotland and England—The Darnley plan—Elizabeth's
hesitation—Lennox goes to Scotland—Melville's mission to
Elizabeth—Mary's pretended sympathy with the Dudley proposals—Dudley's (Leicester's) disclaimer—Mary warned of Elizabeth's
real object—Dissimulation on both sides—Randolph hopeful
still of the Leicester match—Mary's anxiety for an answer from
Spain—John Beaton sees the Spanish ambassador in London—
Philip's refusal unofficially reaches Mary—Her pretence of French
approaches—Her diplomatic play with Randolph—Her determination that recognition of her right to the English succession shall precede
her acceptance of Leicester—Arrival of Darnley in Scotland—
Randolph puzzled—Impression produced by Darnley—Murray's
alarm—He remonstrates with Elizabeth and Cecil on their slow
ungenerous policy—Elizabeth finally refuses to recognise Mary's
heirship—Mary's love for Darnley precipitates her diplomacy—
Randolph still hopeful of Leicester.*

MARY STUART'S AMBITIOUS SCHEME FOR HER MARRIAGE WITH
the son of Spain was sacrificed to greater and more powerful interests than
her own. She knew by experience that Catharine de Medici was always most

dangerous when she spoke fair, and, as we have seen, Mary grew distrustful as soon as sweet messages came thick and fast to her from France, and Cardinal Lorraine and the ultra-Catholics were made much of by the Queen-Mother. She had ample reason for her distrust, though it was probably not based upon an exact knowledge of what was going on at the time. Philip had finally realised (1564) that he must crush Protestantism in his own Netherlands dominions or abandon his dream of the unity of Christendom on Spanish lines. Catharine, too, began to fear that her Huguenot friends were becoming more independent than suited her, so Lorraine and his Catholics once more found themselves in favour, and negotiations under their management and that of Alba soon ended in the famous convention between Catharine and her Spanish son-in-law for the joint extirpation of heresy throughout the world, which was to be finally sealed at the interviews between Catharine and her daughter at Bayonne.

Whenever France and Spain drew together Elizabeth of England softened her tone, and on the arrival in England of the new Spanish ambassador, Guzman de Silva (June 1564), he found the Queen, and especially Dudley, pretending that they were almost Catholic. Dudley began to hint to the ambassador on the very day the latter arrived, that if he could get the countenance and aid of Spain he would remove Cecil, marry the Queen of England, and submit to the Catholic Church;[183] whilst Elizabeth surpassed herself in religious tergiversation and provocative political coquetry towards the broad-minded, amiable Churchman who now represented Philip at her court.[184] In this condition of affairs it was impossible to keep up the pretence that Dudley was a suitor for Mary's hand, in sympathy with Knox and the Protestants, and young Darnley was again ostentatiously brought to the front in the English court. It was Darnley who received the new ambassador on behalf of the Queen at the door of the council-chamber at Richmond, and who conducted him to his barge at the end of his interview; and the first news that had greeted Guzman when he approached England was that Elizabeth was to meet the Queen of Scots and arrange for her to marry 'the son of Lady Margaret Lennox.'

But the negotiations of the Franco-Spanish Catholic league brought about a still more important change in Mary's matrimonial prospects than the substitution of one English candidate for another. It has already been explained why Lorraine and the French Catholics dreaded at this period a Spanish marriage for the Queen of Scots; and now that Catholics through-out the world were to be leagued together for Spanish objects, Philip could allow Cardinal Lorraine's plan for the marriage of Mary with the Archduke Charles to be brought forward officially. In his own hand, therefore, the King wrote to his ambassador in England (8th August 1564): 'As to the Queen of Scots, I understand that Cardinal Lorraine has offered her in marriage to the Emperor for the Archduke Charles; and for this, and other sufficient reasons, the proposal to marry the said Queen with my son Carlos must now be considered at an end.'[185] Mary's hopes were, as we have seen, entirely founded upon this match, and her passionate protest at a later date[186] against the way in which her uncle, Cardinal Lorraine, had betrayed her, proves how deeply she felt the irreparable injury that had been done to her, and, as she said, driven her into the Darnley marriage. We shall see later, however, that the unfortunate union with her English cousin was not entirely caused by her betrayal by her French kinsman.

As soon as Catharine had 'squared' Philip II, and knew she had not to fear a marriage between Don Carlos and Mary that might have made Great Britain Spanish and Catholic, she set about dealing characteristically with the alternative danger of a match that might make Scotland English and solidly Protestant. She chose as her instrument one of the most persuasive diplomatists of the time, Castelnau de la Mauvissière, who in his old age told his own story so gracefully. He had gone to England early in the year (1564) respecting the negotiations for the peace between England and the French Catholics, and had to some extent captured the good graces of Elizabeth. He was now sent back in the autumn with a double matrimo-nial mission; neither of which probably was more than a political device. The proposal of a marriage between the young King Charles IX, now aged fifteen, either with Mary or Elizabeth had several times before been made use of by Catharine for her ends; but the mission intrusted to Castelnau was more complicated both in execution and in aim than any previous proposal of the sort.

Elizabeth, as soon as she knew that Mary's marriage with the Archduke

Charles was officially offered by Cardinal Lorraine, found an excuse for sending (in October 1564) to the new Emperor Maximilian and re-opening the sham negotiations for her own marriage with her old flame the Archduke; and Catharine determined to anticipate this thrust by offering to the English queen the hand of the boy King of France. Elizabeth had laughed at the idea when Condé hinted at it a year before, but when it was suggested, first by Catharine to Sir Thomas Smith in Paris, and soon afterwards by Castelnau de la Mauvissière in London, it was at all events good enough to be used for a time by Elizabeth for her own ends. Guzman, half in joke and to arouse her jealousy of France, told her in October that Mary was much more likely to marry Charles IX than Don Carlos, and Elizabeth indignantly retorted that the French king was offered to her.

When Castelnau had made the offer in August she was very gracious, thanking the King and his mother for the honour done to her; but saying that she found one difficulty in it, namely, that 'her good brother the Christian King was too great and too little. He had so large and noble a kingdom that he could never be expected to reside in England, and her subjects loved to have their sovereigns constantly amongst them. Besides, he was too little, being very young, and she an old woman over thirty.'[187] But though Elizabeth was too modest to give the hint herself, her councillors cleverly endeavoured to stultify the second part of Castelnau's mission, which they knew or guessed, namely, the marriage of Mary Stuart with the young brother of the King, the Duke of Anjou, barely fourteen years of age. Dudley told the Frenchman that there would be no similar objection made if Anjou were offered to Elizabeth, and Castelnau went on his way to Scotland already unsettled with the idea of the new possibilities offered by the hint.

Mary received him graciously, and at once told him of the suggestions that had come to her for her marriage with the Archduke, the Duke of Ferrara, several German princes, the Prince of Condé; 'and with one greater than any of these, the Prince of Spain, whose father King Philip proposed to send him for the purpose to the Netherlands.'[188] This was said some three months before Mary's eyes were opened to her betrayal in this matter, and, in full confidence still of being able to bring about the great match, she answered Castelnau's offer of Anjou by saying that 'though she loved France better than any country in the world, she could never think of returning thither in a lower station than that she had formerly enjoyed there, or risk losing her own realm, which was so gravely divided, in her absence. She loved equal grandeur, and if the Prince of Spain came into Flanders and continued his suit, she did not know what she might do.'[189]

Here spoke the true Mary Stuart. She would marry no prince but one strong enough to assert by force her right to the crown of England, and to compel Great Britain finally to be Catholic. Don Carlos or Charles IX alone possessed the necessary qualifications, and she was willing to marry either of them; but, as we have seen, the courtship-jugglery of Elizabeth, the mutual jealousy of France and Spain, and the determination of Catharine to be mistress of France by balancing one religious faction against the other, made both marriages unattainable by Mary, as she herself feared before many days more had passed.

In the meanwhile the Lennoxes and their tall, pretty stripling of a son were basking in the sunshine of Elizabeth's court. The confiscation of the earl's estates in Scotland, mentioned in an earlier chapter, had never been revoked, and since the arrival of Mary in Scotland Elizabeth had on more than one occasion supported the prayers of Lennox and his wife that the attainder against him might be raised, and his ancestral estates restored. That the English queen should once more take up Darnley as a second string to her bow, at the period when Dudley became temporarily less serviceable as a nominal candidate for the position of Mary's husband, is one more proof of the cunning adaptability of Elizabeth's diplomacy. Failing Dudley, it was evident that no English suitor had the remotest chance of consideration by Mary but Henry, Lord Darnley. Lennox was a weak, unstable man, easily dealt with, and one whose religious convictions were of a mild character; but Lady Lennox was fond of looking upon herself as the Catholic claimant to the English crown, and her intriguing fussiness made her a possibly dangerous personage as an instrument in the hands of Elizabeth's enemies. Elizabeth could therefore only countenance even the appearance of Darnley's candidature on condition of her being able to buy the Lennoxes absolutely. The earl might be gained by making him depend upon Elizabeth for his restoration to the position of a great Scottish noble, and Lady Margaret must be dealt with delicately by holding out the always efficacious bait of the recognition of her own or her children's claim to succeed to the crown of England, failing issue to Elizabeth. So, whilst Lady Lennox was flattered and smiled at, and young Darnley stood near the steps of the throne, Matthew Stuart, Earl of Lennox, was allowed in August to go back to Scotland with Elizabeth's modified blessing to plead for Mary's favour. After the Queen of England had given her permission in July she took fright and revoked it, in consequence of Lady Lennox's imprudent request that she might accompany her husband and take Darnley with them. This was going too fast and too far for Elizabeth, and not without some hesitation did she finally let even Lennox alone go. She knew, of course, that Lady Lennox had never abandoned the hope of seeing her boy married to Mary, and acknowledged as heir to both thrones; and Elizabeth's own now compromising dallying with Dudley had made the countess's hopes stronger than ever, coinciding as it did with Elizabeth's renewed favour to her and her husband. But even if Elizabeth ever meant to allow Mary to marry Darnley at all, which is doubtful, notwithstanding the impression she conveyed to Melville, Castelnau, and others, she certainly was not prepared in the autumn of 1564 to let Darnley go without a hard and fast bond, making him and his parents her humble servants if he married the Scottish queen. So alarmed was Elizabeth by the suggestion of Lady Lennox that she wrote to Mary, as Cecil did to Lethington and Murray, intimating that remonstrances had been sent from the Scottish friends of England against the return of Lennox, as likely to lead to discord, and suggesting that the Scottish queen herself should forbid the earl's coming. Mary was highly indignant at such false dealing as this, which, moreover, she was unable to understand, and wrote protesting passionately to Elizabeth with her own hand. Murray and Lethington also were similarly emphatic to Cecil. They could see no objection, they said, to Lennox's coming to Scotland; and since the Queen of England herself had requested a favourable reception for him, they refused now to be made the tools of an underhand policy, and to forbid the earl's entrance. Elizabeth, thus driven into a corner, was practically obliged to allow Lennox to go, but she did so sulkily and distrustfully, highly incensed at Mary's choleric letter to her and at Murray's refusal to dance obediently to her piping.

Lennox's reception in Scotland increased her distrust. The friends of Knox muttered angrily, and the Catholics bragged that he would go to Mass with the Queen, and that the crown of Scotland would be settled upon him to the exclusion of the Hamiltons, failing issue to Mary. Lennox arrived at Holyrood on the 23rd September; and had hardly removed his riding-boots when he was received in state by Mary and her nobles,[190] all of whom embraced him; and thenceforward the earl lived in the palace in princely fashion, striving to be all things to all men: going to 'sermon' or to 'mass' indifferently, feasting with all and sundry, and himself 'banquetting the four Maries and other delicate dames.'[191]

This was in September, which, it must be recalled, was three months before Mary learned that Philip II had thrown her over, and whilst she was still in the belief that Don Carlos was to come to Flanders to marry her. The loving welcome extended to Lennox by the Queen and her erstwhile Anglophil ministers, in despite of Elizabeth, is therefore explained; since it would have been extremely dangerous to have had the Stuart claimant to the Scottish succession in England, and at Elizabeth's bidding, when the great marriage which was to confound all Mary's rivals suddenly took place. A kindred desire on the part of Mary to disarm Elizabeth's suspicion whilst the great plot was carried through prompted her to feign a desire to proceed with the negotiations for her marriage with Dudley. Randolph, it will be recollected, had gone back to England with what was practically a scornful refusal from Mary, but with dilatory suggestions that a commission of diplomatists should meet on the Borders and discuss the terms proposed for the union. No step to carry out the suggestion had since been made by Elizabeth; but Mary and Murray now found it advisable to say that the proposal of Lord Robert 'was not only well taken, but gently and directly answered as could be'; and to assure the English how willing they were still to discuss the matter by commission. The Protestants and others who were not in the secret of the Spanish negotiation, such as Kirkcaldy of Grange, did not understand it, but the latter, writing (19th September) to his friend Randolph, could at least see that, however Mary might feign compliance, she would never marry Dudley. 'Therefore look on the next, either among you or us; or, if you drive time, I fear necessity may compel us to marry where we may. For I assure you, brother, though she would very fain have a man, and for the same some labours are made by France, and likewise by the Duchess of Arschot (your own Angelo being the convoy there), yet, in my opinion, if ye will earnestly press it ye may cause us to take Lord Darnley.'[192]

In pursuance of Mary's plan to allay Elizabeth's suspicions, by means of a pretended willingness to continue the Dudley negotiations, Sir James Melville was sent south with a mission in the third week of September (1564). He had been brought up abroad, and had passed through London in the spring on his way to Scotland, becoming on that occasion very friendly with Elizabeth, for whom he brought hints of proposals of marriage from Prince Hans Casimir. Elizabeth always smiled on men who brought her offers of marriage which she could safely decline, and Melville, with his courtly foreign graces, was the best envoy Mary could have chosen for the particular mission now intrusted to him.[193] He was to assure the Queen of England of his mistress's desire to please her in all things, to apologise for Mary's angry letter about Lennox, to urge her to appoint commissioners to discuss the marriage proposals made to her and other pending questions, and to watch closely the tendency of the Queen and parliament in the matter of recognising Mary's right to the English succession in conjunction with her proposed marriage.

Melville arrived in London late in September 1564, and before his first interview with the Queen, Mary's friend and true sympathiser, Throckmorton, gave him subtle advice, which he was not slow to follow. If he found Elizabeth hard to deal with, and disinclined to treat the Scottish queen fairly, Throckmorton recommended him to feign intimacy with the Spanish ambassador. This proves, at all events, that Elizabeth guessed, if she did not know, the quarter whence danger might come to her, though really at this date, as we have seen by King Philip's letter, the danger had already passed. With great ceremony Melville was brought into the Queen's presence at Whitehall on the day after his arrival, by Hatton and Randolph, and attended by a retainer of Dudley. Elizabeth was walking in a verdant alley of the garden when the Franco-Scotsman, who had almost forgotten his own tongue, knelt and kissed her hand, addressing her in French and handing to her Mary's letter. He found the Queen still very indignant at the tone of his mistress's choleric answer to the demand about forbidding the coming of Lennox, and Melville skilfully smoothed her ruffled plumes with flattery. 'Has your mistress sent any answer to the proposal made to her through Randolph?' asked the Queen. 'My mistress has thought little or nothing thereof,' replied Melville, 'but expected the meeting of commissioners on the Borders. . . . She will send my Lord of Murray and Lethington, and expects that your Majesty will send my Lord of Bedford and my Lord Robert Dudley.' 'You seem to make very small account of my Lord Robert,' snapped Elizabeth, 'as you mention the Earl of Bedford before him. You will see that I shall make him a far greater earl before long; aye, and before you return home too.' Then, continuing, she said that she looked upon Robert Dudley as her brother and best friend, whom she herself would have married had she ever minded to have taken a husband. But since she had made up her mind to die a virgin, she desired that the Queen of Scots, her sister, might marry him, 'as meetest of all others.' If Mary married him, there would be no danger of any attempt being made to usurp her throne before her death.[194]

Elizabeth was as good as her word; for a day or two afterwards, Michaelmas day 1564, Lord Robert Dudley knelt before his mistress to be made Baron Denbigh and Earl of Leicester, the while she lovingly tickled his neck inside his ruff. Perhaps Dudley, in his fresh finery and personal triumph, looked handsomer even than usual, for the Queen turned to Melville and asked, 'How do you like him?' 'I answered that, as he was a worthy servant, so he was happy to have a princess who could discern and reward good service.' . . . 'Yet, says she, you like better of yonder long lad, pointing to my Lord Darnley, who, as nearest prince of the blood, did bear the sword of honour before her that day. My answer was, that no woman of spirit would make choice of such a man, who more resembled a woman than a man; for he was handsome, beardless, and lady-faced: and I had no will that she should think that I liked him, or had any eye or dealing that way.'[195] But he had, for Mary had instructed him secretly to urge Lady Lennox to obtain permission for her son to join his father in Scotland, to see the country and return to England with him. It has usually been assumed that these instructions of Mary to Melville were based upon her wish to marry Darnley at the time they were given—the middle of September 1564—and there is no doubt that Lady Lennox and her husband were animated by that prospect. I am, however, of a different opinion. Mary was still unaware that the Spanish match had been vetoed by Philip, and the desire to get Darnley to Scotland was probably for the same reason that Mary was anxious to keep his father there, namely, that the Stuart heirs to her crown might not be turned into instruments of attack against her by Elizabeth when by a *coup-de-main* Scotland became Spanish and Catholic. What would have been the fate of Lennox and Darnley in Mary's hands in such an eventuality is a matter which does not concern us here. They were Catholics, and would probably have acquiesced in the change, on the acknowledgment of their claim to stand before the Hamiltons in the Scottish succession, in which case all might have been well with them.

For nine days Melville stayed at court, chatting daily with Elizabeth, and trying to persuade her that Mary was not absolutely averse from the Leicester match, on certain conditions which might be arranged as to Mary's right to the heirship of England. Elizabeth was cool on the latter point. She would have the laws of succession considered by competent jurists. She herself was determined never to marry, 'unless her sister's harsh behaviour drove her to it.' 'Yes, I know that, Madam,' said Melville. 'You think that if you were married you would be but Queen of England: now you are both King and Queen. I know your spirit cannot endure a commander.'[196] But when it came to surrendering her beloved Leicester, even in effigy, to Mary, the hollowness of the diplomatic pretence stood forth clearly. Showing to Melville his portrait and others, carefully wrapped in paper and enshrined in a cabinet in her bedchamber, whilst the Scotsman held the candle, the Queen was asked by Melville to let him carry the earl's miniature to his mistress. 'You have the original, Madam,' he said; 'let me take her at least the copy: or if not, pray send her as a token this great ruby.' 'No,' replied Elizabeth, 'if the Queen will follow my counsel she will in time get all I have.'

And then followed the famous series of manœuvres and intimate conversations, that have so often been quoted, in which Elizabeth exerted all her fascination to win the flattery of the cautious Scotsman. How she dressed every day in the style of a different country, to gain from him a compliment for each costume. How she showed forth her golden hair for his admiration, and urged him to comparisons of her beauty and accomplishments with those of Mary. Whose hair was best? which of them was the fairer? which played the virginal and the lute most perfectly? which was the better versed in foreign tongues? which of the two danced most high and disposedly? and all this with infinite wiles and skittish coquetry, intended to convert the Scotsman into Elizabeth's slave.

The day before Melville left London Leicester himself took him in hand. In his barge on the river, with only his brother-in-law Sir Henry Sidney, the new earl, after much flattery, asked the Scotsman what the Queen of Scots thought of the suggested marriage with him. Melville, as he had been instructed to be, was very curt and cool about it; and Leicester then took an extraordinary course. He declared that he had no thought of such a match for himself. He was not worthy, he said, to wipe Queen Mary's shoes; and the proposal had not emanated from him at all, but from his secret enemy Cecil, so that, if he had jumped at it, he might be made to offend both queens and lose their favour. 'He entreated me to excuse him at her Majesty's hands, and to beg in his name that she would not impute that matter to him, but to the malice of his enemies.'[197] This no doubt meant that the affair was becoming in appearance too real to please Leicester. He was willing to serve as a stalking-horse up to a certain point, but he was aiming at a higher mark than Mary, and at this moment looked like attaining it. He and the Queen were just then positively fulsome in their approaches to Spain and the Catholics, and to pose at the same time as Knox's candidate for Mary's hand might spoil his chance of help from that quarter. Besides, he knew by experience how vain, fickle, and exacting his English mistress was, and he was getting fearful that if affairs were allowed to drift much further she might become jealous of him for playing too well the part she had prescribed to him. So it doubtless seemed to him a prudent move to put himself out of the serious running for Mary, before she proceeded further in the matter. But his strange course did not in appearance have this effect, and it admirably served Mary's interests, because thenceforward she was able with a light heart to appear to acquiesce in Elizabeth's plans for her marriage with Leicester, whilst she was pursuing her own policy and seeking to forward the Spanish negotiations.

Melville carried back to Scotland the usual bland professions of Elizabeth's friendship, but nothing definite about the succession; the only real step in advance being the promise of Elizabeth to send Bedford and Randolph to discuss matters with Murray and Lethington on the Border; but Melville warned his mistress that the Queen of England was playing false. 'There was,' he said, 'neither plain dealing nor upright meaning, but great dissimulation, emulation, and fear.' Elizabeth, he reminded Mary, had been able to hinder the marriage of the latter with the Archduke, and her offer of Leicester, 'whom she could not spare,' was only a feint. From the English Catholics, from Lady Lennox, and from the Spanish ambassador, Melville, however, bore to his Queen messages of a more comforting character; and Mary herself evidently regarded as the principal result of his mission her nominal reconciliation with Elizabeth, as enabling her 'to get intelligence of a great number of noblemen and others, her friends, in England.'

Thus in complete dissimulation on both sides the joint-commissioners met on the Border secretly in the middle of November.[198] Bedford and Randolph were instructed to mention only Leicester's name; but, if the question of the succession as a condition of the marriage was brought forward by the Scots, vague generalities alone were to be held out.[199] Both sides feigned to treat the proposal seriously, for both were playing their own respective games, and both desired delay: Mary in order to carry through her Spanish plan, and Elizabeth in order to delay or prevent Mary's marriage to any one until the dangerous suitors were disposed of, and to distract her counsels in the meantime. When Randolph had first returned to Edinburgh in October, Murray and Lethington showed somewhat less caution than usual, and quarrelled with the English envoy about their mistress's divine right to the English crown, and the unanimous support her claim enjoyed from the English Catholics;[200] but diplomacy soon reasserted itself, and smooth words were resumed, Mary herself using every effort to disarm suspicion, by amiable excuses and palliations of Elizabeth's complaints, and by coy inquiries about Lord Leicester. Randolph, indeed, quite believed that

Mary would consent to the marriage proposed if she were assured that her English claims would be inquired into, 'with all favour.'

In the meanwhile Lennox, now restored to his estates, was ruffling bravely at Holyrood, spending great sums of money, in order to gain friends against the Hamiltons, who were watching him sulkily, and dreading the idea of a possible plan to marry his son to the Queen. The ready apparent acceptance by Mary of the idea of a marriage with Leicester, of which she had learned the falsity from Melville, was, however, somewhat puzzling and disturbing to the English queen, who thought it was time to effect a diversion before matters were carried too far, and this revival of the talk of Darnley's suit seemed a good opportunity for effecting her purpose. Mary had no more intention at this time of marrying Darnley than she had of marrying Leicester, but she was anxious to have him in Scotland with his father for the reasons already explained; and Lennox was prompted to write to Elizabeth that Darnley's presence in Scotland was necessary for a short time, in order that his right to the entail of his estates should be recognised. In answer to the prayer of Lady Lennox that her son might be allowed to go, Elizabeth at first consented with alacrity; for this was at the very time when Randolph's hopeful letters about the Leicester match were arriving in London. But Lady Lennox was fond of intrigue, and was seen to be flitting backwards and forwards to the Spanish ambassador and the disaffected group of Catholic nobles who were jealous of Cecil and the new men, and the Queen withdrew her licence for Darnley's journey as soon as it was given, stricken with fear that a trap had been laid for her, and that she might, when least she expected it, find Darnley and Mary married and acclaimed by the English Catholics as the heirs, if not the rightful possessors of the crown. So the downy-cheeked young gallant was perforce obliged to stay for some time longer within sight of the keen eyes of Elizabeth.

Mary grew more and more anxious as time went on for an answer about the Spanish match that she so ardently desired. When Philip had written to his ambassador, Guzman, in August that the proposal must be considered at an end, he had not instructed him to convey this to Mary; and Guzman, of course, had not done so. The Duchess of Arschot's unofficial intimation, moreover, cannot have reached her before the very end of the year 1564. But the Queen of Scots could not be blind to the fact that her Guise kinsmen were hand-in-glove with Philip, and that they would not now raise a hand to forward her marriage with a Spanish prince, even if Philip was willing to fly in the face of his French allies by proposing it. How bitterly she resented Cardinal Lorraine's selfish diplomacy is seen by her remark concerning him in November, when she received a letter from him, recommending her to marry the Protestant Prince of Condé, with whom peace had recently been made. Lorraine excused his instability in recommending so strange a husband for his niece by saying that he was in great danger from the Protestants unless she did as he wished. 'Truly I am beholden to my uncle,' ironically exclaimed Mary; 'so that it be well with him, he careth not what becometh of me.'[201]

So, whilst she and Murray still continued to profess a leaning towards Leicester, Mary endeavoured to hasten matters with Spain. John Beaton, the brother of the Archbishop of Glasgow, Mary's ambassador in France, had been sent in November to Scotland; and on his return through England in the following month he was secretly instructed by Mary to sound Guzman in London, for whom he had a letter from the Spanish ambassador in Paris. 'How go affairs in Scotland?' asked Guzman. 'Well,' replied Beaton, 'only that my mistress doth not marry.' This was delicate ground, and Guzman made no reply which might give Beaton an opening; so the Scotsman sought out that Luis de Paz, who had been sent to Scotland by the dying Spanish bishop Quadra a year before to tell the Queen that Philip had sent a message for her. To this man at the dead of night Beaton spoke, and asked him (14th December) if there was any answer from Spain yet about the business he had dealt with in Scotland. Guzman the ambassador himself was in doubt as to Philip's present intentions, for many things had changed since the King wrote his autograph note of August putting an end to the Spanish match. Elizabeth's expressed desire to get married especially; and the busy negotiations now going on for her union with a French prince, farcical as they were, seemed to demand the usual counter-move on the part of Spain; so in his desire to leave his master an open course still, Guzman in his answer to Beaton's inquiry through de Paz refrained from dashing Mary's hopes, and pretended to have received no instructions.[202]

In Scotland the Leicester match grew apparently more and more in favour. 'No men in England wish more than they (Murray and Lethington) that the Queen's Majesty's desire of a marriage between this Queen and Lord Robert take sooner effect,' wrote Randolph to Cecil on the 14th December. 'No man is more acceptable than shall be my Lord Robert. More was thought of Darnley before his father's coming than at present. The father is now here and well known, the mother more feared than beloved by those that know her. . . . To think that my Lord Darnley should marry this Queen, and his mother bear that stroke with her that she bore with Queen Mary . . . would alienate as many minds from my sovereign by sending a plague to this country as she . . . drave out of the same when the French were forced to retire, that daily sat on their (the Scots') necks with knives ready to cut their throats. . . . One thing is assuredly known; that Lord Darnley's father told Mr. John Leslie, Lord of Sessions, that his son should marry the Queen. Yet I know, by that which hath been spoken of her own mouth, both of him and his mother, that it shall never take effect, if otherwise she may have her desire.'[203] This letter, written in December, was probably the principal factor in deciding Elizabeth finally to let Darnley go, which she did soon after its receipt, at the earnest request both of Leicester and Cecil; the former because he was anxious to create a diversion from his own marriage with Mary, and the latter because, like his mistress, he wished to embroil her and to prevent her from marrying any one as long as possible; and they thought Darnley might easily be recalled if his chances began to look too favourable.[204]

Mary learned from the Duchess of Arschot in the last days of 1564 that Philip had vetoed the marriage with Don Carlos, and heavy as was the blow to her plans, the Queen of Scots lost no time in changing her tack, in accordance with the new conditions thus created. She had put aside, politely but firmly, as we have seen, the proposal brought to her by Castelnau two months before for a marriage with young Anjou, her brother-in-law; but immediately after the arrival of the Duchess of Arschot's letter, Randolph was surprised at the constant posting backwards and forwards of messengers to France. It was even said that Lethington himself was to go thither, and Elizabeth at once began to grow alarmed, especially when Cecil's spies reported that the Lennoxes had agreed with Mary to call in French armed help and restore the Catholic religion, they being acknowledged heirs to Scotland before the Hamiltons. Considering how really alarmed the English were at this sudden apparent friendship with the French, it is somewhat amusing to see, by Mary's own letter of 28th January 1565 to her ambassador in Paris,[205] that the whole business was simply a diplomatic ruse. He was to pretend to have most urgent business with the Queen-Mother, with whom he was to demand frequent audiences; to write pressing letters about nothing in particular to Cardinal Lorraine; and to do all he possibly could to make the English ambassador believe that negotiations of importance were in progress. All this was, of course, for the purpose of frightening Elizabeth into some important concession in regard to Mary's English claims; and when Randolph was sent by Elizabeth's orders to see the Scottish queen, who was then at St. Andrews, and to demand an answer to the points of the Leicester match left for decision by the hollow conference at Berwick a few weeks previously, Mary, determined to alarm Elizabeth, opened her batteries personally and played her part to perfection.

Randolph arrived at St. Andrews in the first days of February 1565 to deliver his mistress's letter to the Scottish queen. The latter smiled when she read it, but said nothing; and when on the next day the envoy tried to get a reply, she refused point-blank to do anything but make merry. She was staying with a very small train at a merchant's house in the town. Randolph must dine and sup with her, and must join her often in drinking Elizabeth's health; but no business would she listen to. On the fourth day Randolph had had enough of this, and seriously demanded an answer to Leicester's proposal. 'I had no sooner spoken . . . but she said, I see now well you are weary of this company and treatment. I sent for you to be merry, and to see how like a burgess's wife I live with my little troop; and you *will* interrupt our pastimes with your grave matters. I pray you, Sir, if you be weary here, return to Edinburgh, and keep your gravity and great embassade until the Queen come thither: for, I assure you, you shall not get her here, nor I know not myself where she is become. You see neither cloth of state nor such appearance that you may think there is a Queen here, nor would I that you should think I am she at St. Andrews that I was at Edinburgh.' She rallied the poor man in this way until he was completely puzzled; but at dinner next day, though she was very merry, and afterwards when he accompanied her riding, he noticed that, gay as her prattle was, 'she talked to me most of the time of France.' How she loved the country, of which her first husband had been king, and where her people possessed privileges denied to others: how anxious the French were for her to marry a French prince, and much more to the same effect, she impressed upon Elizabeth's agent. 'To leave such friends and to lose such offers as they make without assurance of as good, nobody will advise that loveth me.' She could not, she said, long defer her marriage, but complained that she could get no definite pledge from Elizabeth. She could not be bound to her for nothing. She was willing to treat her as a daughter or a sister should, but there must be some reciprocity, or she must turn to her French friends, though she would prefer to follow Elizabeth's advice alone. 'Remember,' she continued, 'what I have said cometh not upon a sudden. It is more than a day or two that I have had this thought, and more than this that ye shall not know.' 'Oh!' exclaimed Randolph, 'do not cut your talk short here; it is so good and wise, well framed and comfortable to me.' 'I am a fool,' she replied, 'thus to talk with you; you are too subtle for me.' By and by Randolph came to the point again with a leading question. 'How did she like Lord Leicester's suit?' 'My mind towards him is such,' she said, 'as it ought to be of a very noble man, as I hear say he is by very many; and such a one as the Queen, my good sister, doth so well like to be her husband, if he were not her subject, ought not to mislike me to be mine. But marry! what I shall do, it lyeth in your mistress's will, who shall wholly guide and rule me.'[206] Randolph, try as he would, could get no further than this; and it meant, as plainly as diplomacy could speak, that the recognition of Mary's right of succession to the English crown must precede her acceptance of Elizabeth's advice as to her marriage. Whether after such recognition or its promise she would have been willing to marry Leicester, or he to marry her, is another matter. The two queens, in fact, were playing a confidence trick, in which neither of them would make the first deposit.

This was the condition of affairs when young Darnley crossed the Border on the 11th February 1565, to Randolph's utter consternation and bewilderment, openly displayed in his letters. The good man in all sincerity had been pushing the Leicester suit with the utmost zeal, though the earl's irritation in his letters to him had greatly perplexed him; and that this youth, whose father was already suspected of anti-English and Catholic plans, should be allowed to come and spoil a negotiation that seemed prospering, he could not understand at all. 'How to frame or fashion this . . . truly I know not; yet what to think or how to behave myself.' So little was Darnley expected by Scotsmen that many thought the newcomer must really be Leicester. The Hamiltons, the Campbells, the Scotts, the Beatons, the Douglases, the Cunninghames, and many others were alarmed, some for religion and some from ancient feuds, at the bare possibility of the marriage of Mary with her cousin; but Randolph scouted such an idea as out of the question, for he still believed fervently in the success of the Leicester marriage, and his objection to Darnley was mainly religious. Both he and those friends of the English party whom he could advise, however, received the newcomer with great courtesy. Morton and Glencairn, both enemies of Lennox, welcomed him as cordially as they could; and Murray's brother Robert entertained him at Holyrood in the Queen's absence, whilst Randolph lent him horses; when, after awaiting his father's[207] instructions for three days in Edinburgh, the youth proceeded to Wemyss in Fife to salute Queen Mary, whom, of course, he had never seen.

Henry Stuart, by courtesy Lord Darnley, was now in his nineteenth year, and eleven years older than his only brother Charles Stuart. He had been carefully reared in the usual courtly accomplishments of his time, such as dancing, music, riding, and the use of arms, and as we have seen by Melville's description of him, was of tall stature, with the youthful attractions of a fair, smooth face and a graceful bearing. His flat, lymphatic countenance, with its pointed chin and eyes *à fleur de tête*, indicates small powers of reflection and little strength of purpose; but the brow is broad, the perceptive faculties good, and the general expression, though irresponsible, is observant and not unpleasing. Under good tutelage and wise control a youth possessing such a face might well develop into an easygoing, lethargic, self-indulgent citizen, watchful of his own immediate interests, though lacking the moral energy to pursue them with persistence. But Henry Stuart, though carefully taught, so far as accomplishments and graces were concerned, had been unwisely reared. Brought up by his mother, practically as an only son, he had never been allowed to forget that he stood within the shadow of the throne as the first prince of the blood royal, by right of birth, whatever King Henry's eccentric will might say. That he, a member of the sacred royal caste, was allowed privileges and immunities that other young nobles were denied, that a turn of fortune's wheel might at any moment draw him from obscurity into the fullest light, was ever before him; and, as was natural in a lad of his weak sense of moral responsibility, had made him arrogant, petulant, and self-willed, impatient of reproof, and yet without stability or rectitude.

The first impression he made in Scotland was a good one. 'His courteous dealing with all men deserves great praise and is well spoken of.' 'Many resorted to him here, Edinburgh; they liked well his personage—for his other qualities time has not served. A great number wish him well, others doubt him, and deeplier consider what is fit for the state of their country than, as they call him, a fair jolly young man.' But as for Randolph himself, he utterly disbelieved that the coming of Darnley could really upset, though it might impede, the negotiation for the Leicester match, which he innocently prided himself he had brought within measurable distance of celebration. When Darnley received his father's instructions he at once set out on his borrowed horses to salute the Queen at the castle of the Laird of Wemyss, where she was staying.[208]

He first saw Mary on the 17th February. 'He was,' we are told, 'well received, and lodged in the same house.' He only stayed there for a day or so before riding to Dunkeld to join his father; but it was long enough for the Queen to notice, as others had done, at first sight his attractive points. Melville, who was deep in Mary's confidence, says: 'Her Majesty took very well with him, and said that he was the properest and best proportioned long man that ever she had seen.' After visiting his father Darnley rode back in time to enter Edinburgh with the Queen and court a week later. The next day, Sunday, he dined with Murray, and on Monday heard Knox preach.[209] Everybody was charmed with him, for he was evidently on his best behaviour, and was prompt to please those whom he approached. After supper at Holyrood on Monday, he stood watching Mary and her ladies dance, and was challenged by Murray to dance with the Queen. Nothing loth, the tall stripling stood forth and stepped a galliarde with Mary, who, we are assured, notwithstanding her long recent journey through the bitterest winter known for many years, 'looked lustier than when she went forth.'

Up to this period we have seen Mary playing her game with perfect self-command. She was pleasure-loving, light-hearted, and determined to enjoy life to its utmost; but she had so far curbed her inclinations whenever they ran counter to the success of her aims. The kernel of her policy from the first had been the establishment of her prospective or present right to rule England, as well as Scotland, and to restore Great Britain to the Catholic Church. There were two ways by which this might be effected: first, by her marriage with a Catholic prince strong enough to enforce her claims in conjunction with the Catholic party in England; and second, by a transaction with Elizabeth, in which Mary's marriage with an English nominee should be paid for by her formal recognition by Queen and parliament as Elizabeth's heir. So long as Francis II lived Mary had worked in the first direction; but when she came as a widow to Scotland it was with the intention of adopting the second course, under the guidance of her Anglophil ministers, Murray and Lethington. We have seen how, despairing of obtaining definite pledges from Elizabeth, Mary had in 1563 reverted to the first plan, and had attempted to arrange her marriage with Don Carlos, from which Elizabeth's double-dealing intrigue about the Leicester match had never moved her; and she had carried on the negotiations with Randolph in a similar spirit, knowing they were false.

LORD DARNLEY
Painter Unknown. Owner, the Duke of Devonshirre
Photo, Hanfstaengl

When Darnley arrived in Scotland Mary knew, though unofficially, that the Spanish match was 'off'; but it was obvious that whilst she remained unmarried anything was possible; and her best interests were involved in delaying indefinitely any decision, except the one that would ensure the success of her aims, one way or the other. It was quite evident that marriage with Darnley would not do this, unless it were effected as part of a transaction with Elizabeth, and with the support of the Scottish Protestants as well as the Catholics. The only advantage which such a union could bring to Mary otherwise was the co-operation of the two Catholic claimants for the crown of England in case of Elizabeth's death, and the united support of the English Catholic nobles; whilst against this latter advantage were to be balanced the discords and old feuds aroused in Scotland itself by the restoration and elevation of the Lennox Stuarts. It was, therefore, Mary's wisest course to avoid an alliance until she could make an advantageous bargain for herself with one interest or the other, which in changeful times she might always hope to do so long as she remained unfettered. It was on this occasion, the crucial point of her career, that Mary's amorous passion first overrode her diplomacy.

There were, of course, reasons that could be alleged that made the marriage with Darnley appear plausible, or indeed necessary, such as those recited by Mary herself afterwards: her betrayal by Cardinal Lorraine and the consequent failure of the Spanish match, her jealousy of Murray's ambition, and others; but these reasons, though they may excuse the selection of Darnley rather than another, do not establish, from the purely diplomatic point of view, the inevitable need for Mary to have taken a husband at all when she did. We are, then, driven to the logical conclusion that she did so to satisfy her own fancy, which for the time was strong enough to postpone her political interests.

The first doubtful note of alarm about Darnley seems to have come from watchful Murray. There was much talk in Edinburgh still of Cardinal Lorraine's wish to marry his niece, either to her brother-in-law Charles IX or to young Anjou; though Randolph was quite convinced that Mary would end by following the Queen of England's advice, and marry at her bidding[210] Leicester or another. But ten days after Darnley's first sight of the queen Murray dined with the English envoy, and warned him seriously that Elizabeth must promptly agree to acknowledge Mary as her heir, or she would find that the prize of Scotland had slipped through her fingers. Neither Mary, he said, nor her advisers, could afford to 'do all for nought, and neglect the counsel of her friends.' Randolph replied by some fulsome praise of Leicester and an exaggerated estimation of the great sacrifices he would make if he came to Scotland as the Queen's husband, leaving honour, riches, and great hopes in England for so doubtful an advantage as a marriage with Mary would bring him. Yes, Murray replied in effect, Leicester is all very well, and at least we know all about him and his good qualities. But if he come not promptly with conditions acceptable to Mary and the Scots, we shall have another less to our liking: 'for thother yt is uncertayne, and yf yt fell tomorrowe I trowe that yt woulde breede us more trouble than commodity, and no less sorrow to our mistress than to yourselves.'[211] The Laird of Pitarrow, who sat at the table, stern Protestant that he was, pleaded for straightforward dealing. Leicester would lose nothing by coming and marrying the Queen of Scots, and his danger in doing so would be less than in marrying Elizabeth. Let him seize the opportunity promptly, and let fair conditions be granted, in return, to Mary. Above all, in Heaven's name, let us be quick about it, or we shall find our Queen with a papist husband. 'Remember,' he said, 'howe earnestye she is soughte otherwyse. You know her years; you see the lustyness of her boddie, you know what these thynges requere—yt ys all our partes to farther yt—losse of her time is our destruction, and yt is our parte to be most carefull for that which we know to be fittest and most assured for her estate.' Leicester, he told Randolph, was the man desired by Protestants in Scotland, but pray let no time be lost, or things would end badly. Then Murray put in a piteous word on his own behoof. Every one knew, he said, how he had striven to forward Elizabeth's plans for his sister's marriage, and if the English match should fall through after all it would be his ruin. 'Yf she marrye any other, what mind will he bear me that knoweth how much I do myslike therewith? If he be a papist, either we must obeye or fawle into fresh cumbers, and I ever be thought the ringleader.' What was the use, he asked indignantly, of talking any more in this strain. He had said it all a hundred times before, but he saw nothing but drift and delay from day to day. When he left the dining-chamber he whispered in Randolph's ear an impassioned appeal that Elizabeth would save Scotland from 'papystrie,' 'for otherwise it will be worst with us than ever it was.' He had good hopes, he said, of Mary now, for she was offended with the French Queen-Mother and with her uncle Lorraine. Her French physician, a Guisan spy, thank God, was leaving Scotland, and she has no other Frenchman of standing about her. Raulet the French secretary had been dismissed, on suspicion of betraying secrets to the English. 'An Italian Piedmontese, a singer that came with M. Moret, is her secretary for French affairs,' and he had only crept in when Raulet was suspected.[212]

From Murray's talk in this interview it is clear that he was vehemently uneasy, and desirous of precipitating the Leicester match in conjunction with the recognition of Mary's claims in England. Of whom was he distrustful? Who was 'thother' that he dreaded so much? Not a French candidate, evidently, for Mary was on ill terms with Catharine and the Cardinal, notwithstanding the gossip of the Market-place about French suitors. Not a Spaniard, for Murray must have known that Philip had refused the match for his son. There was indeed at the moment no 'thother' but the willowy, flat-faced youth with the pointed chin, upon whom Mary's eyes had rested with desire.

Three days after the interview just related—three days of heavy snow which blocked the roads—Murray gave a great banquet at Holyrood, at which all the gentlemen and ladies of the court were present, Darnley of course included. At the height of the jollity the Queen sent word to the feasters that she wished she was of the company, and was sorry she was not invited. 'It was answered merrily that the house was her own, she might come unbidden: others said they were merriest when the table was fullest, but princes ever used to dine alone'; and Mary thereupon invited all the company to feast with her on the following Sunday (4th March), when 'the lusty Englishman,' Semple, was to marry Mary Livingston, one of the famous four. After Murray's banquet the guests adjourned to the Queen's chamber, and there again Mary and Randolph discoursed interminably upon the inevitable subject. She was as gracious as usual. She would do all that was consistent with her honour to please Elizabeth in everything. Then after some bantering about her religion Randolph suddenly asked her, what about her marriage. 'I am willing enough,' she replied. 'I pray God that your choice may be good,' ventured the envoy. 'He must be such a one as He will give me,' said Mary. Randolph hinted, in answer to this, that God had made a 'fayre offer to her' in Leicester. 'Of thys matter, sayeth she, I have saide inoughe, except that I sawe greater lykelyhood. Nor maye I applye and sette my mynde but where I intende to be a wyfe indeed. And in good faith no creature lyvinge shall make me breake more of my will than the Queen, my good syster, yf she will use me as a syster—if not I must do as I maye.'

Notwithstanding all these hints, and others no less strong from Argyle,[213] Randolph still clung to his belief in the final success of the Leicester match, and in Mary's submission to Elizabeth's will. In vain jealous Protestants pointed out that Darnley was over frequently in the Queen's company, that Mary was gay, bright, and happy when he was with her, and that her eyes followed him as he moved. It was merely natural courtesy, opined Randolph, who had probably forgotten what it was like to be in love. When on the 16th March he handed to Mary another of Elizabeth's procrastinating, enigmatical letters about the succession, instead of the positive pledge that had been so long expected, Mary showed her discontent plainly. 'She wept her fill afterwards,' he was told; but to him she began, as usual, to talk about sending Lethington to France, and rumours pervaded the court at once that a message had reached her from Cardinals Lorraine and Granvelle not to be over hasty in concluding any matter in England.

This was quite in accordance with the usual diplomacy, but Lethington and Murray, who were keener men of the world than Randolph, saw that Mary's fancy for Darnley, if it grew much stronger, would make the old diplomatic methods powerless to serve her, and they vehemently protested against any further procrastination on the part of the English queen. Murray was 'the sorrowfullest man that may be,' and the Scottish nobles who had always supported the English connection were in dismay. 'Some for religion, some for fear of overthrow of their houses, some for doubt of her marriage with a papist, and I never found in my life so many discontented people here.'[214]

And so, swiftly and silently, the stream of events swept Mary Stuart

towards the cataract that was to wreck her life. Elizabeth and Cecil thought they held all the sluice-gates in their hands; that the Lennoxes would not dare to risk the confiscation of their great English estates, and sacrifice the hopes of Elizabeth's recognition of their heirship to the crown by allowing Darnley to marry Mary. The Queen of England and her minister, like their envoy in Scotland, were confident that they could in the end always divert her from a French or Spanish marriage, by the usual expedient that had never failed yet; and that in the utter distraction which they knew their fast and loose policy would bring upon Scotland, Mary would be driven to submit to Elizabeth's will unreservedly, either with or without an undignified marriage; the result, in any case, being to reduce Mary and her realm to a negligible quantity as an international factor. If the ordinary diplomatic game alone was to be played, Elizabeth and Cecil would have been justified in their anticipation of events; but they did not know until it was too late, and their agent in Scotland, cunning as he was, had not enough human nature in him to perceive it for them, that a new element was to be introduced into the contest, against which their ordinary chicane was powerless—the element of the uncontrollable, if transient, passion of an ardent young woman for a particular man.

VII

A GREAT CONSPIRACY

Mary's fancy for Darnley does not blind her to her political object—She resolves to make a last bid to Spain—Fowler sent to London—His interviews with the Spanish ambassador—Carries back a vague answer to Scotland—Alarm of Murray and the Protestants—Scandalous reports about Mary—Lethington goes to London—His intrigues and those of Lady Lennox with the Spaniards and the Catholics—Lady Lennox arrested—Don Carlos finally refused to Mary—Lethington asks for Spanish support for Mary and Darnley—Alarm of Elizabeth—English and Protestant intrigue active in Scotland—The breach between Mary and her people widens—Her gaiety and imprudence—The rise of Rizzio—Murray refuses his consent to the Darnley marriage—Lethington's dissimulation—Throckmorton in Scotland—Darnley's foolish behaviour—Mary's love attributed to witchcraft—Counterplots against Darnley and Murray—Balmerino sent to London—Takes back to Mary the joyous message, pledging Spain to aid her and Darnley—Mary's secret marriage immediately on his arrival—Scandal caused thereby—The public marriage—Love and diplomacy reconciled.

IT IS POSSIBLE TO CONJECTURE WITH SOME DEGREE OF CONFIdence the approximate period when Mary first allowed herself to regard Darnley as an acceptable husband for her. She first saw him on the 17th

February 1565, and expressed her approval of his personal appearance on that occasion. On the 27th of the same month Murray gave his strong hint to Randolph about 'thother' dangerous rival to Leicester; and the following day Lethington wrote a private letter to Cecil couched in the cryptic style which he, like Elizabeth, affected, conveying to those who hold the key a still stronger hint. Cecil had been ill, and Lethington presumes the cause to be overwork. His remedy is one that, he says, he never fails to take himself; namely, always to enjoy at least one merry hour out of the twenty-four. 'Marry! you may perhaps reply, that as now the world doth go with me, my body is better disposed to digest such than yours is—for those that be in love are ever set upon a merry pin.' On the 10th March Lennox must probably have recognised that his son's suit was smiled upon by the Queen; for on that date he wrote a friendly letter to Cecil, begging him to ask the Queen of England to extend his licence to stay in Scotland for three months longer, 'as I cannot proceed so soon as I thought in the assurance of my lands to my son . . . for if I despatch not the matter whilst my son is here his coming were in vain.' 'My greatest care,' he says, 'is not to offend her Majesty; but I trust by my lord of Leicester's good help and yours she will be satisfied therein'; and Lennox concludes by asking permission for Darnley to import three or four geldings for presents.[215] It is difficult to believe that this excuse of Lennox for his longer stay in Scotland was the true one; because, not only by the hints of Murray and others several days before do we know that Darnley had found favour in Mary's sight, but a few days only after the arrival of Lennox's letter in London, Lady Lennox sent word to the Spanish ambassador to tell him how kind the Queen of Scotland had been to her son, and to bid for the support of Spain—rather than that of France, which she said had been offered to her—for the marriage of Mary and Darnley.

The Lennox MS. papers, drawn up for the use of Lennox himself, assert that 'the Queen was stricken by the dart of love, by the comeliness of his (Darnley's) sweet behaviour, personage, wit, and virtuous qualities . . ., as also in the art of music, dancing, and playing.'[216] As all these qualities must have been in evidence within the first few days of Darnley's residence in the Scottish court, it is probable that Mary had been sufficiently smitten with him to make her willing to take him for a consort between the 24th

February, when he entered Edinburgh with her, and the 10th March, when Lennox's courier left for London.

But, withal, Mary, thanks probably to Lethington's advice, did not act rashly at first. This was the most difficult juncture in which she had found herself. Elizabeth's last letter to her had finally convinced both her and her chief advisers that by diplomatic cajolery alone she could never wring from the Queen of England her recognition as next heir to the crown.[217] The only other way to obtain it, as has already been pointed out, was by force or fear. For months Mary had watched eagerly for some definite reply from Spain. Beyond the unofficial letter from the Duchess of Arschot in Flanders received in the last days of the year, and the non-committal answer given by Guzman in London to John Beaton on the 14th December, she had heard nothing since she had been assured that Don Carlos was coming to Flanders to marry her. But however hopeful she might be, it must have been evident to her now that her dream of the great Spanish match was at least problematical of realisation. Catharine de Medici at this period, for the purpose of disarming Elizabeth and at the same time diverting her from the Austrian marriage which had again come under favourable discussion, was pushing with furious warmth the vicarious wooing of Elizabeth by young Charles IX, through Paul de Foix[218] in London; and it was clear to Mary that in these circumstances her marriage with her French brother-in-law was more improbable even than ever; whilst a union with his boy brother Anjou, whilst arousing as much opposition as a more powerful match, would have been perfectly useless for the attainment of her aims by force.

She must have felt keenly, too, the abandonment of her interests by Cardinal Lorraine, who was making desperate efforts at the time to keep a footing at court by marrying his niece to the younger son of France, or to checkmate the threatening Montmorencis by buying Condé and the Bourbons with the price of Mary's hand for the former, suggestions which the Queen of Scots indignantly resented. Given, therefore, the absolute need of an immediate marriage, the only suitor who could have given her any support in enforcing her English claims was Darnley, who at all events enjoyed the sympathy of the large Catholic party in England, and the prestige of his royal blood. Where Mary appears to have made a diplomatic mistake was not so much in marrying Darnley—though that was highly imprudent, unless as part of a bargain with Elizabeth—as in marrying at all when she did.

Her eyes were, however, always fixed on the English succession, and before definitely accepting Darnley she made a last bid to Spain and France for support. Probably at the same time as the courier took Randolph's account to Elizabeth of the grief of Mary and the desperation of Murray at the definite letter from England about the succession (17th March 1565), the Queen of Scots saw Castelnau de la Mauvissiere, the French ambassador, and set before him the reasons why she wished to marry Darnley. Castelnau had noted the growing fondness displayed by the lovers, and foresaw the result; but as his mission had been simply to divert Mary from a Spanish or Austrian match, he had stood aloof during the early progress of the Darnley wooing. The Queen of Scots now told him that she thought the interests of her realm and herself would be best served by her marriage with the young Stuart, but that she would do nothing without the advice of the Queen-Mother, and wished before the match was definitely settled to learn the views of Catharine and her son. That very night an agent of the French ambassador was hurrying south with his message, in which Castelnau privately informed Catharine that he considered the courtship had already advanced too far to be stopped. This move of Mary towards her French mother-in-law doubtless had alternative objects; first, to provoke an offer of marriage at once from Charles IX, or, failing that, to ensure French support, or at all events to avoid opposition to the union with Darnley.

Towards the Spaniards she made a similar, and indeed more significant, advance. Lethington, it was said, was to go to England to carry Mary's reply to Elizabeth's final succession letter; and, with the pretext of asking the English queen for a passport for him, a Scottish agent named Fowler was sent to London on the 17th March. He arrived on the 24th, and, having made his request to Elizabeth, he went at night to see Guzman, the Spanish ambassador, for whom he bore a letter of credence from the Queen of Scots. His verbal message was to the effect that his mistress had learned from Flanders that Guzman had been instructed by King Philip to discuss the business that had been broached to him on a previous occasion. Guzman was suspicious, for he did not know Mary's signature, and the messenger's replies to his cross-questioning were not very definite, so he answered coldly that he had no such orders from the King. Fowler guessed the reason, and said that he would show the Queen's letter to Luis de Paz, who knew her handwriting. He was loth to go back to Scotland, he said, without an answer, as his mistress had been informed that King Philip had instructed the ambassador five months before to treat with her on the matter. If he had done so, retorted Guzman, I should not have waited so long as this before communicating with her. No sooner had Mary's envoy, Fowler, left Guzman to seek Luis de Paz, than a letter from Cardinal de Granvelle, in Flanders, was delivered to the ambassador. The French Queen-Mother, mainly in order to drive Elizabeth into the marriage with Charles IX, which de Foix was so hotly pushing in London, had spread a rumour that the young King was negotiating for the hand of the Queen of Scots. The rumour had reached de Granvelle, and he urged Guzman to make a countermove by reviving the pretensions of the Archduke Charles to Mary. The next time Fowler came to see him, therefore, the Spanish ambassador unbent a little, though he was still very cautious. The coming of Lethington, he was told, was really only to see him about the marriage proposals of Mary; and in order, at least, that the Scottish minister might not be deterred from making the voyage, Guzman wrote a letter to Mary, vaguely professing a desire to serve her, and to speak with Lethington if he came to London. Deeply, therefore, as Mary was smitten with Darnley's charms, she, or perhaps her ministers, did not lose sight entirely of her diplomatic objects. Nor did Lady Lennox, who lost no opportunity of pushing her son's cause with the English Catholic nobles, and with the Spanish ambassador. Philip, she assured the latter, was her mainstay and hope in the case of Darnley's marriage with Mary, or in that of Elizabeth's death, and she and her family would always be his humble servants, though the French, whom she did not trust, were eagerly offering her their support.

Marriages, as de Foix said, were in the air. Elizabeth was flirting desperately with him for Charles IX; she was dropping strong hints that she wanted an offer from Don Carlos; whilst her marriage with the Austrian Archduke was looked upon by many as certain; and Leicester, in his heart of hearts, was more confident than ever that he would finally win the prize. This amorous activity in London was of course mainly intended to divert all possible dangerous suitors from Mary, in which object at the moment Catharine de Medici was, moreover, almost as much interested as Elizabeth herself.[219]

In the meantime, whilst Mary was endeavouring to smooth the diplomatic path, the billing and cooing with Darnley proceeded apace at Stirling.[220] Murray no longer concealed his distress at the course taken by events. The marriage of Mary with a French suitor, such as was still urged by Lorraine, would, he knew, mean a quarrel with England, the strengthening of Catholicism in Scotland, and his own downfall, whilst 'yf she tayke fantacie to this new come guest (Darnley), then shall theie be sure of myscheif, sedition, and debate at home.' Religious feeling in the country was more bitter than ever on both sides, and in her absence in Fifeshire one of the Queen's own priests was like to be hanged by the 'godly' in Holyrood for daring to say Mass for her household. Both Murray and Lethington were therefore opposed more strongly than ever to their mistress's marriage with any foreign prince, unless he was strong enough to dominate Scotland and defy England. Failing their being able to persuade Elizabeth to recognise Mary as her heir as a condition of a marriage with an English nominee, the only solution which presented itself to the two Scottish ministers was to let the Darnley match go on, and to make the best terms they could for it, although they were both deeply distrustful of the young man and his parents.

Elizabeth's cunning diplomacy had, in fact, made it impossible for Mary to marry at all without drawing upon Scotland foreign complications or civil war, and perhaps both. Murray was heartsick of the business when he recognised that not only was Mary bent upon marrying Darnley, but intended to do so under Catholic auspices; and after an angry scene with his sister he rode out of Stirling on the night of 3rd April, retiring to St. Andrews, and leaving Mary to her own devices,[221] as Lethington started a few days afterwards for England, ostensibly to soften Elizabeth, but really with the important secret mission which will be described later. Darnley fell ill of the measles, apparently the day before Murray's retirement, and Mary's attention to her lover on that occasion was a grave cause of scandal

to the virtuous Elizabeth. One of the complaints which Throckmorton was afterwards instructed to make to Mary was, 'that she has so far proceeded in love of him; as he, being sick of the mezells, which is an infectuoos dissease, she could not be persuaded to tarry from him, but attended upon hym with as much diligence and care as any could. Yea! and that she so much desyred to proceed in marriage with hym, as, if others had not been scrupulous and fearful to assist the same, she had been affianced to him.'[222]

Randolph had now fairly taken fright, as well as Murray. He lost no opportunity of whispering incitements to the ducal head of the Hamiltons, but to no purpose, and his Protestant friends were panic-stricken. 'Great expectation there is what shall come of this great favour to Darnley, which makes some muttering amongst us that burst out it must to some men's cost.' The English envoy rode as far as Berwick with Lethington on his way to England (8th April), and how dismal their communings were is evident from Randolph's letter to Cecil of the 15th. Apparently, though he said nothing of this to Randolph, Lethington had persuaded Mary not to pledge herself to Darnley finally until one more diplomatic attempt had been made to gain some political advantage from the match, if nothing better could be done. But it was a forlorn hope, and Lethington's heavy heart told him that his mistress would wed the youth who had captured her fancy, whatever happened. 'The matter is now grown to further ripeness,' writes Randolph from Berwick. 'The Queen's familiarity with him (Darnley) breeds no small suspicion. . . . It is now commonly said, and I believe is more than a bruit, that this Queen has already such good liking of him that she can be content to forsake all other offers, give up all suitors, and content herself with her own choice. I know not what Lethington knows or will utter, but am assured that, with the best of his country, he partakes of their griefs of the inconvenience and danger like to ensue, which he shall as soon find as any.'[223] Darnley remained 'doubtfully sick' all through April, 'lacking no attendance or comfort, oft visited by the greatest and by the fairest, if that may help his malady'; and as Mary and her court travelled in her progress, one noble after another fell away from her, till none but Lennox and the Earl of Athol stayed to witness Darnley's fateful wooing. Even Castelnau, who had been instructed by the Queen-Mother rather to help than oppose the match, was sent by Mary to France to obtain promises of material support, if needed, after the marriage, in return for a renewal of the old Franco-Scottish alliance.[224] No great hope of this can have animated the Queen of Scots, for she knew—and said—that Catharine disliked her more than ever, and the French were flattering Elizabeth to the top of her bent; but appearances had to be kept up, and it was necessary to minimise opposition wherever possible.

Mary's real hope was still fixed on Spain; and if, at any cost, she could get Philip's powerful aid to make her the Queen of Catholic Great Britain, she would triumph over all her enemies—English, French, and Scottish. This was the despairing hope that took Lethington to London in April 1565, and induced Mary to pause, at least until his return, before she wedded Darnley. The letter sent to Mary by Guzman from London three weeks previously was, as we have seen, almost cold and vague enough to have destroyed hope, and, indeed, was only written at all because of Cardinal de Granvelle's remark about the desirability of obstructing a French marriage for the Scottish queen. But, slight as was the hope it gave, Lethington travelled to England solely to see the writer, under cover of fresh negotiations with Elizabeth.

Lethington arrived in London on the 16th April, and one of the first persons he saw was Lady Lennox, for whom he brought a letter from Mary. Almost immediately afterwards the countess sent to the Spanish ambassador, begging him when he saw Lethington to assure him that King Philip wished to favour her (Lady Lennox), as she thought such a declaration might help Darnley in his courtship, of which she was hopeful. Lady Lennox, as usual, was almost treasonous in her professions of obedience to the King of Spain, who, she said, was Mary's main hope for the assertion of her English claims; and, as the ambassador recognised that she had behind her the English Catholic nobility, he decided to keep her in hand, until he learned if the Archduke's suit for Mary was to be urged by Spain or not. A day or two afterwards Lady Lennox entered the presence-chamber at Whitehall, and as she approached Elizabeth with the usual obeisance, the Queen frowned and turned her back upon her: sending a message by a chamberlain almost immediately, to the effect that Lady Lennox must consider herself under arrest in her own apartments, for having received a letter from a foreign sovereign (*i.e.* Mary) without permission. The countess did her best to soften Elizabeth's wrath, but with little success. The letters of Randolph, and the retirement of Murray from court, perhaps also the demands of Lethington, had now fully opened the eyes of Elizabeth to the fact that the Lennoxes could not be whistled back so easily as she had thought, and that the love-making at Stirling was of a more serious description than that which formed her own chief amusement and principal policy.

On the 24th and 25th April Lethington had long conferences with Guzman, in the first of which he spoke bitterly of the enmity of Catharine de Medici against Mary, and of the combination of Elizabeth and Catharine to injure his mistress. On the 25th Lethington came straight to the point with an official message from Mary to Guzman. She had always, she said, desired to be guided by the King of Spain alone, and had been negotiating with the Bishop of Aquila for her marriage with Don Carlos when the bishop died. She had since waited for two years in hope of a reply, and had at last listened to proposals from Darnley. If, however, there were any hopes of the negotiations for the Spanish prince proceeding, she was still of the same mind, and wished to know what Guzman thought about it, as she had learned from Cardinal de Granvelle that he, Guzman, had received King Philip's instructions on the subject. With much sugared verbiage Guzman repeated, in effect, Philip's letter written in the previous August. Cardinal Lorraine, apparently fully authorised to act for her, had, he said, practically arranged the match with the Archduke, and the offer of Don Carlos had therefore been withdrawn. It was all a trick of the Queen-Mother, who hated his mistress, said Lethington. Immediately after the death of Mary's first husband Francis, Catharine had sent for the Guises, and had extracted from them a pledge that they would not forward a marriage between Mary and Carlos, as being dangerous for France. In negotiating with the Archduke, said Lethington, Cardinal Lorraine had acted contrary to Mary's wishes and orders. The Austrian match was detested by every one in Scotland: it would be quite useless, and worse than useless, for the Scottish aims; and the only object of the Cardinal in arranging it, knowing it would never take place, was to wreck Mary's own plan for a Spanish marriage. Well, replied

Guzman, we are very sorry, but it is too late now to talk about Don Carlos. With regard to the proposals of Darnley, continued the ambassador, 'since the Queen will not marry a foreigner, the son of Lady Lennox appears the most suitable person, both on account of his own promise and on account of his parents, for whom, and especially for his mother, my master has especial regard.' Lethington said that he was inclined to think so too, if Mary could not get a foreigner powerful enough to overcome opposition; but if the Queen of England did not take it well, as she showed signs of not doing, it might be inconvenient, because Elizabeth might retort by declaring one of the Protestant claimants her heir, or by entering into a close union with France. But all this difficulty would vanish, continued the Scottish minister, if the King of Spain would take Mary and her affairs 'under his protection, in the assurance that at all times, and in every matter, they shall be considered as his own.' The arrangement might be concluded with the utmost secrecy through Guzman, or through the Spanish ambassador in Paris, and kept quiet till the opportune moment arrived. 'There is no doubt whatever that the majority of the gentry and common people are attached to my Queen, and I can affirm positively that she will follow in every respect the wishes of your master.'[225]

Here we have the edifying spectacle of the Protestant Lethington, speaking perhaps also for Murray, willing to make Scotland as well as England a Catholic appanage of Spain if no other way could be found of establishing Mary's claim to the English crown. Failing the King of France and Don Carlos, who were now out of the question, Darnley was the only man who might be made an instrument to attract a foreign power to enforce Mary's ambitions; and Lethington's course was dictated by the highest diplomacy, whatever we may think of its honesty. He knew that Philip's most vital political necessity was a submissive England, and that Scotland was only interesting to Spain as contributing to that end. Lady Lennox and her son claimed the support of all the old powerful Catholic interests in England; and if Philip had them at his command, with the added advantage of a permanent base in Scotland, he might, by the death of Elizabeth, find himself at any moment the virtual master of Great Britain. The Spanish ambassador therefore smiled upon Lethington's advances, and promised to send post-haste for his King's decision, which he did in terms most favour-able to Mary.

In the meanwhile Elizabeth was in a furious rage, alternately ordering and cajoling Darnley and his father to return at once; and, amongst other things, positively hinting that she might marry Darnley himself if he came.[226] She went to the length of promising Lethington that if Mary would marry to her satisfaction, she would make a clear pronouncement as to the succession; but the promise still was vague; that bait had now lost its savour, and the Scottish minister answered coldly. Elizabeth then angrily asked him if the Darnley wedding had already taken place, to which he answered that he did not know. Lady Lennox, though in disgrace, was jubilant, for she was confident that her son, if not already King-Consort of Scotland, would be so before many weeks had passed. For once the counsels of Elizabeth and her advisers were utterly distracted, and something like panic reigned. They were all sure (28th April 1565) that Mary and Darnley were already mar-ried. Throckmorton was sent off in a hurry to Scotland to stop the match, if not too late, with fresh overtures for the union with Leicester; but he had not gone many miles from London before he was recalled to discuss the matter again. Then the council met Lethington and tried to come to terms with him. The Scotsman now boldly demanded Elizabeth's approval of the Darnley match, and the declaration of Mary as heir of England, on the ground that the bridegroom was an Englishman, as the Queen of England had insisted upon Mary's husband being, and she had actually mentioned Darnley with Leicester as one of those Mary might marry as a condition of the recognition of her claims in England.

Elizabeth endeavoured to meet the new danger offered by a Spanish protection of the Scottish queen and her husband by developing a desper-ate desire to marry the Archduke Charles whilst still negotiating for her union with the King of France; and Leicester tried to turn the matter to his own advantage by asking Guzman to plead his cause with Elizabeth, who he thought might wed him, now that Mary could not marry a dangerous foreign prince. With the forlorn hope of being able either to frighten or wheedle Mary from her resolution, Throckmorton was at last (5th May) sent to Scotland. He was to give to her a choice of any English nobleman, and even to hint at the Prince of Condé if necessary; but his principal lever was still to be Leicester. If Mary would marry him, he should be considered as Elizabeth's brother on her mother's side; and though the definite declaration of a successor to the crown of England was impossible for many reasons, everything short of that should be done to favour Mary's claim; but on no conditions could Darnley be approved of. One item of Throckmorton's instructions shows how determined Elizabeth and her council were to make the most of anything likely to injure Mary's reputation. The Queen had been greatly shocked at certain stories spread by Darnley's relatives 'touching the honour and reputation of our good sister': such, for instance, as the attendance of Mary upon her lover when he was in bed with the measles. Throckmorton was to say that Lethington having assured Elizabeth that these stories were not true, she had forbidden Lady Lennox her presence in consequence of them, and wished to know to what extent Mary desired that those who propagated them should be punished.

In the meanwhile the discontent of a large number of the Scottish gentry with Darnley was consolidating. Mary's tender care of her lover had become the talk of the country, and Murray, sulking apart in St. Andrews, was gradually focussing the dislike of the coming marriage, and of Mary's own proceedings. Her Catholic ceremonies were more ostentatious than ever, and more violently resented by the Protestants.[227] Free also from the firm supervision of Murray and the grave presence of Lethington, she again became imprudently gay in her demeanour. At Stirling, late in April, one Monday night, 'she and divers of her women, apparelling themselves like burgesses' wives, went on foot up and down the town: of every man they met they took some pledge for a piece of money to the banquet . . . and there was dinner prepared and great cheer made, at which she was herself, to the great wonder of man, woman, and child. This is much wondered at of a Queen.'[228] 'She is now in utter contempt of her people, and so far in doubt of them herself, that without speedy redress worse is to be feared. Many grievous and sore words have of late escaped her against the Duke (Chatelherault), she mortally hates Argyle, and so far suspects Murray that not many days since she said she saw that he would set the crown upon his own head.'[229]

Thus the breach between Mary and her people widened. Up to this period she had never been personally unpopular, for, whilst keeping true to her religion, she had not interfered with that of her people; and her brightness and *abandon*, excessive as it had sometimes been, had only given offence to the very dour Puritans. But now that Murray and the Protestant nobles had fallen away from her, and her infatuation for Darnley had thrown her into the hands of the opposite faction, every man feared what next might befall, and what religious persecution, at the points perhaps of Spanish pikes, might follow; for Lennox was openly boasting that 'he was sure of the greatest part in England, and the King of Spain would be his friend.'[230] Darnley, though still ill in bed, was as imprudent as his father, and threatened to break the Duke of Chatelherault's head as soon as he could get up. Murray was, or pretended to be, distrustful of Lethington, Catholics scowled at Protestants, ancient feuds between the families were revived, violence was rife everywhere, no man trusted his neighbours; and Mary's chief instruments were not now those who had steered her so far through innumerable shoals, but proud and foolish Lennox and his son, Athol and Ruthven, 'with David Rizzio the Italian and Mingo the valet de chambre.'

This was the period, probably, when one of her very few real friends, Sir James Melville, read her the little lecture on deportment which he repeats in his memoirs. When he had first returned to Scotland Mary had asked this experienced courtier to warn her if at any time he noticed her 'forget herself by unseemly gesture or behaviour,' or do anything that might make her unpopular. Melville demurred at having such a responsibility placed upon him, but the Queen insisted. Some time previously Rizzio had come to Scotland in the train of Moret, the Savoyard envoy (see p. 148). 'He was a merry fellow and a good musician. Her Majesty had three valets of her chamber who sang three parts, and wanted a bass to sing the fourth. Therefore they told her Majesty of this man, as one fit to make the fourth. Thus he was drawn in to sing sometimes with the rest; and afterwards when the French secretary retired himself to France (*i.e.* December 1564) this David obtained the office.' Melville goes on to say that Rizzio was imprudent in his conduct, often addressing the Queen publicly in the presence of her nobles. This attracted the jealousy of Murray and others of the greater courtiers, who jostled him aside and insulted him whenever possible, which behaviour the Italian revenged by favouring suits and petitions against his enemies, 'whereby in short time he became very rich.' Melville warned him of his imprudence, and recommended to him a more submissive demeanour, and to retire whenever noblemen approached the sovereign. Mary, however, would not allow him to do this; and Melville, reminding her of Chastelard, gravely lectured the Queen herself upon her too great friendliness with a lowborn foreign Catholic, suspected of being a pensioner of the Pope, and prayed her to be more circumspect; which advice she promised to follow. With the coming of Lennox and Darnley, and the rise of the Catholic interest in Scotland, Rizzio's position became more important, and with a keen eye to the main chance he warmly advocated Darnley's suit.[231]

Mary summoned Murray to her side in the first days of May, and when he arrived at Stirling he was, to his surprise, not to say suspicion, overwhelmed with caresses from the Queen and the Lennoxes. The next day he visited Mary, who was in Darnley's room, and she suddenly produced a paper which she begged Murray to sign. It was a pledge that he would aid to the full extent of his power her marriage with Henry Stuart. Murray, taken aback, asked for time to consider, and when Mary refused this, and again urged her request, her brother set forth with brutal frankness in the presence of both lovers his objections to the match. Lethington, he said, had not returned with the Queen of England's answer, which might be a favourable one for Mary. Besides, he asked, how could he (Murray) be expected to forward the Queen's marriage with one who was 'no favourer of Christ's true religion,' but an abettor of papists? Mary railed and stormed at him in vain. Murray was inflexible in his refusal to pledge himself, at least until Lethington's return. Great efforts were made to gain the consent of Chatelherault and the rest of the nobles, in order that Elizabeth's answer, when it came, should be confronted by an accomplished fact; and when Lethington reached Newark on his way home, he was met by Beaton with instructions from Mary for him to return to London again, in order that she might have time to work her will.[232] As we have seen, Lethington—whatever he might profess—was now in favour of the Darnley marriage under Spanish auspices, if nothing better could be devised; and the hopes he carried with him were too important for delay. So he disobeyed his Queen's urgent written command and pushed forward with all speed, overtaking Throckmorton before he crossed the Border. As they travelled north together news continued to reach them from Stirling and Edinburgh of Mary's growing infatuation for this 'disorderly marriage.' Lethington acted his part admirably in the presence of Throckmorton and other Englishmen, feigning violent anger at the prospect of a marriage that, as we have seen, he was secretly advocating. He went so far, indeed, as to deplore to Throckmorton that the latter had not been instructed by Elizabeth 'to threaten this Queen with denunciation of war in case she will proceed in marrying with the Queen's rebels, as the last refuge to stay her from this unadvised act.' The English quite believed in Lethington's sincerity, as they did in that of Murray, but it may be doubted whether this attitude, of the secretary at least, was not prompted by a desire to learn from Throckmorton how far Elizabeth was prepared to go in opposition to the match.

Before arriving in Edinburgh the travellers learned by a letter from the Queen herself that she had summoned a meeting of nobles at Stirling for the following day, 13th May, to create Darnley Lord Armanock, Earl of Ross, and to obtain from those assembled a pledge to support her in her resolve to wed her cousin. Murray and Argyle, almost alone, stood aloof, demanding that the abolition of the Mass in Scotland should be a condition of their consent, to which it is clear that Mary would never agree, since the only good she could hope to gain from the union was the support of Spain and the Catholics to her English claims. The rest of the Scottish nobles, even feeble Chatelherault, came to heel promptly at their Queen's call, for she was a wilful woman determined to have her way. 'Majesty and love can ill sit on the same seat,' quoted Throckmorton; but highly inflamed as Mary's affections might be for Darnley, she was at no loss to find plausible pretexts for the bold step she was taking. A weak foreign prince she would not have, because he would be useless for her ends; a strong one she could not get, for the reasons which have been stated. Three years of experience had proved to her that Elizabeth was playing with her; and she determined to defy England and the Protestants, and throw herself entirely into the arms of Spain and the Catholics, even to the enslavement of her own people. There was no native suitor but Darnley who could have united in her favour the countenance of the English disaffected Catholics and the goodwill of Spain, the two permanent elements of danger to Elizabeth. When love and apparent policy go together it is hard to withstand them, and Mary had her way.

Throckmorton was ill received at Stirling. He found the castle gate shut to him when he rode up, and he had to await Mary's good pleasure for an audience.[233] When he saw her he understood at once that further remonstrance was useless. She had, she said, taken Elizabeth at her word. She was not to marry an Austrian, Spanish, or French prince, but had been told by Randolph that she was free to choose any person within the isle, and she had done so, Darnley being a kinsman of both queens, and in all respects a fitting husband for her. There was, she said, no reason therefore for any complaint on the part of Elizabeth. 'I find her,' said Throckmorton, 'so captivated, either by love or cunning (or by boasting or folly), that she is not able to keep promise with herself, and therefore not most able to keep promise with your Majesty.' Throckmorton saw more clearly than Randolph had ever done where the danger to Elizabeth lay; and his memorandum to Cecil and Leicester as to the best means of counteracting it advises severity and vigilance amongst the Catholics of the north of England, the close confinement of Lady Lennox,[234] and the prevention of any communication between her and the French ambassador; 'but chiefly none with the Spanish, which imports most.'

In the meanwhile the 'young fool' Darnley, though still in bed ill, had lost his head at the greatness of his new prospects, and he, who had gained so much praise for his affability when he first came to Scotland, had already grown insufferable in his wilful arrogance. Randolph affected to pity and deplore Mary's changed character. She who had been, as he says, so wise and honourable, 'hath now so altered with affection for my Lord Darnley, that she hath brought her honour into question, her estate in hazard, and her country to be torn in pieces.' The poor man could not think 'what craftie subtyltie or dyvelyshe devise hath brought this to passe.' 'The Queen in her love is so transported, and he grown so proud, that to all honest men he is intolerable, and almost forgetful of his duty to her already, that has adventured so much for his sake. What shall become of her, or what life with him she shall lead, that already taketh so much upon him as to control and command her, I leave others to think. Darnley,' continues Randolph, 'had even attempted to kill one of his warmest adherents—Lord Justice-Clerk Bellenden—with a dagger, simply for having conveyed to him a message from the Queen which was not to his liking.'

The croaking of Randolph at this time must be accepted with some allowance for a diplomatist who had been completely outwitted, and had failed from the first in his diagnosis of events. He had suddenly seen Mary and most of her councillors change from humble submissive friends of Elizabeth to self-reliant foreigners with awkward hints, that sounded like threats, about Spain and the English Catholics always on their lips; and it was no wonder that he should endeavour to blame devilish devices and enchantment with the events that he had not possessed sufficient penetration to foretell.[235] Mary, he says, was 'seized with love in ferventer passions than is comely for any mean personage—all care of the commonwealth apart . . . I may say to the utter contempt of her best subjects. . . .' 'Shame is left aside, and all regard of that which chiefly pertains to princely honour removed out of sight. . . . David (Rizzio) is he that now works all: chief secretary to the Queen, and only governor of her goodman. . . . The hatred towards him (Darnley) and his house, marvellous great, his pride intolerable, his words not to he borne, but where no man dare speak again. He spares not also, in token of his manhood, to let some blows fly where he knows they will be taken. The passions and furies he will sometimes be in are strange to believe.'[236] Thus the disappointed diplomatist writes from day to day. The worst of the matter is, he says, that most people in Scotland, even the Protestants, think that Darnley was purposely sent by Elizabeth to marry the Queen and produce discord in the country; and evidently Randolph himself had his doubts on the subject. His remedy for the trouble, even thus early (3rd June 1565), was either to have the inconvenient suitor captured or murdered out of hand, or else to subsidise the Protestants and other enemies of the Lennoxes to raise revolt in Scotland. Of course, everybody was to blame but Randolph, who in his querulous complainings of his employers forgot that, again and again, he had assured them that Mary would never marry Darnley, come what might. Whilst Murray, Argyle, and the Hamiltons were plotting with Randolph for the capture of Lennox and his son, Mary was straining every nerve to propitiate her opponents. New titles and grants were showered upon waverers, the Protestants were solemnly assured that no attempt should be made to suppress their religious privileges, though they insolently asked the Queen for much more than that; and another convention of nobles was summoned early in June at Perth to confirm further the Queen's proposed marriage. But the mustering of clansmen on both sides, especially that of Murray and Argyle, was so threatening, and the rumours of plots so rife, that the assembly was promptly countermanded in fear. There seems to be no doubt that, with the consent of Elizabeth (who instructed Randolph to assure Murray and his friends of her support), evil was intended to the Lennoxes, if not to Mary personally; whilst Murray never wavered in his assertion that a plot had been divulged to him, which aimed at his murder at Perth by Darnley's friends. Mary even pretended to make another effort to mollify Elizabeth by a fresh embassy to London. The man she chose for her envoy was a Protestant of the Lethington school, John Hay of Balmerino; but we shall see that his apparently hopeless mission to Elizabeth was not the only object of his journey.

He arrived in London on the 23rd June, and was greeted with the news that on the same morning Lady Lennox had been sent to the Tower. When he saw the Queen at Whitehall the next day, Elizabeth flew into a rage as soon as he opened his mouth about the marriage. When he ventured to beg that he might be furnished in writing with the reasons why she objected to Mary's union with Darnley, or otherwise that she would appoint a commission to discuss the matter on the Border, the Queen peremptorily refused both requests. Nor would she allow Mary's letter to be delivered to Lady Lennox, unless it were first read. How could the Queen of Scots think such a thing possible? she asked. Lady Lennox had lied and betrayed her. Lennox himself and his son were traitors, and she would treat them as such. They should be sent back to England, or they should be demanded of Mary as English rebels.

No doubt all this had been expected by Hay and his mistress, and the real object of his journey came when he left Whitehall and went to the Spanish ambassador, for whom he had a letter from Mary. Had any reply from the

King been received, he asked Guzman, with regard to the matter that had been discussed with Lethington? By great good fortune, only an hour or two before, a letter from Philip, written on the 7th June, had reached the ambassador. For once there was no trimming or shilly-shally. The King of Spain saw that this was the best chance that had been offered to him of securing a Catholic Great Britain under his protection since the death of his wife Mary Tudor, and he came as near to jumping at it as was possible by his methods. 'The bridegroom and his parents being good Catholics and our affectionate servants, and the Queen (Mary) having so good a claim to the crown of England, to which Darnley also pretends, we have arrived at the conclusion that the marriage is one that is favourable to our interests, and should be forwarded and supported to the full extent of our power. We have thought well to assure the Queen of Scotland and Lord Darnley's party, which we believe is a large one in the country (*i.e.* England), that this is our will and determination; and that if they will govern themselves by our advice, and not be precipitate, but will patiently await a favourable juncture, when any attempt to frustrate their plans would be fruitless, I will then assist and aid them in the aim they have in view.'[237] The official message was to be sent to Mary through Archbishop Beaton in Paris; but Guzman was to assure Lady Lennox, and any of Mary's confidential agents who might ask, that Philip's aid and favour should positively be extended to them, if they would be controlled and guided by his advice. The Catholic party in England was to be animated and encouraged 'to carry the business into effect, with Philip's assurance of help at the critical moment; and every resource of diplomacy was to be employed to prevent Elizabeth from appointing as her successor any of the Protestant claimants.'

Hay, Protestant and English partisan though he ostensibly was, was overjoyed at the news. 'His Queen,' he truly said, 'desired nothing so much as that your Majesty should take her under your protection, and that she should follow your Majesty's orders in all things, without swerving a hair's-breadth from them. I urged him to prevail upon his Queen to manage her affairs prudently, and not to strike until a good opportunity presented itself.'[238] Hay asked whether Mary ought to marry at once or suspend the matter somewhat. She might wait, said Guzman, until she received the

King's official pledge through Beaton; but, above all, she should temporise and conciliate the English as much as possible. Hay only stayed one day longer in London after this, for the great wish of Mary's heart he knew was now to be granted; and though he pulled so long and grievous a face at the 'evil success of his long journey,' when he arrived in Scotland, as to arouse the pity even of Randolph, it must have been with a merry heart beating beneath his doublet that he bore his welcome message to Mary at Holyrood on the 7th July.

Mary was, as we have seen, in love with her young suitor, and had already decided to marry him, happen what might. Her caprice for him, and her determination to supplant Elizabeth on the throne of England, had together driven her thus basely to promise to submit herself and her realms, present and prospective, to the dictation of a foreign monarch, who was the traditional enemy of the France she pretended to love so well, and whose aim was to overthrow utterly, in both kingdoms over which she aspired to reign, the religion held by the majority of the people. But it must have been a sweet triumph for her that the support of Spain, for which she had been bidding since the death of Francis, was at last promised to her as a condition of her marriage with the man to whom she had taken so violent a fancy. For once, inclination and policy seemed to go together, for Mary was blinded by love and blunted by Lorraine's teaching. She could not see in its true aspect the treachery, the wickedness, of her aims. That the hideous methods of religious enslavement characteristic of Spanish Catholicism were to be employed in crushing her own subjects; that foreign pikemen were to deluge England and Scotland in blood rather than religious liberty should prevail; that French interests should suffer irretrievably, was all nothing to Mary if she could call herself Queen of Britain, and enjoy the man she thought she loved.

The danger to Elizabeth was great; but she dealt with it in her own clever, cold-hearted way. The King of France was suddenly, but politely, discarded as a suitor for her hand; for she knew now she had not to fear the marriage of Mary with a Frenchman. But the vain, boastful talk of Lennox, his wife's known intriguing with the English Catholics and Spain, and the visits of Lethington and Hay to Guzman, were sufficient proof of what was being plotted; and Elizabeth became in appearance feverishly anxious to marry the Archduke, and so to draw nearer to Spain. Imperial ambassadors flitted to and fro. Leicester's enemies prayed the Queen night and day to make up her mind and marry the Austrian, and so banish her danger. But, though in appearance she was all eagerness to do so, she exercised every fascination she possessed to draw from suave Guzman some sort of assurance that, if she did marry the Archduke, Philip would smile upon the union, and regard the bridegroom as his son rather than his cousin. But, as we know, Philip, distrusting his Austrian kinsmen, had put his money on Mary and Darnley, and all that Elizabeth could obtain from the Spaniard were bland generalities, which she was far too wary to act upon.

Mary, when the news had come to her at Perth that conspiracies were hatching and the nobles of both factions mustering their retainers, hurried back to Edinburgh, successfully avoiding a plan that had been laid by Murray's friends for her capture. For two months previously rumours had spread that she was actually married to Darnley, and the assertion has been seized upon by her apologists, as an explanation of her attendance upon him during his long confinement to bed by illness. There is, however, nothing in the form of proof that the wedding took place in April or May, except the assumed familiarity of the pair, and the confident hints of Lady Lennox and others that the union was now indissoluble. But the arrival of Hay of Balmerino, on the 7th July, with Philip's assurance must have satisfied Mary that she might now safely indulge her fancy without sacrificing her great ambition; and there is every probability that the alleged private wedding on the 9th July actually took place. Randolph wrote hurriedly to the Queen a week later that on that day 'this Queen was secretly married in her own palace to my Lord Darnley, not above 7 persons being present, and went to their bed to Lord Seton's house. This is known by (means of) one of the priests present at the Mass.'[239] In his letter to Cecil of the same day (16th July) Randolph wrote: 'That whole day (*i.e.* 9th July) was solemnised, as I do believe, to some divine God, for such quietness was in court that few could be seen, and as few suffered to enter. Her horses having been secretly prepared at 8 o'clock that night, she and the Lord Darnley . . . rode to Seton. Hereupon rose many foul tales, where liberty enough is given for men to speak what they will. Two nights she tarried there (at Seton) and the next day came to the castle of Edinburgh to dinner. It was said that she would remain there. That afternoon she and my Lord Darnley walked up and down the town, disguised, until supper-time, and returned to the castle again; but lay that night at Holyrood. This manner of passing to and fro gave again occasion to many men to muse what might be her meaning. The next day in like sort she cometh after dinner on foot from the Abbey (Holyrood), the Lord Darnley leading her by the one arm, and Fowler by the other.[240] In that troop being Lady Erskine, old Lady Seton, the Earl of Lennox, Signor David (Rizzio), and two or three others. These vagaries made men's tongues chatter fast.'[241] This being immediately after the receipt of King Philip's message, was practically the earliest date upon which Mary could have married Darnley with safety, or the hope of carrying through her ambitions, and there can be little doubt that then, if not previously, she began her marital relations with him. The papal dispensation had not arrived, and the ceremony could not be publicly performed; but when the Pope's permission came, not an unnecessary day was lost, the banns being published in the Canongate Kirk, St. Giles's, on the 22nd July,[242] Darnley having received his coveted dukedom of Albany the day before.

On the 28th July, at nine o'clock at night, to the surprise and indignation of many, three heralds stood at the Market Cross of Edinburgh, and with a flourish of trumpets announced that the Queen had resolved to wed, in face of the holy kirk, 'with the rycht nobill and illustris Prince Henry, Duke of Albany; in respect of quhilk marriage, and during the time thereof, we ordain and consent that he be named and stylit King of this our Kingdom.'[243] This last provision was illegal without the consent of the Scots Parliament, but Mary could refuse her bridegroom nothing, and there was nothing his pride did not covet. The next morning, Sunday, 29th July 1565, before six o'clock, Mary, clad in deep mourning robes, with her wide widow's hood, walked between Lennox and Athol into the chapel of Holyrood. There she was left alone, whilst Darnley, clad in splendid garb and glittering gems, was led in by his father. The banns were proclaimed for the third time; and then the fateful words were spoken that made the nineteen-year-old hobblede-hoy King-Consort of Scotland. Rich rings were exchanged and the troth plighted, and then, after prayers and blessings over the wedded pair, the young bridegroom kissed his wife upon the lips, and left her whilst Mass was being said. That finished, she joined him in her own chamber, blushing and smiling, at first unwilling to put off her garb of woe and don her bridal finery: 'more for manners' sake than for grief of heart,' says Randolph, with every probability of truth. 'Then she suffereth them that stood by, every man that could approve, to take out a pin; and so, being committed to her ladies, she changed her garments, but went not to bed, to signify unto the world that it was not lust that moved them to marry, but only the necessity of her country, not, if God wills, to leave it long destitute of an heir. Suspicious men, or such as are given of all things to make the worst, would that it should be believed that they knew each other before they came there. I would not your Lordship should so believe, the likelihoods are so great to the contrary, that if it were possible to see such an act done, I would not believe it. After the marriage followeth commonly cheer and dancing. To their dinner they were conveyed by the whole nobility. The trumpets sound, the largess cried and money thrown about the house in great abundance, to such as were happy to get any. They dine both at one table, at the upper hand, and there served her these earls: Athol was server, Morton carver, Crawford cupbearer. These serve him (Darnley) in like offices: Elgin, Cassilis, and Glencairn. After dinner they danced a while and retired till the hour of supper, and, as they dined, so they supped. Some dancing there was, and so they go to bed.'[244]

The great conspiracy against Elizabeth and Protestantism was at last complete. The political system of Catharine de Medici and the religious situation in France had deprived Scotland of the ally that had always been its safeguard against England, whilst the acceptance of the reformed doctrines by the Scots had created an affinity between them and the Protestant power of Elizabeth, such as had never before existed. In the new set of circumstances thus created there were two courses open to the sovereign of Scotland: either to accept Protestantism and become a vassal of England, or to make common cause with the great enemy of the Reformation, submit to be the humble servant of Spain, and restore the lost balance of Europe by making both England and Scotland Catholic under one crown. The effect would have been to reduce France to insignificance, to secure supremacy for the papal church throughout the world, and to place Europe under the heel of Philip.

It had been Mary Stuart's golden dream thus to vanquish her enemies ever since the death of Francis took from her the hope of using French national arms for the purpose of asserting her claim to England; and, so long as hope remained that the heir of Spain might be her husband, she would accept no other advances. When Darnley's suit, as first urged by his mother, seemed to be saddled by English conditions and safeguards, Mary would have none of it, for it would have been useless to her; but when she learned later from the Lennoxes that it was to be part of a widespread Catholic conspiracy in England to overthrow Elizabeth, she smiled eagerly upon it, and was able, as we have seen, by means of Lethington and Lady Lennox, to enlist Philip in the plot, and to secure his pledge of powerful aid when the moment came to strike the blow.

It is perhaps too much to say that Mary was dragged upon the dangerous slope solely by her fervent love for the youth she married; for she was desirous with a similar object of wedding the deformed lunatic Don Carlos whom she had never seen; but, putting aside her possible adoption—real or feigned—of the other alternative, political submission to England, the Catholic conspiracy, which was her principal aim, was not served in any important degree by her hurry to marry Darnley, whilst it consolidated and brought to a head all the Protestant distrust against her, both in Scotland and England. If she had not been precipitated blindly by her love she would have seen, as Elizabeth always did, the enormous advantage of keeping herself free, and shifting the balance as required by circumstances. Murray, Argyle, and the Protestants might have been made to counteract Athol, Glencairn, the Gordons, and the Catholics. The Hamiltons and the Lennoxes might, by hatred of each other, all have been made humble servants of the Queen; and, following the example of Elizabeth, Mary might have attracted or repelled one suitor after another, whilst the plan for the capture of England by the Catholics with the aid of Spain was fully matured, and all the parties pledged, the trump card in Mary's hand, her own marriage, being kept unplayed until everything was ready for decisive action. At another time Mary herself would have seen this; but her love, or caprice, hurried her into prematurely disposing of herself upon a verbal promise of Philip and hopes from the fussy plotting of Lady Lennox: conditional and problematical results to be balanced against the certain defection of Murray and the Scottish Protestants, the discontent of the Hamiltons and their friends, the enmity of Elizabeth, and the fact that, the question being disposed of, no more political capital could be made out of Mary Stuart's marriage.

VIII

REVOLT OF THE PROTESTANTS

*Murray's opposition to Darnley—Rising of the Protestant lords—
Elizabeth's intercession—Darnley and Knox—Murray enters
Edinburgh—His flight—Renewed appeal of Mary to Spain—
Darnley's ill behaviour—Murray visits London—Elizabeth's
attitude—Philip decides to protect Mary—Yaxley's unfortunate
mission—Mary places Darnley in the background—Quarrels in
consequence—Darnley's conspiracy—Murder of Rizzio—Mary
escapes to Dunbar—Flight of the murderers.*

SO LONG AS THERE HAD APPEARED TO BE A POSSIBILITY OF CARRY-
ing through the Darnley match in conjunction with an arrangement with
Elizabeth, Murray had not opposed it; but as he gradually understood
that Mary intended to make it part of a conspiracy against England and
Protestantism, his objection to it developed in strength. In the first stages of
Mary's intrigue with Spain through Lethington, it is probable that Murray
connived with the intention of using it as a means of bringing pressure to
bear upon Elizabeth to recognise the right of Mary to succeed to the English
crown, failing direct issue to herself. But when he found, as he must have
done before Lethington left Scotland for London in March 1565, that entire
submission to Spain and a Catholic revolution in England and Scotland
were intended, he must have taken fright; for he was too far pledged to the

Reformation to side with such a policy as that, which, moreover, it was obvious, must cause incalculable turmoil and bloodshed, even if it succeeded. His firm refusal in May to assent to the match, except on rigid religious conditions, and Mary's violent anger with him on that occasion, marked the parting of the ways. Whatever tortuous diplomatic course Lethington might take, Murray thenceforward broke with the policy which he saw was to overthrow Protestantism in Europe and make Mary merely a vassal sovereign of a Catholic Great Britain. Mary's apologists have ever been ready to heap abuse upon Murray for his desertion of his sister at this juncture, and for his subsequent action with regard to her. He was more cautious, but no better than other Scottish nobles of his time; most of them were willing to murder and forge and lie as often as their personal interests seemed to recommend such a course; but we need look no further for the mainspring of Murray's action in opposing his sister's marriage and her subsequent policy, than the fact that he was naturally unwilling to be a party to a course which would not only have been destructive to him personally if it were successful, but would have dragged his country through seas of blood, only to establish the supremacy of a foreign despot, whose methods filled all enlightened men with horror and alarm.

As early as the beginning of May, nearly three months before the marriage, the nobles began to range themselves on either side. Murray and Argyle, with the aid of Randolph's half-promises that Elizabeth would stand by the Protestant lords to the last, had drawn towards them most of the Hamilton partisans, Maxwell, Rothes, and the Puritans; whilst Athol, Ruthven, Hume, and the Lennox followers were arming to oppose them. Morton, the son of that shifty George Douglas, the erstwhile friend of England, was for sale, his price being the forfeited inheritance of his Angus kin; Glencairn was wavering between his allegiance to the Stuarts and his attachment to the 'religion'; and Lethington, thinking above all things of the aggrandisement of Scotland and his Queen, was plotting in the background the obscure intrigue which was to lay them both at the feet of Spanish Philip. Whether the Protestant lords actually intended to capture Darnley and send him into England or kill him on the 1st July, and perhaps also to sequester Mary, cannot be asserted positively, though the existence of such a plot was generally believed by Mary and her friends;[245] but certainly the alarm of the ministers and the Protestants in the country generally had by that time been so far aroused that they were ready for any desperate course which might avert what they instinctively felt, rather than knew, was the dire danger threatening them by the Darnley marriage. At the end of June a Protestant convention demanded of Mary the total abolition of the Mass and papistry in Scotland, and that all persons should be compelled to attend the kirk every Sunday. This, of course, Mary would not grant, though, short of doing so, she made every effort to assure her subjects that she would never force her own religion upon them. But the Protestants were not to be tranquillised by professions, for the spectre of Spain lurked behind Darnley, and Spain and toleration were known to be strangers. And so the armed forces of the nobles, according to their views and party, gathered, some around Mary in answer to her call, some to support Murray and his friends at Stirling, who were sending beseeching messages through Randolph to Elizabeth's ministers, praying them not to desert the Protestants in this their hour of need. Murray was summoned to court to give proof to Mary of the truth of his pretext for taking up arms, namely, that a plot had been formed by the Lennox Stuarts for his destruction. He promised that he would appear before Mary, and personally justify himself, on receipt of assurance for his safety. The safe-conduct was sent, signed by the Queen and her privy council, but Murray came not. Three days after the marriage a peremptory command for him to appear within six days on pain of outlawry was issued, but again he disobeyed, and was pronounced in open rebellion, flying with his followers to join his armed friends in the west.

Mary's conduct at this juncture was queenly indeed. However unwise had been the step she had taken in marrying so hastily, there was no drawing back now. She must fight for her sovereignty, perhaps for her faith, against Murray, and if necessary against the English as well. The stake was a great one, and she was determined to run the risk. So when, on the very day that she took up Murray's gage and proclaimed her brother a rebel, Leicester's friend Tamworth, the Groom of the Queen's Chamber, came from Elizabeth with all sorts of complaints and minatory warnings to Mary for having dared to marry Darnley, the Queen of Scots no longer spoke with bated breath and whispering humbleness. 'I find her,' says Tamworth, 'marvellous stout, and such a one as I could not have believed.' She would listen to no intercession for Murray or the rebels. The latter continued to implore Elizabeth's aid, and the fulfilment of her promise given through Randolph; but the Queen of England dared not go to war with Scotland in support of open rebellion, and affairs on the Continent still made it necessary for her to avoid driving the Catholics into the field against her; so the Protestant lords besought and protested in vain, whilst Mary grew in strength and confidence. 'The lords are in great perplexity, so mortally hated by the Queen and that faction that it is not possible to reconcile them. Some greater matter there is in it than is fit to be written. The more I travail in the Queen's behalf for them, the worse I speed. She hath utterly refused that her Majesty (Elizabeth) shall meddle . . . between her subjects and her . . . and hateth the Queen's Majesty, as she doth them. Therefore, to be short, if ye intend to save or do any good to these noblemen, look about you.'[246]

Mary was bold, nay, imprudent enough in her answer by Tamworth to throw Spain into Elizabeth's teeth. She had seen no reason, she said, to defer her wedding; and 'had perfect knowledge of the allowance of the principal and greatest princes of Christendom of her marriage.' This fact it was that gave Elizabeth pause; for she was straining every nerve to propitiate Spain at the time, to counteract the dangerous new Catholic league between Catharine and Philip. Mary was as well aware as was her opponent, that, for the time at least, the former had triumphed,[247] and this knowledge prompted her to make a last attempt to drive Elizabeth to acknowledge her right to the English succession. Mary and Darnley professed themselves willing to make no claim during Elizabeth's life, and to enter into no foreign league against her, and would, in the case of their succeeding to the English crown, make no innovation in religion, on condition that an Act of the English parliament established them as next heirs after Elizabeth's issue.[248] Mary's main object was always the same, the English succession. If political expediency drove Elizabeth into acknowledging her claim peacefully, well and good. The Protestants in England and Scotland would remain unmolested, and the Catholic powers might make the best of it; but if the English queen faltered or remained obstinate, then it must be war to the knife between them;

and the ultra-Catholic party in England and on the Continent must be the weapon by which the road of Mary to the thrones of Britain must be carved.

Mary's high spirit, and her appeal to the loyalty of her lieges, drew to her side an army of seven thousand men, and through the month of August the preparations went on to enable the Queen and her husband to pursue and destroy Murray and the lords who had dared to disobey their sovereign. Even the Protestants of Edinburgh, stirred by their old fealty to the crown, were ready to side with the plucky young woman, who in this hour of danger showed herself a worthy daughter of her race; and she for her part did her best to dissipate their fears.[249]

On the 19th August Darnley was with this object sent to St. Giles's Church to hear Knox preach. As usual, the divine was aggressive and inopportune. Whilst the young consort shifted uneasily on the special throne prepared for him, Knox preached interminably at him and his wife. 'I will give children to be their princes, and babes shall rule over them,' he quoted. God had punished Ahab because he did not correct his idolatrous wife Jezebel, but in these degenerate times Ahab joined with Jezebel in her idolatry. Darnley in a rage flung out of the church, too much upset even to dine, and went out hawking instead. Mary was more confident now, for Scotland in the main was with her, and she determined to read Knox himself a much-needed lesson. He was brought before her at Holyrood the same evening, and was told that as he had insulted the King he must refrain from preaching whilst the sovereigns remained in the capital. He had only spoken the word of God, he replied, and would speak or keep silent as the Kirk might command him. 'As the King had gone to Mass and dishonoured the Lord God to please the Queen; so should He in His justice make her the instrument of his (Darnley's) overthrow.' Mary burst into tears at the cruel prophecy, for apparently she was still in love with her husband of a month; but her inhibition against Knox's preaching was practically inoperative, for on the following Sunday, 26th August, Mary sallied from Edinburgh with her army, horse, foot, and artillery, to attack the rebels, some of whom were in Argyle and some under Murray at Ayr. 'I never hearde more outragieus wordes than she spake agaynst my Lord Murray,' wrote Randolph on the same day, 'and sayde she wyll rather lose her crown than not be revenged upon hym.'[250] She knew, indeed, that she was playing for her crown, and that boldness alone could win. Whilst Mary and her forces travelled by Stirling towards the west, Murray and his party, much inferior in strength to those of the Queen, and with no arquebusiers or artillery, by a skilful flank move approached Edinburgh, Murray depending for a favourable reception upon the influence of Knox and the ministers over the Protestant majority of townsmen. With hypocritical professions of loyalty, and of a determination not to attack the Queen in the field, Murray and Chatelherault with 1,200 horsemen rode into the royal burgh before dawn on the 31st August. But they found the Protestants lukewarm towards them, alarmed at the idea of treason or open rebellion. The castle on its beetling cliff, with grinning cannon dominating the city, held firmly for the Queen, and Murray's cause began to look desperate. Beseeching messages went speeding to the Earl of Bedford at Berwick for him to send English reinforcements, and Randolph almost indignantly added his prayers to the same effect. But Elizabeth dared not countenance open revolt against a Scottish sovereign, with the two great Catholic powers friendly with each other, and plotting, as she knew, the destruction of Protestantism throughout the world; and Murray prayed for English help in vain.

Whilst Mary was hurrying back from the west country distraction fell upon the counsels of the rebels. First they would await and fight her outside the city, away from the guns of the castle, then they would take boat at Leith, then they would march by Hamilton to Dumfries. And as Mary's host tramped through the tempestuous weather to give them battle, the rebels first sent to her whining messages protesting their loyalty, and their sole desire 'to maintain the true religion';[251] and then, panicstricken at her approach, they fled towards Dumfries, only just escaping capture by the Queen's force. Thus they hurried from place to place, whilst the great cannon from the castle ramparts banged and battered all the stiffness out of their friends in Edinburgh; and even bullying John Knox, a self-conscious Simeon, anxious to depart in peace when the guns began to speak, whimpered: 'Lord, into thy hands I commend my spirit, for the terrible roaring guns and the noise of armour do so pierce my heart, that my soul thirsteth to depart.' No doubt it did, and his body too. Mary was the 'best man' in Scotland at this juncture.

Keeping the saddle through the foulest weather, and on execrable paths, for twenty miles a day, leaving all her ladies far behind her, save one of exceptional strength. It was said, indeed, that the Queen herself was armed with a pistolet, and Darnley by her side was, his fine gilt corselet notwithstanding, a poor fribble in comparison with his royal wife.

Whilst Murray and his friends were unavailingly begging for English help, Mary lost no time in claiming the Catholic support, which had been promised on her marriage with Darnley. Her first appeal was to the Pope. If he would furnish her with a contingent of 12,000 men, paid for six months, she would undertake to 'settle' the question of religion for good. This was a large order all at once for Paul IV, and the Scottish envoy was put off with suave generalities until the views of Philip could be obtained.[252] But the Queen of Scots knew that this, or never, was her opportunity, for the rebels were alternately whining to her and running away from her, and Elizabeth's hands were tied by the Catholic league then being so ostentatiously settled between Catharine and her Spanish daughter at Bayonne.[253] All the Catholic north of England were straining in the leash for the revolt of which they had been dreaming so long. If Philip had been prompt at this juncture Britain might have taken the Catholic road—for good or for evil—and the history of civilisation would have been changed. A Catholic courtier, named Francis Yaxley, a dependant of Darnley's parents and an agent of Spain, had left London for Scotland by way of Flanders in July, for the purpose of serving Mary's consort as secretary, and as a means of communication with the Catholics. Less than a fortnight after his arrival he was sent on a mission from Mary to Philip. The letter he carried, dated the 10th September 1565,[254] sets forth the danger that threatens the Catholic faith, and prays for Philip's effective help: '*qu'il nous importe, autant pour la couronne et la liberté de l'Eglise pour jamais; pour la quelle maintenir nous n'espargnerons ni vie, ni état, etant supporté et conseillé de vous.*' At the same time John Beaton was sent to Cardinal Lorraine and to the Scottish ambassador in Paris with instructions that the Spanish ambassador there should be kept well posted on Scottish affairs. After an unsuccessful attempt to reach the Continent by sea, Beaton was obliged to pass through England; and whilst he was in London met Castelnau de la Mauvissière, who was on his way to Scotland with a mission from Catharine. It was as important for the latter as it was for Elizabeth that Mary should not place herself under the protection of Spain, and Catharine's object was to bring about a pacific arrangement to render this unnecessary. Naturally Castelnau and Paul de Foix found Elizabeth ready enough to help their object if she could do so without a sacrifice of dignity. She could not well despatch another envoy to Scotland, she said, for Mary had sent her back a rude answer by Tamworth; but still, if the Scottish queen desired it, she would appoint an English gentleman to accompany Castelnau in his peaceful mission. Mary was in the stirrups now, and haughtily replied to the hint that she did not need any one to intervene between her and her rebel subjects, and Castelnau went north alone.

Elizabeth, indeed, was in a puzzling quandary. If she went to war with Scotland by helping Murray in his rebellion, Spaniards or French, or both, might set foot in Great Britain, and then the foundations of her throne might crumble. Mary was defying her, and making her own case good before the world, and Elizabeth strove desperately to convince the Spaniards that *she* was the aggrieved party. In an interview with Guzman in the middle of September she started the subject by pretending that she believed he was negotiating to send Spanish arms to Scotland. The good man protested, quite sincerely, that this was not the case, and Elizabeth broke out in bitter complaints of Mary and the Lennoxes. It was all a pretence of Mary's, she said, that the trouble had arisen from religious differences. She had invented this fiction, in order to be able to claim foreign intervention. 'Well,' replied Guzman significantly, 'in any case it was a very bad precedent to aid rebels against their lawful sovereign.' 'God forbid that I should do that,' retorted Elizabeth, who had just sent a fresh remittance in gold to Murray; 'but Murray and his friends should not be crushed unheard.' 'It was all Darnley's fault,' she continued. 'Mary had no quarrel with her brother, but she was persuaded to refuse him a hearing because her husband was jealous.' 'He was only a lad, and did not know how political affairs should be conducted.'[255] Thus Elizabeth was obliged to assume the, for her, unwonted apologetic attitude; whilst Mary, with activity and confidence, hunted the rebels from pillar to post, and met English threats with warnings of Spanish aid that paralysed her opponents.

Castelnau arrived in Scotland late in September, and found the Queen in no melting mood. She would have no interference, she told him, from any foreign prince between her rebel subjects and herself: as she had ample means to punish them and bring them to reason.[256] 'She will agree to no accord with them,' wrote Castelnau to de Foix; 'her courage and stoutness being such, that she would rather lose her crown and sceptre than make terms with them.' On the contrary, she claimed with ready tears of self-pity, and almost vehemently, the aid of France, if the Queen of England attacked her or aided Murray; and Castelnau, astonished at her firmness, could only beg his King to prepare for eventualities, since Mary threatened, if French aid were not promptly sent, she would throw herself into the arms of Spain.[257] As we have seen, she had done this already; but it was, she knew, the rod which would awe both England and France into letting her have her own way; and the mere hint of it made Elizabeth almost lachrymose in her protestations to the Catholic powers that she would not help the Scottish rebels.

The hopes of Murray and his friends in Dumfries waned, as they saw that Elizabeth's hands were tied, and that no effectual aid reached them. A last desperate attempt he made to find favour with his sister at the expense of Darnley, whom he refused to recognise as King. Mary's reply to his letter was that he was a bastard, a rebel, and a traitor, and should be promptly punished as such. On the 8th October the dauntless Queen sallied from Edinburgh at the head of her troops, and attended but by one woman. She was armed, and wore steel, it was said, and with her rode her stripling husband in his fine gilt corselet; but close behind followed a stronger than he—the square martial figure of James Hepburn, Earl of Bothwell, newly called back from exile.[258] Rough and hirsute, shaggy and stern, the strong man took the place of leader at once. He had insulted the Queen verbally in the hearing of others many a time; and Randolph and his friends had rolled the choice epithets over their tongues, as they pawkily repeated them to Mary herself. But she wanted a strong man now, for Athol alone of her great nobles stood by her, and she knew already that her husband was a painted lath instead of a trusty blade, and she forgave Bothwell's slurs, because for her great aims she needed such as he. So we are told thus early that 'Bothwell takes great things upon him, and promises much: a fit captain for so loose

a company as now hang upon him.'[259] Young Darnley, in the short period of his married life, had sufficiently shown his quality. Quarrelsome, petulant, and vicious, he had begun to wrangle with his wife before the honeymoon had gone. The first question was that of the crown matrimonial, which he demanded for himself. Then disputes arose with regard to the appointment of a lieutenant-general of the realm, Darnley violently demanding the appointment for his rapacious father, and Mary insisting upon the superior capabilities of Bothwell, in which she was right.[260]

The opinions of Randolph and the rebels upon the persons that now surrounded the Queen can only be accepted with much reserve, but they would naturally possess, at least, a germ of truth. They speak of 'jars' between Mary and her husband frequently now. *She* was bad enough, said Randolph, but it was the duty of her subjects to put up with her; 'but to live under him that in all these things that in her are grievous, but in him outrageous, they think it intolerable.' 'This man, whom she hath chosen for her husband and made a king, showeth himself altogether unworthy of that to which she hath called him.'[261] 'I may well say that a wilfuller woman, and one more wedded to her own opinion, without order, reason, or discretion, I never met or heard of. Her husband, in all these conditions, and many worse, far passeth herself.' All this, be it recollected, is the testimony of men whose every hope and prospect Mary's new policy and firmness were ruining; but there was enough of truth in it to show that Mary had already found her husband unworthy of her.

Lethington, always a timid man, was frightened at the effects of the intrigue of which he had been a chief contriver, and avoided the council as much as possible, waiting upon events. Rizzio, Fowler, an Englishman, and Francesco, another Italian, 'crafty, wily strangers,' we are told, were now the Queen's principal advisers. Than David (Rizzio) especially, 'no man so great with her, the whole governor of this estate.'[262] At this time it was that Mary's enemies first began to drop black hints about some disgraceful connection between the Queen and David Rizzio. The Italian secretary was no beauty, and was of mature age; and although from the first, as we have seen, he had been detested by the jealous Scots for his presumption and his foreign blood, and Mary had been imprudently familiar with him, he had never been suspected of being the Queen's lover. So far as can be traced, the slander was first started by Murray at Dumfries. It was the safest possible stick with which to beat Mary, for the Italian had no friends; and the tippling young booby of a consort, who was Murray's principal obstacle, could as easily be separated from his wife on Rizzio's account as on that of a man who could retaliate. Both Bedford at Berwick and Randolph at Edinburgh began almost simultaneously to write to London hints that they 'could, an' if they would,' tell some disgraceful story about Mary, 'but for the honour due to the person of a Queen.' 'The hatred conceived against Murray was because he would not allow or authorise Davy in his abuses.' 'It was neither for his religion, nor for that that she now speaketh, that he would take the crown from her, as she said lately was his intent; but that she knoweth that he understandeth some such secret part, not to be named for reverence-sake, that standeth not with her honour, which he so much detesteth, being her brother, that neither can he show himself as he hath done, nor she think of him but as one she mortally hateth. Here is the mischief, this is the grief.'[263]

Murray and the Protestant lords did not wait for Mary's attack, but fled over the Border to Carlisle before she left Edinburgh, whilst the Queen's troops laid waste the country towards Dumfries, which Bothwell held in awe when Mary hurried back to Holyrood. So far the Queen had triumphed all along the line. She was for the first time Queen of Scotland indeed, freed from tutelage and humiliation; her power was proved to be strong enough to deal with her own subjects without dictation, and above all she had successfully bidden defiance to the insolent attempts of Elizabeth to treat her as a vassal. But no one knew so well as Mary that this was only the first skirmish of a great campaign, the necessary preliminary to the struggle that she hoped might make her Queen of Britain. The Archbishop of Glasgow had come to a perfect understanding at Bayonne with Alba, who represented Philip;[264] and though, contrary to the assertion of many of her historians,[265] Mary was not a signatory of the great Catholic league then negotiated, there is no doubt that the other parties to it were cleverly led to believe that Scotland would join it, the real intention of Philip and Queen Mary being to come to a separate arrangement behind the back of Catharine, to the benefit of Spain and the detriment of France. The great fight was to come when the crown of England was to be wrested from Elizabeth and placed by the hands of Spain and the English Catholics on the brow of the Queen of Scots.

In the meanwhile Elizabeth's tortuous gyrations to extricate herself from her danger, though extremely ingenious, were certainly not dignified. Murray wrote to Cecil and to Leicester from Carlisle, on the 14th October, eight days after his arrival, reminding them that the Scottish lords had only risen against their Queen, 'but being moved thereto by the Queen your sovereign and her council's hand, writ direct to us thereupon';[266] and on the 16th October the fugitives travelled to Newcastle on their intended way to London to pray for Elizabeth's intervention on their behalf. This did not at all suit the English queen. To be seen welcoming at her court the rebels against a neighbouring sovereign would have confirmed the suspicions, almost certainty, of the Catholic allies that she had been the moving spirit in the rebellion, and she sent swift couriers up the north road to stay the Scotsmen coming south. Murray, perhaps suspecting some such step, had hastened away before the others, and met the Queen's messenger at Royston with 'her Majesty's plain resolution, that it was not meet for him to come at this time, but to forbear such open dealing with her Majesty till further consideration be had.' So the rebel earl stayed at Ware that night (21st October), though on private hints from the Council he entered London at dusk on the following day. Elizabeth pretended to be deeply offended and shocked at a 'rebel' daring thus to approach her; 'but it is all make believe,' wrote Guzman to Philip, 'for he arrives at night, and is received next morning.' It is indeed asserted, with full probability, that Elizabeth, Murray, and Cecil were closeted together that same night to arrange the comedy for the morrow.[267]

Castelnau was in London on his way back from Scotland, and he and Paul de Foix, the regular ambassador, were informed by Elizabeth, in horrified tones, that Murray had arrived. The Queen was, so she said, much shocked at the rebel's boldness, but would not receive him except in the presence of the two Frenchmen, who might hear how he justified himself. De Foix demurred, saying that if anything fell from Murray derogatory to the Queen of Scots, he must retort. If Murray dared to say anything of the sort, said Elizabeth, she herself would cast him into prison. The same afternoon

(23rd October) Murray, modestly dressed in black, and with grievous countenance, entered the presence at Whitehall, the Frenchmen standing by. Bending his knee before the Queen, James Stuart began to address her in Scots. Elizabeth stopped him at once, and told him to speak in French. 'I have grown so unused to it, your Majesty, that I cannot express myself in the tongue.' 'Well,' retorted the Queen, 'you can understand it, at all events; so I shall employ it to speak to you.' And in her own majestic way she did speak to him, as if all she said was true. She was astounded that he, being in rebellion against his sovereign, her good sister, should presume to present himself before her. Here were Monsieur Castelnau and the French ambassador, who had tried to bring Scottish matters to a peaceful issue; let them hear what he had to say for himself. She desired to do nothing that could give the Queen of Scotland any just cause for going to war with her. . . . Many people were saying that her country was a common refuge for all the seditious subjects of neighbouring princes; and she had even heard rumours spread that *she* had caused or favoured the rebellion in Scotland, which she would not have done for the world. She well knew that God, being a just judge, would punish her with a similar plague of sedition if she gave any help to the rebel subjects of other monarchs.' Murray set forth his side of the question as he knew it: the Queen's unwise and hasty marriage with Darnley, the rumoured intention to destroy 'the religion,' the design against his own life, and the rest of it; after which relation Elizabeth scolded Murray soundly in French for the benefit of the ambassadors, and then told him that she would take counsel as to what she should do; but she warned him that he was in a very grave position, and by the laws of England might be cast into prison. Murray probably remained silent from policy, though he held, as Elizabeth well knew, her written pledge to help him in his rising, and had received large sums of her money for its promotion. She prayed the Frenchmen to write an account of the interview to their sovereign,[268] and then sending for Guzman, who was just starting for Flanders, she assured him of her detestation of all rebellion, and her anger with Murray.[269] Considering that she had actively helped the French Huguenots, and soon afterwards supported the Flemish revolt against Philip, the true value of her virtuous protestations may be gauged. With such cold comfort publicly, but doubtless not without a close understanding between him and Cecil for future action, Murray was fain to return to Newcastle.[270]

In the meanwhile the great conspiracy against which all this double dealing was directed was developing apace. It will be recollected that Yaxley, with his secret mission to Philip, left Scotland in September, but before his arrival (22nd October 1565) the Spanish king had elaborated his answer to Mary's petitions for aid that had reached him through Guzman. As usual, his statement of motives and intentions is a tremendous rigmarole, fenced and qualified with precautions on every side, in order that he may in the end work his will, without himself being compromised. The Queen of Scots is so good a Catholic that he has decided to help her in her object of preserving her realm in the Catholic faith. He is delighted at her marriage with Darnley, and congratulates her much upon it. But the Spanish help must be given secretly, and in the form of money, so that other princes may not be made jealous. If the Queen of England supports the Protestants by force of arms, effective aid in men or money shall be given to Mary by Spain and the Pope, but entirely in the name of the latter. But, above all, said Philip, Mary must be cautious, 'endeavouring always to retain the support of her party in England, and I will do my best to assist her there with such adherents as I may have; but she must try at the same time not to irritate the Queen of England or press her to an extent that may make her strike.'[271] Do not let her (Mary) force the Queen of England to declare a successor, but keep the discussion open 'until more ground has been gained, and I have placed myself in a position to help her more easily than I can at present. Let her consult me before she takes any decisive step'; and, as an earnest of his future help, Philip tells his ambassador that he is sending him a bill of exchange for 20,000 crowns, to be used in helping Mary against the rebels, according to his discretion. Secrecy, and the establishment of ample means for conveying intelligence, are imperative, and Mary must avoid, above all things, letting Elizabeth imagine that there is any idea of claiming the English crown during her life; and thus, with a last warning against French intrigue in Scotland,[272] Philip's letter comes to an end. It suffices to lay before us the whole conspiracy which Mary herself, with admirable diplomacy, had arranged, in spite of Cardinal Lorraine, France, and England, as well as in defiance of Murray and the Protestants: a marvellous instance of persistent, patient statecraft for a young woman, unaided, except by the skill of Lethington and Rizzio. With good fortune, and a continuance of the cool craft which had carried it so far, it bade fair to place the crown of England on Mary's head before many years had passed, and to crush or cripple the Reformation. But a woman's passion, and, it must be confessed, utter bad luck, ruined it all.

Before Philip's letter quoted above was despatched Francis Yaxley rode over the bare Castilian plain into Segovia. He was at once admitted to an audience of the King, and told his story of Mary's hopes and fears, her faithfulness, and her sole reliance upon Spanish guidance in all things. If Philip would help her with men and money, 'not only would it enable the rebels to be destroyed, but would confirm the King and Queen in their hope of succeeding to the English throne.' Philip repeated to Yaxley his promise of effective aid, and, instead of sending the 20,000 crowns through Guzman in London, ordered the amount to be paid in gold to Yaxley in Antwerp; and then, late in October, with a light heart the young envoy hastened northward with his important message. Guzman, the ambassador, was in Flanders when Yaxley arrived there on the 9th November, and they secretly met at the dead of night in Brussels, to arrange for the future cipher communications between Scotland and the Spanish agents. Receiving the 20,000 crowns in gold at Antwerp as arranged, Yaxley sailed at once for Scotland, dodged by English pirates on the watch to capture him. Alas! in the midst of Mary's anxiety there came, as an additional blow to her, the news that his dead body had been washed up by the sea on the Northumbrian coast; and the gold that was to have enabled Mary to buy and bribe on her way to the English throne, became the bone of contention, to be wrangled over for many a month, amidst the jeers of English courtiers, by the Earl of Northumberland as lord of the foreshore, and by the crown as the claimant of treasure-trove.[273]

We must now turn back somewhat and trace the events in Scotland that dissipated Mary's golden dream even more ruthlessly than the loss of Philip's treasure. The news of Murray's treatment at the English court was loudly proclaimed by Mary's friends in Scotland as an evidence of Elizabeth's fear and impotence, and dismay fell upon the Protestant faction: Lethington made up his mind to seek favour again, the false scoundrel Morton shifted his balance towards the Queen's side, Chatelherault at Newcastle sent his humble submission, and prayed for pardon, and all the rebels but Murray and Kirkcaldy were encouraged to hope that their mistress would not prove implacable if they humbled themselves in time. Mary was diplomatic in her triumph. She smiled on Randolph again, and readily agreed to receive envoys from Elizabeth, and to settle all difficulties and disputes with her good sister, whose displeasure grieved her so much. Kirkcaldy warned the English that Mary was playing false. 'Send as many ambassadors to our Queen as ye please, they shall receive a proud answer: for she thinks to have a force ready as soon as ye do, besides her hope of friendship (of the Catholics) in England, of which she brags not a little; so driving time is to her advantage.' As we can see now, Kirkcaldy was right in his view. Counting upon Spain and the English Catholic party—towards which she learned that the Duke of Norfolk was now drifting—Mary was in high hopes; but, following the urgent advice of Philip, she was ready to go, in appearance, almost any lengths, to conciliate Elizabeth until the propitious moment for action came.

Obviously there was no way in which the English queen could be more effectively flattered and disarmed than by throwing Darnley into the background. His constant absence and devotion to trifling pleasures, hawking, roystering, love-making, and what not, and his petulant distaste for the hard work of kingship, seemed almost to invite the process of minimising him. When, therefore, Randolph saw Mary early in November, to ask for a passport for Elizabeth's proposed new embassy,[274] the Queen of Scots surpassed herself in amiability. 'She found nothing strange (in Elizabeth's message), except naming her husband Lord Darnley, whom, above all other things, she desires to call King.' But, after much pressure from Randolph, who said he could only regard the consort as a disobedient English subject, the passport was issued *signed by Mary alone*. From the first Darnley had been jealous and discontented that the promise given to him of the joint crown with his wife had not been fulfilled. Francis II had been of no better blood than himself, he said, and yet he had enjoyed the crown matrimonial, making him king of Scotland for life, even if his wife died. Why could not Darnley have as much? The 'young fool,' immersed in his frivolous pleasures, could not, or would not, see the immense importance diplomatically of lulling Elizabeth's distrust, until the great plan for her ruin should have matured; and, in a pet at what he thought an insult to himself, sulked away from court for weeks together.

Mary was understood to be pregnant early in November, and in addition to this she fell ill of her old malady in the side, which confined her to her bed for some time. Darnley carelessly pursued his pastimes in Fifeshire, whilst Mary was in ill-health, and surrounded by the difficulties inherent to the tortuous diplomatic course to which she was committed. Traitors surrounded her, men such as Morton, ready to betray her again, but whom she could not afford to alienate unnecessarily. There were few Scotsmen whom she could trust to be proof against English bribes or their personal prejudices; she got no help from her husband; and to the man who had been her instrument in successfully concluding the plans with Philip and the Pope, the Italian secretary Rizzio, almost alone could she turn for counsel; for he, at all events, was unable to change sides and sell her. Darnley's frequent absence had needed the making of a stamp, by which his signature might be affixed to formal documents, and, naturally, this stamp, in the keeping of Rizzio, was impressed upon many documents of which the young consort knew nothing.[275] The pardon of Chatelherault and the Hamiltons, with only five years' exile, was granted and stamped in his absence, to his violent anger; for they were his rival claimants to the Scottish throne, and the enemies of his house. Mary was growing tired, too, of the constant complaints she received of Lennox's extortions in Glasgow, and 'wished he had never come to Scotland.' Either in pursuance of the policy of pleasing Elizabeth by putting Darnley in the background, or else because of his neglect of business, the consort's name was sometimes dispensed with or placed after, instead of before, that of the Queen in official papers; 'the Queen's husband' he was usually called now, and not King; and the coins which bore their joint effigy were ordered to be recalled.

When, therefore, at the beginning of December, Mary was well enough to travel in a horse-litter to Linlithgow to meet her husband, matters were ripe for further dissension between them. Nor was it long coming. For the

first time since he came to Scotland Darnley devoutly attended Matins and Mass at Holyrood on Christmas Eve;[276] and whilst Mary sat up all night playing at cards with her friends, Rizzio amongst them,[277] only retiring when it was near morning, her husband rose before day and listened on his knees to three Masses in the chapel of Holyrood. Randolph on the same day represents the court as all in discord, and Mary and her husband with 'private disorders amongst themselves, but which may be lovers' quarrels.'

Desperate efforts were being made by Murray himself, and the English government for him, to obtain forgiveness for his rebellion; and at first it was understood that Darnley was the principal obstacle to its being granted. But when Philip's reply reached Mary, and news of the completion of the Catholic league in Europe (February 1566), she, too, hardened her heart, and summoned parliament to forfeit the lands of the fugitives. It was clear to Elizabeth, and also to the Scottish Protestants, that the latter had nothing to hope for from Mary's clemency. The Catholic plot in England was maturing,[278] and the league in Europe seemed to shake the very basis of Elizabeth's power. All the world saw that the English queen dared not move for her life; and Mary's attitude towards her became suddenly more independent than ever. Even Randolph's misdeeds were at last dealt with, and he was expelled from Scotland for furnishing money to the rebels.[279]

But, beaten at every other point, Murray and his friends bethought them of a plan, by which Darnley's boyish ambition and foolishness might be turned to their advantage. The ground was well prepared. Morton, who was still at court, though profoundly distrusted by Mary, was busily whispering doubts into Darnley's ear, and he, poor muddled wretch, weakly irritated at the disregard into which he had deservedly fallen, eagerly walked into the trap baited for him. Drury, writing to Cecil on the 16th February, says that Darnley was then drinking too much, and had quarrelled with the Queen at a merchant's house in Edinburgh, where they dined: 'she only dissuading him from drinking and enticing others, in both of which he proceeded, and gave her such words that she left the place in tears, which they that know say is not strange to be seen. These jars arise, among other things, from his seeking the crown matrimonial, which she will not yield to. Darnley is in great dislike with the Queen, and she is very weary of him, and, as some judge, will be more so ere long. As true it is that those who depend wholly upon him are not liked of her, nor they that follow her of him, as David Rizzio and others.'

Nine days after this was written Randolph[280] conveyed the intelligence to Cecil that a political plot was brewing. Lennox, as weakly ambitious as his son, was to see Argyle, who had 'wobbled' backwards and forwards, willing to submit if the others would, but was still unreconciled in his own country; and Lennox was to propose, that if Murray and the Protestants would guarantee the crown matrimonial to Darnley, he would restore them to their estates, and firmly establish Protestantism in Scotland. To this it was said Darnley had already set his hand. Nothing surely could be more foolish than this. With infinite skill and pains, as we have seen, Mary had been able to negotiate a close alliance with the strongest power on the Continent, and had entered into negotiations with the English Catholics, with the joint object of ultimately raising herself and her husband to the throne of Britain, the essence of the whole business being the adhesion of Mary and her consort to Catholicism. Elizabeth, for almost the first time in her reign, was at her wit's end, and could do nothing effectual to countercheck the powerful combination against her; and yet this young simpleton, at the instance of his and his wife's enemies, was willing to sacrifice everything and change sides to feed his silly self-esteem, or perhaps to avenge his drinkmused jealousy.

'The suspicion of this King towards David is so great that it must shortly grow to a scab amongst them,' wrote Randolph in the same letter as that quoted above, and already we begin to see the poisonous effect of the hints started by Murray and Randolph in September that the relations between the Queen and her Italian secretary involved a disgraceful secret. The only way by which Murray and Elizabeth could hope to avoid the disaster to them, threatened by the Spanish and papal protection of Mary, was to begin by removing from her side her principal foreign minister. Murder was an ordinary incident of party politics at the period, and the simple removal of Rizzio by the hired dagger of an assassin would have been easy. But to render it effectual for the purpose of its plotters it was necessary that it should be accompanied by a separation of interests between the Queen and her husband. The plan of making Darnley's jealousy the pretext for Rizzio's murder was devilish in its ingenuity. It ensured the separation of Darnley from the great combination in which all his future and that of his wife was bound up, it alienated Mary from him, and effectually prevented Spain or the Pope from intervening in Scotland by force of arms whilst he or his new friends had any voice in the government of the country. This meant a free hand for Elizabeth and the ruin of Mary. It was the consciousness that she had Spain and Rome behind her that had enabled her for a time to snap her fingers at her enemies. Stripped of that resource, with her husband and the Lennox faction on the other side, and the English Catholics disgusted at Darnley's apostasy, she had no force to withstand her opponents. The Hamiltons, who might have counterbalanced the Lennoxes, were in exile. The newly restored Earl of Huntly and his just married brother-in-law Bothwell were, it is true, on her side, but both of them had obstinately refused to go to Mass, though she had entreated them to do so; and Philip would not spend a ducat or risk a pikeman to uphold a sovereign whose friends did not swallow Catholicism whole and unquestioned.

Darnley and his father saw none of these things, though the wisest head of them all, Lethington, cannot fail to have done so. But he had his own cause of complaint against Rizzio. As we have seen, it was he who had first carried on the successful negotiations with Spain, and he had earned the distrust of England and of Murray in consequence, but, after all, he found that he was pushed aside by Rizzio as chief secretary, and he was one of the first persons to put in writing a hint that his rival should be killed.[281] On the 13th February Randolph wrote to Leicester that Lennox and his son were plotting to obtain the crown (matrimonial) against Mary's will. 'I know if that take effect which is intended, David with the consent of the King shall have his throat cut within these ten days,'[282] and he goes on to hint that the plot to murder may even be directed against Mary herself. Morton too, the chancellor, had his special grudge against the Italian, for it was said to be Mary's intention to give the latter the seals of Morton's great office, and the earl was the busiest of the conspirators to convince Darnley that the Queen's relations with the secretary injured her husband's honour. Morton's jackal was his illegitimate kinsman, George Douglas, a man steeped in every crime; and this creature was sent on the 10th February by Darnley to

Ruthven to draw him into the plot to avenge the consort's dishonour by killing the Queen's paramour, making her husband king for life, and bringing
back Murray and the exiled lords with England's benison.

On the 1st March the deed of association was signed by Argyle,
Morton, Boyd, Ruthven, and Lethington, and, according to Darnley's statement, was acquiesced in by a large number of Scottish gentlemen of all
ranks. The exiled lords in England, Murray, Rothes, and Kirkcaldy, and of
course Randolph and Bedford, were also cognisant of the plot, and pledges
of pardon and mutual support and protection were given by Darnley and
the whole of the other conspirators. The government in London was fully
informed of every stage of the proceedings by Randolph and Bedford,[283]
and on the 9th March 1566 the black deed was done. Mary was in the sixth
month of her pregnancy, and as it had always been a feature of the plan that
the secretary should be murdered in her presence, the object was certainly
to discredit her morally, if not to cause her injury or death from the shock.
The details of the crime have been so often set forth that they need not be
fully described here, where we are more concerned with the objects and
results of the act than with the act itself, but a brief glance at the attitude of
the various parties during and immediately after the crime will enable us to
understand more clearly the significance of what followed.

The day chosen was three days prior to the meeting of the Scottish parliament, in which the forfeiture of the fugitive lords was to be proposed. It
was Saturday evening past seven o'clock, when the Queen sat at supper—or,
as we should now call it, dinner—in a little twelve-foot closet adjoining her
sleeping apartments in the palace of Holyrood. In the tiny chamber there
was a low couch and a small table, at which the party sat: the Queen with
her natural sister, the Countess of Argyle, her brother, Lord Robert Stuart,
and David Rizzio,[284] with the laird of Creich (Robert Beaton) and Arthur
Erskine, captain of the guard, in attendance, and some servants in waiting. Morton and Lindsay, with about one hundred and sixty armed men,
having occupied the approaches of the palace, Darnley led up the private
staircase into the Queen's apartments Ruthven, who was in the last stage of
consumption, George Douglas, and two other men, all in armour. Leaving
his companions in the outer room, Darnley entered the little cabinet alone,

and took a seat by his wife's side at table. Almost immediately afterwards the door was opened and Ruthven stood unbidden upon the threshold, his armed companions behind him. Pointing at the Italian, who sat opposite the Queen, Ruthven bade Rizzio 'come forth from the Queen's chamber, where he hath been overlong.'

Mary, alarmed and indignant at the intrusion, asked what offence he had committed. He had offended, replied Ruthven, against her honour, her husband, her nobles, and her commonwealth; and with that the speaker advanced to seize the secretary. The Queen sprang to her feet, whilst Rizzio, having drawn his dagger, shrank behind her into a window embrasure, clinging fast to the pleats of her skirt. Is this your work? asked the outraged Queen of her husband, who gave no answer, but at Ruthven's direction threw his arms around her to prevent her from aiding the doomed man, at whom Ruthven and his companions struck over her shoulder, throwing down the table and its contents, candles and all, in the struggle. In vain the Queen ordered the assailants, on pain of treason, to leave the room; in vain she promised to submit Rizzio to judgment: Darnley still held his wife, whilst Lord Robert and Erskine turned upon Ruthven, who defended himself with his dagger. Then at a signal there rang out in the courtyard and corridor the warcry, 'a Douglas! a Douglas!' and soon the Queen's chamber was filled with armed men from below. Saved from his attackers, but exhausted, and almost moribund, Ruthven sheathed his weapon, whilst Rizzio, panting and bleeding, was dragged out of the little room through the bedchamber and despatched at the head of the stairs from the presence-chamber. George Douglas, either by accident, or more likely by design, snatched Darnley's own dagger from his side and dealt the fatal blow, leaving the weapon in the wound and the body to be hacked in fury by others. Morton and Lindsay were present at the deed, and professed a desire to save Rizzio to be hanged next morning, but, if such was really their wish, it was overborne by the blood-lust of others.

When the deed was done, Ruthven, fainting with exhaustion, entered the Queen's cabinet again with Morton and others. Mary was just recovering from a swoon, and her first order was that the dead secretary's cipher-chest with her secret foreign correspondence should be brought to her; and then, turning to her unworthy husband, she upbraided him for the outrage, to which she knew he had consented. He retorted that since the Italian had been so intimate with her she had avoided the society of her own consort; and Ruthven sought to justify what had been done by attributing to Rizzio the blame for what he called Mary's tyranny in favouring Catholics, and forming leagues with foreign powers to the detriment of Scotland. The banished lords, he said, had been pardoned by the King, and would join the assailants, so that wellnigh all Scotland was on their side.[285]

Mary through the shameful scene saw the wreck of all her great hopes: the diplomatical skill and patient effort of years wasted and scattered in an hour by the ineptitude of the hulking simpleton who stood by her side; and she turned upon the creature that she had once loved so fiercely, glowing with indignation now that she saw the depth of his iniquity, and in answer to his whining complaint that she had avoided his companionship she cried, between her tears, 'Well! ye have taken the last of me, and so, farewell!' Ruthven dared to lecture her on conjugal duty, but she told him that he and others had been divorced, and so might she be. Whilst they disputed, Ruthven, overcome with weakness, sank upon a seat, and begged for a cup of wine to save him from fainting; and the Queen turned her back upon him with a threat that if Rizzio's blood had been spilt, 'it should be dear blood for some of you.' But in answer to Darnley's continued reproaches of her conjugal coldness towards him, Mary scornfully told him at length that he could enjoy his privileges that night; and she was at last left alone with her ladies, whilst Darnley and Ruthven went below to calm the frightened courtiers as to the feared results to them of Murray's return. Bothwell and Huntly, somewhat unheroically, escaped out of a back window and fled. Athol and others were with Darnley's permission spirited out of the way by Lethington; and Mary, a prisoner in her own apartments, passed the night pacing in indignant grief, additionally angry, though probably not sorry, that her husband should after all go to sleep in his own room, and forget to keep the conjugal appointment for which he had pretended to be so anxious.[286]

Darnley at once assumed regal authority, forbidding the magistrates of Edinburgh to see or communicate with the Queen, and dissolving the parliament that had been summoned. The next day Murray, Kirkcaldy, Rothes, and the rest of the fugitive lords rode to Holyrood in triumph. Before they arrived assurance of Mary's pardon reached them, for she thought at least that her brother would save her life. Anything was better than the unchecked control of a puerile hothead like Darnley, surrounded by men who had proved themselves traitors and cut-throats.[287] A council of the lords that night decided to isolate the Queen in the castle of Stirling until she had approved of all the acts committed.[288] Almost any other woman would have given up the game as lost; for her Catholic champions had run away, her most trusted instrument was murdered, her husband had joined her enemies, and she was a defenceless prisoner of those who had sworn to defeat the dearest hopes and wishes of her life.

But Mary was no ordinary woman. After all her resources as Queen, politician, and diplomatist had been defeated, there still remained to her the abundant armoury of her personal fascination, her feminine wiles, her ready tears, her persuasive caresses; and to these she turned now, as ever, in her hour of greatest need. First she readily granted everything that was required of her by Murray, Morton, and the rest of them, and then she opened her batteries upon Lethington. She was in fear, she said, of the rough soldiery that kept ward over her; pray let them be withdrawn. There could surely be nothing to fear from her now; commit her to the guard of her dear husband for the night; he would answer for her. Darnley, proud of her renewed affection, added his prayers to hers, and as she walked to her own chamber, with her husband and her brother supporting her on either side, the guards that were posted about her to prevent escape were withdrawn.[289] Already, earlier in the day, a message had reached her from Bothwell and Huntly that they were gathering forces, and had arranged a plan for her escape that night by having her lowered over the walls by ropes. But this scheme was full of danger, considering Mary's condition, and was rejected for a better one.

When Mary was alone with him in her room, she took her husband in hand. He was, we know, vain and a coward, and as clay in her skilful hands. She was in fear for him, she said, for if the rebels triumphed over them, he himself would be miserably handled by them; and she set before him the splendid dream she had for both of them, and how his faithfulness to the Catholic Church was the pivot upon which it all turned; and so, conquered by the caresses and entreaties of his wife, the unstable creature again consented to change sides and betray his companions. Yes; he would fly with her that very night if they could get away, and once in safety he would denounce and condemn the men who had calumniated and outraged his wife. And so, when all in the palace and the royal burgh were wrapped in sleep, a way was found through the basement of Holyrood, and so to the open under the light of the moon. Led by a single chamberlain to the place of tryst, Mary and her husband found awaiting them with swift horses Arthur Erskine and Stuart of Traquair; and through the night the dauntless Queen fled to Seton. There she rested a space, and partook of refreshments, surrounded thenceforward by two hundred stout Seton clansmen ready to defend her; and almost before the dawn began to light the east the strong walls of Dunbar were between the Queen of Scots and the deadly enemies of her policy. Snatched by her own address from captivity, perhaps from a violent death, Mary was mistress of her fate once more.

As for the 'noble and mighty Prince Henry, King of Scotland,' he crumbled down completely. He had in the flight been so eager to get away that he had ridden in advance of his wife, and had flung back over his shoulder craven reproaches that she could travel no faster.[290] Now in Dunbar, with Huntly, Bothwell, and Athol rallying to the Queen, he surpassed himself in mean cowardice, swearing his own innocence of Rizzio's death, but inculpating every one else.[291] Some passionate words, said to have been uttered by Mary as she passed Rizzio's newly-made grave in her escape from Holyrood, were afterwards interpreted to mean a threat of murder against her husband by the family of the latter,[292] but to all appearance Mary believed Darnley's protestations at the time, and endeavoured with statesmanlike acumen to reconcile interests and personages in a way that would allow her, by holding the balance between them, still to have her own way, and to carry out the policy which had been so rudely disturbed by her husband's ineptitude and her brother's religious leanings. Her task of bringing events back to their normal channel was immense. Surrounded by her armed anti-English nobles, she might, it is true, again have driven Murray and the whole of the Protestant leaders into exile; but she was too wise to do so. Murray, Glencairn, Rothes, and Argyle promptly sent their submission to her when they found that

Darnley had betrayed them, and, with the other nobles, were summoned to a convention at Haddington; but Ruthven, Morton, and their immediate accomplices in Rizzio's murder fled across the Border, and were publicly proclaimed traitors and their property forfeit.

How far Darnley's jealousy of Rizzio was warranted has been a subject of fierce controversy. The Italian, it has been admitted, was elderly; though a contemporary portrait of him presents him as not altogether ill-favoured. We have seen from Melville's admission that from the first Mary had been very confidential with him; but, as has been shown, there was good political reason for her being so, the correspondence for the great Catholic alliance with Spain, Rome, and Florence being entirely in his hands after Raulet's dismissal. De Foix, who it must be recollected, however, was a 'politician,' provides the most injurious testimony against Mary in the matter. He says that Darnley 'a few days before the murder knocked at the door of the Queen's chamber, but received no answer. Hereupon he called out aloud and begged Mary to open the door, but in vain. At last he threatened to break it open, and found the Queen, when she let him in, quite alone in her room: but looking about, he found Rizzio in a closet, who had thrown a morning gown over him, having nothing else on but his shirt.' But de Foix only spoke at second hand, for he was not in Scotland at the time; and the great balance of probability is that Darnley's suspicions against his wife were deliberately aroused and fostered, in order that they might be turned to political advantage by those who wished to upset Mary's great Catholic scheme. With the whole evidence before us, it is impossible to condemn Mary of flagrant immorality with Rizzio; though it must be admitted that the imprudence and perversity of her favour towards him provided her enemies with the means they sought for injuring her.

IX

BOTHWELL AND DARNLEY

*Mary returns to Edinburgh—Renewed quarrels with Darnley—
Mary's plan of revenge—Birth of James—Elizabeth's alarm—
Catholic aid to Mary—Rise of Bothwell—Alleged amours with the
Queen in Edinburgh—Proposed flight of Darnley—His attempted
conspiracy—Mary's disgust of him—Mary at Jedburgh—Bothwell at
Hermitage—Craigmillar—The proposal to kill Darnley—Extent of
Mary's complicity—Her political caution in the matter—Baptism of
James—Darnley at Glasgow—Mary's visit—Return to Edinburgh—
Kirk-o'-Field—Darnley's murder.*

ON THE 17TH MARCH 1566 MARY RODE INTO EDINBURGH, DIS-
daining to be carried in a litter, notwithstanding her condition. By her side
rode her husband like a whipped cur, and around her were Bothwell, Huntly,
Marischal, Hume, and Seton, with some three thousand of their armed
retainers. To blood-stained Holyrood she would not go, but lodged, first in
a private dwelling in the High Street, and afterwards in a house belonging
to the Humes, until Erskine, having hanged some of the humbler instruments in the Rizzio murder, made ready the Castle for the reception of his
sovereign (5th April). Soon there joined her Argyle and Murray, the latter
still at feud with Huntly and Bothwell, undisguisedly scorning Darnley, and
bearing but little love for his own shifty ally Argyle. With infinite pains and

entreaty Mary patched up some sort of apparent truce between the jarring elements around her, and tried with skill and patience to pick up the broken thread of her policy.

Elizabeth was all amiability and pity now, weeping crocodile tears at her dear sister's troubles, and wearing a portrait of Mary pendant from her girdle,[293] for couriers were busily running backward and forward between Scotland and the Catholic powers, and Elizabeth was still afraid,[294] though delighted at the blow that had been struck at Mary's prestige; and she even made something of a grievance that Mary had warned Darnley that she could count upon the friendship of the kings of Spain and France, and other princes, but had not mentioned Elizabeth, the nearest friend of them all. Darnley, weak and wavering, was already dissatisfied at the shabby part he had played and its results to himself; for Mary was scornful and cold towards him, and Murray passed him by and looked to the Queen alone for authority. The wretched young man was, moreover, in mortal fear that Murray would in the end have his way, and persuade Mary to pardon Morton and the rest of the Rizzio murderers[295] whom he had betrayed, and from whom he could hope for no good. This fear drew him closer to Murray's enemy Bothwell, the strong man of war, snarling at England across the Border, upon whom the Queen depended increasingly for support for her future plans.

Mary's love for her husband had vanished before the repeated proofs of his folly and levity. As we have seen, she had married him because her fancy for him seemed to run parallel with her political interests. But the personal caprice had been sated, perhaps killed, by his mental and moral insufficiency; whilst his ineptitude in allowing himself to be drawn by his enemies into a coalition with the Protestants, for the purpose of frustrating his wife's deeply-laid plans, had convinced Mary that he was no longer to be trusted as a political partner. For her eyes never left the goal at which she aimed. Free, now, from the passing passion that had for a time warped her judgment and hastened her into a plausible-looking marriage, her mind had regained its predominance over her heart; and her first object was to get the management of affairs entirely into her own hands, by reducing Darnley to the position of a cipher. The more he was distrusted and contemned by all parties, and the further discredited he became, the more entirely dependent would he be upon her, and the less likely to be able to interfere with her policy out of fickleness, personal ambition, or malice. The only use he could ever be to her was to conciliate a certain number of English Catholics, who looked to him, or rather to his mother as their candidate for Elizabeth's throne; so that at the moment (namely, April 1566) it was not policy to remove him altogether, so long as he could be reduced to the position of a nonentity in the government of Scotland.

But, like all petulant, vain men, Darnley was hard to manage. He chafed and rebelled against the Queen's treatment of him. In April he quarrelled with her, and left her for a time, because she had been shown the bond signed by him for the Rizzio murder, and reproached him for his double deceit.[296] It was even said that Mary had sent to Rome to obtain a divorce from him;[297] and when the French envoy, Castelnau, again arrived in Scotland (April 1566) to pacify matters, if possible, he found the consort coldshouldered by every one, and did not even speak to him for days after he came to court.[298] 'He (Darnley) is,' wrote Randolph on the 25th April, 'neither accompanied nor looked upon by any noblemen, but is attended by certain of his own servants, and six or eight of the guard, at liberty to do and go what and where he will.'

Every day fresh proof was given of Mary's determination to deprive her husband of credit and influence. With Castelnau there came to Scotland Joseph Rizzio, the murdered favourite's brother, a mere lad of twenty years or so, who was made Mary's foreign secretary; and Darnley, so chagrined was he, even threatened to fly to Flanders and publish his grievances to the world. At a later period he told his father that, at this time, a few weeks previous to the birth of Mary's child, the Queen—perhaps disgusted with him personally, perhaps the further to embroil and discredit him—advised him to take a mistress, and if possible to make the Earl of Murray 'wear horns.' 'I assure you,' she said, 'I shall never love you the worse.' The father seems to have been somewhat shocked at this, and advised the King-Consort never to be unfaithful to his wife. 'I never offended the Queen my wife,' replied Darnley, 'in meddling with any other woman, in thought, let be in deed.'[299] Darnley, we know, was a liar, and it was to the interest of Lennox when he recounted this story to make out Mary to be as black as possible; but from other and more trustworthy evidence it is clear that Mary did her best thenceforward to sow secret discord between her husband and her brother.

There is nothing surprising that she should have done so, when we consider that her political interests needed the dwarfing of Darnley, if not his disappearance; and if by fomenting hatred between him and Murray she could, without reproach to herself, compass his destruction, and perhaps that of Murray too, if he proved recalcitrant, it would have been a master-stroke of policy. Lethington, who was still unpardoned but tolerated in Scotland, and not unhopeful of future favour, thanks to his staunch friend Athol, was the wisest of her statesmen, and could be trusted to carry out her schemes, if once the masterful influence of the more consistent Murray was conciliated or removed. Bothwell, upon whom her eyes must have already looked with approval, perhaps with desire, seemed to be a good instrument to be used in the forcible part of her programme. With these two ministers, Lethington and Bothwell, the forces of the Catholic lords, the support of the English Catholics, her own popularity, and the aid of Spain, she might yet triumph; but Murray might perhaps be an obstacle, and Darnley was a constant difficulty and danger, by reason of his instability. If they could be made mutually destructive and she blamelessly rid of them, she would be a step nearer to success.

But, withal, she had to move warily. She must keep up appearances and avoid scandal; for she had not yet lost her head over Bothwell, and was mainly concerned with political considerations. She could not fly in the face of Elizabeth and the Protestants by seizing Murray, nor could she trust him far out of her sight in the time of her weakness, or he and his friends the English might join on the Border, invade her realm, and end her dream. So, when her time approached, and it became a question as to who should remain in the Castle beside her husband when the looked-for event took place,[300] Mary wisely resisted the distrustful hints of Darnley, Bothwell, Huntly, and the Bishop of Ross that Murray should be put under lock and key during her illness, to prevent his bringing back the Rizzio murderers; and it was Murray and Argyle and their wives, and not Bothwell, who stayed in charge of the Queen's safety, with Erskine (Mar) the keeper of the fortress. Bothwell, who hated the English with all his heart, was a safer man than Murray on the Border; and to his own lands, accordingly, he was sent, salved with the great fief of Dunbar. In her apprehension of her coming trial Mary made her will; and in this, too, she had regard for the proprieties, leaving to her husband, amongst other things, the ring with which he wedded her; and as Castelnau told Guzman on the way back to France (in May), though they did not trust each other, the Queen and her husband now dwelt for a short time together at least without open scandal.

On the morning of the 19th June Mary's child was born; and Mary Beaton ran with the glad news to the waiting courtiers, amongst whom was James Melville, praying night and day, as he tells us, for a happy delivery of his Queen. Hardly had the news passed Mary Beaton's lips before Melville was in the saddle and scouring southward as fast as a horse could gallop. On the fourth day afterwards, 23rd June, he rode into London, and to his brother Sir Robert's house with the intelligence. Cecil learned it the same evening at his house in Canon Row, and whispered it into Elizabeth's ear an hour later at Greenwich. Dancing and music were going on at the time, but with Cecil's whisper a shadow fell, and all mirth ceased. Elizabeth, blazing with spiteful jealousy, uttered her oft-repeated saying that, whilst Mary was mother of a fair son, she herself was a barren stock. But the next morning when she saw Melville diplomacy asserted itself, and she clothed her face in smiles.[301] Yes, marry! she would be godmother to the infant,[302] and would send some of her greatest lords to represent her at the ceremony; but when Melville suggested Leicester as her proxy, she vouchsafed no reply; for Leicester, she knew, was now deep in the plot with the conservative and Catholic nobles to upset Cecil and the new men, and to get Mary declared Elizabeth's heir.

Fortune seemed, indeed, to favour the Queen of Scots just then; and this will sufficiently account for Elizabeth's amiability to Mary, and her desperate attempts to seem friendly to Spain. Only a few days before James Melville arrived in London with his news, his brother Sir Robert had formally repeated the request that Mary's rights to the English succession should be recognised, Lady Lennox released from the Tower, and her husband and son pardoned. Elizabeth dared not refuse point-blank, but showed herself yielding. If Mary would formally renounce all claim during

Elizabeth's lifetime, the latter would by word of mouth acknowledge her claim to succeed; and about Lady Lennox, too, she was not so obdurate as previously. She expressed herself as quite shocked, however, that Mary should help the Irish rebels and plot with the English Catholics as she did, both of which accusations Melville strenuously denied, though his brother Sir Robert and he took care to convey everything that passed to the Spanish ambassador in London.

Guzman saw on the same day, 24th June, another person of importance to Mary. A Scottish Catholic, Thornton, who had been sent as her emissary to Rome, came with the great news to London on his way back to Scotland that His Holiness had sent his mistress 20,000 crowns, and had provided a subsidy of 4,000 crowns a month to pay for soldiers for the attainment of her objects; and that more money still should be sent as soon as the war with the Turk was over.[303] Renewed promises of Spanish aid were also sent to Mary at the same time; and Robert Melville, Protestant though he was, and as we now know in the pay of Cecil, told Guzman that not a Scotsman of any sort would follow Elizabeth after her shabby treatment of Murray and his friends; and he agreed with the Spaniard that caution must be used by Mary in her communications with the Catholics, until her subjects were united, and the great blow might be struck in her favour. Thus, notwithstanding Darnley's temporary defection from the Catholic party, Mary, In the two months that had passed since the Rizzio misfortune, had managed, partly by good luck and partly by diplomacy, to restore the Anglo-Catholic-Spanish conspiracy to vigour, and Elizabeth was once more compelled to speak humbly to the Queen of Scots, to feign a new desire to marry the Archduke, and to smile sweetly on Philip and all his works.

In the meanwhile the relations between Mary and her husband did not improve as a consequence of the birth of their child. Although some of Mary's enemies at a later period threw doubt upon the paternity of the infant, and Darnley himself is said to have questioned it, receiving the reply from Mary that it was shown to be 'too much his child' by the shameful blemishes upon it, the consort, in his letter written to Cardinal Lorraine on the day of the child's birth, acknowledges himself as the happy father. Harry Killigrew, who arrived in Edinburgh on a mission from Elizabeth a week after the birth of James, found Darnley and his father (the latter being sick and sorry at Holyrood, whilst the consort lodged in the Castle) neglected and of little account. Bothwell was still in strength on the Border, 'his credit with the Queen being more than all the rest put together,' whilst Huntly remained in Edinburgh. The Bishop of Ross was deep in the Queen's confidence; and the most powerful nobles in Scotland, Murray, Argyle, Athol, and Mar, had for once forgotten old feuds, and were linked together in reality to resist Mary's Catholic projects. Murray himself complained to Killigrew that 'his credit was but small,' not much better, he said, than when he expected banishment, and it appears evident that Mary kept him by her, not out of affection or confidence in him, but the reverse.

Darnley in the meanwhile was serving as Bothwell's jackal, intent upon any course that could ruin Murray and prevent the return of Morton. With this object he endeavoured to persuade Mary to pardon the most heinous of the Rizzio fugitive murderers, the scoundrel George Douglas, in order that he might testify, as Darnley said he would do, that Murray and some others then unsuspected had been prompters of the crime. Mary had not forgotten her resentment, and she was unwilling to pardon Douglas. The plan, moreover, was discovered by Morton in England before it could be carried out, and Douglas swore to his kinsman that he had not promised to denounce Murray; but if confronted with Darnley would declare that the latter, instead of being innocent, was really the originator of the murder. Douglas's oath, of course, was worthless, but the story at least shows the length to which Darnley and Bothwell would go to ruin Murray.

Before the end of July, when Mary was convalescent, Bedford wrote from Berwick: 'Bothwell carries all the merit and countenance at Court. He is the most hated man among the noblemen; and therefore may fall out to his cumber one day'; and a few days later the same writer reports that 'Bothwell's insolence is such that David (Rizzio) was never more abhorred than he is now. The Queen and her husband are after the same manner, only rather worse. She seldom eating with him, and keepeth no company with him, nor loveth any such as love him.'

Suddenly at the end of July 1566 Mary, without knowledge of her husband, left Edinburgh. She had been 'overbold' during the first days of her illness, and had consequently suffered from a 'hollow cough.' She was still in delicate health, barely six weeks after her delivery, and quite unfit for arduous travel; but she had apparently conceived a violent repugnance to her unhappy consort, and left him. What she said of him just previous to her departure, writes the Earl of Bedford, 'cannot with modesty, nor with the honour of a Queen, be reported.' Her journey was more like a flight than a pleasure-trip, and all men wondered to see her, with but a few followers of low rank, hurry to the waterside at Newhaven, and embark upon a vessel awaiting her, manned by Bothwell's retainers—robbers and pirates, Buchanan calls them. Sailing for the castle of Alloa, she there took up her residence. In what particular way she offended whilst there is not clear— for Bothwell does not appear to have been present—but Buchanan, whose bitter invective must be accepted with caution, talks of her 'unprincely licentiousness,' and 'lack of modesty in all her words and doings.'[304] Probably the poor lady was thirsting for a little of the gay abandonment and self-indulgence she loved so much, after her six weeks' illness in the gloomy castle on the cliff, and thought that the sea trip and change of scene would be beneficial. In any case she did not enjoy her pleasure long undisturbed, for her husband took horse as soon as he heard of her departure, and rode to Alloa by Stirling to join her; but he met with a repellent reception, and left her a few hours later.

Thus from day to day the distance between them grew. Occasionally for a short time some sort of reconciliation was effected, as it was soon after his repulse at Alloa; but Darnley's jealousy and petulance knew no bounds. Murray and the Protestant lords had, he thought, played false with him, as he most certainly had with their associates. They were to make him all-powerful if he brought them back and into favour. He had done so, and had gained the hatred of his wife by killing Rizzio as part of the plan; and after all he was more of a cipher than before, contemned by every one. Revenge upon Murray, and fear of the pardon of Morton, were the principal motives of his actions; and when he saw Murray and Argyle still by the Queen's side he could not master himself, and either fell into foolish rage, or sulked away from court at Dunfermline, Stirling, or elsewhere.

In the first week of August one night he was with the Queen in the castle

of Edinburgh, and told her that he meant to kill Murray, as she was favouring him too much. Mary, alarmed and angry, sent immediately to her brother to come urgently to see her. Waiting only to cast a gown over his night garb, Murray hurried to the Queen's chamber, to be told that his assassination was planned by the King-Consort, and to be bidden to tax Darnley with it. This action of Mary would seem to be deliberately directed to the exacerbation of the ill-will already existing; and when the earl, in the presence of the Queen and many others, publicly accused Darnley of his criminal intent, the unhappy young fellow was obliged tearfully to confess it and seek to excuse himself as best he might with feigned repentance, and to be soundly rated before the whole roomful of people both by Murray and the Queen herself, who said that she would permit no one, not even her husband, to slight Murray. And with this Darnley again flung away from court to sulk at Dunfermline, 'having at his farewell such countenance as would make a husband heavy at heart.'

But he was soon back again, and was admitted by Mary to conjugal life once more. It is clear to see that he was unhappy away from his wife, and crazy with jealousy and wounded pride whilst he was with her. He had enough sense to see that his folly and instability in the Rizzio affair had condemned him to death, if ever Murray brought back the exiles; as, sooner or later, he would certainly do. There was no one to save him but Mary and Bothwell; for he himself had no friends, and his father by his extortions and greed had alienated even his own people. The one and only hope for Darnley was now humbly to follow his wife, as a satellite rather than a husband, and to strive, in season and out of season, for the ruin or death of Murray. His only ally, Bothwell, was growing almost as unpopular as himself. The earl had always been rough and masterful with the other nobles, and his sea-roving and Border-rieving methods were considered hardly respectable; there was still a rankling feud between him and Murray, though they were occasionally obliged to meet at court; he had been condemned more than once by his own Queen for lawlessness, and had escaped serious punishment by his boldness or evasion. He did not belong to the Catholic party, and had refused to attend Mary's Mass, whilst he was at issue with the friends of England.

Standing thus alone, hated by his fellows, it would appear at first sight somewhat curious that Mary should have selected him especially for her instrument, unless she was captivated by him personally from the beginning, as she certainly was afterwards. But really he had one quality, apart from any personal attraction or ability, which made him the one man in all Scotland the fittest for Mary's purpose. The other nobles had, almost to a man, at one time or another succumbed to the bribes or blandishments of England. From the first, and unwaveringly, Bothwell had been England's bitter enemy, and might be trusted to remain so. This in Mary's eyes must have outweighed much that was to be urged against him, and may well account for her first close association with him. With the greater hopes for the success of Mary's plans, inspired by the remittances and promises from Rome, Flanders, and Spain, and by Elizabeth's evident helplessness, Bothwell's favour steadily grew, to the dismay of Murray and his friends. There was even a plot to assassinate him when he went to Edinburgh in August. 'Bothwell,' writes Bedford on the 12th August, 'has grown of late so much hated that he cannot long continue. He beareth all the sway, and though Murray be there and has good words, yet can he do nothing.' He and Murray came almost to blows in the Queen's presence at this time, because Murray wished to bring Lethington back into the Queen's favour; but Mary knew the men she wanted, and cleverly managed soon afterwards to reconcile Bothwell to the astute secretary's reappointment.

For some days, from 13th to 19th August, Mary, with her husband, Murray, Bothwell, and Mar, were hunting somewhat unsuccessfully in south Peebles, Darnley repaying by his loutish behaviour the neglect and indifference with which his wife treated him.[305] On her way back to Edinburgh (20th August) Mary arranged that her child should be placed in safety at Stirling with Lady Murray, and thither she went herself on the 28th to instal him, and to receive Lethington with his friend Athol. What arguments she used to reconcile Bothwell to this may well be guessed. She had only to tell him that the secretary had been her first powerful instrument to conclude her Spanish alliance against Elizabeth. In any case the Queen diplomatically managed a fortnight afterwards to bring them together, with Murray and herself, secretly in a private house in Edinburgh, and at her request Bothwell graciously made friends with the restored secretary, and came also to some sort of working agreement with Murray and the lords. This private house, of which Lethington himself speaks,[306] was doubtless that adjoining the dwelling of John Balfour, mentioned by Buchanan in his scandalous story of Mary's amours with Bothwell at this time. Previously nothing had been said implying that Mary was in love with the Border earl; but Buchanan tells the story coarsely enough, and with a tone of conviction that has carried credit with it, even to those most disinclined to believe it.

His account is to the effect that the Queen moved from the private house into the Exchequer, the garden of which had a door into the house of Bothwell's servant Chalmers.[307] By the mediation of Lady Reres (or Mrs. Forbes of Reres), an infamous woman, now obese and elderly, but formerly Bothwell's mistress, who had been made one of the Queen's bedchamber ladies, Bothwell was brought from Chalmers's house to the Queen's lodging, and there, according to Mary's later statement, forced her against her will. With hollow mirth Buchanan scoffs at this latter statement, and says that a few nights afterwards Mary sent Lady Reres to fetch Bothwell again to her chamber. The communicating door in the garden was this time closed, and as the corpulent Reres was being lowered over the wall by Mary and one of her maids, the rope broke, and the massive procuress came down a crash. Nothing dismayed, however, she waddled to the room in which Bothwell was sleeping with his young wife, and brought him, halfdressed, to the Queen's chamber. Buchanan, to substantiate this story (which he tells with a frankness impossible to be repeated here), says that George Dalgleish, Bothwell's chamberlain, declared it in his confession, made just before his execution for Darnley's murder; but it is certainly not in his confession as printed by Buchanan himself in the *Detection*.

The fact that Mary did lodge in the Exchequer house between the 11th and the end of September is testified to by Sir J. Forster, who says that she was busy there at the time about her revenues;[308] although she must have gone sometimes to Holyrood, as we hear of her there sorting and arranging her finery for the coming christening, and ordering the new clothes for her courtiers.[309] Her husband, we are told, she 'held in light estimation' now, and she had never even seen Lennox since Rizzio's death.[310]

On the 24th September Darnley seems to have come unexpectedly from Stirling, where he had been staying, to Edinburgh. Mary, when she heard of his coming, 'purposely fled out of the chekker-hous and passed to the palace of Halyrudehous.'[311] Why she should have fled from the Exchequer if there was nothing wrong is not clear; and although the positive assertion of Mary's amour with Bothwell having commenced then and there depends entirely on Buchanan's and Lennox's statements, it may have as well been then as later. Her subsequent demeanour before her council and the French ambassador de Croc, who had arrived in July, may be attributed either to conscious innocence or bold dissimulation.

Darnley had found his position becoming more and more intolerable: he was deservedly scorned by his wife for his bodily viciousness and his mental instability; even Bothwell could do without him now; and he declared to his father at Stirling on the 29th September his intention to fly to France in a ship which was then awaiting him. Lennox was shocked, and at once wrote to Mary warning her; but he would have been even more shocked and angry if he had known, as we do, the depth of his son's folly.[312] Seeing that Bothwell and Lethington had been reconciled, and that Murray, Athol, Huntly, and even Argyle were rapidly, in appearance at least, coming round to Mary's plans,[313] the foolish young man now endeavoured to raise an extreme Catholic counter conspiracy by appealing to the Pope, and denouncing Mary's religious lukewarmness in consorting with heretics like Murray; and he had the turpitude to claim for himself the purely Catholic aid that was to be sent to Scotland. The idea was not without cunning, combined, as it was, with the intention to look to France instead of to Spain, and to make use of their national jealousy, in order to place him in the position of a rival to his wife's claims: to the crown of Scotland in right of his son, and to that of England in right of his mother.

But his letters to the Pope had been intercepted, his tentative advances to France were laughed at; and the poor creature, distracted and feeble of purpose, instead of embarking on his waiting ship, suddenly appeared at Holyrood at ten o'clock at night of the day that his wife had received the letter saying that he was going to France (29th September). He was in a penitential mood; but, in answer to Mary's reproaches and inquiries as to what he complained of, he would say nothing. Late as it was, she summoned a meeting of her council and nobles, with the French ambassador, to hear what her husband had to say for himself. She again, before them all, demanded the reason of his proposed flight; and besought him, solemnly and with clasped hands, to say whether he had any fault to find with her. The lords likewise said that they saw he looked at them askance. Had they done anything to offend him or give reason for his flight? Then the French ambassador, a stout Guisan, took him in hand, and lectured him roundly. If he was moved, said de Croc, by anything the Queen had done, it was his duty to her and to himself to say what it was; if otherwise, his object in flying abroad could not fail to be reprehensible. Darnley remained pouting and silent for a long time; but at length declared that he had no reason to allege for his proposed flight. Mary said she was satisfied with this; and the rest of those present promised to bear witness to Darnley's declaration in her favour; but the young man could do nothing graciously, and he skulked out of the room without kissing his wife, muttering as he went that it would be a long time ere she saw him again; and before the night was passed news was brought to her that he still meant to sail away if he could.

But he lacked resolution either to go or to stay; and a few days afterwards, whilst the Queen was on the Border, he wrote begging de Croc to meet him and his father a few miles from Edinburgh. 'I see,' writes the Frenchman, 'that he does not realise his position. He wishes the Queen to send for him, but I told him that he had left her without reason. The Queen, I said, was very good; but there were very few wives who would send for him in such case. I see that he would like to temporise until after the christening, in order not to be obliged to be present at the ceremony. There are two things that, in my opinion, cause him to despair: the first is the reconciliation of the Queen with the lords, which makes him jealous, because the latter pay more court to the Queen than to him; and, as he is haughty and proud, he does not like foreigners to see this; the second is that he knows that the person who may come from the Queen of England to be present at the baptism will take no notice of him, and he is afraid of receiving a slight. If he were well advised he would not presume too far, and he would avoid the trouble in which he now is.'[314]

It is evident to us now, as it no doubt was to him, that Darnley was a lost man from this time. He had not a single friend, not even himself. Morton, and the other accomplices he had betrayed, were certain to kill him sooner or later, if no one else did so. Murray would not lift a finger to save a man who had never ceased to plot his destruction. Bothwell had no longer any need of his help, but on the contrary was now, of all men in the world, the most interested in his prompt removal from the living. Even in the not improbable event that Mary had, as she afterwards alleged, been forcibly induced to cede to Bothwell's lust in the first place, there is no doubt that she was now being swept off her feet by the rush of her passion for him; and she, too, could not desire the prolongation of the life of a husband who had disgusted and affronted her personally, had perversely thwarted her politically, had betrayed her interests, joined her enemies against her, and now seemed to stand fair in the path of her happiness as a woman, and her success as a Queen.

Mary yearned for the full enjoyment of life; she had always been pampered and flattered, and she resented any obstacle to the attainment of her ends. Her great dream of a Catholic Britain under her sceptre was never long absent from her mind, though the steadfastness and sacrifice needed for its realisation were sometimes hard for her pleasure-loving nature to endure. But when unnecessary and wanton difficulties were interposed by the very man whom she had chosen for her husband in order the better to carry through her policy; when, in addition to this, the yoke-mate she had thought she loved, repelled and disgusted her; then she would have not been self-indulgent Mary Stuart, bred in the Guisan school and at the court of France, if she had not, like another Pilate, washed her hands of him and left him to the scant mercy of his enemies, from whom, in any case, she would have been powerless to save him without sacrificing herself. And Mary Stuart never willingly sacrificed herself for any one, least of all for one who was in her way.

Soon after the scene with Darnley at Holyrood above described, Mary started on her tour of assize and pacification on the Border, as had been settled two months before, the assize being fixed for the 8th October at Jedburgh. The earlier, and some of the later, of Mary's historians have been so unjust to her in the matter of this purely official journey to Jedburgh, that a comparison of dates will prove how necessary it is to demand independent confirmation before accepting even her contemporary Buchanan's statements to Mary's detriment. He talks of her 'flinging away like a mad woman to Jedburgh in the sharp time of winter' when she heard that Bothwell had been wounded in a Border affray. 'There, though she heard sure news of his life, yet her affection, impatient of delay, could not temper itself, but needs must bewray her outrageous lust: and in an inconvenient time of year, despising all discommodities of the way and weather, and all dangers of thieves, she betook herself headlong to her journey, with such a company as no man of any honest degree would adventure his life and goods among them.'[315] This is an exceedingly unfair statement of the case, and that of Robertson is not much better. Bothwell, in execution of his office, had gone to the Liddesdale district a day or so previously, to bring the Border thieves into something like order. On the 7th October—the day before that fixed for the assize at Jedburgh—he had sallied from his stronghold the Hermitage for the purpose of apprehending a notorious robber, one John Elliot of the Park, whom he shot with a pistol. The freebooter, wounded but not disabled, turned upon the earl, and, it was believed at the time, killed him.[316] The supposed corpse was placed in a cart and carried to Hermitage, the news being sent to meet the Queen, who was on the way to Jedburgh. She learned of his supposed death either on the way to, or on her arrival at, Jedburgh on the same day, 7th October; and instead of rushing off, as alleged, to Hermitage to see her lover, who she soon learned was not dead, but only badly wounded in the thigh, she attended to the business of the assize until she adjourned it on the 15th October.

On the day previous to this, 14th October, she rode out with Murray and her other nobles privately to witness a conference between the English warden of the eastern marches and her officers; and on the 15th, a week after his misfortune, she saw Bothwell for the first time, he having been carried from Hermitage to Jedburgh in a horse litter, a journey of five-and-twenty or thirty miles. Bothwell seems to have remained at Jedburgh that night, and on the following morning Mary, escorted by Murray and others, rode to Hermitage with Bothwell, returning to Jedburgh the same evening.[317] Now, there is nothing very shocking or compromising in this, certainly nothing indecorous. It is a proof of Mary's endurance that she could ride fifty or sixty miles over the moorland in a day; but there was no reason why she should not have done it, even if Bothwell had never been her lover, for he was one of her principal and most trusted officers, General of the Marches, upon the business of which she was on the Border. The Liddesdale district, moreover, was still turbulent, and had next to be dealt with, and in pursuance of Mary's avowed intention to visit the whole of the Border her ride to Hermitage to escort Bothwell on his return was quite a natural act.

On the 21st October Bothwell again came to Jedburgh in a horse litter, and the intention was for Mary to travel thence to Hume Castle, and so along the frontier to Eyemouth. But the plan was upset by the sudden and dangerous illness of the Queen (on the 17th October), who the day after Bothwell's arrival (22nd October) was believed to be *in articulo mortis,* as she was again on the 25th October.[318] Illness kept her at Jedburgh until the 15th November, Darnley remaining, except for one day's tardy visit to his wife, sulky and neglected at Linlithgow, Glasgow, and Stirling the while; and Mary, surrounded by Murray, Bothwell, Huntly, Hume, Lethington, and five hundred horsemen, then rode on her way to Dunbar and Edinburgh to prepare for the stately christening of her child. On her way she passed by Coldingham through a strip of English territory, where she was courteously greeted by the English general,[319] and on Halidon Hill heard the salute of all the ordnance on the walls of Berwick fired in her honour. 'There have been many cumbers between these two realms,' she said, as she turned to Sir John Forster, the English warden, 'but I will never give occasion for war between England and Scotland.' She charged the Border nobles, Hume, Bothwell, and Ker of Cessford, to keep order in their bounds, and then, knowing that it would give pleasure to the Englishman, she made a remark, a mere passing politeness it seemed—but it was the death-warrant of her husband. 'She was,' she said, 'a favourer of the Earl of Morton and his company.'

The murder of Rizzio was forgiven that it might be avenged. The interests of every one demanded the removal of the unhappy young man who was so superfluous; what better way of getting rid of him than to pardon the Rizzio murderers, and let them work their will upon the accomplice who had betrayed them. If they failed, there was always Bothwell, with his great ambition to reach supremacy by the Queen's love for him; nay, there was always Mary herself, loathing the man she had wedded,[320] and momentarily postponing even the ruling motive of her life to her passion for the virile ruffian who had subdued her by his strength.

From the time of Mary's stay at Jedburgh Bothwell became all in all to her. During her grave illness, caused as she told Lethington by her grief at Darnley's conduct, the consort pursued his pleasure at Glasgow for days before thinking of coming to see her, and when he did so, on the 28th October, he only stayed at Jedburgh one night, being dissatisfied with his welcome,[321] and then rode to Stirling. There were those about Mary who noted openly the contrast between her demeanour to her husband and to Bothwell. Buchanan, as usual, makes the worst of it, calling the Queen's treatment of Bothwell 'dishonourable to themselves, and infamous among the people'; and says that the earl was, 'as it were in triumph over the king, gloriously removed in the sight of the people into the Queen's own lodging, and there laid in the lower parlour, directly under the chamber where she lay sick. There, while they both were yet feeble and unhealed, she of her disease, and he of his wound, the Queen being very weak of her body, yet visited him daily. And when they were both a little recovered, and their strengths not yet fully settled, they returned to their old pastime again, and that so openly as they seemed to fear nothing more than lest their wickedness should be unknown.'[322] Other less violent authorities agree that the Queen's conduct at Jedburgh was 'very suspicious,' and 'that the world in those same days began to speak of it.'[323] Mary as we have seen was, however, seriously ill most of the time that Bothwell was at Jedburgh, and the earl himself was disabled with a smashed thigh, so that, however much the pair may have been in love with each other, their circumstances were hardly favourable to successful gallantry.

Mary rode along the Border by Tantallon to Craigmillar, where she arrived on the 20th November, still ailing,—fretting with grief it was said,—wishing constantly that she were dead. On her way—at Kelso—indeed, she had hinted at suicide. Reading a letter she had received from Darnley, she said (according to Calderwood), 'unless she was freed of him, one way or another, she would put a hand into herself.'[324] 'Unless she were quit of the king by one means or another she could never have a good day in her life, and rather than that to be the instrument of her own death.' We have seen that five days before she arrived at Craigmillar Mary told Forster that she was inclined to favour the refugee Morton and his company, so that the suggestion of this being made part of a bargain, of which the other part was the Queen's divorce from Darnley, could not have arisen so spontaneously amongst the nobles, or have come so suddenly upon Mary at Craigmillar, as is represented in the document drawn up by Leslie three years afterwards, to be signed by Huntly and Argyle, for the inculpation of Murray and the exculpation of the Queen. According to my view, the precise steps by which the project for the elimination of Darnley was matured are of quite secondary importance. By all the rules and practice of Scottish politics of the day he was certain to be removed, with or without the expressed connivance of the Queen; and it is quite probable, as the declaration says, that the proposal of Murray, Argyle, Lethington, Huntly, and Bothwell, at Jedburgh and Craigmillar, that the Rizzio murderers should be pardoned, was principally urged upon and accepted by the Queen because it was likely to expedite the process by which she might be liberated from her husband; otherwise there was no reason for uniting the two proposals. It is certain that the nobles at Jedburgh in October had signed a bond of union of some sort against Darnley, and which of them it was who took the lead in formulating a plan at Craigmillar does not matter.

According to the exculpatory document, which is the main authority on the subject,[325] Lethington answered Argyle, when the latter remarked that he did not know how the Queen was to be divorced from Darnley: 'My lord, care ye not, we shall find the means well enough to make her quit of him.' When they all went to Mary's apartment to broach the matter to her, Lethington was the spokesman, and said they could so arrange a divorce that Mary 'need not meddle therein.' 'It was,' he said, 'necessary, both for the sake of the Queen and the country; for (Darnley) troubled her Grace, as us all, and would not cease until he did her some other evil turn, when her Highness would be much perplexed to put a remedy thereto.' Mary is stated to have replied that she might consent, but on two conditions: first, that the divorce should be a lawful one, and next that it was not to the prejudice of her child, otherwise she would endure all torments and perils that might ensue to her. Bothwell remarked that he had no doubt the divorce might be made without any prejudice to the prince, and instanced his own case, his father having been divorced from his mother without any prejudice to his own succession.

It was suggested by one of them that Mary and her divorced husband should live in different parts of the country, or Darnley might reside abroad. Mary replied to this that perhaps he might alter his mind, and that it would be better that she should leave Scotland (as she had wished to do when her child was born); but Lethington had his pregnant answer ready: 'Madam, care ye not. We are here the principal of your Majesty's nobility and council; who shall find the means that your Majesty shall be quit of him without prejudice of your son; and, albeit my lord of Murray here present, be little less scrupulous for a Protestant than your Grace is for a papist, I am sure he will look through his fingers thereat, and will behold our doings, saying nothing to the same.'[326] 'I will have you do nothing,' the Queen is represented as saying, 'whereby any spot may be laid to my honour or conscience; and therefore I pray you rather let the matter be in the state it is, abiding till God in His goodness put a remedy thereto, than ye try to do me service, that may possibly turn to my hurt and displeasure.' 'Leave it all to us,' said Lethington, 'and you shall see nothing but what the parliament will approve of.'[327]

Here we see Mary in the attitude which she frequently assumed towards the various plans for the murder of Elizabeth in after years. She was acute and experienced; she knew the significance of diplomatic language as well as any one living; and it is incredible that she should not have understood perfectly what Lethington meant. The avoidance of any direct responsibility for violent acts was one of the primary points of a sovereign's trade. She had learned all that years before. Do Mary's thick-and-thin defenders expect that her accusers could in any case produce her plain compromising acquiescence in writing, giving her orders for a crime like the murder of her husband? Such a demand proves an entire ignorance of the procedure then usually adopted. Sovereigns were always safeguarded by perfectly well understood protests on their part that nothing illegal must be done, and by an avoidance on the part of their instruments of over-plain speaking in their presence. But they knew what was meant, nevertheless. It is an insult to the intelligence of readers to attribute either ignorance or lack of penetration to Mary in this matter. Elizabeth, Catharine, Philip, and most other princes of the time connived at outrage and murder over and over again by their agents; knowing broadly what was intended, but never being told in plain brutal words, in order that, come what might, their ermine might not be too openly soiled. They thus usually avoided scandal; and Mary was unable to do so, not because she was less cautious than they, but because her councillors were at deadly feud amongst themselves for the spoil; and because she offended them all by falling in love with one of them, the rudest, and marrying him.

Mary went to Stirling from Edinburgh for her child's baptism on the 12th December 1566. 'Bothwell was appointed to receive the ambassadors; and all things for the christening are at his appointment; and the same scarcely liked by the rest of the nobility.'[328] Darnley, at the urgent request of the French ambassador and Guzman, had joined the Queen before she went to Stirling, and he remained in the castle during the festivities and ceremonies of the baptism, though he took no part in any of them; and, indeed, was not seen by the ambassadors. He prayed several times that de Croc would come and speak to him, but the French ambassador was disgusted with him, and refused to do so; and when Moret, too late for the baptism, arrived at Stirling from the Duke of Savoy, he also was persuaded by Mary not to see the consort. In this his utter isolation his father warned him by private letter from Glasgow that he had been informed of an agreement made by the nobles at Craigmillar to seize and imprison him, and if he resisted to kill him, but that the plan had been postponed at Mary's request until after the special ambassadors had departed.[329] In hourly fear, therefore, he fretted in his chamber, whilst the fine doings in the other parts of the castle were progressing. The fullest Catholic ceremony was performed (17th December 1566), the infamous Archbishop of St. Andrews, Chatelherault's brother, performing the ceremony. The Puritan Bedford, proxy for the Queen of England, stood outside the chapel door with Bothwell, Murray, and Huntly during the papist rites; but nothing that could be done to promote pleasure and cordiality afterwards was omitted. Splendid presents were brought from abroad, a great gold font from Elizabeth; Bothwell, in his fine blue suit, the gift of the Queen,[330] took the lead in all the gaiety, and even Murray must now have begun to realise that his old foe and new ally was likely to be a dangerous rival to him. Seven days after the baptism Darnley took horse and fled to his father at Glasgow, intending as soon as possible to put the sea between him and those he was told were planning his capture, perhaps his death.

In the meanwhile Mary was never losing sight of her political objects. The condition upon which she might hope for Spanish aid was that her Catholic friends should be willing to declare for her in England when the opportune moment came. The first recommendation that Darnley possessed as a husband for her was that his mother influenced a large number of the Catholics of the north of England; and it must not be supposed that a stateswoman as ambitious and able as Mary was willing to lose this necessary support when the pending disappearance of her husband should take place. Robert Melville, though a 'political' Protestant, receiving pay from Cecil, was nevertheless, like other Scotsmen of his class and time, zealously desirous of forwarding the views of his sovereign, whatever they might be; and he took care that Mary's share in the matrimonial discord should be presented in a favourable light. He saw Guzman in London at the end of October, when Mary was on the Border, and after a long talk with him the ambassador wrote to his master that 'the Queen (Mary) is so popular with good people in this country that they lay the whole blame on the husband.' The Pope, the Spanish Governor of Flanders, and other leading Catholics were asked to write to the disunited couple, urging harmony upon them; but there was never a question for a moment on the part of the English Catholics, and much less on that of Spain and Rome, of transferring their support from Mary to Darnley or his mother in case of a separation.

Shortly afterwards Melville told Guzman that Mary had written to Cardinal Lorraine, saying that she had friends in this country who would help her to her rights, and that the Cardinal had replied, dissuading her from any such course as that suggested, the French ambassador having urged her to the same effect. It is very doubtful that Mary would have written thus to her uncles. They were French again now, and for the time strongly opposed to Mary's becoming Queen of England, which they knew she could only do under Spanish auspices, to the detriment of France. The active and cordial understanding now being cemented by Mary personally with the Pope, the Spaniards, and the English Catholics was as usual being combatted by Elizabeth and Catharine in their characteristic fashion. Elizabeth, for her part, began to discourse amiably about the desirability of an arrangement with Mary as to the succession; and to raise a fresh issue she offered to make an alteration in the still unratified Treaty of Edinburgh in a sense favourable to Mary's pretensions. In order to bring Mary into a tractable frame of mind, too, poor Lady Katharine Grey's claim to the heirship of England was much talked about, and Catharine, as her contribution to the defeat of Mary's Spanish objects, did her best to promote Katharine Grey's cause in parliament; until finally Melville, on the advice of the Spaniard, and supported by him, asked Elizabeth to defer the whole question of the succession for the present. The Queen of England once more took up the Archduke, and gave out unhesitatingly that she had quite made up her mind to marry him.

But such futile dust-throwing was quite in the order of things, and the old tricks did very little harm to Mary now. People had got to understand that Elizabeth would neither marry nor declare a successor if she could help it, and the English Catholics were becoming daily more convinced that if England were ever to revert to the faith, it must be by means of a widespread revolt, supported from abroad, and headed by a popular leader who could command such support. After Darnley's inept vagaries and vacillations it was evident that he was useless for such a purpose, and there only remained Mary. Of this she received full assurance both from the English Catholics and from Rome and Spain during the last few months of 1566,[331] and it was not until she knew that she would receive the same help without Darnley as with him that she abandoned him to his enemies.

On the very day that Darnley fled from Stirling to his father's castle at Glasgow (24th December 1566) Mary signed the pardon of Morton and all the Rizzio murderers. Even the most brutal of them all—with the exception, perhaps, of George Douglas—Andrew Ker of Faldonside, was forgiven.[332] All of them were free to come to Scotland, and if they could, or would, to sate their vengeance on the miserable simpleton who had betrayed them. He stayed sick in Glasgow, whilst Mary, free now even from the overlooking of Murray, who was entertaining Bedford at St. Andrews, stayed for a week or so at Drummond Castle, Tullibardine, and Callander, in complete aban- donment to her love for Bothwell.[333] Mary must have known, in effect, that her husband was doomed. She had ceased to feel any affection for him; his removal, she had now satisfied herself, would not injure her political aims, but rather the contrary. There had been some plausible excuse for her mar- riage with Darnley, even before she conceived any passion for him; and if he had been a good partner and a stable character he might have helped her powerfully with the English Catholics. But what possible pretext could there be for Mary's attachment to Bothwell, other than her passion for him? He was a recently married man, whose close association with her could only tend to her personal discredit; he was disliked by the Scottish nobles, who would naturally be alienated from the Queen by the favour she extended to him; he was a Protestant, and as such would deprive Mary of that which she had striven for so long, namely, the support of the English Catholics and of Spain; he was a determined enemy to England, and would arouse the opposition of Elizabeth and her friends. He had, in fact, hardly a recom- mendation as a source of political strength to Mary, either as a minister or as a husband; and only personal and passing infatuation for him could have blinded so able and ambitious a stateswoman as Mary to the fatal sacrifice she was making in taking him to her arms.

Rumours came to her of evil designs on the part of Darnley and his father upon her child or herself; and even from abroad warnings reached her of impending dangers from the same quarter. According to one story, when Mary sent a messenger to Glasgow to offer to visit her husband in his sickness, the latter gave a reply, to the effect that she must please herself: 'but this much ye shall declare unto her, that I wish Stirling to be Jedburgh, and Glasgow to be Hermitage, and I the Earl of Bothwell as I lie here, and then I doubt not but she would be quickly with me undesired.'[334] That such a message was really delivered would appear improbable, in view of Mary's travelling to Glasgow immediately afterwards, and Darnley's reconciliation with her on her arrival; but the fact of its being set forth by Darnley's father, whilst yet the events were recent, proves that at this time, the middle of January 1567, the amours of Mary and Bothwell were fairly well known, and that one other, and a crowning reason for discontent was believed in by the Lennoxes, which would justify the evil designs said to be harboured by Darnley and his father against the Queen.

Mary carried her infant from Stirling to Edinburgh on the 14th January. About the 19th, on the eve of her departure to stay with her sick husband, she was visited by Archibald Douglas, the cousin of Morton, who since his return to Scotland had been staying at his cousin's (William Douglas's) house of Whittinghame. Archibald's message was a strange one. It was to the effect that Bothwell and Lethington had visited Morton at Whittinghame, to ask him to join them in the conspiracy to kill Darnley, and that he had consented to do so, if the Queen would give him a signed warrant acquiescing in the act. We need not suppose that Douglas put it thus bluntly to Mary. It is almost certain that he would not do so; but, however he put it, Mary at once, and in accordance with all the rules of the kingly tradition, refused to give her signature, or even to discuss the matter at all.[335] But though she refused, and Morton consequently declined to sign the murder bond, as also did Murray with his usual cleverness in avoiding personal responsibility, the fact of the message from Morton being delivered proves that when Mary started the next day, 20th January, for Glasgow, she knew that an association of some of her nobles existed, whose object was the murder of her husband.[336] But she went, nevertheless, to bring him from the security of his father's castle and the Lennox followers to a place where none could stand between him and those she knew were pledged to murder him.

The interminable wrangle as to the genuineness or otherwise of the compromising letters found opportunely in the casket taken by Dalgleish from Edinburgh Castle seems to lose its importance beside these unquestioned facts. If Mary wrote every line of the letters, it would prove that she was a heartless, lascivious wanton, who had forgotten mercy and humanity in her adulterous passion; but it would not make her one whit more morally guilty of Darnley's death than we know her to have been from the irresistible logic of facts and probabilities. It must be admitted, in extenuation, that, even if she had wished to do so, she could not for very long have prevented the removal of the man who was in everybody's way, and who had succeeded in alienating every individual interest. But it is equally evident that she did not try, her main object being to avoid the personal compromise of herself in the matter.[337] Before she started for Glasgow Mary wrote to Archbishop Beaton in Paris, a letter full of resentment and bitterness towards the man she was about to betray. 'Always we perceive him occupied and busy enough to have inquisition of our doings, which, God willing, shall aye be such as none shall have occasion to be offended with them, or to report of us any ways but honourably: howsoever, he his father and their fautors speak, who we know lack no goodwill to make us have ado, if their power be equivalent to their minds.'[338]

As Mary rode towards Glasgow she was met four miles from that place by Darnley's gentleman, Crawford, who had come to conduct her to the castle. On the way Crawford presumed to say, on his master's behalf, that it was not pride but bodily illness that had prevented the consort from coming to meet and conduct her; and also because he did not dare to venture into her presence after the hard words she spoke to his servant Cunningham at Stirling. Mary's reply was haughty and repellant. 'There is no recipe against fear,' she said; 'he would not be afraid if he were not culpable'; and when Crawford replied that Darnley only wished that the secrets of every creature's heart were written on their faces, the Queen turned angrily to him, and asked if he had been instructed to say anything else. 'No, your Majesty,' he replied. 'Then hold your peace,' said Mary.

Bothwell himself appears to have ridden with the Queen out of Edinburgh, accompanying her until the next day, 21st January;[339] and late in the evening of that day she probably arrived at her destination. Lennox was ill and in disgrace, with good reason, and did not see the Queen; whilst Darnley was still in bed, but convalescent, apparently very weak, and an uninviting object to look upon, disfigured, as he must have been, at that stage of his malady. There was little demonstration of affection on the part of Mary as she entered. What was the meaning, she asked him, of his letters, complaining of the cruelty of 'some' people? He had good cause to complain, he replied, as she would admit when she was well advised. Then he whimpered that she was the cause of his illness. 'You ask me what I mean by the cruelty specified in my letters. It proceedeth from you only, who will not accept my offers and repentance.' He knew he had acted badly in some things, he said. But he pleaded his youth, and reminded her that she had forgiven others for worse things than he had been guilty of. 'You will say that ye have forgiven me divers times.' But he had lacked counsel, he pleaded, and though he had fallen twice or thrice, yet he was repentant now, and had been chastised. 'If I have made any fail, that ye but think a fail, howsoever it be, I crave your pardon, and protest that I shall never fail again. I desire no other thing but that we may be together as husband and wife, and if ye will not consent, I desire never to rise forth of this bed.'

And so, tearfully, the poor wretch maundered on. God knows, he said, how he had been punished for worshipping his wife as he had done. If she had only let him come to her and tell his grievances frankly, he would never make a confidant of any one else. But he had been obliged by her coldness to keep his troubles in his own breast, and this had brought him to his present state. Mary replied that this attitude of his was seemly; she was sorry for his illness, and would seek a remedy as soon as she might. 'But why did you want to sail away in the English ship?' she asked. He denied that he really meant to go, but said he had good reason for going, seeing how badly he had been treated. Then she opened up another rankling wound. How about Heigate's story that Darnley had learned that the lords at Craigmillar had proposed a plan to her, at her own instance, for his capture, which, however, she had refused to sign? 'Well,' replied Darnley, 'I was told so by the Laird of Minto,' but, he continued, he could not think that his own wife would do him harm, if others would; and he wanted to be near her, but she always found, he said, some pretext for retiring to her own apartments, 'and would never abide with him past two hours at once.' Mary was still cold and distant, and Darnley began to grumble again. Why had she brought a horse litter with her? he asked; to which she replied that she had brought it that he might travel the easier. He did not want to travel in such cold weather, he said. He was too ill to do so. She would take him to Craigmillar, so that she might be near him and their child, she replied. Well, 'if they might be at bed and board as husband and wife, and she to leave him no more, he would go where she pleased—without this he would not go.' He must be purged of his sickness before they came together, said Mary.

She then asked if he bore ill-will to any one. No, he replied, he 'hated no man, and loved all alike.' The next question, like the former one put by the Queen, seems to prove that she was trying to discover if he had any grudge against Bothwell. 'How do you like Lady Reres?' to which Darnley gave an unsympathetic but non-committal reply; and then, harking back to his own safety, he prayed his wife not to 'move any against him, as he would stir none against her. Let them work together, or it would be bad for both. It was rather late in the day for him to urge this, as no doubt Mary thought, for she told him that it was he who had been in fault, which was quite true. And so, with this half-reconciliation, it was settled that Darnley should leave Glasgow with his wife. He and his friends in Glasgow were deeply distrustful still. 'They thought he was going more as a prisoner than a husband,' the only safeguard being the word of the Queen, which, if they had noticed it, even as recorded by themselves, was not very emphatic or binding. 'Yet he would put himself in her hands, if she cut his throat,' replied Darnley to his friends.[340]

The long and important letter (No. 2), said to have been written by Mary from Glasgow to Bothwell, gives an account of this interview strikingly similar to that given by Darnley to Crawford. The resemblance is too close to be accidental, and would seem to indicate that this portion at least of the letter was added subsequently by a forger. The consideration of whether the whole letter was a forgery or not is outside the scope of this book,[341] though I may express my own belief that Mary did write a letter of some sort to Bothwell at the time. There are many passages in the letter as published which could only serve the object of the forgers—namely, a desire to inculpate Mary in the murder. 'He would not let me go, but would have me watch with him. I made as though I thought all to be true, that I would think upon it, and have excused myself from sitting up with him this night, for he sayeth that he sleepeth not. You have never heard him speak better nor more humbly; and if I had not proof of his heart of wax, and that mine were not as a diamond, no stroke but coming from your hand could make me but to have pity on him. But fear not, for the plan shall continue to death. Remember also, in recompense thereof, not to suffer yours to be won by that false race that would do no less to yourself. I think they (*i.e.* Darnley and Lady Bothwell) have been at school together. He hath always the tear in his eye. He saluteth every man, even to the meanest, and maketh much of them, that they may take pity of him.'

If these words and others hinting at Darnley's danger from Mary and Bothwell were written by the Queen herself, there would have been no need for the forgers to have added the comparatively innocent account of her interview with her husband. The passage about 'cursed be this pocky fellow that troubleth me so much,' containing also offensive allusions to the poor creature's state, are certainly not such as Mary would be likely to write, and I am inclined to believe that the letter was concocted out of a much more cautiously worded epistle, by the aid of the notes or headings that are now incorporated in it. Even if we eliminate this, the most damning of the letters produced against Mary, and regard it as a forgery throughout, my contention is that her moral guilt for the murder remains the same. She knew that the lords were banded together to kill her husband, and she brought him out of safety, as she alone was able to do, and placed him within reach of his destroyers. He was doomed in any case; and her complicity, tacit or overt, in his death would have had little or no influence in her political position but for the jealousy of the nobles at her connection with Bothwell, and their fear of the Queen whilst he was by her side.

Mary had intended carrying her husband to Craigmillar. He was sensitive as to being seen in his disfigured condition. He wore a silken covering over his face, and wished to take a course of baths before appearing publicly. The Lennox people at Glasgow objected to Craigmillar, and urged that the consort should be taken to Holyrood. This would not suit the conspirators, and it was suggested that Hamilton House, just outside the walls of Edinburgh, where the University now stands, would be a fitting place. It was said that that side of the city was more salubrious than the low-lying palace of Holyrood. But the wicked old Archbishop Hamilton, and his nephew Lord Claude, were living there at the time, and would not vacate it for the accommodation of the enemy and rival of their house; besides which, according to at least one confession, the Archbishop was well aware of the murder plot, and would hardly relish the idea of his brother's palace being blown up.

Either for this reason or some other, Bothwell and his accomplice, Sir James Balfour, had during Mary's absence in Glasgow thought of a much more convenient place for the committal of the crime. The ruined Dominican church, standing in a field adjoining Hamilton House, possessed, still attached to it, the old conventual quadrangle of lodgings, of which the principal and most habitable was a small house abutting on the town-wall, through which a door led into a narrow by-lane. The house, built over an arched crypt, contained two principal rooms, both very small, one over the other.[342] When Darnley found himself taken into this house instead of to Hamilton House he appears to have demurred, but his objection was overcome. He was installed there on the 31st January 1567, being lodged in the upper room, which had been sumptuously furnished for him, the lower or ground floor room underneath being similarly fitted as a bedroom for the Queen, in which room she slept on the Tuesday and Friday, the 4th and 7th February.[343] There was a door leading direct from this lower room into the old quadrangle, and another into the enclosed garden at the side, where Mary, we are told, walked and sang with the saintly Lady Reres.

From the moment Darnley entered the semideserted quadrangle the shadow of the tragedy closed in over his head. Bothwell and Sir James Balfour obtained duplicate keys of all the doors: it matters not whether Paris filched them or Sir James had them cut—both statements are made. We may put aside, too, the confused and mutually contradictory minute details of which Paris, long afterwards, was so lavish in sight of the rack. We know that the men who signed the bond were Bothwell, his brother-in-law Huntly, Argyle, Lethington, and probably Sir James Balfour. Morton and Murray confessedly knew all about it, but were too cautious to commit themselves, carefully withholding their signatures, and providing *alibis* for themselves.[344]

On Thursday or Friday, 6th and 7th February, Bothwell enlisted the men who were to perform his part of the task. According to their own confessions they were naturally loath to engage in such a deed, but were overborne by their master. In the meanwhile Mary was treating her convalescent husband with unwonted kindness, visiting him daily; and on Friday, 7th February, the doomed man wrote a cheerful little letter to his father, thanking God for his wife's renewed love for him, 'who hath all this while, and yet doth, use herself like a natural and loving wife.'[345]

On the following day, Saturday, Mary having slept at Kirk-o'-Field on Friday, she had her velvet bed taken away from the lower room and a poorer bed put into its place,[346] saying that the state bed should serve as a renewed bridal bed for her and her reconciled husband. One note of alarm was sounded in the midst of this harmony. Lord Robert Stuart, Mary's base brother, Earl of Orkney, seems to have whispered to Darnley that the latter was in danger and should fly. Instead of doing so, he weakly told Mary. Upon this is founded by Mary's enemies a story to the effect that she urged Bothwell thereupon to bring Lord Robert and Darnley together, and raise a quarrel between them, so that Darnley might be killed without compromising any one very seriously. On Sunday night Mary stayed late at Kirk-o'-Field, affectionately chatting with her husband; but in the course of their loving talk she dropped a sinister hint that just a year had passed since Rizzio's murder; and when she had gone Darnley, in the hearing of his pages, expressed his uneasiness that she had recollected it, for he at least had not forgotten her threat over Rizzio's grave. But by and by a message was brought to her that she had promised to honour with her presence that night at Holyrood the marriage-feast of one of her French servants, Bastien, and a favourite maid who had been a confidante of her first amours with Bothwell. Murray told Guzman afterwards that she had petted and fondled Darnley on that last night, and had given him a ring as a token before she left him for ever, and then, turning away, she traversed by torchlight the quiet streets of her capital to the wedding-feast. But of the nuptial gaiety she soon was tired, and went to her own apartments and to such rest as might be vouchsafed to her. Whilst she was charming her husband with her sweetness in the upper chamber, Bowton, Ormiston, Hay of Talla, and perhaps another of Bothwell's men, piled the powder in the lower room where the Queen had slept; and when Darnley, having sung a psalm and drunk a cup of wine to his servants, one of whom only, Taylor, slept in his chamber, had retired to his fine velvet bed, wrapped in a velvet and sable gown, all was ready for the tragedy, and many ears awaited the coming boom that would tell of murder.

Those who afterwards related the miserable story were mostly Bothwell's men, for Murray's only need was to inculpate Mary and her lover, and all other accomplices were spared by him out of policy. But there must have been at least two parties besides those who laid the powder. Lethington and Huntly must have had separate gangs to do other work—to guard the approaches, to fire the train—and probably the Douglases, under the worthy parson and judge Sir Archibald, who doubtless strangled the consort and his page Taylor before the explosion, and carried the bodies across the back lane to an adjoining field, though why they did so is not clear. Bothwell, leaving the wedding-feast for his own apartments, changed his velvets and satins for rougher garb before going to witness the last scene of his plot; but some of the gentlemen who went with him, Archibald Douglas especially, still wore their velvet shoes, one of Archibald's being lost in his flight from the scene.

Suddenly, at two o'clock in the morning of Monday, 11th February, a great shock rent the air of sleeping Edinburgh, and awoke the frightened townsmen. Those living in the Cowgate, hard by, rushed to their windows, and some of them saw, sallying from the narrow wynd leading from the Kirk-o'-Field to the Cowgate, a party of thirteen armed men hurrying away. 'Traitors! traitors! what have ye done?' cried the citizens after the retreating murderers. An affrighted woman, rushing from the gates of Hamilton House, caught one of a flying party by his silk cloak, beseeching him to say what had happened, but he shook her off roughly and fled. What Mary thought when the reverberation that told her that she was a widow shook the ancient palace in which she lay, none now may tell. If she could have foreseen the extent to which those who had promoted the deed would have sought to place upon her and her paramour the whole of the odium of it, she might well have wished that she had been included in the holocaust. The poor, foolish lad—he was less than twenty-one—whose pride and ineptitude had made him unfit for the great task he should have shared with her, had paid dearly for his insufficiency. Mary was free again to make, if she could, a powerful political match that should help her to realise her life-dream; or she was free to become the slave of a passing passion, to take the unhappy course that should unite the strongest in her realm against her, and drag her down to ruin and disgrace. For once passion in her was stronger than politics, and she fell.

X

INFATUATION AND DISGRACE

IN THEIR HURRIED RETURN THROUGH THE NETHERBOW GATE after the explosion had awakened the town, and in passing the sentries at the gates of Holyrood, Bothwell and several of his followers had been recognised. When half an hour later he feigned to be aroused out of his sleep to hear the news, and led an armed body of men to the seat of the crime, in order to warn curious citizens against near approach to the spot where the dead bodies of the king and his page still lay, men, haggard with horror as the dawn lit up the ruin around, looked askance and shrank away as the Earl of Bothwell passed, and his name in bated whispers already trembled upon blanching lips. The Queen sat 'sorrowful and quiet' in a darkened room where none might see the grief with which she was supposed to be prostrated; but before the morning passed she was well enough to confer with Bothwell and Lethington, the two men who had taken the lead at the conference of Craigmillar when Darnley's removal had been proposed to her.

The first care was to prevent the odium of the crime from falling upon the Queen personally, and to avoid, so far as might be, any coolness with the Catholic interests in consequence of it. Beaton's courier from France arrived on the day of the murder, bringing warning of the mischief said to be plotting against Mary herself from Darnley and his friends, and a hasty answer by swift courier left Edinburgh before sunset giving Mary's (or rather Lethington's) account of what had happened. 'The matter is horrible and strange, as we believe the like was never heard in any country.' 'By whom it was done, or in what manner, it appears not yet. We doubt not but, according to the diligence which our council has begun already to use, the certainty of all shall be known shortly, and the same discovered, which we wot God will never suffer to lie hid; we hope to punish the same with such rigour as shall serve as an example . . . for all ages to come';[347] and then the hypocritical opinion is expressed that the intention of the conspirators had been to sacrifice the Queen as well as her husband; but that by God's special providence she had, 'by very chance,' not slept there that night, and had so escaped. She never had, as we know, any intention of sleeping at Kirk-o'-Field on the night of the crime.

But people in Edinburgh were not all influenced by diplomatic fictions; and by word of mouth there went flying to all quarters the rumours that the Queen's favourite, the Earl of Bothwell, was the chief regicide, and that Mary herself was a party to the murder. The Spanish ambassador in London even, on the very day he heard the news, sounded the note of distrust against Mary; and Moret the Savoyard envoy, who left Edinburgh only thirty-six hours after the crime, carried to London and to the Catholic courts still graver suspicions of her.[348] It is evident, from all the remarks in continental

Catholic quarters, that Mary's complicity was believed in by her friends; but it is equally evident that they did not intend to allow their suspicions, or even the certainty, to disturb the political relations which bound them to her.

When Elizabeth gave an audience to Guzman, ten days after the murder, she feigned deep sorrow; 'but she could not,' she said, 'believe that the Queen of Scotland was to blame for so dreadful a thing, notwithstanding the murmurs of the people.' Of course the Spaniard agreed with her—although we know by his letters to Philip that he himself suspected Mary. The rumours, he said, were set afloat in order to estrange her from the English succession, and to favour the Puritans and Katharine Grey. 'I told her (Elizabeth) that certain persons were not without suspicion that the whole affair might have been arranged by those who wished the Queen of Scotland should be married in France.' Thus, almost before Darnley's body was cold, the diplomatic intrigues for the disposal of Mary in marriage were begun again by people who gravely suspected her to be a murderess.[349] The distracted Lady Lennox had no need to respect diplomatic convention, and loudly proclaimed that her boy had been sacrificed by his wife. The Protestants in England, influenced of course by the feeling in Scotland, were of the same opinion. 'The (English) Catholics are divided: the friends of the King holding with the Queen's guilt, and her adherents to the contrary.'[350] This, be it recollected, is the testimony sent in the strictest secrecy of cipher by the Spanish ambassador in London, Mary's greatest well-wisher, to King Philip, her principal supporter.

Meanwhile in Edinburgh the sky darkened over Mary. Bothwell, at whom all fingers were pointing as the chief murderer, was ever by her side. Instead of staying in seclusion, as was the custom with widows, and as she had done for four weeks when Francis died, she attended the wedding ceremony of her waitingmaid, Margaret Carwood, on Tuesday, whilst yet Darnley's body remained unburied in the care of the treacherous groom Sandy Durham, at a humble house near the spot where it had been discovered; and after huddling the corpse at night, with no ceremony, into the grave of Rizzio on the 15th February, the bereaved widow hurried off to Seton, for change and relaxation, accompanied by Bothwell, Huntly, Argyle, and Lethington,[351] and guarded by Captain Cullen, whose hands had drawn tight the fatal napkin that strangled her husband.

Deeper and deeper grew the indignation of the people of Edinburgh at the slackness of the court in the prosecution of the murderers. It is true that two days after the deed a proclamation was issued in Mary's name, expressing abhorrence of the crime and offering a reward of £2,000, a free pardon, and a life-annuity to any person who would discover the criminals; but none dared to claim the reward openly, as had been foreseen by those who offered it. Every night anonymous placards appeared on the Market Cross and in other public places, even on the very gates of Holyrood, denouncing Bothwell, Balfour, Chambers, Ormiston, Bastien, Joseph Rizzio,[352] and others of Bothwell's or the Queen's underlings as the chief murderers. Portraits of Bothwell, and even of the Queen, with incriminating inscriptions, were spread broadcast; and the Protestant preachers were ceaseless in their hints from the pulpit at the criminality of the highest people in the land. In vain Bothwell rode with fifty men-at-arms clattering up the High Street, and threatened to wash his hands in the blood of any man who dared to accuse him; but when Murray, brother of the Laird of Tullibardine, avowed the authorship of one paper, and offered to sustain the accusations in it by ordeal of combat, he was proclaimed a traitor and silenced.

Poor old Lennox clamoured to the Queen and council that the persons thus publicly denounced as his son's murderers should be brought to justice. Elizabeth and Catharine de Medici almost indignantly urged Mary in scandalised letters, and by special envoys, to insist, for the sake of her own impugned honour, upon having due investigation made; and at last, on the 23rd March 1567, the Queen wrote to Lennox, after many previous subterfuges, promising him that the persons accused by him should be brought to their trial before a special assize during the coming parliament.[353] Lennox at once accused Bothwell and others; but when the day for the trial came (12th April) the accomplices of the accused sat upon the bench, with Argyle as their president. Edinburgh was crammed with Bothwell's rough borderers and hired bravoes, whilst Lennox was forbidden to bring with him more than six men-at-arms out of the three thousand he had at his bidding. He came not at all to this mockery of justice, but by proxy protested against the finding of a court so convened and so conducted. Of course Bothwell was 'cleared and acquitted, by some for fear, some for favour, and the greatest part in expectation of advantage.'[354] This way being assolsied, he remained still the greatest favourite at court.'[355]

But acquitted he was, and a decree was issued imposing the death penalty upon any man who should see a slanderous placard and not destroy it; whilst Bothwell himself challenged to mortal combat any who questioned his innocence.[356] The consideration which will occur to the reader is that, whilst Darnley was really a Catholic, looking to the papal party alone for support, and all his principal murderers were Protestants, the outcry and scandal that were raised both in Scotland and England about his murder came almost entirely from the Protestant party. The Catholics, as we have seen, though some were swept into the movement against Bothwell, were disposed to stand by Mary through thick and thin, let her be guilty or otherwise. This fact marks the purely political character of the agitation against her for her complicity in the murder. We must admit that the Catholics as such were no more likely to condone murder than the Protestants were, and yet we see that Catholics who believed Mary to be, at least, a consenting party to the crime, were still desirous of using her for their ends as if nothing had happened; whilst the Protestants, even some of those concerned in the murder, during the rest of Mary's life never ceased to make capital out of it, to her detriment and to their own advantage. The loud indignation at the murder expressed both in Scotland and abroad was, indeed, to a great degree artificial and political, and in all probability would have been easily overcome by the usual political means but for the jealousy aroused by Mary's insensate passion for Bothwell. This it was that turned against her, it must be confessed with an utter want of chivalry, the men who, like Murray, Huntly, Morton, and Lethington, were more deeply compromised than she was in the crime for which they endeavoured to make her alone suffer.

The dastardly meanness, of Murray especially, in seizing upon the opportunity presented to him by Mary's weakness, to drive home to her alone the charge of murder in order to serve his own ambition, was satanic. All that might tend to inculpate others in the crime, except Bothwell, who was out of his power, was carefully eliminated from the evidence produced at York and subsequently published to the world. Lethington and Morton, Huntly and Balfour, and of course the stainless Murray himself, were shielded; but all that existed, or could be invented or forged, to blacken Mary's consenting share of the crime, was made the most of by the leaders of the Protestant party; not necessarily because they abhorred murder more than others, for principal agitators were quite as guilty of it as Mary herself, but because they saw in it a chance of thus defeating the objects which they knew she cherished; and she, by her blind, unworthy love, had, for a time at least, lost the friends who otherwise would have stood by her.

Mary's infatuation for Bothwell was boundless. The faithful Mar was deprived of the keepership of Edinburgh Castle in favour of a creature of the Queen's lover. The castle of Blackness and the Inch were surrendered to Bothwell, who also obtained the superiority of Leith, which ensured him, if necessary, a retreat by sea. Jewels, church embroideries, splendid furs, formerly belonging to her mother; nay, even poor Darnley's finest garments, were made over by Mary to her lover.[357] The objections justly urged against much of the text of the Casket Letters cannot with equal force be opposed to the sonnets that accompanied them. They appear, to me at least, to bear upon them undoubted signs of authenticity, and if they present a true picture of her feelings towards Bothwell when she wrote them, the favours crowded upon the earl by his sovereign are more than explained. She appears to have been self-tortured with jealousy, and reveals herself in one hundred and sixty lines of passionate verse as a woman fiercely and insatiably pursuing the lukewarm object of her desire, at one moment bewailing the vast sacrifice she has made for his doubtful love, at the next protesting her abject submission if only he will be faithful to her. Poor Lady Bothwell, who appears to have been of an accommodating disposition, fares badly at the Queen's hands; and nothing more clearly shows the handiwork of a desperate woman in love than the lines devoted to Bothwell's lawful wife. No forger, especially if he were a man, would have put so much gall in his pen when referring to her as is contained in several of Mary's sonnets.

'She for her honour's sake obeyeth you—
I, obeying you, my dishonour seek.
No wife, alas! am I, as she to you;
Yet shall she not excel me, e'en in this.
Constant she be, for profit to herself,
For great her honour is to rule your state,
Whilst my dear love with scorn alone be paid;
Yet shall she pass me not in duty leal.
Tranquil she sleeps and dreams not of your ill,
Whilst I in torment toss, lest evil fall.
She did enjoy you with her friends' consent;
I, in despite of mine, will love you still.
And yet, dear heart! my loyalty you doubt,
And firm assurance bear that she be true.'

Her utter abandonment and subjection to her love are well expressed in the following sonnet:—

'Mon amour croist, et plus en croistra;
Tant que je vivrai, et tiendra à grandeur.
Tant seulement d'avoir part en ce cœur,
Vers qui, en fin, mon amour paroitra
Si tres á clair, que jamais n'en doutra.
Pour luy je veux rechercher la grandeur,
Et faira tant qu'en vray connoistra,
Que je náy bien heur, ni contentement,
Qu'a obeyr et servir loyammant.
Pour luy j'attends toute bonne fortune;
Pour luy je veux garder santé et vie;
Pour luy tout vertu de suivre j'ay envie,
Et sans changer me trouvera toute vie.'

In another of her sonnets she seems to hint, as inimical forgers certainly would not have done, at violence having been used by Bothwell in his *first* intercourse with her:—

> 'Pour luy aussi, je jete mainte larme,
>
> Premier quand il se fit de ce corps possesseur;
>
> De quel, alors, il n'avoyt pas le cœur.
>
> Puis me donna un autre dure alarme
>
> Quand il versa de son sang maint drasme.358
>
> Dans de grief il me vint laisser doleur,
>
> Qui me pensa oster la vie, et la frayeur
>
> De perdre lá la seule rempart qui m'arme.
>
> Pour luy depuis j'ay meprise l'honneur,
>
> Ce qui nous peut seul provoir de bonheur.
>
> Pour luy j'ay hasardé grandeur et conscience;
>
> Pour luy tous mes parents jay quisté et amys;
>
> Et tous aultres respects sont apart mis.
>
> Brief, de vous seul, je cherche alliance.'

In this poem, it will be noticed, Mary asserts that, until Bothwell had possessed himself of her by violence, she had not been in love with him; but that from that time she had, for his sake, disregarded honour, the sole source of happiness, had risked the loss of her great position, had imperilled her conscience, abandoned her friends and kin, and had cast aside all considerations but her love. It is perfectly true that she had done so, and with her eyes open to the sacrifice she was making. Carried away by the passion with which Bothwell had been able to inspire her, perhaps for the first time in her life, she was ready temporarily to place in the background even the great aims that had thitherto been the absorbing interest of her existence. Later, as we shall see, she endeavoured to pick up the broken thread; but during the spring of 1567 she disregarded all things and considerations for the overpowering passion that dominated her.

As Bothwell rode on Darnley's charger out of the gates of Holyrood to stand his mock-trial (12th April), followed by thousands of armed horsemen to overawe possible opposition, Mary waved him a smiling farewell from her window; and people were already saying in the town that the twain would be married notwithstanding Bothwell's wedded wife.[359] When he had been duly absolved from the accusation against him, he carried before the Queen her crown and sceptre at the opening, and the sword of honour back to the palace after the closing of parliament; and the Border earl then gave to the nobles that famous supper-party at Ainslie's tavern. Bothwell was irresistible. The rest of the nobles had received their rewards for conniving at, or shutting their eyes to, Darnley's murder; Bothwell now claimed his guerdon, the hand of the Queen. His men-at-arms swarmed in the town, the fortresses were in his hands; and, either by persuasion or threats, he induced the whole of the lords present, except the Earl of Eglinton, who 'slipped away,' to sign a bond pledging themselves, with their bodies, gear, and kin, to defend his innocence and maintain his quarrel. 'And as her Majesty is now destitute of a husband, in which solitary sort the common-weal cannot permit her Highness to continue, if it should please her so far to humble herself by taking one of her own born subjects, and marry the said earl, they will maintain and fortify him against all that would hinder or disturb the said marriage as common enemies, and therein bestow their lives and goods, as they shall answer to God' (19th April 1567). Murray had with his usual prudence left for France and avoided the trap, though it was afterwards alleged that he signed the bond; but the Earls of Argyle, Huntly, Cassilis, Morton, Sutherland, Rothes, Glencairn, and Caithness, and all the bishops and barons present, pledged themselves to this,[360] 'so far as it may please our sovereign lady to allow.' We shall see later how Mary, under different impulses, first accepted[361] and later repudiated this bond, as she did Bothwell himself.

At this period, at least, just before the comedy of her abduction, the evidence points strongly to the probability that she was even more eager for the marriage than the proposed bridegroom. Rigid Protestants, untouched by courtly effeminacy, like Kirkcaldy of Grange, were horrified at the scandal, and already saw the inevitability of an armed struggle in the near future to secure the punishment of those who had committed or condoned regicide. There was no religious reason for a Protestant rising, for great concessions to the reformers had been made by Mary and the Parliament just closed. To their last demand alone, that Darnley's murderers should be punished, Mary returned an angry refusal. It was the Queen's ostentatious favour to a murderer that was arming the feeling of Protestants against her much more than the murder itself, which, if the actual perpetrators had lain low or fled, would soon have been forgotten. Kirkcaldy, on the 20th April, writes to Bedford asking what help they (the Protestants) may hope for from Elizabeth, who had treated them so badly the last time they rose. The Queen (Mary), he says, intends to take her child out of the hands of the Earl of Mar (Erskine), 'and put him in Bothwell's keeping, who murdered his father.' Kirkcaldy is sure Mary will marry Bothwell, 'for she said she cared not to lose France, England, and her own country for him, and will go with him to the world's end in a white petticoat, rather than leave him. Yea, she is so past all shame that she hath caused make an Act of Parliament against all that set up any writing that speaks anything of him. Whatever is unhonest reigns presently at court.'[362]

On the 24th April, four days later, Kirkcaldy again wrote to Bedford. 'Bothwell's wife is going to part with her husband.' 'The Queen rode to Stirling this last Monday, and is to return on Thursday. I doubt not that ye have heard Bothwell hath gathered many of his friends; some say to ride in Liddesdale; but I believe it not, for he is minded to meet the Queen this day (Thursday) and to take her by the way, and bring her to Dunbar. Judge ye if it be with her will or not! But ye will hear more at length on Friday or Saturday.'[363]

Thus we see that people in Edinburgh knew before the event the purpose of Bothwell to abduct the Queen, and, supposing for a moment that the latter had not connived at her seizure, she might have escaped it by staying at Stirling or proceeding to Edinburgh by another road. As Kirkcaldy predicted, whilst Mary was returning from visiting her child at Stirling, and on arriving at Almond Bridge, between Linlithgow and Edinburgh, six miles from the latter place, attended by Huntly, Lethington, and Sir James Melville, with a small escort, she found Bothwell with a strong body of eight hundred horsemen blocking the way. Seizing her bridle, he led her with him to the stronghold of Dunbar, which had just been given to him; and as Captain Blackater, one of Darnley's murderers, took prisoner Sir James Melville, he whispered to him that the thing was being done by the Queen's consent.[364]

Riding, surrounded by Border ruffians, to Dunbar, Lethington alone of all the party had cause to fear, for Bothwell distrusted and hated him. He was too clever, and knew too much, to suit either the Queen or her lover at this juncture; and shortly afterwards he would have fallen to Bothwell's dagger in the Queen's chamber had not Mary stepped between them.[365] Lethington, Huntly, and Melville were released from Dunbar the next day, but Mary, in appearance a prisoner, remained in the hands of Bothwell. That she was really a consenting party was the general opinion at the time, both amongst the friends of Mary and her foes. On the 26th April honest Kirkcaldy writes: 'This Queen will never cease till she has wrecked all the honest men of this realm. She was minded to cause Bothwell to ravish her, to the end that she may the sooner end the marriage which she promised before the murder of her husband.'[366] Drury, writing on the following day, expresses a similar opinion. Guzman the Spanish ambassador thought so too. He wrote to King Philip (3rd May 1567)[367] that when the Queen's escort displayed an intention of defending her against capture, 'the Queen stopped them, saying she was ready to go with Bothwell wherever he wished, rather than bloodshed and death should result. She arrived at Dunbar at midnight. . . . Some say she will marry him . . . as they are informed by the highest men in the country who follow Bothwell. They are convinced of this, both because of the favour the Queen has shown him, and because he has the national forces in her hands. Although the Queen sent secretly to the governor of the town of Dunbar to sally with his troops and release her, it is believed that the whole affair has been arranged, so that, if anything comes of the marriage, the Queen may make out that she was forced into it. This Queen (Elizabeth) is greatly scandalised at the business, and related it to me. I also heard it . . . from the man who brought the news, who is a good Catholic and an intimate acquaintance of mine.' Thus both Mary's friends and her enemies believed that she and Bothwell understood each other, though the Catholic party, perceiving that their opponents were busy turning the rumours about her to political account, very soon began to attribute the spreading of rumours themselves to party rancour, and alleged that they were deliberately made the most of by Cecil's orders[368] where they tended to Mary's discredit.

Mary returned to Edinburgh from Dunbar on the 3rd May. The high-handed proceeding of carrying her off, ostensibly without her consent, had aroused great indignation in the country; and many of the nobles who up to that period had seconded Bothwell's action turned violently against him, not really so much because they learned that, during her week of seclusion at Dunbar, the Queen had promised to marry him, as because they now saw that he aimed at a monopoly of power. At the time of the capture Mary had sent a message to the townspeople of Edinburgh ordering them to come to her rescue. But Dunbar was strong, and the burgesses of Edinburgh divided; and their half-hearted muster could do nothing effectual. Mary's attitude appears somewhat paradoxical in thus demanding aid if she consented to the abduction. But it must be remembered that it was of the first importance to her that she should be protected personally[369] against responsibility, particularly in sight of friends abroad; and the least she could do to keep up appearances, already gravely compromised, was to ask for aid, which she knew would be powerless if given. A pardon from her to Bothwell would, moreover, at any moment have absolved him from any blame that he might have incurred, and, as Buchanan points out, such a pardon would also have covered the accusations against him for the murder of Darnley.

There was another possible reason for Mary's connivance at her own abduction, namely, her hurry to marry the man with whom she was so madly in love. In the hearing of James Melville at Dunbar Bothwell boasted that he would marry the Queen, 'who would or who would not; yea, whether she would herself or not'; and, as Melville adds, 'the Queen could not but marry him, seeing that he had ravished her and lain with her against her will.'[370] It is probable that this latter statement may have been to some extent true, though the act must presumably have been committed some time before the abduction to Dunbar, apparently even before Darnley's death. Whenever it took place, and however far Mary may have resisted at the time, it was soon condoned by her. Contemporary public opinion was probably not far wrong when it ascribed the abduction to a desire on the part of Mary to avoid personal responsibility for past transgressions, and for the subsequent hasty marriage which she desired, or her condition rendered necessary.[371]

If the fifth and sixth casket letters be genuine, Mary's connivance in her abduction is proved by her written word; but again I prefer to rest the case upon her own actions rather than upon a disputed text, and, whatever may have been her motives, it is impossible to get away from the prevailing probability that Mary might, if she had pleased, have avoided capture, and from the conviction that her subsequent attitude towards her abductor was not that of a proud princess who had been imprisoned and outraged against her will.[372] On the 3rd May, the very day upon which Mary and Bothwell returned to Edinburgh, the collusive divorce between Bothwell and his wife was published by both churches, and on different grounds: the ineffable scoundrel Hamilton, Archbishop of St. Andrews, granting it—for a valuable consideration—on the allegation, that he knew to be false, that no papal dispensation[373] had been granted for it; and the Presbyterian jurisdiction dissolving the marriage on Lady Bothwell's petition, founded on the admitted adultery of her husband.

When Mary, with Bothwell by her side humbly leading her bridle, and surrounded by his spearmen ostentatiously unarmed, rode into Edinburgh Castle, now held in Bothwell's interest by his accomplice Sir James Balfour, the thunder of quickly coming contest rumbled around her. The lords had been at one with Bothwell so long as the question had been the removal of obnoxious Darnley; they had acquiesced even, more or less willingly, in the proposal for the Queen's marriage with their accomplice. But when the abduction showed them that the latter intended to use the marriage as a means of monopolising power and the Queen's influence, to the exclusion of his associates, then jealousy and self-interest rebelled against the union. Bothwell had been acceptable as an instrument, even as a political partner; but as an arrogant superior the lords could not tolerate him. The common people too, especially those of the capital, with whom Bothwell was intensely unpopular, added strength to the movement of the nobles to separate the Queen from her captor; and when Argyle, Morton, Athol, and Mar met at Stirling soon after Mary's capture, they had behind them practically the whole of the nobility except Crawford, Errol, and Huntly, Bothwell's complaisant brother-in-law.

JAMES, EARL OF BOTHWELL.
(Artist Unknown.)
Enlarged from a Reproduction in "The Stuarts" by J. J. Foster

At Stirling another bond was made, pledging them to liberate the Queen from Bothwell, to defend the child-prince in Stirling, whom they asserted Bothwell wished to kill,[374] and to punish the murderers of Darnley. As Morton and Argyle at least were accomplices in the latter crime, it may be taken that the inclusion of this item in their pledge was for the purpose of attracting public opinion in their favour, and to make Bothwell a scapegoat, he having been specially associated with the actual commission of the crime in the minds of the mass of the people. For their own sake, however, they could have had no real desire to bring him to justice, for in that case their own guilt would have come out; as indeed it did, to a great extent, in the last confessions of the subordinate actors, who were soon afterwards brought to the scaffold. To their respective estates the lords scattered to raise their retainers, except Mar, who guarded the prince at Stirling, whilst the Queen and her captor in Edinburgh strained every nerve in their warlike preparations to meet force with force. Demands for aid from the Protestant section of the lords flew daily to the English court, whilst de Croc, the French ambassador, made most of his opportunity to urge the nobles to look to France, the old friend of Scotland, to help them to liberate their Queen. De Croc even implored Mary herself to leave Bothwell and refuse to marry him, or she should have no friendship with his master Charles IX. But unhappy Mary had gone too far now to retreat. De Croc told the lords that 'she would give no ear to him,' and thenceforward he attached himself to them instead of to Mary, in the hope of obtaining for France the custody of the Prince. Melting her plate into ducats, even the great gold font sent by Elizabeth for the christening of James, raising loans in Edinburgh and mustering men-at-arms, the Queen and Bothwell organised their defence with energy. On their entry into the town Mary had formally pardoned her captor, and three days before the marriage she appeared publicly before the Lords of Session and assured them that she was a free agent. The lords, however, refused to consider her free, 'so long as she be in the said earl's company, albeit he may persuade her Majesty to say otherwise.'[375]

A few days after her return Mary ordered the banns of her marriage with Bothwell to be published according to law. John Craig, who held Knox's charge in his absence, at first indignantly refused; but being assured by the

Queen in writing that she was neither abducted nor a prisoner, and being demanded legally by both parties, he reluctantly and under protest published the banns of the ill-fated union at St. Giles on the 11th May. 'I took heaven to witness,' he says, 'that I abhorred and detested that marriage, as odious and scandalous to the world, and, seeing that the best part of the realm did approve of it, either by flattery or by their silence, I desired the faithful to pray earnestly that God would turn to the comfort of the realm what was done against reason and conscience.'[376] That no determined attempt was made by the lords to prevent the marriage by force, if they really believed that Mary was being compelled to marry under duress, is one of the most disgraceful details of the shameful episode. It is true that Bothwell held the fortresses and the stores of warlike material, but a general cry coming from a whole people against the outrage would have made even him hesitate before he went to the extreme of forcing the Queen to marry him against her will. That no demonstration of protest was raised, and no attempt made to disturb the ceremony, seems to prove, if further proof be needed, that the opinion of the people was that no compulsion was exercised by Bothwell, and that Mary was as anxious for the marriage as was her husband; and this view is certainly borne out by her own words. When the lords at Stirling wrote simply remonstrating with her against the proposed marriage, which, be it recollected, they had sworn to promote, she answered that 'it was true that she had been evil and strangely handled, but since so well used as she had no cause to complain; willing them (the lords) to quiet themselves.'[377] To this they replied that, unless she dismissed the soldiers who surrounded her, and admitted the nobles to attend her, they would not believe that her writings were spontaneous. This provides a key to the whole problem. They hated and feared Bothwell's monopoly of power more than the marriage.

In the meanwhile the unhappy Queen was already awakening to the fatal position into which she had been led. Once inside Edinburgh Castle, with only Bothwell, Huntly, and Lethington (the latter in hourly fear of death, pretending to side with the Queen's action, but betraying her the while), Mary found that Bothwell when out of the public eye was no longer a humble slave, but an overbearing and arrogant master. 'There are often jars between the Queen and the Duke,'[378] writes Drury to Cecil. 'There has been great unkindness between them for half a day. He is held the most jealous man that lives, and it is believed that they will not long agree after the marriage. . . . The Queen walking abroad will hang upon his arm'; and Sir William Drury's modesty is so shocked that he dares not repeat to Cecil what Lady Buccleugh says was the way she 'bred Bothwell's greatness with the Queen;[379] nor the speech of the Queen, nor of his unsatiateness towards women.' Bothwell was evidently a truculent, sensual tyrant, who watched Mary jealously, fearing treachery; whilst she, always in tears now, was wearing her heart out with unavailing regrets, jealous on her side at Lady Bothwell's[380] stay in the neighbourhood, and feeling, for the first time in her life, the heavy hand of a master.

On the morning of Thursday, 15th May 1567, in the old chapel of Holyrood, Adam Bothwell, Bishop of Orkney, performed the mournful marriage ceremony according to the rites of the Reformed Church.[381] Mary was in deep mourning, as she had been at her wedding with Darnley; and there was none of the feasting customary at the wedding of princes. Some of Mary's zealous friends have sought to adduce from her sorrow at and soon after the marriage proof that she had been from the first an unwilling victim. That she was terribly distressed is undoubted. Drury wrote that he had been told that 'the Queen was the most changed woman of face that in so little time without extremity of sickness they have seen.'[382] De Croc, the French ambassador, refused to attend the wedding, but visited the bride the same day at her request. 'I noticed,' he writes,[383] 'something strange in the manner of her and her husband, which she sought to excuse; saying that if she was sad, it was because she wished to be so, and she never wished to rejoice again. All that she wished for was death. Yesterday whilst she and her husband were together, shut up in their cabinet, she cried out aloud for a knife with which to kill herself. Those who were in the outer chamber heard her.' Sir James Melville[384] also refers to this incident. 'The Queen was so disdainfully handled, and with such reproachful language, that in the presence of Arthur Erskine I heard her ask for a knife to stab herself, or else, said she, I shall drown myself.' That Mary was profoundly unhappy after she had taken the false step is evident; that, indeed, is what happens to most people who take false steps; but it does not prove that she had not taken it willingly.

She had for passing love of this lustful, foul-mouthed desperado[385] cast aside for a space the political object of her life. She had forgotten, if only for a week, her high interests and her good name. But the infatuation could not last long, and she soon again became the ambitious, keen, diplomatic Mary, proud of her royalty, loving luxury and comfort, and essentially selfish in her outlook upon life. Being such, how could she fail to be wretched when, after the first violence of her passion was spent, she saw in its prosaic hideousness the awful position into which it had betrayed her, a position in which she, for the first time perhaps in her life, had sacrificed everything and gained nothing, not even personal happiness? She, the light-hearted woman who loved gaiety and popularity, saw herself, as a result of her own folly, surrounded by treacherous enemies, execrated in the streets as she passed for a murderess and an adulteress, knowing that for this rough tyrant at her side she had sacrificed her all, and yet jealously doubting even of his love for her now that his first passion was sated. The ghastly nightmare that must have pursued Mary Stuart in those dreadful days was indeed reason enough to have driven a less high-minded woman than she to despair and death.

In public Bothwell played the royal consort as well as he was able.[386] A week after the wedding he entertained her at a 'water triumph,' where he himself tilted at the ring; but it was noticed that wherever she went she was guarded by soldiers. 'The Duke,' wrote Drury to Cecil, 'openly uses great reverence to the Queen, ordinarily bare-headed, which she seems she would have otherwise, and will sometimes take his cap and put it on his head.' But it must have been as plain to him as to Mary that a tragic mistake had been made, and that he had overestimated the power of his own boldness, and of the complaisance of the lords. The principal people had all fallen away from them. Lethington was only biding his time tremblingly until he could fly; Huntly, himself in secret treaty with the lords, was also looking for an opportunity to desert the sinking ship, to Mary's tearful indignation; Sir James Balfour, the keeper of Edinburgh Castle, with that insatiable itching palm of his, was listening eagerly to Sir James Melville's talk of patriotism and bribes, and undertook to hold the castle for the lords, and not for Bothwell, when the critical time came. The venal scamp was not a little influenced by the argument that, if he stood through thick and thin by Bothwell, the people would conclude that he was deeply concerned in the Darnley crime—which, in fact, he was; whereas, if he deserted him, he would be supposed innocent. James Balfour knew as well as any man the most profitable moment to desert a cause, and when he saw that the stronger party had decreed that Bothwell was to be scapegoat for the crime of all, he arranged to desert him with characteristic alacrity, preferring like the rest of the false scoundrels to be a hound rather than the hunted quarry.

In these circumstances, how could Mary avoid being beside herself with remorse that she had flung away her high hopes, her good name, her freedom, and her happiness, for the passing enjoyment of a sensual caprice? Elizabeth, she knew, was sniggering joyfully behind her pawky mask over the false step her rival had made. The English queen could, in fact, have wished for nothing better than Mary's marriage with Bothwell, discrediting as it was to her in the eyes of the Catholics to marry a Protestant, and a man of rough manners, bad character, and inferior rank. Elizabeth could afford now to write cold stiff letters to the lords, reminding them of their duty to their sovereign; for Mary had lost her international prestige through her marriage, and for the moment was not to be feared. Catharine de Medici was much more shocked than Elizabeth, for though the Bothwell marriage conjured away much of the immediate Spanish danger, it brought Scotland nearer to Protestant England than to France. Both Catharine and Elizabeth tried their hardest to persuade the lords to deliver the infant James to them, but Mar kept him tight in Stirling; and the baby pledge, that would have given a pretext for French or English intervention in Scotland, was withheld, in spite of bribes and blandishments innumerable. The treacherous lords knew full well the babe's value to them as an instrument against his mother, and would not part with him.

Mary lost no time in endeavouring to repair some of the injury which her marriage had done to her prospects. Chisholm, Bishop of Dunblane, was sent to France and Robert Melville to England with a similar story. It was necessary, said Mary, for her to marry; the state of the country demanded it, and her nobility had urged her to do so, specially mentioning Bothwell as a fit match for her. She was young, and desired more offspring, and had consented. Bothwell, it is true, had used her roughly, but had afterwards purged his offence by submission. He had been legally divorced, and had been acquitted of the murder of Darnley, and Mary had acted for the best, and begged their friendship for her husband. The defence was a weak one, and was received both by Elizabeth and Catharine with contemptuous coolness, the great effort of each of the queens being, by special envoys and trimming messages to Mary, to prevent the influence of the other from becoming paramount in Scotland. From Spain Mary heard nothing direct, the action of the ambassadors in London and Paris being confined to throwing obstacles in the way of French intrigue in Scotland.[387] But Mary was a diplomatist too experienced not to see that the all-powerful support of Philip, for which she had intrigued so long to aid her in obtaining the English throne, would never be at the command of a woman married in a heretic Church to a divorced Protestant. Connivance at murder would have been in Philip's sight a very venial offence in comparison with this; and it was only long afterwards, when the persecution of Mary had assumed an essentially Protestant character, and she was driven again to look exclusively to Catholics for support, that Philip once more slowly and cautiously pledged the power of Spain to aid her at the critical moment of a Catholic rebellion in England and Scotland.

At length, in the early days of June 1567, all was ready for the final struggle that was to decide the fate of Scotland, perhaps of Europe. The lords had said that, so long as Bothwell did not attempt to capture the Prince by force, they would not move against him; and Mar, when the demand for James was made in the name of the Queen and her husband, replied that he would only give him up if he were to be placed in Edinburgh Castle in proper custody. Perhaps some inkling of James Balfour's intended treachery came to Bothwell at the same time as this answer; certainly he received warning of the intention of the lords to surround Holyrood with their forces and capture him. In any case, he and the Queen came to the conclusion that even Edinburgh Castle in Balfour's hands was no longer a safe refuge for them, and suddenly, on the 5th June, they rode together from Holyrood to the castle of Borthwick, a few miles from the capital, towards the Border, whither Mary had convened a muster of men to repress disorder there. But the levies came not, for the Humes and other Border men were out under their chiefs, sworn to destroy the man who had used the Queen's weakness to engross the power of the Scottish nobility. Chagrined at finding that none flocked to his standard as they had been ordered to do, Bothwell hurried back from Liddesdale to Borthwick.

As evening fell on the 10th June a few men came flying to the castle gate, crying in feigned alarm that the rebels were pursuing them. Bothwell on the battlements was suspicious, and denied them entrance. The demeanour of the men soon proved that he was right, and that they were in fact but the forerunners of a great force of horsemen under Morton and Hume, coming to capture him. Borthwick could not stand a siege, and only just in time Bothwell fled, accompanied by young Crookstone, the son of the owner of the castle. Even as they rode they saw a party of the Humes pursuing them, and they separated, both flying different ways. Young Crookstone was caught, and truly told which road Bothwell had taken. He was but a bowshot off, and might have been captured, but the Bordermen disbelieving Crookstone's story went the contrary way, and missed him, perhaps not altogether unwillingly, for he would have been a most inconvenient prisoner for some of them. But they shouted after him insults and challenges, of 'murderer,' 'butcher,' and the like, which probably relieved their minds. Nor did they spare Mary in their verbal outrages, to which we are told she replied in similar fashion, 'wanting other means for her revenge.'[388]

Finding their bird flown, the forces of the lords, joined by Mar, proceeded to Edinburgh, which they entered without opposition, the disinterested Balfour delivering the castle to them without a shot, as had been arranged beforehand (11th June). They had risen, they told the cheering townspeople, only to avenge the murder of Darnley. De Croc, the French ambassador, was active in endeavouring to bring about some arrangement between the Queen and her nobles, pointing out to the latter that they themselves had sanctioned the marriage, and had acquitted Bothwell of murder. But there was more at issue now than the question of Bothwell's guilt, and the Frenchman's efforts came to nothing, Mary answering him that if 'the lords meant to attack her husband she desired no agreement with them.'[389]

At no period of her career did Mary show more pluck and constancy than at this. If she had pleased she might have rid herself easily of Bothwell now. He had fled towards Haddington, and she was alone at Borthwick, with an army of his enemies within call of her. But she still clung to her love for him, the father of her unborn child; and as soon as Lord Hume's force had turned away, though the night was late and dark, she dressed in a soldier's garb, mounted her courser, and scoured off to join her husband, who lurked in hiding awaiting her a few miles away. Just as the dawn of the 12th June was breaking, these two, almost alone, rode into the strong castle of Dunbar. Mary had thrown down the gauntlet, and was at war with all the world, and with her own fate, for the sake of a coarse blackguard, whose masculinity had mastered her.

In the meanwhile the forces of the lords in Edinburgh were mustering apace, and Bothwell on his side had called together in Dunbar such of his Bordermen as would follow him. Thinking, doubtless, to take the rebels by surprise, the Queen and Bothwell on the 14th June rashly abandoned the walls of Dunbar and hurried by forced marches towards Edinburgh with 3,500 men. On Sunday morning Mary's little army halted at Gladsmuir, and a proclamation was read to them giving the Queen's version of the dispute in which they were asked to fight. The rebels, she said, lied when they claimed as their object her own liberation from captivity, the revenge for the murder of her former husband, and the security of her child. None desired more than she to avenge Darnley; her present husband had proved his innocence, which even the rebels had acknowledged in writing. As for her alleged captivity, that was disproved by her public marriage, at the recommendation of the very men now in arms against her. With this allocution, and promises of rich reward if her men fought for her bravely, Mary herself, clad in a red coat and velvet cap, and mounted on her charger, preceded by the royal standard of Scotland, rode at the head of her troops to offer battle to those who defied her. With her were Bothwell, and Seton alone of the peers, and the Lairds of Yester, Ormiston, and Borthwick.

Alarmed at midnight by the news of her coming, the lords set out from the capital before dawn on Sunday morning with their little army under Kirkcaldy of Grange, bearing before them the famous banner of white silk, upon which was painted the dead body of Darnley, with the infant James praying before it for vengeance upon his father's murderers. With almost religious fervour the troops of the nobles marched to consummate this sacred retribution, led thereto by some of the men deep in complicity in the crime. At Carberry Hill, overlooking Musselburgh, the Queen's army was halted, the two forces facing each other half a league distant, separated by a running brook. As the armies were forming, de Croc, the French ambassador, in much trepidation as to what he ought to do, rode up to the rebel force from Edinburgh, and besought the leaders to allow him to mediate before they drew a blade against their sovereign. There were only two ways of avoiding a conflict, they told him: first, for the Queen to leave the wretch she consorted with, and they would all serve her loyally on bended knee; and second, for Bothwell to come out before the army and meet in single combat a lord who would maintain that he murdered the Queen's former husband. De Croc demurred at being made the bearer of these suggestions, and asked them rather to allow him to go and hear what the Queen had to say. They at first objected to this, but finally Lethington—who had fled from Mary and joined the lords some time before—spoke for his colleagues and consented, giving the Frenchman an escort of fifty horse under a flag of truce.

When he reached Mary he found her haughtily indignant at the treachery of the lords, who had asked her to marry Bothwell, and now dared to make a crime of her having done so. If they would ask her pardon she would forgive them, but would make no other concession. Just then Bothwell rode up, and shouted, loud enough for his men to hear: 'Is it me they spite?' The Frenchman replied aloud that the lords professed entire loyalty to the Queen; and then, sinking his voice to a whisper, said they were his (Bothwell's) mortal enemies. Bothwell blustered noisily that he had done no harm to any of them. They were jealous of his rise, and there was not one who did not wish himself in his place. Fortune was free for those who grasped it, as he had done. And then, assuming a quieter tone, he prayed de Croc to do his best to extricate the Queen from her trouble. If any of his enemies would meet him in single combat, he was ready. 'No, no,' interposed Mary, 'I will not suffer that': she would, she said, fight out the quarrel by his side.

The colloquy was suddenly cut short by Bothwell, who noticed that the enemy were approaching as they talked, and had already crossed the brook. He banteringly told de Croc that if he stood and looked on, he would see more fun in the next hour or so than ever he had in his life; and the Frenchman, full of admiration for the ruffian's bravery, could only foretell, in his own mind, that such a soldier as this was sure to win, if his men would stand by him; and so with a word of praise to Bothwell, and a low bow to the Queen, who was in tears, de Croc rode off to the lords again, whom he found more determined than ever not to submit.

For hours the two forces watched each other, both unwilling to commence the onslaught, which would have necessitated an unfavourable change of position for the attacking force. There is nothing that tries troops so much as inactivity such as this; and, as the sun sank towards the west, Bothwell's rough levies began to break their ranks, and to murmur that terms had better be made. It was at length, after many parleys, agreed that Bothwell should meet an opponent single-handed between the two armies, both of whom consented to abide by the result. Bothwell, apparently nothing loath, consented, and the Queen was at last persuaded. The Lairds of Grange and Tullibardine challenged him; but Mary would not hear of a simple laird fighting her ducal consort. A peer, at least, it must be: and a peer, Lord Lindsay, stood forth for the combat. Before the fight could begin the Queen's troops became quite disordered; and seeing the hopelessness of her cause in any event, Mary sent for the brave Kirkcaldy of Grange, a staunch Protestant, but, as she well knew, an honest man, and asked him what terms could be made. 'None for your husband,' replied Grange; 'we have all sworn to die or to obtain possession of Bothwell.' As he was speaking to the Queen Bothwell secretly sent one of his men to shoot him; but Mary, with a cry of horror, protested indignantly against such treachery. Kirkcaldy professed the readiness of all the lords to submit to her if she would leave her husband, the murderer of her former consort; and as Bothwell listened, his heart began to fail him, for Lindsay was standing ready, and his adversary had no stomach for the fight. There was but one course now open for Mary. Her troops would not stand by her; Bothwell, the man for whom she had risked all, was losing his nerve,[390] and her respect, as the moments fled.

With a glance of contempt at the rabble around her, she turned to Grange and accepted his terms: loyalty and obedience to herself, their sovereign, and separation from the man she had made her husband, who, however, must not be harmed. Bothwell waited to hear no more. Mounting his horse, with a hasty word of farewell to the woman who had ruined herself, and a great cause, for love of him, he fled, surrounded by thirty spearmen, leaving the Queen to face her calamity alone. To have died with his face to his accusers might have touched with one ray of heroism the base memory that for ever will be his; but to seek his own safety at such a crisis of his life as this proves him to have been unworthy of the place to which Mary's love had raised him.

With a breaking heart, but yet with queenly port, Mary watched the Duke of Orkney as he turned his back upon his and her foes; and if anything could add to the bitter anguish of her humiliation, it was the knowledge that the gilded idol, before which she had sacrificed her happiness, had been proved before a mocking world to be the veriest dross. There was no pursuit of him, for his lordly accomplices were only too glad not to have to catch him, and Kirkcaldy had promised the Queen that he should not be injured. Sitting proudly erect upon her jennet, the defeated Queen was led down the hill to meet her conquerors; Kirkcaldy and others, who still remembered they were gentlemen, chastising the sordid knaves who dared as she passed to revile her with coarse words. Morton and Lethington on bended knee, and in the name of their associates, professed their loyal duty and obedience in answer to the Queen's dignified surrender: 'My lords, I am come to you, not out of any fear I have of my life, nor yet doubting of victory, if matters had come to the worst, but to save the effusion of Christian blood. I have come to you, trusting in your promises, that you will respect me, and give me the obedience due to your native Queen and lawful sovereign.'[391] But, even as she spoke, the rebels closed around her, and held aloft, full in her sight, the banner demanding from God vengeance upon Darnley's murderers.

Many writers have dwelt unfavourably upon Mary's haughty scornfulness at this scene. She would have been more than human had she not been scornful. At her feet there grovelled, with lying protestations of loyalty and faith, the most hypocritical caitiff alive, demanding vengeance for the crime which he himself had planned; and in Mary's pocket there lay the paper that at the last moment Bothwell had handed her — the bond for Darnley's murder—signed by Lethington and known, at least, to Morton![392] With rising indignation and excitement Mary was led to Edinburgh, not as a queen, but as a prisoner. She did not spare her captors who thus treated her, swearing that she would have Lindsay's head for that day's work, and declaring vociferously against the indignity to which she was subjected. But half-demented words, and tearful appeals to passing strangers for rescue, were drowned by the howls and execrations of the rabble by which she was surrounded; and, fainting and hysterical, the unhappy woman was lodged in a strong room in the provost's house, with the horrible banner of vengeance fluttering above her window.[393]

In the middle of the night she cried in her rage from the casement that her subjects should release her; but, though many flocked to hear her cries, no hand was raised to help her. Seeing Lethington, her erstwhile secretary, pass beneath her window, she begged him to come to her; but he pulled his hat over his brows and slunk away.[394] The imprisonment of a monarch was no light matter for the lords, and the position was full of danger for them. Kirkcaldy, upon whose promise Mary had surrendered, indignantly demanded that the promise should be kept. But the keeping of promises was not in Morton's nature, and he had gone too far to look back. He had other plans now. Murray, he knew, was hurrying home from France, and though Huntly, Argyle, and a few Hamiltons and Catholics were inclined to desert them for the Queen, it was evident that the specious cry of vengeance against Darnley's murderers had given to the rebels the support of the great majority of the people; and so long as Mary was out of the way, there was apparently nothing to prevent Murray, Morton, and their friends from ruling Scotland at their will for the next twenty years in the name of the infant whom they proposed to crown.

But somehow, the lingering sympathy of the people for a captive queen must be alienated still further as an excuse for deposing her. When, therefore, Kirkcaldy grew threatening, Lethington was able to produce what purported to be a letter written by Mary to Bothwell that night and intercepted. 'Dear heart,' it ran, 'I will never forget or abandon you, though I need be absent from you for a time. Be comforted, and on your guard: for your safety's sake did I send you away from me.' Whether Mary wrote the letter or not, who shall say? for it was never produced subsequently: but it served its turn; and the very children in the streets cried shame upon the woman who thus clave to the murderer of her husband. Kirkcaldy pleaded still. Give her time, he said, she will forget him by and by; and she had already left him. When she did forget him, replied Morton, they would think about it; but their lives and lands depended upon her being in safe keeping in the meantime. Mary, in her pride and anger—and still with a lingering love for Bothwell—may well have refused in the first days of captivity wholly to abandon thoughts of the man she had married. The lords, at least, gave out that she swore she would never consent to his punishment, and had vowed to touch no meat until she should see him again.

With such stories, true or false, the traitors worked their will. The streets rang with the cry, 'Burn her! kill her! drown her!'[395] and, late at night on the 16th June, the Queen of Scots was smuggled out of the city to the island fortress in Lochleven, to ponder at her leisure on the base treachery of which she had been a victim. To add one more touch to her martyrdom, she was warded at Lochleven by Murray's mother, her own father's mistress, and her son, William Douglas, Morton's close kinsman. Mary's conduct in shutting her eyes, if she did nothing worse, to what she must have known was the intended murder of Darnley, was shameful; and according to the ethics of to-day monstrous. But she did not suffer for this offence her pun-ishment at the hands of men more guilty of the crime than she. That was the excuse they needed to arouse against her the indignation of the people both in Scotland and abroad; to afford Murray and Morton the opportunity of usurping power; and afterwards to provide Elizabeth with a means of reducing Mary's international importance. Her real offence, in the eyes of the mass of the nobles who persecuted and deposed her, was in clinging to the blackguard with whom she had fallen in love, even after he had shown by his actions that he intended to use his position as consort for the purpose of dwarfing his wife, of ousting from the government the rest of the nobles, and of monopolising the power himself.

The providential discovery of the Casket Papers in the hands of a retainer of Bothwell's,[396] who had obtained them from the Castle by his master's orders only three days after Mary's deportation to Lochleven, placed in the hands of Morton and the rest of the lords the very evidence they required to alienate the sympathies of the world from the Queen, and enable them to exclude her from the government of her realm. Whether the papers were wholly or only partly forged does not to a great extent affect the question of her guilt, so far as concerns her prior knowledge of the intended crime, and her attachment to Bothwell before and after its commission; but without some such documents as those said to have been discovered, Morton, Lethington, Balfour, and the rest of them could not have persecuted her without inculpating themselves; not to mention the 'stainless' Murray, though he only 'looked through his fingers' afar off whilst the deed was done, and took care to sign no bond sanctioning the murder.

With the devilish weaving of the web around Mary whilst she was a prisoner by Morton, Murray, and Lethington, and their successful usurpation of the government in the name of the infant James, this book cannot deal. The seizure and judgment of sovereigns by subjects in the sixteenth century was a matter so grave that no ordinary transgression on the part of Mary would have been considered by other crowned heads a sufficient pretext for it. But, as we see by Murray's interview with Guzman in London in July,[397] when the former knew that some letters, horribly compromising Mary, were in the hands of Morton, every indignant remonstrance against the impiety of Mary's treatment was met by hints that her guilt in the murder, and her adulterous attachment to the chief murderer, made her unworthy of consideration by her subjects.

It soon became apparent that Mary's chief friends outside Scotland were the throughgoing Catholic party. Catharine de Medici and her son, whilst professing to be shocked at Mary's treatment, surpassed themselves in their efforts to gain a footing in Scotland through Murray and the lords. Villeroy, Lignerolles, and other envoys sent from France, ostensibly to see and comfort Mary, were almost rudely refused access to her; but they continued to be fulsome in their court and offers of aid to Murray. The policy of Cecil and the English Protestants would have been the same, but Elizabeth's superstitious respect for royalty, as against subjects, sadly hampered her ministers. She scolded Murray soundly as he passed through London, and almost commanded him to release his sister as soon as he arrived in Scotland. Murray for the time was in no mood for submission. He was being assiduously courted by the French, and he promptly let Throckmorton and other English agents understand that he would allow no dictation from England, and if Elizabeth would not aid the Protestants Catharine would. Bedford and Throckmorton, and even Cecil himself, were in despair that their hands were thus tied by Elizabeth's royalist traditions,[398] and only with much remonstrance could they persuade her formally to receive an envoy from the Regent after the infant James was crowned. But though Elizabeth's personal leanings somewhat weakened the action of her government, the general tendency in England, as elsewhere, was for the Protestant element to accept readily the statements that made Mary appear so guilty as to justify her gaolers in permanently disabling a Queen whose dream it was to make Great Britain Catholic. The Catholic party, whilst scandalised at Mary's marriage with a divorced man, were inclined to minimise her faults, and to gather around her as their only hope of saving the ancient faith in Scotland, and perhaps of restoring it in England.

During her imprisonment in Lochleven, indeed, the forces for and against Mary gradually ranged themselves on more or less religious lines. Mary's French Dominican confessor, on his way home in July 1567, had a long talk with Guzman in London in which this tendency was observable. His one and only subject for reprobation of Mary's conduct was her marriage with a divorced man, against which he (the confessor) had vehemently pro-tested. 'She was not only a good, but a very devout Catholic, and he swore to me solemnly that until the question of the marriage with Bothwell was raised, he never saw a woman of greater virtue, courage, and uprightness . . . though she declared to him that she contracted the marriage with the object of settling religion by that means. Those who had risen against the Queen had not been moved by zeal to punish the King's murderers, as they had been the King's enemies . . . nor in consequence of the marriage, as they had been all in favour of it, and had signed their names to that effect without exception, either lay or clerical, apart from the Earl of Murray; but their sole object had been a religious one.'[399]

The unsophisticated confessor secretly amused the diplomatist to whom he was talking by suggesting that the two great Catholic powers, France and Spain, should jointly demand Mary's release. He little knew, good man, that in the struggle then going on between England and France respectively to utilise Mary's troubles to gain a footing in Scotland, Spain was rather on the side of Protestant England than on that of Catholic France. Anything was better for Philip than the strengthening of French influence in Britain. In this clash of interests, in which to a great extent the fate of the Reformation was involved, the personal sufferings and troubles of Mary Stuart were quite a secondary consideration. She, a prisoner and an outraged Queen, might be pitied platonically by other crowned heads, as she was, especially by Elizabeth, for the reasons already stated; but whilst she was a prisoner she could be of no use to their respective policies, and it was the actual government of Scotland, and not the Queen, that for a time became the centre of intrigue for the contending powers.[400] In this contest Elizabeth's government obviously possessed the great advantage of neighbourhood and of having been for years the paymaster and defender of the leading nobles who had deposed their Queen, namely, Morton, Lethington,[401] and Murray, with their strong Protestant supporters.

Whilst political anarchy raged without, Mary, secluded in her island prison, with only two or three menial servants to accompany her, passed the first few days of her confinement in irreconcilable indignation, eating nothing, and taking not even the scanty exercise possible to her; but soon news reached her that the Hamiltons were resenting her imprisonment, and that Huntly, Argyle, Herries, Seton, Fleming, and other nobles, more or less Catholic, had joined them at Dumbarton, pledged to liberate the Queen; and once more her courage rose. Lord Ruthven, the son of that peer who had presided at the murder of Rizzio, was for a short time placed in joint charge of her; but the gaolers soon noticed that the young man was softening under Mary's pathetic glances,[402] and he was hurriedly removed, a very different man, Lord Lindsay, assuming, with the Laird of Lochleven, Sir William Douglas, the chief ward of her. To all appeals to renounce Bothwell for good she gave a haughty reply in the negative. 'She will live and die with him, and says that, if it were put to her choice she would leave her kingdom and dignity to live as a simple damsel with him, and she will never consent that he shall fare worse or have more harm than herself.'[403] To Lindsay's suggestions on behalf of his colleagues, that she should agree to

a divorce, she replied—as she did to a similar hint from Throckmorton—
that she would rather die, 'as she was seven weeks gone with child, and if
she renounced him she would acknowledge herself mother of a bastard.'[404]
She prayed that she should have better treatment, and offered to commit
the government to Murray when he should arrive, or to old Chatelherault;
but this did not suit Morton and his friends, and on the 24th July her act of
abdication was placed before her for signature. When it had first been proposed to her she had angrily refused to sign it; though artful Lethington, to
curry favour in case she should ever be released, sent Melville to tell her that
whatever she signed in duress would not be binding when she was free; and
Throckmorton, though he was not allowed to see her, succeeded in conveying similar assurance to her. At first she refused to resort to subterfuge; but
when swaggering Lindsay roughly demanded her signature to the abdication, she deigned to contend no more, and by the stroke of her pen James
Stuart at the age of thirteen months became King of Scotland, with Murray,
who was still absent, as first Regent.

But still the rebel lords grew daily more uneasy. Elizabeth coldly held
aloof and hectored them haughtily upon their insolence to a crowned queen.
Mary stood firm in her refusal to abandon Bothwell; and the Hamiltons,
with Huntly, Argyle, and the Catholic lords, were threatening them from
Dumbarton. If ever Mary regained her freedom, Morton and his friends
well knew that their shrift would be a short one; and until Murray's arrival
Mary was in hourly danger of death. Throckmorton again and again prayed
Elizabeth to speak less harshly to the lords, in order that they might not
be driven out of fear to end the Queen's life. Tullibardine positively told
Throckmorton that the Hamiltons, Huntly, and their friends were only in
arms against the lords because the latter did not kill the Queen. 'If she be suffered to live, she will be free some time, and they will suffer. But if the lords
will kill her, all will run the same course.' Throckmorton said they could put
her to better use than that, by marrying her to one of them. 'Yes,' replied
Tullibardine, 'that has been discussed by us, but her death is really the only
way out of the difficulty. The Archbishop of St. Andrews and the Abbot of
Kilwinning have both urged it within the last forty-eight hours.'[405]

Once in the middle of July the lords fell into a panic, and Lethington incontinently fled, on the news reaching them that Mary had escaped. It was nearly true. With her inexplicable charm she had already captivated hearts even in Lochleven; and a boat had been left loose and unguarded on the shore where she walked. Entering it alone, she essayed to reach the mainland, but she had not gone far when a lookout on the castle espied her and raised an alarm. Thenceforward her imprisonment was made more rigorous, and she was confined in the tower of the castle.[406] When Murray arrived in Scotland and saw his sister in August, her danger became somewhat less acute. He dared not release her, even if he had wished to do so,[407] for he had to depend upon the other lords for his authority; but he succeeded in persuading Mary, not without some foundation, that he alone stood between her and death; and she herself begged him to accept the regency. Thenceforward it was almost as much to his interest as to that of Morton that Mary should never again be free.

Nothing proves more strongly the extraordinary personal fascination of Mary Stuart than the events that followed her incarceration at Lochleven. She went there surrounded by Douglases and enemies, warded by Murray's mother and his half-brother, a close kinsman of Morton. She was broken-hearted and desperate, in delicate health, and her condition was aggravated by the frequent agues and low fevers induced by a damp residence. Most women in such circumstances, in hourly fear of death, outraged and betrayed as she had been, would have pined and lost heart. Not so Mary Stuart. After her nearly successful attempt at flight in July she was for a time shut up in the strictest seclusion; and yet on the 5th August, only three weeks later, Throckmorton reported that the lords were desperate, and at their wits' end to know what to do with her. 'The occasion is that she has won the favour and goodwill of the house, men as well as women, and thereby she means to have great intelligence, and was in towardness to have escaped. Also they would have her relinquish Bothwell; whereof I do not now so much despair as heretofore.'[408]

Mary's passion for Bothwell was passing. He was wandering afloat, seeking a safe refuge and finding it not, and was shortly to fall into Danish hands to be kept in prison as a pirate for the rest of his life. There had been nothing heroic or magnanimous in his behaviour towards Mary. Even in the dire trouble that now surrounded her she yearned for enjoyment and personal pleasure: her obstinate refusal to give up Bothwell at the dictation of the lords was mainly the result of pride; but when it was evident to her that her own wellbeing would be served by putting aside the memory of him, she philosophically did so, and turned her fascination to the conquest of others, who could better than he minister to her present comfort. She had now been provided with proper attendants of rank, and personal servants. Lady Murray had visited her affectionately, and they had shed many tears together, and evidently before the end of September Mary had surrounded herself with friends, and with such comfort and elegance as her situation allowed.[409] Murray reported to Bedford, on the 25th September, that she was 'in as good health of person, as lusty, and to appearance as merrily disposed, as at any time since her arrival in the realm'; and shortly afterwards Robert Melville told Drury that she 'waxes fat, and instead of choler makes show of mirth, and has already drawn divers to pity her who before envied her and wished her evil, Murray's mother for one.'

On the 28th October comes a piece of information from Drury, which shows us that Mary was still herself, even in this captivity, 'The suspicion of over great familiarity between the Queen here and Mr. Douglas, brother of the Laird of Lochleven, increases more and more, and worse spoken of them than I may write.'[410] George Douglas, Murray's uterine brother, was very young, a mere lad of eighteen, and was, I presume, the youth mentioned by Guzman in August as being in the habit of conveying messages for Mary; but his love for the Queen, whether purely platonic, or as hinted by Drury of a warmer character, led him to risk his life more than once for her service, and doubtless sweetened many of the weary hours of Mary's seclusion.

Some time in February 1568 Mary must have given birth to Bothwell's child—or children, according to Nau, who obtained his information from the Queen herself. The matter was kept quiet, probably in view of a future nullification of the marriage. Mary was reported to be ill of a fall, and Elizabeth said that, even if she got over that, she would still be in danger. Little was afterwards said of the infant, and Le Laboreur was probably right in his assertion that she was educated in France as a nun. Early in March

Murray visited Lochleven 'to give her some comfort'; and then Mary appears to have suggested to him that she might be married to some person agreeable to him, on condition of her release and retirement, her confirmation being given of his regency during the minority of James. Drury suggests that Murray was growing somewhat tired of the struggle. Elizabeth would not recognise him: her agent had refused to be present at the coronation of James, and had declined Murray's present at his departure; the Hamiltons, his hereditary enemies, with Argyle, Huntly, Herries, Seton, and the Catholic lords, were gathering a strong party that threatened to overthrow him at any moment; he knew that if the French obtained a footing in the country the Hamiltons, and not he or his friends, would be their favourites, and he endeavoured to make terms with Mary that might ensure him continued power.

After long cogitation he saw Mary again on the 19th March. The first suggestion brought forward, hardly a serious one surely, was that Mary should marry the scoundrel Morton. To this she gave a firm negative. Then Murray proposed the young man of his choice. It was necessary that the consort should be a person of no power or great ambition, amenable to Murray, and yet that he should be of fitting rank and family. Lord Methven, an amiable young Stuart, kinsman of Murray, twenty-two years of age, was proposed to Mary, on condition that she should be liberated, give an act of indemnity to all who had offended her, and confirm Murray's regency. Mary demurred, and asked for time for reflection; and soon afterwards, upon being pressed by Murray as to whom she wished to marry, to his intense surprise she answered George Douglas. George was his own half-brother, but he was out of the question as a consort, and Murray would not give his consent, the youthful lover being forbidden any longer to reside in the castle.[411] Mary, angry at being thwarted, cleverly used Lady Douglas's ambition for her younger son to set her against the elder. 'Look,' she said, 'what a kind brother George hath of Murray'; and although young George was forbidden the house, 'yet it is thought that he hath secret recourse there, and the affection is great. The Queen's liberty by favour, force, or stealth is speedily looked for.'[412]

This was written on the 20th March, and the prediction in it soon became true. Mary had already turned all her enemies at Lochleven into friends. On the 14th April she changed garments with her laundress, and whilst the latter remained in the Queen's apartment Mary entered her boat to be conveyed to the mainland in the character of the laundress. George Douglas with horses was awaiting her on the opposite shore. The boatmen had strict orders from the laird to see the face of every woman that left the island, but Mary was closely veiled, and they insisted upon her putting aside the silk that hid her features. She refused, and when they attempted to force the veil apart, she put up her hand in defence. Alas! no laundress's hand was like that which had inspired the verses of a score of poets. The beautiful white hand betrayed her; and though she threatened the boatmen with death if they disobeyed her commands to land her on the mainland, the anger of their chief was a more immediate danger than the threat of a captive queen, and Mary, in tears of rage, was rowed back to the castle. But, even so, the boatmen loyally kept her secret from the laird, and the way was still left open for a more fortunate opportunity.[413]

George Douglas, aided by his mother and by many of Mary's servants, was tireless in his plotting with her adherents, and it was certain that, sooner or later, the Queen must escape, if she were not murdered to prevent it. Her party in the west had grown in cohesion. Individually the leaders were a poor lot. Hamilton, Argyle, Herries, Huntly, and the Archbishop of St. Andrews, all of them either feeble fools or faithless wretches, but they were powerful in their own lands, and, whilst united, quite able to hold their own against Murray and the distracted lords in Edinburgh. The third attempt of Mary to escape was more successful. All the arrangements for flight to safety had been carefully organised by George Douglas, who, late in the evening of the 2nd May 1568, stood upon the shore opposite Lochleven Castle with the Laird of Riccarton (a Hepburn), John Beaton, and ten horsemen, with a spare horse saddled for Mary.

Sir William Douglas and his household sat at supper, doubtless disarmed of suspicion by his mother; and in the gathering darkness a trusted retainer, Willie Douglas, born in the house, a humble member of the family, stole the keys, and quietly led the Queen from her chamber to the outer air, locking all the gates after him, and preventing pursuit by carrying with him the Lochleven horses and scuttling all the boats but one barge, in which

Mary and her maid entered with Willie Douglas as sole oarsman. Doubtless money had been spent in plenty in silencing servants and guards, and all was managed so swiftly and noiselessly that Mary was far on her way and out of danger before her flight was discovered. Loving George Douglas carried the Queen ashore, and in the gathering darkness the little cavalcade set off, carrying with it, as it seemed, the fate of Scotland, perhaps of the Reformation. Two miles away they found Lord Seton and one of the Hamiltons with thirty armed horsemen. A few miles further on Lord Claude Hamilton with twenty horsemen joined them, and without halting they sped on to Niddry, Lord Seton's place. Here Mary stayed a few hours, but rested not. She was a Queen again, free now from the wretched passion that had obscured her political judgment, and intent upon recapturing the position she had temporarily sacrificed. John Beaton was sent flying south to England and to France to inform the sovereigns of her escape. But, even in this crisis of her fate, Mary did not forget that her hopes must rest not upon Elizabeth or Catharine, but upon Philip; and though she dared not write to the latter with watchful Scottish eyes upon her, she gave to Beaton a verbal message which Guzman in London was to convey to his master. She had, she told him, escaped, thank God! and would now show how blameless she was of the evil acts attributed to her; and that those who had kept her in durance were the principal culprits. She prayed for advice; and said that she was as firm and constant a Catholic as ever. She was, however, penniless, and had no garments but the servant's disguise in which she escaped; and she begged that if Murray tried to sell or pawn her jewels in Flanders, the Duke of Alba would embargo them for her.[414] The distance from Lochleven to Niddry had worked this change—Mary was herself again.

From Niddry she rode with an escort led by Lord Herries to Hamilton; and there, as if by enchantment, from all sides the nobles flocked to salute their liberated sovereign. Murray was holding an assize at Glasgow when he heard the news (3rd May). He immediately summoned the lieges to the King's assistance, and proclaimed as rebels all Mary's abettors; whilst 'Mary by the grace of God, undoubted and righteous Queen of Scotland,' issued such a counterblast as few crowned heads have ever set their hands to. Murray is scourged with scorpions. 'A beastly traitor'; 'a spurious bastard';

and 'a bastard traitor': he was to blame for everything,—for the destruction of the Gordons, for Bothwell's violation of the Queen, and for all the conspiracies against her. Everything that had been done by the lords, and the signatures extorted from herself whilst in prison, were revoked; Chatelherault, 'her dearest adopted father,' and his heirs were to be for ever accepted, after her issue, as sovereigns of Scotland; and she charged all good subjects to aid her in punishing 'these vile usurpers.' 'The unworthy traitor' Lethington comes in for his share of the castigation, as he richly deserved to do. 'The ingrate traitor, James Balfour,' is not spared; nor is Morton's base cousin, the 'shameless butcher,' George Douglas, with other 'hell hounds and bloody tyrants, and a great number of godless traitors, common murderers, and throat-cutters, whom no prince, be he neither heathen nor Turk, could pardon or spare.'

On the 8th May, at Hamilton, the nobles of Mary's party signed their bond to aid her; and their signatures prove that the dividing-line had now become mainly religious. Of the nine earls who subscribed it, the only one belonging to the traditional Protestant English party was Argyle, nearly all the barons, lairds, and bishops belonging also to the conservative or anti-English party. The moving spirit in the assembly was that bad Hamilton bastard Archbishop of St. Andrews, who had been 'everything by turns and nothing long,' and who was eventually beheaded by Lennox for complicity in the Darnley murder, as Morton was subsequently by James. Not nobles alone flocked to Mary's standard, for within a week of her arrival at Hamilton some five or six thousand rough clansmen had joined her. They were a savage, undisciplined host of western men, inferior in arms and efficiency to the force that Murray and Morton were able to bring into the field; and considerable difference of opinion prevailed in Mary's counsels as to the wisdom of at once risking battle. The Queen wisely advocated a retirement into the strong castle of Dumbarton, until by diplomacy and conciliation her party in the country should be rendered irresistible; but the fiery old Archbishop, who only a few weeks before was represented by Tullibardine to have urged her immediate murder, had the interests of his own house to serve: his idea being to overthrow Murray by a prompt battle, marry the Queen to his nephew, Lord Abroath, Chatelherault's second son, and himself become paramount ruler of Scotland. Unfortunately, the majority of the lords agreed with him, and it was decided to risk everything on the hazard of combat.

On the 13th May 1568 Mary and her army set out from Hamilton to march to Dumbarton, the intention being to accept battle if it was offered by the Regent on the way. Murray's force, though numerically smaller than that of his opponents, was much stronger in artillery, the guns from Stirling having been sent by Mar, and the spearmen being better mounted and armed. Murray and Kirkcaldy, moreover, were commanders far more able than any in the service of the Queen, and the choice of the battle-ground by the former proved their superior generalship. Stationing the main body of his force on the hill of Langsyde, overlooking Govan Moor on the outskirts of Glasgow, Murray was in a position to bar the way of Mary's army to Dumbarton. The ground commanded by the hill was broken and much divided by hedges, buildings, and enclosures, and the Queen's undisciplined but numerous cavalry were hampered in their onward movement. The Queen's advance-guard of two thousand mounted Hamilton men was ambushed and enfiladed in a narrow passage through the village, and was thrown into confusion. An attempt was made to charge uphill the main body of the Regent's force, but the assailants reached the fray panting and exhausted by their climb; and, though they fought stubbornly, they never had a chance of victory. Mary's main force, moreover, was badly led—Argyle, the commander-in-chief, fainting with fright at the first shock, and being thenceforward useless. On the other hand, Kirkcaldy, the best leader in Scotland, enjoyed the full confidence of his men; whilst Murray, Morton, and Hume were cool, brave, and skilful generals. The result of the fight in such circumstances was inevitable. After three-quarters of an hour of furious struggle on the hill the Queen's men were driven headlong down in flight. The rest was confusion, pursuit, and slaughter, lasting for hours. Three hundred of Mary's troops were captured and as many killed; and the Queen, recognising long before the fight was over that all was lost, fled precipitately from the eminence from which she witnessed the ruin of her hopes, accompanied only by Lord Herries and a small guard.

Mary had been as brave as a lioness at Dunbar, Borthwick, and Carberry, so long as she had a strong man with her; but at Langsyde, perhaps recognising to the full the awful significance of the struggle, her heart failed her, and she fled without awaiting the issue. For sixty miles she rode on that dreadful day without rest to Dumfries; and then, travelling by night only, snatching such sleep as she might upon the bare ground, feeding upon beggars' fare, haggard, travel-stained, and wellnigh in rags, the Queen pushed onward still for many miles away from the scene of terror she had left. With no woman near her, guarded only by the few companions of her flight, this pleasure-loving, great-hearted woman fled, beaten, helpless, and nearly hopeless, cursing her fate and the treachery and folly that had brought her to it. When she arrived at the banks of the Solway, there before her, just across the strip of water, England and safety from pursuit lay before her eyes: far away over the waste of sea was the land of her youth that she had loved so well.

To which country should she appeal for pitiful shelter in her trouble; since to stay in the realm that once was hers meant certain death now? The vengeful Medici, she knew, hated her, but would hardly dare to harm her, though the French diplomatic efforts during her imprisonment had been directed more to the conciliation of the rebels than to her release. On the other hand, Elizabeth's regard for the sacredness of royalty had made her active and sympathetic personally whilst Mary lay a captive in the hands of subjects. She would, surely, for once allow pity to conquer policy, and treat her cousin courteously! Herries was a cunning knave, and a good Catholic, and besought his mistress to beware of trusting heretics. Let her, he urged, stay yet on Scottish soil for a space—he would answer for her life with his own—and a fitting ship could be obtained to carry her to France or Spain if needful.

But Mary was half crazy with long travel, poignant emotion, and continual danger. Repose and safety were for the moment all to her, and these seemed to beckon her so near and temptingly—beckoned her, as it proved, to her destruction; and she, with eyes blind to the future, chose the fatal easier alternative. On the 16th May 1568 Mary stepped from her own land, which she was to tread no more, into a humble fishing-boat that was to ferry her across; and as it left the shore, and the Queen with streaming eyes bade farewell to her country—full for her of memories of crime and horror—the first volume of her life-story was closed. It had been a history whose bright and splendid earlier pages had been succeeded by others sullied with passion, tears, and blood; and the lesson it taught to all the ages to come was, that a woman, be she queen or peasant, who allows her passion to override her duty, hands herself over defenceless to her enemies, to deal with as they will. For the next sixteen years the lesson was to be seared deep by fire upon the heart of Mary Stuart.

XI

MARY IN ENGLAND

*Mary's unwise attitude on her arrival—Elizabeth's suspicion of her—
Herries's mission to London—The conference at York—Lethington
and Norfolk—Suggestions for Mary's marriage with the Duke—
Norfolk and the Casket Papers—Murray dissembles—The match
promoted by the English conservative nobles—Co-operation of Spain
and real objects of the conspiracy—Mary's complicity in the rising of
the North—Her love-letters to Norfolk—Norfolk's protestations—
Norfolk's collapse—The rising of the North—The nobles misled by
de Spes—Defeat of the rising—Mary's persistence in the Norfolk
match—Revival of the plot—The Ridolfi mission—Spain's support
to be given after Elizabeth's murder—The unmasking of the plot—
Execution of Norfolk—The ambitions of Don John—His plan to
marry the Queen of Scots—His disappointment and death—The end.*

MARY HAD LEARNED BY EXPERIENCE THE POWER SHE EXERCISED
by her personal fascination, especially in pathetic appeal; but she probably
did not fully realise how infinitely stronger it was over men than over women.
The first letter she wrote to Elizabeth on touching English soil contained a
prayer for aid against her rebel subjects, and an apparently confident request
that the English queen would grant her an immediate personal interview. 'I
pray you send for me as soon as you can: for I am in piteous case, not only
for a queen but for a gentlewoman. I have nothing in the world but what I

stand upright in, having escaped by riding sixty miles the first day across country, and having dared only to travel at night since then; as I hope to explain to you if you will have pity, as I hope you will, upon my extreme misfortune.'[415]

There was little room for personal sentiment in Elizabeth's political methods. She was perfectly well aware, of course, that Mary had been intriguing for the possession or succession of the crown of England ever since she was capable of intriguing at all; and Elizabeth could not afford to lose a point in the game of which her throne, her life, and the Reformation were the stakes. High as was her reverence for royalty in the abstract, she did not allow it to hurry her into consenting to a compromising meeting with Mary Stuart. Her first impulse was to treat her with full royal honours, and if possible to make some arrangement that should leave her the nominal sovereignty of Scotland, whilst securing to Murray and his Protestant friends unchecked power. But the majority of the English council viewed the matter in a different light from the Queen. It was almost as important for the paramount Protestant party in Elizabeth's counsels as it was to Murray and Morton that Mary should be so dealt with as for ever to be excluded from the English succession, and Elizabeth's ministers had to bear in mind what would happen to them in the case of the Queen's death. Even whilst Mary and Murray were in arms in Scotland, and Elizabeth was sending sympathetic messages to the former, confidential communications to the detriment of the Queen's party were passing from Cecil to the Protestant lords;[416] and when the news came to London of Mary's arrival in England, Bedford, Cecil, and the other strong Protestant partisans in Elizabeth's council continued to press upon her the urgent necessity of preventing the Queen of Scots from leaving England, for the purpose of appealing for the introduction of armed foreign aid into Scotland.

By great misfortune, Mary when she crossed the Solway just missed Elizabeth's envoy, Leighton, who had been sent to promise English aid to the Scottish queen, on condition that the latter would pledge herself not to appeal to the French;[417] and if Mary had remained long enough in Scotland to receive Leighton, she might have made a fair bargain with Elizabeth. On English soil, however, she had nothing in hand to bargain with, so long as she could be prevented from escaping; and this fact, which was promptly made patent to Elizabeth by her Puritan advisers, did not come home fully to Mary in time to prevent her from falling into the fatal mistake of arousing Elizabeth's distrust, and threatening to adopt an inimical course, which the English queen could prevent by retaining her in England. Mary first struck this unfortunate note in the second letter she sent to Elizabeth on the 28th May by Lord Herries, a strong Catholic. Elizabeth's cousin and vice-chamberlain, Knollys, had personally carried to Mary the day previously his mistress's answer to her first pathetic appeal. Knollys was a strong Puritan and did not soften his message. Apparently Mary was surprised, and not a little indignant, at its tone. 'After delivering your Highness's letters, she fell into some passion, with the water in her eyes; and, taking us into her bedroom, complained that you (*i.e.* Elizabeth) did not answer her expectation to admit her at once to your presence, where, on declaring her innocence, you would either without delay aid her to subdue her enemies, or else, she being now come of her goodwill, and not of necessity, into your Highness' hands, . . . you would at least give her passage through your country to France, not doubting that both the kings of France and Spain would help her.'[418] Knollys credited Mary with having 'an eloquent tongue and a discreet head; and it seemeth by her doings that she hath a stout courage and a liberal heart.' But in his interview with her the latter qualities are certainly the more conspicuous. He told her that Elizabeth was sorry that she could not do her the honour of receiving her 'by reason of this great slander of murder, whereof she was not yet purged . . . but he was sure that, whether she purged herself or not in that behalf, yet if she would depend upon your Highness' favour, without seeking to bring strangers into Scotland, the imminent danger whereof your Highness could not suffer, your Highness would use all convenient means you could for her comfort and relief.'

Mary's hopeless position would seem to dictate the need for a conciliatory reply to Elizabeth's condition; but the Scottish queen, instead of lulling suspicion, complained bitterly to Knollys of the delay in answering her, which she said was only to serve her enemies; and the Englishman at once wrote off to his Queen warning her of the danger of Mary's longer stay in the Catholic north of England, where the gentry were flocking to salute her, and eagerly listening to her pathetic account of the sad events that had befallen her. Knollys's remedy was a cruel one; namely, to give Mary the choice of going back to Scotland at once, or of remaining in England entirely at Elizabeth's devotion. But, he adds, if Murray were given a private hint when his sister was to go back to Scotland, she would not trouble any one again.

Mary's choice of an envoy to express her indignation to Elizabeth was unwise. Herries was an outspoken Catholic, subtle and false enough naturally, but given to outbursts of temper, which made him a bad negotiator. He carried south an imprudent, threatening letter from Mary, saying that if the Queen of England would not receive and aid her, she would seek other allies who would do so: '*Car, Dieu merci, je ne suis denuée de bons amis ni voisins en ma juste querelle.*' When Herries arrived in London and learned that the Queen refused to receive him, he was more imprudent and haughty than even his mistress had been. He protested angrily that he was watched and guarded like a prisoner, whilst Murray's envoy was free; and he violently demanded a prompt answer, 'as he could not suffer the long delay usual here, nor would the nature of his business permit it. He wished to learn whether the Queen (Elizabeth), as she always had promised, would help his Queen. . . . If she did not, he would go and beg the aid of the King of France, the Emperor, your Majesty (*i.e.* Philip), and even the Pope.'[419] This was said to the Earl of Bedford, one of the most pronounced Puritans in Elizabeth's council; and when, in shocked remonstrance, the earl held up his hands and exclaimed, 'The Pope!' Herries burst out, 'Yes! and even the Grand Turk, or the Sophi himself, seeing the need my Queen is in.'

In view of such talk as this, Elizabeth, quite naturally, refused to allow Fleming, who had accompanied Herries, to proceed to France; and sent them both back to Mary with a cold intimation that she must clear herself of the slur of murder before she could be received as a sister queen. The position was an extremely difficult one for Elizabeth, and her perplexity is admirably indicated in her many conversations with Guzman on the subject at the time. She was anxious to treat Mary as a queen, but the threats to appeal to the Catholic powers for the introduction of armed forces in Britain must be prevented from realisation at any cost, since the whole tendency of English policy had been for many years to prevent such an eventuality; and Elizabeth's throne, England's independence, and the Protestant Reformation depended upon it. The Spaniard for whom, and for the Duke of Alba, Fleming had brought letters from Mary, did his best to soften matters for her; but even he was obliged to confess that, having regard to her own safety, Elizabeth could hardly act otherwise than she had determined to do, namely, to bring Mary away from the Catholic north and from near proximity to the Border, and endeavour, by conference and negotiation, to bring about a settlement that should restore the Queen of Scots to her own country, whilst disabling her for ever from acting against English interests. Mainly, therefore, owing to Mary's slowness in realising the sudden change wrought in her negotiating power from the moment she stood on English soil, the evil seed was thus early sown; and Elizabeth's heart hardened as Mary's unwise threats of foreign armed intervention convinced the English queen that the woman, who in her hour of agonising distress had sought her pity, had never for a moment abandoned the ambition to seize her crown.

For the rest of Mary Stuart's unhappy life she was plotting ceaselessly with this end. The invasion of England, the murder of Elizabeth, revenge, dire and bloody, upon her enemies were ever before her eyes as the great goal of her existence. With the discontented English nobles, with Scottish Catholics, with her son James, with her cousin Guise, with the Jesuits, with Alba, with Don John, with Spanish agents innumerable, with the Pope, with traitors and spies, with wretched hired assassins, with anybody, Mary Stuart was thenceforward ready to plot and plan for carrying out, at any cost of life and suffering, the dream that animated her from her girlhood to her death. Finally, ready to disinherit her own son, and become herself a mere puppet of Spain; determined to hand over England and Scotland to the foreigner, and to make gloomy Philip and his Inquisitors masters of Europe, because masters of England, Mary lost all title to consideration from Elizabeth long before her tragic death.

The story of these long years of sombre intrigue must be left mainly to be told in a future volume, but on two occasions the plots to overthrow Elizabeth and the Protestant *régime* in England were interwoven with marriage projects that properly bring them within the scope of this book.

Regarded as love affairs they were cold, calculating courtships, involving murder in one case at least; but even in this case a semblance of sentiment was imported into it by Mary, probably in order to inflame her suitor with spirit and determination to go through with the dangerous business for the sake of her love, if for no other reason.

For months Mary stood out against the suggestion that she should prove herself innocent before an English tribunal of the accusations informally made against her by Murray and the Protestants. She, an anointed sovereign, would, she said, acknowledge no judge of her actions but the Almighty. At length she and her advisers were gradually won over by the specious pretext that the inquiry would be no trial, but a conference in which Murray would be called upon to justify his rebellion, and that reconciliation, not condemnation, was the object. This Conference at York in the autumn of 1568 was a scene of more subtle, self-seeking intrigue than perhaps was ever centred at one time and place in England. All the actors but the principal one, Mary, were there: Murray and Lethington, accompanied by Morton, Lindsay, Buchanan, and others; old Lennox, clamouring only, but in vain, to secure the punishment of Mary for the murder of his son; Herries, the Bishop of Ross, Boyd, and Fleming representing Mary, each with his own interest to serve, as well as those of his Church and his Queen; and the Queen of England's commissioners, headed by the first noble of the realm, Thomas Howard, Duke of Norfolk. Robert Melville was secretly running backwards and forwards from Murray in York to Mary at Bolton, trying to frighten her into silence and an acceptance of the regency by threats of disclosing the incriminating Casket Papers. Lethington, pretending to her to be desirous of softening the case against her—he is even said to have sent her surreptitiously a copy of the Casket Papers—was in private at York condemning her with the bitterest venom; desirous of making himself secure, whichever side came uppermost, and of preventing Mary in her desperation from making disclosures about *him*. Infinite chicane and falsity were on all sides, each party endeavouring to force the hands of the others, and to gain their ends without involving themselves; and for a time nothing was done but fencing.

The Duke of Norfolk, though a professed Protestant, had for some time been drifting towards the party of discontented Catholic nobles, of which his father-in-law, the Earl of Arundel, was the chief:[420] enemies, all of them, of Leicester and the new men who surrounded Elizabeth. His sister, Lady Scrope, was the wife of the nobleman who, jointly with Knollys, now guarded Mary, and the latter had been assured by her that the duke was favourable to her cause. In effect, it was evident from his letters when he first arrived in York that he hoped that a compromise, rather than a condemnation, would be the result of the meeting. Murray and Lethington were probably, for their own ends, animated by a similar desire, and delayed the production of the murder portion of their charges against Mary. But, finding that she was less amenable to threats than they had expected,[421] Lethington appears most unfairly to have shown the incriminating letters and the Ainslie bond, privately, to the English commissioners on the 11th October, with an alleged warrant from Mary directing the nobles to sign such bond.

To judge from Norfolk's letter, written the same day to Elizabeth,[422] he was shocked at the letters, the worst of which he calls 'horrible,' containing 'foul matter, and abominable'; discovering 'such inordinate love between her and Bothwell, her loathsomeness and abhorring of her husband that was murdered, in such sort as every godly man cannot but detest the same.' The duke seems to have raised at the time no question as to the genuineness of the papers shown to him. He was told they were in the Queen's own handwriting; and if that were the case there could be no doubt that Mary was an active accomplice with Bothwell in the murder of her husband, and that she had lived in adultery with the murderer before the commission of the crime. Norfolk was an amiable and popular nobleman, a widower of thirty-three, of the highest rank and great possessions, and a kinsman of Elizabeth. Whatever may have been hinted previously by intriguing friends or accepted by him, as to the possibility of his marrying Mary, and rallying to her cause the discontented conservative English nobles, it may be concluded that the sight of the Casket Papers on the 11th October, and the assurance that they were genuine, would drive out of his mind any floating idea he may have had of marrying the woman whose 'ungodly marriage' with Bothwell he was convinced had been settled a week before the bridegroom's mocktrial and acquittal for Darnley's murder, and before Bothwell's divorce.[423]

That on the 11th October, after he had seen the compromising papers, he had no fixed thought of his own marriage with Mary seems probable from his remark as to the need for including the Hamiltons in any reconciliation between Mary and her nobles that might be effected, but saying that this was only possible if Chatelherault, who was then in London, was willing to abandon his plan for marrying his second son, Lord Abroath, to the Queen of Scots. But, withal, it is evident that Norfolk, even when he believed Mary to be guilty, was anxious to save her from condemnation, and to patch up a reconciliation which should enable the conservative English nobles still to regard her as their candidate for the English succession. This result would have suited Lethington also if he were to be allowed to join in the negotiation; but it would have been ominous of ruin for Murray, because the accession of his sister to the throne of England, by the death of Elizabeth or otherwise, would have meant his own immediate overthrow in Scotland.

Norfolk took Lethington aside one day in York, and said he wondered how he and his friends could be so unwise as to raise the horrible scandal about the mother of their child-king, and suggested that the murder charges, at least, should be hushed up. Lethington, as usual—and this time, no doubt, truly—disclaimed any intention of proceeding to extremities against Mary, and asked Norfolk's permission to consult Murray on the subject. The next day Murray had a long private conference with the duke in the gallery of the house where the latter was staying. We nobles of England, said Norfolk, are anxious as to what is to happen when our Queen dies. She cares nothing about it, and has always been angry when we have endeavoured to settle the succession. But we must look ahead, whether she likes it or not. What, asked Norfolk, could be Murray's motive in coming there and blackening Queen Mary's character, injuring not only her own great hopes of the English succession, but those of her son after her? And then he proposed a subterfuge by which the accusations against Mary might remain in abeyance; and after some other interviews,[424] in which only Lethington and James Melville accompanied Murray, an agreement was effected between them to render the conference at York abortive as against Mary, Norfolk pledging himself to obtain from the latter a confirmation of Murray's regency. However sincere Norfolk and Lethington may have been in the matter, Murray probably was not so. Mary unguardedly showed to one of her friends Norfolk's letter to her informing her of the arrangement, and the friend conveyed the intelligence to Morton, who at once reproached Murray for his betrayal. It was no betrayal of Morton, however, for Murray, through his precious secretary Wood, divulged the plan to Cecil, for the purpose of having it frustrated.

Before this happened the two sincere conspirators, Norfolk and Lethington, carried the negotiation into a still more dangerous stage. We have seen that the subject of a possible marriage between Mary and Norfolk had already been mooted by the English conservative nobles, with the object of forcing Elizabeth's hands in regard to the succession, and of eclipsing the Cecil influence at court. After Norfolk's approaches to Lethington about hushing up the murder charges, Lethington, Melville, and the Bishop of Ross sat up nearly all night on Saturday trying to devise some safe scheme of reconciliation. In the course of the discussion Lethington remarked that Norfolk seemed to bear great goodwill to Mary, and 'that it appeared to him that the duke had some intention of marrying the Queen, as the bruit was.'[425] It will be recollected that, only a few days before, Norfolk had been shown the Casket Papers, and if he believed them genuine, it is incredible that he then should have desired to marry a woman who was capable of writing them. Norfolk himself asserts, indeed, that on Saturday, after dinner, Lethington took him aside, and earnestly proposed that he should marry the Queen, 'which I utterly refused.'[426] During the long ride to Cawood next day (Sunday, 16th October), Lethington's efforts appear, therefore, to have been mainly directed to casting doubts upon the genuineness of the papers that formed the damning evidence against Mary; the very papers that only a week before he had privately shown to Norfolk for the purpose of incriminating her. What arguments Lethington may have used during the ride we know not; but somehow he managed to persuade the duke that, after all, Mary was not so black as she was painted, and that the marriage suggested might provide a solution of all the difficulties both in England and Scotland, whilst ensuring to Norfolk a regal future. At once the whole Catholic intrigue was actively revived.[427] Lady Scrope broke the matter to the Scottish queen at Bolton, who approved of the plan. The Bishop of Ross and Liggons, a Catholic agent of Norfolk's, carried messages backwards and forwards to Mary; the Spanish ambassador was drawn into the secret, and the English conservative nobles, Arundel, Lumley, Northumberland, and the rest of them, were all agog with new hopes for the future; for, with the highest and most popular of them as consort of the future or present Queen of England, the old nobility and the old faith might come to their own again, and the new men, the Cecils, the Bacons, the Bedfords, the Hunsdons, and their like would be ousted from the place they occupied.

The new danger, suspected if not known precisely, was parried by Elizabeth and Cecil in characteristic fashion. The Conference was removed from York to Hampton Court without Norfolk, in order that the Queen herself might conduct it; and simultaneously Knollys was instructed to sound Mary at Bolton as to her willingness to marry one of Elizabeth's English kinsmen. He seems on his own account to have specially mentioned his cousin, George Carey, son of the Puritan Lord Hunsdon, and Mary, without committing herself, conveyed the idea that in order to gain Elizabeth's favour she would not reject such a match. Considering that the plot to marry Norfolk was at the time in full negotiation, it is certain that Mary never intended to mate with one of the newest of the new men, an enemy of her cause, without a single recommendation except the very doubtful one of his kinship with the Queen of England.[428] Murray himself affected to fall in with the plan for the marriage of Norfolk, and later, when he was taxed angrily therewith by Elizabeth, he excused himself by saying that, though Norfolk had pledged him to secrecy, he had divulged the proposal to Leicester at Hampton Court, who was also privy to Norfolk's plans, and, understanding them to be directed only against Cecil and his party, at first approved of them.[429] Murray, probably with truth, declared that his own consent was only feigned, because he had learned that if he had not given it Norfolk had arranged to have him murdered on his way back to Scotland.

Whilst the adjourned Conference was slowly lingering onward to inevitable abortiveness at Hampton Court, for it would have embarrassed all parties to condemn Mary for conspiracy to murder without confronting her with her accusers, which was undesirable for them, the new political matrimonial conspiracy was maturing. The letters which crossed between the political lovers, Mary and Norfolk, were mutually returned to the writers, but a few of them remain, and demonstrate the nature of the courtship. On one occasion, early in May, Mary forgot to return one of her suitor's letters to him, and in reply to his reproaches she wrote from Wingfield (11th May): 'I would have been gladder than I am, if the assurance of my carelessness in anything touching you might have prevailed against suspicion in the contrary. Always I am glad that ere now ye may know that my great haste to answer to your satisfaction might cause a fault to be done without danger, for the letters remained, but my keys are not in that peril you take them to be in. I pray you be sure I have none I trust in shall oversee them, nor do I trust in none more than I am able to do. . . . I write as much as I may do, and spare not my travail; for I have none other matters in head than those that you have in hand to be occupied with: and I fear that it is too busy upon me presently, that I have not taken much ease this last night, so that I am not able to write further; and this in pain, being in a fever. I pray you not to take it in evil part, for I mind it not. I thought yesterday to have sent you the token you sent, to pray you not to leave your care of me for any extremity. I may write no more. As soon as I be anything amended I shall write more plainly. I pray God preserve you, and if you send me any news I pray God it be more comfortable. From my bed, 11th May. My trembling hand will write no more.'[430]

Mary entered with zest into the conspiracy. In January 1569 de Spes, enraged at the capture of the Spanish treasure, wrote to his king, as usual, urging him to help the English Catholics to rise. 'In the meanwhile many means will be found to bring this country to its senses, and convert it to the Catholic faith. Those who have spoken to me about a rising for the Queen of Scots will be sure to return to the subject, and I will inform the Duke of Alba. . . . The day before yesterday the servant I sent to the Queen of Scots returned. . . . She certainly seems a lady of great spirit, and gains so many friends where she is that, with a little help, she would be able to get the kingdom into her hands. . . . Last night, at midnight, the Bishop of Ross came to offer the goodwill of his mistress, and of many gentlemen of this country, and I have reported this to the Duke of Alba. . . . The Queen of Scots herself gave my servant the following message for me: "*Tell the Ambassador that, if his master will help me, I shall be Queen of England in three months, and Mass shall be said all over the country.*'"[431] 'The Earl of Northumberland came to see me disguised at four o'clock in the morning, and is ready to serve your Majesty.'[432] By April the plot had so far progressed that all was ready to capture Cecil and his friends, and change the government by a *coup de main*. Leicester, however, grew alarmed when he gained an inkling of the ulterior objects in view, and threatened to warn the Queen. Cecil had also learned of the plan, and cleverly persuaded Norfolk and Arundel that he also desired a reconciliation with Spain; and so the conspirators for a time were thrown into confusion. In June, however, they informed the hot-headed Spanish ambassador, through the Bishop of Ross, that they now understood how they had been hoodwinked by Cecil, and would proceed more cautiously in future. Leonard, Lord Dacre of the North, promised de Spes at the same time that whenever the King of Spain would send a sufficient force to England, the north-country nobles would undertake to raise a body of fifteen thousand selected troops for his service in England, in order that the Catholic Church might be restored under Mary and her consort Norfolk.[433] On the following day Ridolfi, the Florentine banker and papal agent, came to de Spes from Norfolk's brother-in-law, Lord Lumley, with fresh pledges of what the nobles would do for Spain and Catholicism if they succeeded in their plot.[434]

That Mary was the head and front of this conspiracy, the most dangerous that ever threatened Elizabeth, is seen also in her interesting letter from Wingfield to Norfolk of 24th June 1569, a letter much warmer in tone than the one just quoted. 'Considering how much I am beholden to you in many ways, I am glad the grant of my goodwill is so agreeable to you. Albeit I know myself to be so unworthy to be so well liked of one of such wisdom and good qualities: yet do I think my hap great in that; yea much greater than my desert. Therefore, I will use myself so that, so far as God shall give me grace, you shall never have cause to diminish your good conceit and favour of me, whilst I shall esteem and respect you in all my doings as long as I live, as you would wish your own to do. Now, my good Lord, more words to this purpose would be unseemly in my present condition, and importunable to you in your many businesses.' After speaking of her illhealth from her old malady in the side, Mary continues: 'I write to the Bishop of Ross what I hear from the Duke of Alba, governor of the Netherlands. Let me know your pleasure at length in writing what I shall answer. Now, my good Norfolk, you bid me command you: that would be beside my duty in many ways. But to pray you I will, that you counsel me not to take patiently my great griefs, except you promise me to trouble you no more for the death of your ward. I wish you had another in his room to make you merry, or else I would we were out of both England and Scotland.'[435] And so with many kind, almost affectionate, words Mary takes leave of her new lover.

The aristocratic conspiracy, of the success of which the only final result could have been the death or deposition of Elizabeth in favour of Mary, as its contrivers well knew, could only succeed with the aid of great armed forces provided by Philip and the Pope. The incredibly rash and imprudent de Spes violated his precise instructions, which were of a temporising character, and unquestionably encouraged the English conservative nobles to believe that if they rose Spanish aid would be sent to them.[436] From the first day of his arrival in England he had tried to force his master's hand and to precipitate the war which Philip had always striven to avoid. At the present juncture the resources of Spain were absolutely exhausted. Elizabeth had seized the treasure that was being sent to Flanders to pay Alba's troops, and it was more impracticable than ever it had been for a Spanish army to be sent to help the English Catholics to substitute Mary for Elizabeth on the English throne. In February 1569 Philip wrote to Alba in reference to the appeals which, as we have seen, for months previously de Spes had been sending to Spain for aid to Mary and the English nobles. The King says that de Spes assures him that the opportunity is now ripe for deposing Elizabeth and placing Mary upon the throne, and he leaves to Alba's discretion whether or not to undertake the business. But Alba had a very poor opinion of de Spes's judgment, and could only assure his master that he had neither men nor money to conquer England, and could only pursue a mild, conciliatory course with the heretic Queen and her ministers.

On the urgent prayer of Arundel, Lumley, and the other conspirators Alba managed to scrape together and send them six thousand crowns during the summer, but it was accompanied by a stern order to the ambassador to the effect, 'that though he might at unsuspicious hours listen to the servants of the Queen of Scots,' he must, on no account, take any part in conspiracies directed against Elizabeth or her government. But de Spes never ceased to do as he was forbidden to do. The Italian agents of the English nobles came to him almost nightly; and on the 25th July 1569 he reported that the Bishop of Ross had gone to see him at Winchester House at three o'clock in the morning, 'to assure me of the wish of the Duke of Norfolk to serve your Majesty. He said he was a Catholic, and has the support, even in London, of many aldermen and rich merchants.'

A week later the ambassador wrote that 'Norfolk and the other adherents of the Queen of Scots are busy trying to get her declared the Queen's successor, and this Queen (Elizabeth) has already grown suspicious of the duke. There certainly will be some turmoil about it. They all assert that if they succeed religion shall be restored.'[437] Whilst Norfolk was thus humbling himself to foreigners and Catholics, he vainly imagined that he was winning Murray and the Protestants as well. Writing to Murray on the 1st July,[438] he promised him all sorts of favour and reward, 'as a natural brother,' and sought to reassure him as to the results of the marriage with Mary. 'To come to that which you desire to be satisfied of, my marriage with the Queen, your sister, I must deal plainly with you . . . as my only friend. I have proceeded so far therein, as I can with conscience neither revoke that which I have done, nor never mean to go back from it: nor with honour proceed further, till such time as you shall there remove all stumbling-blocks to our more apparent proceedings.[439] Which, when by you it shall be finished, upon my honour the rest shall follow to your comfort and contentment. . . . My very earnest request is that you proceed with such expedition as the enemies (which shall be no small number) to this good purpose of uniting this land into one kingdom, in time coming, and the maintenance of God's true religion, may not have opportunity . . . to hinder our determination; against which there will be no practice by foreign princes omitted. . . . You shall not want the furtherance in this enterprise of the most part of the noblemen of this kingdom, whose faithful friendship in this cause, and all my other actions, I have . . . proved.' Thus Norfolk was both Catholic and Protestant; a humble servant of the kings of Spain and France,[440] and an opponent of 'foreign princes'; a friend of Murray and a lover of Mary!

Elizabeth and Cecil were well aware of the danger; which, in effect, was very great. A caucus majority of the council had met privately and decided in favour of Norfolk's marriage. 'The signatures of the principal people in the country have been obtained to this effect.'[441] Mary was to be released; the French ambassador had been reconciled to the plan,[442] and de Spes expected from day to day a formal visit from Norfolk, to request the King of Spain's approval of the match. Mary herself had already informally asked for it, and the ambassador opined that 'the business is so far forward that it will be difficult now to prevent it, but I think it will be better that it should be done with your Majesty's consent . . . as it will bind them more closely than ever to your Majesty's service. The Queen of Scotland says that, if she were at liberty, or could get such help as would enable her to bring her country into submission, she would deliver herself and her son entirely into your Majesty's hands; but that now she is obliged to sail with the wind, although she will never depart from your Majesty's wishes in religion or other things.'[443]

The only person whose approval of the match was apparently not desired was Elizabeth herself; and she generally had to be reckoned with in matters concerning her own interests. So, when Leicester in a fright went and made a clean breast of the whole affair to her,[444] the heavy hand of the angry Queen fell upon Mary and her faint-hearted suitor. Suddenly in September Mary's confinement was made much closer under the Puritan Huntingdon, Norfolk and the conservative lords being peremptorily summoned to court. Norfolk was a weak reed. He came as far as London, the Queen being at Windsor, but what he heard at Howard House frightened him. Feigning illness for the first two days, he fled on the third (24th September), bewailing in his letter to Elizabeth that she was so angry with him. He never meant any harm. 'On his honour he never dealt with the Queen of Scots further than he declared to the Queen and some of her council.'[445] And so the poor creature, lying and prevaricating, sought safety in his own county at his castle of Kenninghall—the third unworthy man who had been betrothed or married to Mary Stuart. Elizabeth well knew how to deal with such thread papers as Norfolk. Fever or no fever, she said, he must come to her instantly, even if he have to be carried; and on the second summons the duke, with trembling steps and as slow as he dared to make them, came to his raging mistress, and was promptly reduced to a condition of lachrymose submission.[446] He was ordered into arrest, as were Arundel, Lumley, Pembroke, and Throckmorton, the only conspirators within reach. Leicester was reproached with alternate tears and railing at having for a moment consorted with such traitors, whilst Mary, protesting against the renewed rigour of her imprisonment under Huntingdon, and unable to send her messengers as she had intended to Alba, was still as haughty and defiant as ever.[447]

There were, as we have seen, other nobles in the north less pusillanimous than Norfolk, and not so easy to reach from London. In the very letter of de Spes which reports Norfolk's collapse the ambassador says that a servant of the Duke of Northumberland had been to him again to ask for armed aid for the Catholic revolt in the north in favour of Mary. For many months the imprudent ambassador had been encouraging the nobles in their plots; but now, in the face of an imminent rising, he could only refer them to the Duke of Alba. If only a small number of arquebusiers were promised to them from Flanders, said Northumberland, Westmoreland, and their friends, they would undertake to release Mary, master the north of England, restore Catholicism, and make friends with Spain. 'I feel sure they will attempt the task, and it will be better carried through by them than by the Duke of Norfolk, as they are more fit for it, and the Queen of Scotland will have more freedom afterwards in the choice of her husband.'

This was the most dangerous moment of Elizabeth's reign. If the aid the northern lords daily craved from Alba had been sent promptly, the government of Elizabeth would have in all probability been defeated, and Mary Stuart would have become, as she herself predicted, before the end of the year 1569 Queen of a Catholic Britain under Spanish protection. But Alba, like his master, was slow and poor. The eternal lust for inquiry, and the avoidance of sporting risk, blighted most of his promising enterprises. It is true that he sent the fat, unwieldy, but masterly general Ciappino Vitelli, with fifty experienced officers, under the guise of a commercial embassy, to Elizabeth, really to spy out the land. But the northern lords could not wait. The Italian commercial general's military companions were promptly packed off again to Flanders; and whilst Norfolk, Arundel, Lumley, Throckmorton, and their friends were trembling for their necks in prison in London, and Mary was hurried off to the strong castle of Tutbury, the northern lords were scattered by the Earl of Sussex—Westmoreland and others to lifelong poverty and humiliation in Spanish territory, Northumberland to Scotland and thence to the scaffold; and Elizabeth, her foot on the necks of all her enemies, was mistress of her realm again, and let her disloyal Catholic subjects and their real leader, Mary Stuart, know it.

Terrible as must have been the disappointment to the Queen of Scots, she never lost heart. The weakness of Norfolk, and the imprudent encouragement given to her party by de Spes, had ruined for a time the hope of success for the one great object of her life. But, whilst yet the lords were in full flight from Elizabeth's pursuing soldiers, the Bishop of Ross still brought messages to the Spanish ambassador that his mistress 'was firm and in good heart; and that the Catholics of England were as determined as ever to carry through their plan. As soon as they learn that they will have the help of foreign princes, and good arrangement is made for support to reach them, they will all rise at a day's notice, and persevere until this country is again Catholic, and the succession is assured to the Queen of Scots.'[448]

Mary's letters to Elizabeth and her ministers continued, through it all, to be full of hypocritical professions of attachment and faithfulness—'the sincerity of our perfect inclination towards her' (Elizabeth)—as had been agreed between the writer and Norfolk, with whom during his imprisonment she kept up a close secret correspondence. Once it was whispered to the duke that Mary had spoken words of disparagement of him, and on his reproaching her she was very indignant. 'I have sworn to you I never meant such a thing; for I feared your evil opinion of me. . . . And therefore, when you say you will be to me as I will to you, then you shall remain my own good lord, as you subscribed once, with God's grace, and I will remain faithfully yours, as I have promised. On that condition I took the diamond from my Lord Boyd, which I shall keep unseen about my neck till I give it again to the owner of it and of me both.[449] I am bold with you, because you put all to my choice. Let me hear some comfortable answer again, that I may be sure you will mistrust me no more; and that you will not forget your own, nor have anything to bend you from her; for I am resolved that weal or woe shall never remove me from you, if you cast me not away. And if I be suspected by you, meaning so truly, have I not cause to be sorry and suspicious? . . . And yet, if you be in the wrong I will submit me to you for so writing, and ax your pardon therefor. But that fault I could not forbear for very joy.' The Queen then tells her lover that Huntingdon has been hinting again to her of a marriage with Leicester, which she said should never happen. Huntingdon had then wagered that Norfolk would be her husband. 'And where he said afore, that the Q. of England would never let you out unless you refused me, I said that you were not worth a want if you did; and that shortly you should be out. If you forget me, yet I will be glad of your weal. Much more if you have your liberty and your own granted. You may have better, but never nothing straighter, and more bound to obey and love you, than yours faithfully till death, and I should never rest so long in prison.'[450]

Though often at great risk and danger for both, Mary continued to write from Tutbury to her lover, animating and encouraging him not to abandon the great plan that was to crown with success so many heartbreaking failures. In her love-letters to Norfolk every art of the diplomatist and the woman is displayed; but, whilst urging him to high endeavour and a stout heart, whilst warning him to beware and be cautious, the dominant note of all the letters is the almost provocative assurance of her personal love and faith. 'Last of all, I pray you, my good lord, trust none that shall say that I ever mind to leave you, nor to anything that may displease you, for I have determined never to offend you, but to remain yours: and, though I should never buy it so dear, I think all well bestowed for your friendly dealings with me, undeserved. So I remain yours till death conform, according to my faithful, dutiful promise.'[451] Soon after this (31st January) she suggested that she should attempt an escape.[452] 'If it please you, I care not for my danger: but I would wish you would seek to do the like: for if you and I could both escape, we should find friends enough. . . . Our fault were not shameful; you have promised to be mine, and I yours. I believe the Queen of England and the country should like it. . . . If you think the danger great, do as you think best, and let me know what you please that I do; for I will ever be for your sake perpetual prisoner, or put my life in peril, for your weal and mine. . . . As you please command me, for I will for all the world follow your commands, so that you be not in danger by my doing so.'

Mary, weary with close confinement, for some weeks in the spring had professed to entertain thoughts of declaring her entire submission to Elizabeth's demands. That the main object of this feigned desire was to prevent her deportation into Scotland at the request of the new rulers[453] appears probable; but, even in this peril, she assured Norfolk that she would not abandon him, even to save herself. 'If you mind not to shrink at the matter, I will die and live with you. Your fortune shall be mine, therefore let me know in all things your mind.' The murder of Murray shortly before had thrown Scotland into anarchy, and Mary's friends there were in open revolt against the young king's so-called government. Whilst Lennox was travelling north to obtain the regency, Morton, Mar, and their friends sent an envoy to Elizabeth to beg for Mary's surrender. This would have meant certain death for the latter, and the Queen of England desired at the moment nothing better, for affairs had taken a turn against her. But she dared not bear the responsibility of delivering Mary to such a fate, without exacting some appearance of guarantee for her safety. This the Scots would not give; though Elizabeth hinted very strongly that she desired Mary's death.[454] This was the juncture or never, wrote Mary to Norfolk, when the Spaniards should be urged to help her friends in arms in Scotland, or she would be obliged to become a Protestant, and submit utterly.

The Bishop of Ross had been in prison for a time upon suspicion of plotting with Alba on Mary's behalf, and the Catholic party in England and Scotland were again raising their heads, in view of the Pope's bull excommunicating Elizabeth and absolving her subjects from allegiance to her;[455] a peace between the religious factions had been patched up in France, and a strong Spanish fleet was in the Channel, ostensibly to convey Philip's new bride to Spain. In these circumstances Elizabeth was forced once more to smile upon Mary, and enter into negotiations with her for a reconciliation and alliance in the autumn of 1570. The negotiations were insincere on both sides, especially upon that of the English queen, whose only object was to gain time until the Spanish fleet had passed, and the English party in Scotland had again become irresistible.[456]

Whilst these negotiations were pending, the reanimated English Catholics, the Bishop of Ross, de Spes, and Mary herself never ceased for a moment plotting and planning for the *coup* which was to liberate the Queen and change the government of England. Norfolk alone of the conspirators was timorous, and the other nobles began to sneer at his timidity and, above all, his doubtful Catholicism, although Arundel and Lumley assured them that when he had succeeded in his designs he would be as true a Catholic as any of them. 'His desire to reign,' wrote de Spes, 'might well wean him from bad paths to good ones'; and the brilliant prospect held before him at last stirred up a little stiffness in him, especially when talk began to prevail that the Duke of Anjou was to be a French suitor for Mary's hand. The Spaniards were now in favour of any candidate chosen by Mary and the English nobles, Norfolk, for choice, if he could be got to toe the Catholic line firmly. There was no longer any pretence that the threatened revolution was merely to oust Cecil. 'It is certain,' wrote de Spes to Philip, 'that the release and marriage of the Queen of Scots carries with it the tranquillity of Flanders and the restoration of religion in this country'; and, not once but a score of times, the imprudent ambassador begged his master to take the English revolution under his direct patronage, and become virtual master of a Catholic Britain through Mary Stuart.

This, however much the fact might be wrapped up, could only be effected by the imprisonment or removal of Elizabeth. It was clear that, whilst the great Queen lived, a Spanish protectorate and a change in the religion of England was impossible; and gradually all or most of the principal parties to the conspiracy, understanding that Philip, with his blighting caution, would only support an accomplished fact, and would not risk responsibility in case of failure, came round to the inevitable conclusion that Elizabeth must be cleared out of the way before Mary and Catholicism could reign.

On the 23rd March 1571, by which time Norfolk was again free, Rodolfo Ridolfi, the Florentine banker in London, visited de Spes at Winchester House. From the first this man had been the confidential go-between of the English conservative nobles and the ultra-Catholic powers, and he now told the ambassador that he was at once starting for Flanders, Rome, and Madrid with letters of credence and an important mission from Mary and Norfolk.

'The Queen of Scotland and the Duke of Norfolk, in the name of many other lords and gentlemen who are attached to your Majesty's interests and the Catholic faith, are sending Ridolfi to offer their services to your Majesty, and to represent to you that the time is now ripe to take a step of great benefit to Christianity, as in detail Ridolfi will set forth to your Majesty. The letter of credence from the Duke is in the cipher that I have sent to Zayas (the King's secretary), for fear it should be taken.'[457] In a private letter to Zayas by the same courier de Spes lifts the curtain a little more for us to see the dark secret behind it. 'It is necessary that Ridolfi should have audience of his Majesty with the utmost secrecy, as you will be able to arrange on so important a matter as this.'[458]

The written instructions given by Mary and Norfolk to their envoy still further enlighten us. The Queen's instructions contain an impassioned statement of the evil treatment that she had been subjected to, and the determination of the English Catholics to strike a blow to restore the Catholic religion. Ridolfi is to set forth the miserable condition of the Queen, in daily peril of death, and to say that the Duke of Norfolk and the nobles of England are resolved to risk everything, and, with the aid of Christian princes, to assert the right of Mary to the throne, and make England Catholic. The plan is for Norfolk to continue for the present to feign Protestantism, in order not to lose the support of his Protestant friends, but he is pledged to restore the Catholic religion after success has crowned the enterprise, and to follow the orders of the Pope and King Philip in all things. The Pope and the King are to be prayed to favour the marriage of Mary and Norfolk,[459] and not that with Anjou which has been proposed, and the envoy is to assure them that France is to be entirely excluded from the proposed attempt. Above all, Spanish armed help must be sent from Flanders, and success is then assured. Norfolk's instructions to Ridolfi are to profess his full adhesion to Catholicism, to beg for the approval of his marriage with Mary, and to solicit 6,000 arquebusiers, 4,000 arquebusses, 2,000 corselets, and 25 field-guns with munitions, 3,000 horses, and a sum of money to aid his revolt. The forces should be sent to Harwich or Portsmouth, and the duke undertakes to join them at once on their landing with 20,000 infantry and 3,000 cavalry. He also wisely urges upon the Spaniards the need for excluding French influence, and counteracting the Anjou match for Mary; and offers to become in all things the humble servant of Spain only.[460] Even if the Scottish crown be restored to Mary, Norfolk says that the nobles are determined to fight for her right to that of England, *and to obtain possession of the person of Elizabeth.*[461]

Ridolfi was first to go to the Duke of Alba in Flanders, and obtain his opinion on the whole matter before proceeding to Rome and Madrid; and he carried with him orders from Mary 'to expound verbally the secret part of his mission, adding thereto what the Bishop of Ross will tell him verbally.' As the written portion of the instructions deal with the Catholic rising, the restoration of religion, the marriage with Norfolk and the armed forces required, the secret part to be verbally imparted by the bishop must have been something beyond these. We shall see by Alba's report to Philip, and the consultation of the Spanish council of state, that this most secret part was the murder of Elizabeth, proposed by Mary Stuart and Norfolk, through Ridolfi, 'the real remedy for all the ills,' as de Spes soon afterwards called it.

Ridolfi arrived at Brussels early in April, and saw Alba at once. When the envoy talked about seizing Elizabeth and the Tower of London, Alba became interested, but objected the difficulty of doing it, seeing the failure of the previous conspiracies against her. Ridolfi replied that all was ready and assured this time, and there would be no failure, 'but the lords saw that they could not carry out the full intent without the support and aid of a powerful prince and the Pope.' Alba's first care was to warn Ridolfi that the French must have nothing to do with it; but beyond enjoining secrecy, above all things especially from the French, he could give to the envoy nothing but vague words, and refer him to the personal decision of the remote little despot in the middle of Spain. When, however, he himself wrote to Philip, he was much more explicit. This, he urged with unwonted warmth, was an opportunity which must not be missed of revenging themselves upon the Queen of England. As usual with him, he set forth interminably all the difficulties and objections to the sending of the armed force openly to England, as proposed by Mary and Norfolk, seeing the penury with which Spain was cursed, and the difficulty of keeping secret the necessary armed preparations; 'and if the enterprise were discovered it would probably cost the life of Mary and Norfolk at least.' He was a little doubtful, too, of Ridolfi's trustworthiness, seeing that he was a Florentine. But, after giving full rein to his doubts and fears, he sends to his master his final advice. 'But in case the Queen of England were to die, *either of a natural death or otherwise*, or if these lords were to seize her person, without any interference on the part of your Majesty, I should then find no difficulty whatever. It therefore appears to me that in case the Queen of England dies, *naturally or otherwise*, or she should fall into the hands of the Duke of Norfolk, your Majesty ought not to miss so good an opportunity to gain the object aimed at'; and, with this, the Duke of Alba recommends his king to reply to Ridolfi's message that within twenty-five or thirty days after Elizabeth's death the six thousand soldiers demanded by Norfolk should be sent to him.

Ridolfi arrived in Madrid from Rome early in July, with fervent letters of recommendation from the Pope; and on the 7th July the whole question of his mission was discussed by the council of state. The point submitted for decision was as follows: 'That it is advisable that the associated lords in England should commence by killing or capturing Queen Elizabeth during her progress.' Ridolfi, it was stated in the course of the discussion, had assured them that the conspirators had trustworthy persons near the Queen for the purpose; and, after an exhaustive consideration, the council resolved that the course proposed should be adopted, the invading force to be forthwith prepared in Flanders, on the pretext of the going thither of a new governor, who was to carry to Alba 200,000 ducats to defray the expenses. But the first and most important point, in the opinion of the council, was that the Queen of England should be assassinated as soon as possible, 'for when that has been done the whole thing will be over'; and that immediately the news reached Flanders saying that the 'principal execution' had been effected, the troops and material requested by Norfolk should be sent under experienced generals to force Mary upon the throne and impose Catholicism by push of pike upon the English people.

But again it was too late. The deadening centralisation of Philip's methods made it impossible for his officers to do anything without reference to him personally in far-off Spain, and all his enterprises failed because watchful opponents had ample time to foresee and parry his blows. Cecil well knew that the Bishop of Ross in London was Mary's principal intermediary with the Catholic powers. His every movement was spied. Ridolfi's visits to the Spanish ambassador, and his departure for Flanders, were duly reported; and also the fact that the Bishop of Ross's Flemish secretary, a young man named Charles Bailly, had accompanied him. Ridolfi's interviews with Alba at Brussels were known to Cecil as soon as the wind could waft the news, and every port in the south and east of England was closely watched by Cecil's agents. About the 12th of April Charles Bailly landed at Dover from Flanders. He was found to be carrying in his baggage a number of copies of a book that had recently been issued at Liége in favour of Mary Stuart's claim to the English crown; nor was this all, for upon him was found a bulky packet of correspondence in cipher addressed to his master, the Bishop of Ross. The unfortunate young man was himself sent in custody to the Marshalsea in London for inquiry, whilst his packet was taken by Lord Cobham, governor of Dover Castle, for transmission to Cecil.

The Cobhams belonged to the party of conservative nobles, and, by a trick of one of the younger brothers of the house, the real packet was sent to de Spes, whilst a dummy imitation of it was what reached Cecil. The imprisoned secretary wrote from his prison an imprudent letter to the Bishop of Ross, which, of course, was intercepted. 'Now that Rodolfi's letter and the decipher had reached their destination, he had no fear,' he said. 'He would confess nothing, though they pluck him into a hundred pieces'; and he begged the bishop to tell him how to answer the questions put to him. The bishop was just as imprudent as his agent, animating him to stand firm, threatening the villain that had betrayed him, and saying how much Queen Mary's cause would benefit by Bailly's sufferings. The poor wretch knew but little of the particulars of Rodolfi's mission, but he had written the letters for him to the principals in England, and gradually what he knew was wrung out of him on the rack.[462]

Every day fresh letters went from him, with agonising appeals to the Bishop of Ross; until at last, half crazy with terror and pain, he confessed that Alba had received Ridolfi favourably, and had sent him on to Rome and Madrid; that the object of his mission was to demand armed assistance in behalf of two persons in England unnamed. It was sufficient to draw the Bishop of Ross into the Tower, and within sight of the rack, in spite of his cloth and his diplomatic standing. From him, too, in his agony and terror, some extraordinary admissions were wrung, and thus gradually the net was widened, and swept into Cecil's clutches, one after the other, many of the confidants and tools; and the plot to make Mary Queen of England was patiently unravelled. But still there was no actual proof against Mary and Norfolk, for their names in the writings were always indicated by cipher numbers, of which the key was unknown.

At length, in August, a large sum of money[463] was found in the possession of one of the Duke of Norfolk's retainers, with a cipher letter. The money and letter, it appeared on inquiry, were to be forwarded to Lord Herries and Mary's friends in Scotland; and all those who were known to have handled it were at once arrested. The Duke of Norfolk's secretary, Hickford, and his steward, Bannister, were first laid by the heels, and all their secrets twisted out of them. Barker, the duke's confidential servant, gave evidence that condemned his master; the Bishop of Ross, seeing that all was lost, his most confidential correspondence with Mary deciphered, and Norfolk's proceedings known, made a clean breast of the whole business, and, according to his examiner, Dr. Wilson, surpassed Mary's bitterest enemies in vituperation of her.[464] Then Norfolk was caught in the toils, and made as poor an exhibition of himself as a baffled conspirator well could do. He only hoped to wed Mary, he declared, by the favour of others, and with Elizabeth's blessing. He was very sorry he had acted so falsely, and would never do it again. He had never been a Catholic, and yielded wholly to her Majesty. *He*, good man, had not dreamed of bringing a foreign force into England, or of touching the sacred person of his sovereign. The Bishop of Ross, he said, was the real conspirator; and, with such sorry stuff as this, the first and most beloved noble in England whined for mercy and his bare life.[465] Elizabeth was loath to sacrifice him, and withdrew her warrant for his execution more than once. But at length, on the 2nd June 1572, Norfolk's head fell on Tower Hill, and Mary Queen of Scots was free to undertake another 'love affair,' if she had heart to do it. De Spes was expelled from England, with every circumstance of ignominy, for his futile plotting; Philip and Alba were defied by the English queen; and the Catholic nobles, trembling for their necks, shrank into abashed obscurity; whilst Mary Stuart, threatened openly with death, ill and heartbroken at the downfall of her hopes, confined to two small rooms in Sheffield Castle, and spied night and day, was yet haughty and defiant, ceaselessly demanding through La Mothe her full sovereign privileges, replying vigorously to Elizabeth's accusations against her, and still plotting with Alba for the invasion of England in her favour.[466]

One more political love affair, with a man she never saw, was interwoven into Mary's ceaseless plots to gain her end. Unlike the rest of her similar intrigues, in this last case the initiative was due to the ambition of others rather than of the Queen herself. Philip of Spain had found himself in 1571 not only at death-grip with the forces of the Protestant Reformation in his own Netherlands dominions, but forced to defend the supremacy of Christianity in the Mediterranean against the aggressive power of Islam. His own illegitimate brother, Don John of Austria, the most splendid and ambitious young prince in Europe, thirsting for fame, begged to be allowed to lead the hosts of the Cross against the infidel. Philip, as usual, was cold and doubtful. He could not allow the ambition of others, even of his brother, to become a factor of his policy; and when at length he sent Don John to command the Christian fleet, he went surrounded by sage mentors, fenced in by precise limitations, and bound by strict instructions. But when in September the great fleet of galleys swept out of Messina, to find and beat the Turk, who could think of the niggard injunctions of the King far away, when the young prince, gallant in white velvet and gold, with his fair curls floating in the sun, stood erect in the stern castle of his gilded barge, with the sacred banner of the Pope fluttering over him, and the prayers of all Christendom wafting his fleet to victory?

The battle of Lepanto made Don John the darling prince of Catholic Europe. The soberest ministers were carried away with the enthusiasm of the victor; and when Tunis was captured by him there opened before the prince the dream of carving for himself a great new Christian empire in Africa and the East, which should rival the glories of Alexander's realm. The Pope blessed the project, and all Italy and Spain rang with the echoes of the new crusade. But one man, and he the chief, was cold and unmoved. Philip would not, even if his struggle with Protestantism had allowed him, employ his power for the advancement of others; and to all beseeching prayers he turned a deaf ear. Tunis must be dismantled and abandoned, if dreams of a new empire for his brother were to be the result of its capture. In vain Don John protested, and at last disobeyed. Philip's method in such cases was invariable and efficacious. He stopped supplies, left Don John's letters unanswered, and abandoned Tunis to its fate. Within a year the fortress fell to the Turk again, and Don John's garrison of eight thousand men were put to the sword.

The young hero, in bitter resentment, stayed in Italy until his brother needed him for a task which would surely, thought Philip, give no scope for his mad ambition. Alba's system of blood and iron had failed in Flanders. Hellish cruelty had only made the stubborn Dutchmen still more dour. The unpaid Spanish and Italian soldiery had broken loose and become a murderous rabble; and Hollanders, Flemings, and Walloons, Protestant and Catholic alike, were all banded together now to defend their homes from rapine. Bitter as was the pill for him to swallow, Philip had but one possible course, if he would save even the appearance of his sovereignty over Flanders—the conciliation of the Flemings on any terms, and the immediate departure of all the foreign troops from the land they had outraged. He chose Don John for the task, and to his surprise the prince accepted it with alacrity. The reason was evident when Don John, instead of travelling with all speed direct to Flanders, disobeyed orders and rushed to Spain to see his brother. Let him, he prayed, send the fierce soldiery, the wardogs of Alba, away from Flanders by sea, instead of marching them to Italy by land. Let him suddenly descend upon England with these old campaigners, marry the captive Queen of Scots, crush the heretics and their Queen, and reign over Britain with Mary as the humble servants of Spain.

Philip listened with a grim face to the heroics of his brother, and sent him on his way with fair words, but with a determination not to be driven to fight Elizabeth, except at his own time and in his own way; and, what is more, for his own sole advantage. The news of the design came to Orange and to Elizabeth long before Don John appeared on the Flemish frontier; and the States insisted more sternly than ever that the bloodthirsty ruffians should march away by land before Don John should enter Flanders as governor. Hoping against hope that at last he might have his way, Don John alternately raved in anger and wept in despair; and in the meantime obsequious friends were soon able to establish communications with Mary.

She was always ready to clutch at the veriest straw that might float her into the harbour of her hopes; and no wonder, when the new proposals involved marriage with the victor of Lepanto, the prince of romance that Europe idolised, that she smiled from her sad captivity at so tempting a prospect. The Spanish agent in London at the time was a merchant named Antonio de Guaras;[467] and this man, doubtless in the belief that he was serving King Philip's objects in the matter, became the intermediary for the correspondence between the Scottish queen and her new suitor. Guaras was justly proud of the secrecy of his cipher, for most of his letters even yet remain undeciphered; and certainly none of his letters about Mary had been intercepted so early as the 20th January 1577, before Don John's entry into Brussels. But on that date Mary herself mentions in a letter to the Archbishop of Glasgow, in Paris, that Elizabeth and her people were extremely jealous of the idea of her marriage with Don John.[468] A little later (18th March), when Don John had patched up his short, hollow truce with the Flemings, Mary writes how suspicious the English queen is of the pacification, 'fearing that there may be an understanding between the kings of France and Spain, to trouble this realm; and that I, with Don John, may have entered into it. With such talk as this, founded, as I think, on surmise, without any precise knowledge, they have become so alarmed they are already preparing for war, and doing their best to avert the storm, by stirring up the French rebels to fresh disturbances.' Mary expresses her fear that the fresh severity with which she is being treated may be caused by this alarm, and that worse treatment may be in store for her, 'if it should happen that Don John were to make a descent upon this country, in accordance with the general plan you describe to me, even if such descent be without my knowledge or consent. So that you must keep your eyes open, and let me know all the details you can learn of the project; and if it is still being persevered in; for I can assure you I have not been informed of it, further than you have written to me.'[469]

When Poulet and Wilson went to Flanders, shortly before this letter was written, to reconcile Don John with the States, the prince affected to laugh at the idea of a marriage between himself and Mary; but before Wilson returned home he was able to obtain possession of some of Guaras's letters to the prince.[470] They were partially, and with great difficulty, deciphered; and sufficient was understood to prove that the Spanish agent was in constant communication with the captive Queen. He was closely watched thenceforward by Cecil's spies. In September 1577 a letter of his to Zayas, Philip's secretary, says: 'I have received the enclosed letters from the Queen of Scotland. I will continue to entertain her with letters. I have very secure arrangements by which I can send and receive letters from her, however important. The world hopes that God is reserving her for some great service to His cause, and this Queen (Elizabeth) and her friends fear that this is the case.'[471]

In October the same man writes to Don John's secretary about some 'great service,' which is being prepared. And then the suspended sword fell upon Guaras. Most of his secret papers, including all of those from Mary, were hustled away before Cecil's police could seize them; but Guaras was carried to the Tower, and with the rack and the gallows always before him for the next two years, he lay in a dungeon, to be at last contemptuously expelled from England as a conspirator against the Queen. He was stouthearted, and the examiners could gain but little information from him. The nature of the charges against him are, however, plain from the inquiries put to him.[472] 'What letters have passed between you and the Queen of Scots?' 'What letters have passed between her and Don John?' 'How far did Don John proceed in the marriage treaty with the Scottish queen; and who were the principal dealers therein?'

But the danger of the Don John marriage soon passed away. The King frowned at his brother's wild beseeching letters, and left him without money; once more Don John quarrelled with and defied the States, and shut himself up in Namur. The foreign troops marched out of Flanders by land, and the prince, without money, credit, ships, or men, was not only powerless to invade England and marry Mary, but was unable to subdue the Flemings themselves, and died miserably in despair. It was almost as if a malison accompanied the matrimonial regards of Mary Stuart. One after the other, her husbands and suitors had died prematurely and unhappily: Francis in his early youth, Darnley cruelly murdered, Bothwell a prisoner in exile, Norfolk on the scaffold, and Don John of a broken heart; all dead but Mary and her great ambition, which could never die whilst she breathed. Once only did she seem to waver. In 1583, when the Catholic party was paramount in Scotland, and a great conspiracy against Elizabeth and England was being hatched by Mendoza, the Guises, the Jesuits, and Lennox-d'Aubigny, the Queen of England as a diversion sent to propose terms for Mary's release, with permission for her to go to France or Scotland. Mary was ill and old, she herself told Beal, and needed peace; and she wrote to Mendoza, the Spanish ambassador, to ask his advice as to whether she should make terms with Elizabeth for her liberation. He thought nothing of the wretched woman or of her freedom, and advised her, as he says, 'with the greatest artifice,' to refuse all offers of freedom or reconciliation; because, as he wrote to his King, her release might be injurious to Spanish aims in England, especially if Mary were in a place where French influences could reach her.[473]

Thenceforward, until her death, Mary was the centre around which revolved the great Spanish intrigue to obtain possession of England, in order that Philip might triumph over the Reformation. Under the cunning guidance of Mendoza all other ends, even her own best interests, were set aside by the Queen of Scots. The ties of blood, the claims of humanity, the tolerant pity of an ageing woman, who herself had suffered much, all were dwarfed and deadened in her by the ever-growing ambition to triumph over her foes, and sit on the throne of Catholic Britain before she died. For that she was willing that the foundations of her regal state should be set deep in blood, that foreign pikemen should interpose an impassable barrier between her and the people she sought to rule, and that, after her, there should succeed, not her own child, but the narrow, sinister despot, whose very name made Englishmen shudder.

The amorousness, which in her earlier years had sometimes for a space caused her to forget her overpowering ambition, was itself conquered now. Once it pleased the cantankerous virago, Bess of Hardwick, Countess of Shrewsbury, to accuse her henpecked husband, the guardian of Mary, of falling a prey to the wiles of his prisoner, and softening her captivity for love of her. Perhaps Shrewsbury, who was always kind and considerate to Mary, did fall under the dominion of her plaintive smile: most men did when Mary deigned to exercise her fascination upon them. But with the death of Norfolk, Mary's attempts to use the resources of courtship as an element in her diplomacy came to an end. Thenceforward the hope of triumph over her foes by any desperate means monopolised her caged activity; but love and marriage formed no part of her plans. At that game she had measured herself with Elizabeth, and had been beaten; for she had found that, for her, political love affairs had been but Dead Sea fruit, that had blighted all her own fair prospects, and had brought her lovers, one by one, to sorrow and to death.

Well it would have been for her and her cause if from the first she had been able to recognise the disadvantages under which she laboured, in competing with Elizabeth in the employment of her own disposal in marriage as an instrument of her policy. She was warm-hearted and trustful: Elizabeth was cold and suspicious. Elizabeth had always by her side the judicious, clear-sighted Cecil to save her from herself in her hours of weakness, and Leicester as a permanent matrimonial possibility and a foil to other suitors: Mary was surrounded by the most self-seeking set of traitors and scoundrels the world ever saw, and both the men she thought she loved were utterly unworthy of her; and, above all, Elizabeth had strength to remain single, whilst Mary had not. The contest was an unequal one, and the weaker competitor lost because she was the more human of the two and the less fortunate.

INDEX

Mary, 251, 254; denounced by
Mary, 270.

Banner of vengeance, the, 258, 259.

Bannister, the duke of Norfolk's steward, arrested, 298.

Barker, a servant of the duke of
Norfolk, arrested, 298.

Bastien, Mary's valet, 231, 237.

Bayonne, the meeting at, 126, 182,
186.

Beal, his visit to Mary (1583), 303.

Beaton, archbishop of Glasgow,
Scottish ambassador in Paris, 169;
agrees with Alba at Bayonne, 186,
226, 235.

—— cardinal, 8, 9; regent, 9; arrest
of, 10; released, 17; triumph of, 18;
murdered, 21, 22.

—— John, his mission to Guzman,
138, 153, 182; sent to France, 269.

—— Mary, 108, 206.

Bedford, earl of, warden of the
marches, 64, 65, 66, 123, 133, 136,
181; at James's baptism, 221, 262.

Blackater, captain, 243; hanged for
Darnley's murder, 359n396.

Borthwick Castle, Mary at, 253–255,
271.

—— laird of, 255.

Bothwell, James Hepburn, earl of,
75, 83; Arran's plan to murder
him, 87; joins Arran's plan to
kidnap Mary, 87, 88; returns to
Scotland, 184–186; escapes after

Rizzio's murder, 198, 199, 202;
not to remain with Mary when her
child was born, 205, 206; in great
favour, 208; his unpopularity,
210, 211; his alleged amours with
Mary, 212; wounded on the border, 216; visits Mary at Jedburgh,
217; stays with her there, 218;
scandalous reports thereon, 218; at
the Craigmillar conference against
Darnley, 219; at James's baptism,
221; rumours of his amours with
Mary, 225; arranges the murder
of Darnley, 230; after the crime,
235; suspected of complicity, 235;
accompanies Mary at Seton, 236;
publicly accused of the murder,
236, 237; his trial and acquittal,
238–241; Mary's infatuation for
him, 239; grants him Dunbar,
etc., 243; seizes the queen, 243; at
Dunbar, 244; boasts that he will
marry the queen, 245; divorces his
wife, 246; the lords revolt against
him, 246; bond signed against,
at Stirling, 248; preparations for
defence, 248; his behaviour to
Mary, 249–251; marriage, 250;
after the wedding, 251–252;
threats of the lords against, 253;
flight to Borthwick, 254; flight to
Dunbar, 255; at Carberry Hill,
256; flight, 258; Mary refuses to

abandon him, 259; his wander-
ings, 265.
—— countess of (Jane Gordon),
239–242; divorced, 246.
Bourbons, the, 34, 56, 59, 60, 61, 67,
153.
Boyd, lord, signs the Rizzio bond,
196; at York, 279.
Brantome, 4, 27, 35, 37, 41, 62, 64, 74,
76, 102.
Buchanan, George, 37, 92; his statements to Mary's detriment, 209,
212, 218; at York, 279.

CAITHNESS, earl of, 242.
Calais, loss of, 47; Mary sails from, 73,
74, 75, 77.
Carberry Hill, 256.
Carey, George, proposal to marry him
to Mary, 283.
Carlos, Don, suggested marriage with
Mary, 65, 67, 68, 70, 86, 87, 89, 93,
96, 98, 103, 106, 111, 112, 113, 117,
119, 120, 122; Philip declines the
match, 127, 139, 155, 159.
Carwood, Margaret, her marriage,
236.
Casket Papers, 3, 5, 225; the sonnets,
239; Murray's talk with Guzman
about them, 260; produced at
York, 279.
Cassilis, lord, 43, 173, 242.
Castelnau de la Mauvissière, French
ambassador, 127–130, 139,

154, 157, 183–184; present at
Elizabeth's reception of Murray,
187, 206.
Cateau Cambresis, treaty of, 47.
Catharine de Medici, queen of
France, 2, 6, 26, 27, 28, 29, 31,
34, 41, 45, 53, 54, 55, 56, 60;
queen–regent, 61, 65, 66, 70; her
intrigues against a Spanish match
for Mary, 89; attempts to estrange
Mary and Elizabeth, 92; smiles
upon Lorraine, 121, 125; stops
the Spanish match, 127, 153, 183;
shocked at the Bothwell marriage,
252; endeavours to obtain possession of James, 252; attempts to
conciliate Murray, 261.
Catholics, English, 50, 117, 136, 137,
167, 170, 187, 194, 195, 204, 205,
207, 222, 223, 224, 236, 284, 286,
293, 294.
Catholic lords, Scottish, 10, 15, 17,
68, 79, 92, 205, 259, 261; resent
Mary's imprisonment, 264, 267.
Cecil, William, lord Burghley, 48, 71;
his dealing with Lethington, 94,
116; plots against, 126; conveys
to Elizabeth the news of James's
birth, 206; his policy thwarted by
Elizabeth's regard for royalty, 262,
275; plots against, 283, 285; dis-
covers the Ridolfi plot, 297.
Cesford, laird of, 217.
Chalmers, David, 212.

her counter intrigues, 161; is shocked at Mary's behaviour with Darnley, 162; her anger to Hay of Balmerino, 168; her approaches to Spain, 170; her treatment of the Scottish protestants, 179–182; her difficult position, 184; receives Murray, 187–189; approaches made to Mary, 188–189; her danger, 193; her reception of the news of James's birth, 206; difficulty of her position, 207–208; temporises with Mary, 223; her feigned sorrow at Darnley's murder, 236; her secret delight at the Bothwell marriage, 252; endeavours to obtain possession of James, 252; her respect for royalty, 261; her attitude towards Murray, 261; her attitude on Mary's arrival in England, 275–278; the great conspiracy against, 282–290; proposal to deliver Mary to Morton, 292, 292; the Ridolfi plot to murder her, 293–297; beheads Norfolk, 298.

Elizabeth of Valois, queen of Spain, 26, 27, 31, 32, 45, 51–52, 67; Mary's letter to, 361n427.

Elliot, John, of the Park, wounds Bothwell, 216.

England, relations with Scotland, 7, 8, 9, 10, 11–13, 14–19, 20, 22, 58, 59, 66.

Eric, King of Sweden, a suitor for Mary, 84, 87; rejected, 114.

Erskine, Arthur, captain of the guard, present at Rizzio's murder, 196, 197; plans Mary's escape after Rizzio's murder, 200.

—— lord, 23.

—— lady, 172.

Erskine of Dun, French plot against, 54.

Exchequer House, Edinburgh, 212.

FALKLAND, death of James V at, 8–9; submission of Arran at, 17.

Ferrara, duke of, a suitor to Mary, 84, 86.

Fleming, lady, 23, 26, 37.

——lord, 43, 263, 277–278.

Forster, Sir John, Warden of the Marches, 217.

Fowler (Catholic agent) sent to London, 154, 172, 185.

France, relations with Scotland, 8, 18–19, 20–22, 28, 37, 38, 44, 51, 56.

Francesco, a Catholic agent of Mary, 185.

Francis I, king of France, 11, 20, 22.

—— II, king of France, 23, 24, 26, 30, 36, 37; married to Mary, 39–41, 44; his letter to Elizabeth, 47, 48–49; succeeds his father, 55; illness, 61; death of, 61.

French troops in Scotland, 15, 22, 56, 57, 71.

Fyvie, laird of, 17.

GLASGOW, Darnley's interview with Mary at, 228, 271.

Glencairn, earl of, welcomes Darnley, 142, 173, 174, 201, 243.

Gordons, the rising of the, 90–92.

Gordon, John, in love with Mary, 90; his disobedience, 91; his revolt, 91; executed, 92.

Granvelle, Cardinal de, 118, 120, 155, 158.

Grey, lady Katharine, her claim to the English succession, 223, 236.

Grimani, papal legate, 19.

Guaras, Antonio, Spanish agent in the plot to marry Mary to Don John, 301–303.

Guises, the, 29, 28, 30, 33, 40, 42, 44, 47, 50, 53, 56, 57, 59, 60, 64, 67, 84, 89, 93; prefer an Austrian match for Mary, 111.

Guise, duke of (Claude), 10, 11, 28.

—— duke of (Francis), 28, 30, 40, 54, 55, 66, 67, 73; enters Paris in triumph, 88; murder of, at Orleans, 94.

—— the dowager of (Antoinette), 25, 26, 27, 37, 67, 68.

Guzman de Silva, Spanish ambassador in London, 126, 136, 137; his interviews with Beaton, 138, 152; his interviews with Fowler, 154–155; receives Lethington, 159; receives Hay of Balmerino, 169; his conversations with Elizabeth, 183, 188, 207; believes in Mary's prior knowledge of plot against Darnley, 236; his interviews with Murray, 261; his opinion of Mary, 262–263, 277.

HAMILTON, 181, 269, 270, 271.

—— House, Edinburgh, 229, 232.

Hamiltons, the, 9, 30, 39, 50, 131, 134, 137, 140, 142, 157, 167, 174, 175, 192, 195, 259, 263, 264, 267, 269, 281.

Hamilton, archbishop of St. Andrews, 221, 229, 246; urges Mary's murder, 264; sides with her on her escape, 270.

—— lord Claude, 229, 269.

Hampton Court, conference adjourned to, 283.

Hay of Balmerino, sent to London, 168; carries good news to Mary, 169.

Hay of Talla in the Darnley murder, 231.

Heigate's story, 227.

Henry II, king of France, 26, 29, 38, 40, 52; death of, 54.

—— III, king of France, 2. See also Anjou.

—— VIII, king of England, 7, 9, 11;

his attempts to obtain possession of Mary, 11, 22.

Hepburn of Bowton in the Darnley murder, 231.

—— captain, insults the queen, 107.

Hermitage, Bothwell at, 216; Mary visits him at, 217.

Herries, lord, 263, 267; at Langsyde, 271; accompanies Mary in her flight, 272; sent to London, 276, 277.

Hertford, earl of. *See* Somerset.

Hickford, a servant of the duke of Norfolk, arrested, 298.

Howard of Effingham, lord, his embassy to France, 48, 49.

Huguenots, the, 6, 56, 60, 61, 65, 66, 67, 84, 89, 96, 98, 102, 103, 106, 188.

Humes, the, 16, 202, 253, 254.

Hume, lord (Alexander Hume), 177, 202, 217; at Langsyde, 271.

Huntly, George Gordon, fourth earl of, 9, 10, 14, 16, 18, 33, 44, 69, 79; will set up the Mass in three shires, 82, 90; his rebellion, 90–91; his death, 92.

—— fifth earl of, 195; escapes after Rizzio's murder, 198, 202, 217, 219, 221; in the Darnley murder, 232, 236, 238, 242, 243, 246, 259, 263, 264.

Huntingdon, earl of, 288, 289, 291.

JAMES V, king of Scotland, 8.

—— VI, king of Scotland, 206; kept by Mar at Stirling, 252; competition for possession of him, 253; crowned, 262, 264.

Jedburgh, Mary at, 215–218.

John of Austria, Don. *See* Don John.

KILWINNING, abbot of, urges Mary's murder, 264.

Kirkcaldy of Grange, 56, 88, 131, 191, 196, 198, 242, 243; at Carberry Hill, 257, 258, 259; at Langsyde, 271.

Kirk–o'–Field, 231–232, 235.

Knollys, Sir F., his mission to Mary, 276, 277, 280; proposes George Carey to Mary, 283.

Knox, John, 24, 34, 43, 44, 76, 77, 79, 80, 81; his interview with Mary, 82, 83, 92; his indignation at Mary's behaviour, 105, 108; his suspicions of a Catholic marriage, 117, 131; offends Darnley, 180; his fear and flight, 181.

LA BROSSE, French envoy, 19.

La Mothe Fénelon, French ambassador, 299.

Langsyde, battle of, 271.

Leighton, English envoy to Mary, 275.

Leith, sacked by Somerset, 20; French troops in, 58; siege of, by

Elizabeth's troops, 58; Mary lands at, 77.

Lennox, Margaret, countess of, 19, 20, 85; in favour with Elizabeth, 113, 124, 126, 129–130, 133, 137, 152, 155, 158, 159, 160, 166; sent to the Tower, 168, 206; accuses Mary of Darnley's murder, 236.

—— Matthew Stuart, earl of, 11, 15, 18, 19, 20, 85, 129; goes to Scotland, 129, 137, 140, 150, 202; Murray plots to capture him, 168; Elizabeth calls him a traitor, 168; at Mary's private marriage, 172, 177; plots with Darnley, 194, 195, 213, 237; regent of Scotland, 292.

Lethington, William Maitland, laird of, 47, 56, 68; his fears of Mary's coming, 76, 77; sent to England, 80, 83, 84, 86, 88; another mission to England, 92; his intrigue with Spain, 93 *passim*; his change of policy, 97–99; changes again, 113, 116; favours Leicester's suit, 139; alarmed at Darnley, 149, 152; more Spanish intrigue, 154, 157; sees lady Lennox and Guzman, 159; bids for Catholic support, 160; his return to Scotland with hopes of Spanish aid, 165, 177; he fears results of his own policy, 185; signs the Rizzio bond, 196; reconciled to Bothwell, 211; with Mary on the Border,

217; his suggestion for removing Darnley at Craigmillar, 219–220; in the Darnley murder, 232; his account of it sent to France, 235, 237, 239, 244; prepared to betray Mary, 249; at Carberry Hill, 256, 258; deaf to Mary's appeal, 259; panic and flight, 264; denounced by Mary, 270; at York, 279, 281, 282; proposes Mary's marriage to Norfolk, 282.

Liggons, a Catholic agent, 282.

Lignerolles, French envoy to Scotland, 261.

Lindsay, earl of, at Carberry, 257; at Lochleven, 263; at York, 279.

Linlithgow, Mary born at, 9, 17; meets Darnley at, 217.

Lisle, lord (John Dudley), 10.

Livingston, Mary, marriage of, 148.

Livingstone, lord, 23, 24.

Lochleven Castle, Mary at, 260–268; escape from, 269.

Lorraine, cardinal (Charles), (*see also* Guises), 27, 30, 31, 33, 34, 38, 40, 48, 49, 55, 58, 59, 61, 66, 67, 68, 86; he betrays Mary, 110; urges the archduke's suit, 115, 120; in favour with Catharine, 121, 126; stops the match with Carlos, 127, 128, 138; proposes Condé for Mary, 138, 146, 153, 159, 182, 207, 222.

—— cardinal (John), 40.

Darnley's jealousy, 193–195; at the murder, 197; flight to England after Rizzio's murder, 201; pardon of, 217; will sign bond for Darnley's murder if Mary authorises him, 225; privy to Darnley's murder, 230, 238, 246, 254; at Carberry Hill, 258, 259; his fear of Mary, 264; at Langsyde, 271; at York, 279, 281.

Murray, James Stuart, earl of, regent of Scotland, 6, 18, 43; plot against in France, 54, 69; his fears of Mary's coming, 76, 79, 80; offended at the Mass, 82; his moderate course, 84, 86; fresh attempts to settle the English succession, 92, 98; his anger with Chastelard, 105; disclaims to Cecil the Spanish match, 117; refuses to stay the coming of Lennox, 130; leans toward Leicester, 137, 139; alarmed about Darnley, 146–148, 156; retires to St. Andrews, 156; focuses the Protestant discontent, 162; distrusts Lethington, 163; refuses to sanction the Darnley marriage, 164; plots with Randolph to capture Darnley, 168; his revolt, 178; defeat and flight, 181–182, 186; seeks interview with Elizabeth, 187; Elizabeth's reception of him, 187–188; seeks forgiveness, 193; plots with Morton and Darnley, 193; privy to Rizzio's murder, 201; returns to Edinburgh, 202; submits to Mary, 203; remains with Mary on birth of James VI, 206; endeavours to secure Morton's pardon, 208; with Mary on the Border, 216; accompanies Mary to Hermitage, 216; with her at Jedburgh, 217; his presence at the conference of Craigmillar, 352n326; entertains Bedford at St. Andrews, 224; did not sign the Darnley murder bond, 225; privy to Darnley's murder, 230; his treacherous dealing with Mary, 239; leaves for France, and escapes signing the Ainslie bond, 242; return after Carberry, 359n394; his interview with Guzman in London, 261; made regent, 264; sees Mary at Lochleven, 265; combination against him, 266; approaches Mary, 267; denounced by Mary, 269; at Langsyde, 271; at York, 279, 280, 281; feigns approval of the Norfolk match, 283; approached by Norfolk, 287; murder of, 292.

Murray, countess of, 205, 266.

—— James, brother of Tullibardine, denounces Bothwell, 237.

NAVARRE, Anthony de Bourbon,

—— lady, 171.

—— lord, 202, 263, 267, 269.

Shrewsbury, countess of, jealous of
Mary, 303–304.

—— earl of, accused by his wife of
flirting with Mary, 303–304.

Sidney, sir Henry, 90, 107.

Solway Moss, battle of, 8.

Somerset, duke of, protector of
England, invades Scotland, 19, 20,
22–23.

Stirling, castle of, 16, 23, 156; meeting
of the lords at, to oppose Bothwell,
246, 248; James VI at, 248, 249.

Strathbogie Castle, 90, 91.

Stuart of Traquair, 200.

—— lord John, 85.

—— lord Robert, abbot of Holyrood
(earl of Orkney), 24, 78, 85; present at Rizzio's murder, 196, 197;
warns Darnley, 231.

Sutherland, earl of, 242.

TAMWORTH, his mission to
Scotland, 178, 179, 183.

Tantallon, II, 218.

Taylor, Darnley's page, murdered,
232.

Thornton, Scottish Catholic envoy,
207.

Throckmorton, Sir N., 48, 50, 51, 53,
55, 57, 61, 62, 63, 65, 66; interview
with Murray in France, 69, 70;

interview with Mary, 72, 73; sent
to Scotland to stop the Darnley
match, 161, 164–165; his warning
to Elizabeth, 166; sent to Scotland
after Carberry, 261, 263, 264;
arrested for the Norfolk conspiracy, 289.

Tullibardine, laird of, 257, 264.

VASSY, massacre of Huguenots at,
88.

Villeroy, French envoy to Scotland,
261.

WAR of religion begins in France, 88,
89.

Warwick, earl of (Ambrose Dudley),
Elizabeth suggests him for Mary,
99.

Wemyss, castle of, Mary first sees
Darnley at, 143.

Westmoreland, earl of, his share in the
northern rising, 289–290.

Whittinghame (William Douglas),
proposal to Mary from sent by
Morton, 225.

Wilson, Dr., 298, 302.

YAXLEY, his mission to Spain, 182,
189; his death, 190.

Yester, laird of, at Carberry Hill, 255.

York, the conference at, 279–283.

ENDNOTES

1 *Calendar of State Papers, Henry* VIII., vol. xvii. p. 657.

2 John Knox.

3 *Hamilton Papers,* p. 276.

4 They were Earls Cassilis and Glencairn, Lords Maxwell, Fleming, Somerville, and Grey, Robert Erskine, Oliver St. Clair, and the Lairds of Craigy and Carssie.

5 *Calendar, Henry* VIII., vol. xviii. p. 54.

6 *Calendar, Henry* VIII., vol. xviii. p. 85.

7 *Sadlier State Papers.*

8 George Douglas told Sadlier 'that they had agreed well together, and though in the beginning one began to grin at another, there was none that would bite, nor fall out amongst themselves whereby they might make themselves prey to enemies.'

9 Arran's falsity is evident here. Beaton was already partially at liberty, being only confined in his own castle of St. Andrews, and soon to be restored to the Regency by Arran's voluntary act, as will be seen.

10 He had ample cause for suspicion even thus early. The copy of a pledge taken by the Cardinal and his adherents when they were at Linlithgow (24th July), to prevent Mary's removal to England, was sent to England by Sadlier on the 10th August. This pledge was signed by several of the ex-prisoners who had been ostensibly favourable to English influence, and though Arran solemnly denied that he knew of it, subsequent events would seem to render his statement doubtful. Mary was removed to Stirling on the 26th July, and a month afterwards Henry's brother-in-law, Suffolk, was instructed to hold himself in readiness on the Border to invade Scotland with 16,000 or 20,000 men.—*Hamilton Papers,* vol. ii.

11 *Calendar, Henry* VIII., vol. xviii. pt. 2, p. 11.

12 *Hamilton Papers,* vol. ii.

13 *Hamilton Papers,* vol. ii.

14 A counter intrigue to this was started by the Cardinal (November 1543), in order to seduce Lennox from the English connection. It was proposed that Arran should divorce his wife and marry Mary of Guise; and, whilst remaining nominally Regent, should hand the real power to Lennox, who was to be betrothed to the infant Mary: 'And so they shall be friends and join together as one party with France against England.' The proposal was probably never anything but a feint; but, patriotism apart, it was obviously less favourable to Lennox than his immediate marriage with a beautiful bride of full age, well dowered, and in near succession to the crown of England (*Hamilton Papers,* vol. ii.).

15 *Spanish State Papers, Henry* VIII., vol. vii. p. 34.

16 *Ibid.* p. 60.

17 Full accounts of the engagement, from Hertford and Russell, are in *Spanish State Papers,* vol. viii. (now in the press). The Cardinal, we are told, appeared upon the field dressed in a frock of yellow velvet slashed and puffed with white spangled silk (see also *Hamilton Papers,* and Teulet (Bannatyne Club), *Papiers d'Etat).*

18 Rymer, xv.

19 *Hamilton Papers,* vol. ii.

20 *Spanish State Papers,* vol. viii. (in the press), and *Diurnall of Occurrents.*

21 So hardly driven was Francis, that he was forced to strike a special debased coinage of 150,000 crowns to send to Scotland to pay the troops taken thither by Montgomerie (*Spanish State Papers,* vol. viii. p. 147, in the press).

22 *Ibid.*

23 *Ibid.*

24 *Spanish State Papers, Henry* VIII., vol. viii. (in the press).

25 Bishop of Ross's *History of Scotland* (Bannatyne Club).

26 *Hamilton Papers,* vol. ii.

27 *Hamilton Papers,* vol. ii. Henry Jones to Somerset, 9th August 1548. The same writer says: 'The old Queen doth lament the young Queen's departure, and marvels that she heareth nothing from her.' It is difficult to see how she could have heard so soon, as the squadron can hardly have sailed more than a day or two before.

28 The Earls of Lennox and Kildare, a Danish prince, etc.

29 Many authorities give Brest as the place, but for several reasons I consider that the

balance of proof is in favour of Roscoff, where a chapel to commemorate the event was soon afterwards erected, the ruins of which still exist.

30 *Balcarres Papers.* The Dauphin, of course, was the child Francis, destined husband of Mary, and the two princesses, Elizabeth, afterwards third wife of Philip II, and Claude, afterwards Duchess of Lorraine.

31 In support of this opinion, it may be mentioned that both Elizabeth, Queen of Spain, and Claude, Duchess of Lorraine, her school-fellows, were paragons of propriety, whilst their younger sister Margaret was just the reverse.

32 Jebb (Conæus).

33 If we are to take literally the account of Conæus (in Jebb), the child of eight years, when taken to Rouen with the court to receive her mother, Mary of Guise, in 1550, replied to the Queen-Dowager's maternal embraces by inquiring: 'What factions continued to subsist in the noble families of Scotland, at the same time inquiring by name for those who had evinced most attachment to the ancient faith. She then proceeded to ask, with all the usual expressions of royal benevolence, whether the English still harassed her native country; whether worship remained pure, and the prelates and clergy did their duty.'

34 *Calendar of Foreign State Papers, Edward.*

35 Labanoff, vol. i. p. 5.

36 Writing shortly after this, the Venetian ambassador, Capello, reported that 'she is most beautiful (*bellissima*), and so accomplished that she inspires with astonishment every one who witnesses her acquirements. The Dauphin, too, is very fond of her, and finds great pleasure in her company and conversation' (*Relations des Ambassadeurs Venetiens*).

37 Labanoff, vol. i. p. II.

38 *Latin Themes of Mary Stuart* (Anatole de Montaiglon).

39 Labanoff, vol. i. p. 21.

40 *Ibid.*

41 Mary to her mother, 28th December 1555 (Labanoff, vol. i.).

42 Cardinal Santa Croce to the Pope, quoted by Cheruel: Catharine, however, a profound dissembler, who at this period made no open attempt to dominate, followed the lead of her husband in showing public consideration for Mary. Cardinal Lorraine writes (8th April 1556): 'I can assure you, madam (*i.e.* Mary of Guise), that there is nothing more virtuous or beautiful than your daughter, and she is very devout also. She quite governs the King and Queen.' In reality, as was afterwards made plain, Catharine was the last

person in the world to allow a girl whom she hated to 'govern' her; but it was for the moment her policy to 'lie low.'

43 The Cardinal to Mary of Guise (Labanoff, vol. i.).

44 *Venetian Calendar,* Sorzanzo to the Doge, 9th November 1557.

45 Brantome, *Dames Illustres.*

46 Brantome says he was '*éperdument épris*' of her. Even when they were both children (in 1548) Constable Montmorenci wrote to Mary of Guise: '*Je vous asseuray que Monseigneur le Dauphin en est soigneulx et amoureux come de s'amye et sa femme, et qu il est bien ayse a juger que Dieu les a faict naitre l'un pour l'autre. Je vous souhaict souvent ici pour les veoir ensemble.*'

47 In the midst of the splendid turmoil of her wedding-day (24th April 1558) Mary found time to scribble a long, dutiful, and delighted letter to her mother (first printed by Mr. Hay Fleming in his *Mary Stuart),* in which she does not hide her triumphal happiness in her marriage. '*Je ne vous en diray rien, sinon que je m'estime l'une de plus heureuses fames du monde, pour avoir et le Roy et la Reine, et madame* (i.e. Margaret), *et messieurs et medames* (in the Princes and Princesses of the blood) *tant que je les sauroys souhaiter, et le Roy mon mari, me fait une estime comme telle que je veus vivre et mourir* . . . (here follows a list of the beautiful presents made to her). *Quant a messieurs mes oncles il n'est possible de me plus faire d'honneur et d'amitie qu'ils ont tous fait tant aises et contents que rien plus, et surtout monsieur le Cardinal mon oncle qui a eu la paine de tout, et tout avance si onestement que on ne parle d'autre chose.*'

48 Bad as was Cardinal Lorraine (Charles of Guise), he was not so bad, or bad in the same way, as the elder Cardinal Lorraine, his uncle John, for whose vices he is sometimes blamed. Bothwell's coarse reference to Mary after her arrival in Scotland as '*the Cardinal's whore*' must surely have been unwarranted.

49 The patent is cited in Labanoff, the Scottish ambassadors being the Archbishop of Glasgow, the Bishops of Orkney and Ross, Lords Cassilis and Rothes, James Stuart, Prior of St. Andrews, James Fleming, John Erskine of Dun, and George Seaton.

50 They are published in Labanoff, vol. i., but were first printed in Purton Cooper's *Correspondance de La Mothe Fénélon.* The originals are in the Archives Nationales Paris.

51 It was stipulated that the elder son of the marriage should be King of France and Scotland, and that if only a daughter was born she was to be Queen of Scotland with a dower of 400,000 crowns from France, and only to be married with the consent of the King of France. A widow's jointure of 60,000 livres Tournois was secured to Mary.

52 For accounts of the marriage festivities see *Discours du grand et magnifique triomphe*, etc. Paris, 1558, Teulet's *Papiers d'Etat*, etc.

53 *Venetian Calendar*, vol. vi.

54 *Dames Illustres*.

55 In the hastily written letter from Mary to her mother, dated on the day of her marriage with Francis (first printed by Mr. Hay Fleming), a most significant passage occurs which shows how ready and eager Mary was to subordinate the interests of Scotland to the aims of the Guises: '*Quant a vous dire ce je fait avec mes Ecosois je espere que vous vous contenteres de moi, car comme je pense que Monsieur le Cardinal mon oncle vous aura fait entendre . . . j'en ay a peu pres fait tout ce que je voulois.*'

56 Buchanan, *History of Scotland*.

57 In Mr. Hay Fleming's *Mary Stuart* several other authorities for this belief are quoted.

58 *Dieu ha voulu que les ambassadeurs qui vont presentement vers vous etant a mi chemin ayent esté repousés jusqu'a Dieppe: la ils sont tous malades, et Monsieur d'Orcenay mort.*— Labanoff, vol. i. p. 58.

59 Labanoff, vol. i. p. 57.

60 For particulars of these intrigues, see the *Courtships of Queen Elizabeth* by the present writer.

61 *Calendar of Spanish State Papers, Elizabeth,* vol. i.

62 The same ambassador, the hot-headed Feria, at a subsequent period (1560), after his retirement from England, told Throckmorton that Cardinal Lorraine had assured him that when the Regent Arran had consented to the marriage of Mary and Francis in their infancy, he had agreed to a stipulation that Scotland should in future be an appanage of the French crown, and ruled by the successive heirs to the realm of France, even though no issue were born of Mary's marriage.—Forbes, 4th May 1560. This story is extremely unlikely, and in view of Feria's personal hatred of Elizabeth, and his ardent desire to embroil England with France, it may safely be disbelieved.

63 Cardinal Lorraine was apparently to blame for first bringing forward the idea in a form offensive to Elizabeth. In a memorandum of Cecil's (*Hatfield MSS.* vol. i. p. 154) it is stated that when the peace commissioners met at Cateau Cambresis, Cardinal Lorraine expressed a doubt as to whether they ought to 'treat with any for England but with the Dolphin and his wife.' But the speech was repudiated, and the Cardinal reproved, by the Constable Montmorenci.

64 *Foreign Calendar, Elizabeth* (March 1559).

65 *Foreign Calendar, Elizabeth* (March 1559), and Forbes's *Public Transactions.*

66 Lord Howard of Effingham, the principal English special ambassador, also mentions very different scutcheons in a letter to the Queen (24th May). He was entertained splendidly on his way from Amiens to Paris at various houses belonging to Constable Montmorenci. At that of Escouan, near Paris, they noticed 'upon the gate, as in divers places within the house, were set uppe three scutcheons; the middlemost conteyninge the armes of Englande; that on the right hande conteyninge a rose half whyte and half redde, and the thurd conteyninge a great E, as it seemed to me for your Highness' name. The lyke we found at our lodgings at Paris.' It is evident that this was intended by Montmorenci as a counterstroke to the Guises' scutcheons quartering England on Mary's arms, and it demonstrates how profoundly the nobility of France was divided between the Guisan-papal party and the 'politicians' who favoured toleration and friendship with England. When, later, Throckmorton showed to Montmorenci and protested against the escutcheons bearing the English arms quartered on those of Scotland and France, the Constable, whilst evidently disapproving of them, endeavoured to minimise their significance, and pointed out that Elizabeth quartered the arms of France upon her own, as her ancestors had done.—See letters in Forbes's *Public Transactions,* etc.

67 Forbes, vol i., 24th May 1559.

68 Forbes, vol. i. p. 118.

69 Throckmorton, writing early in June 1559, urges the Queen 'to nourish and entertain the garboil in Scotland as much as may be.'

70 That Mary personally was an approving party to the intrigues for which Cardinal Lorraine is usually held responsible, and of which Throckmorton says young Francis himself was the head, is proved by the reply given by her to M. de Monpesson, who was ordered to capture Arran. The Frenchman apologised to the Queen for having to take such measures against a kinsman of hers, and she replied that he could do her 'no greater pleasure than to use the Earl of Arran as an arrant traitor.' Throckmorton, when telling this story to Cecil, recommends that it should be 'insinuated' as much as possible into the ears of the Duke of Chatelherault and the Hamiltons, in order to irritate them and the Protestants against France.

71 Throckmorton to Cecil, 21st June 1559.

72 Throckmorton to Cecil, 21st June 1559. *The Constable, it must be recollected, was England's friend.*

73 Mary to her mother (Labanoff, vol. i. p. 72).

74 Labanoff, vol. i. p. 71.

75 The entrance of Francis and Mary into Arran's forfeited town of Chatelherault is thus described by Throckmorton (29th November 1559): 'The Quene, who came first, was received by the burgeois and convoyed to the palice, having a canapy of crimson damask, the arms of England, France, and Scotland quartered thereon, carried over her by foure of the townsmen. The King, coming after, was in like sort received, and had carried over him a canapy of purple damask with the armes of France only. There were two gates of the towne painted, through which they passed; on the right sides whereof were set forth the armes of France with the King's name, and on the left sides the armes of England, France, and Scotland, quartered, with the Quene's name. Upon which gates, underneath the King's and Quene's pictures, were set forth the verses in golden letters which we send your Majesty here enclosed.' The following was one of the verses:—

'Gallia perpetuis pugnaxque Britannia bellis.
Olim odio inter se dimicuere pari,
Nunc Gallos totoque remotos orbe britannos,
Unum dos Mariæ cogit in imperium.
Ergo pace potes Francisce quod omnibus armis,
Millie patres annis non potuere tui.'

Francis and Mary had gone to Chatelherault to accompany thus far Elizabeth of Valois on her journey to wed Philip II.

76 See Les Triomphes de Chenonceau, a contemporary tract, reprinted by Prince Galitzin, Paris, 1857, and Poplinière, Histoire de France, 1550-1581.

77 Cardinal Lorraine approached Throckmorton first in February, and had a long interview with him at Amboise, in which he artfully minimised his action in Scotland. He also sent his henchman, Monluc, Bishop of Valence, to Elizabeth with a similar object in March. Mary herself turned angrily upon her uncles and said they had lost her realm.

78 The correspondence of the special Flemish agent Glajon sent to England for the purpose is calendared in vol. i. of the Spanish State Papers of Elizabeth (Hume).

79 Diurnal of Occurrents.

80 Venetian State Papers, vol. vii.

81 Mary of Guise herself on her deathbed recognised how fatal had been her brother's

ambitious policy with regard to England and Scotland. She saw James Stuart (Murray) and other leaders of the Congregation, and admitted the unwisdom of the policy she had been forced to carry out, begging them as a last resource at least to be loyal to their sovereign, her daughter.

82 By parliament was understood an assembly of the bishops, titular abbots, and nobles, with a few members to represent the burgesses of the greater towns, but in practice the higher nobles, each attended by an armed retinue, usually disposed of matters as they pleased.

83 *Venetian Calendar*, vol. vii.

84 Teulet, *Papiers d'Etat,* vol. i. p. 605.

85 *Foreign* Calendar, Elizabeth, *vol. iii.*

86 A week before his fatal attack he had fainted at vespers in the palace chapel, from mere weakness.

87 Throckmorton to the Queen, 6th November 1560 *(Foreign Calendar).*

88 Sir James Melville says that the King of Navarre, his brother the Prince of Condé, and others were to have been executed three days later, the scaffold having been already erected *(Melville Memoirs).* Throckmorton, too, told Elizabeth that she had cause for rejoicing.

89 Melville asserts that she was glad of his death.

90 *Hatfield Papers,* vol. i.

91 *Venetian Calendar,* vol. vii.

92 *Foreign Calendar,* Throckmorton to the Council, 31st December 1560.

93 Throckmorton, for instance, writing on the 6th December, speaks of her as already speculating upon a political second marriage.

94 *Foreign Calendar,* vol. iii., 6th December 1560.

95 *Sur quoy ne faut doubter nullement, si lors de son (i.e. Mary's) partement, le feu roy Charles, son beau frère, fust esté en age accomply, comme il etait fort petit et jeune, et aussi s'il fust esté en l'humeur et amour d'elle, comme je l'ay veu, jamais il ne l'eust laissée partir, et resolument il l'eust espousée: car je l'en ay veu tellement amoureux que jamais il ne regardait son pourtraict qu'il n'y tinst l'œuil tellement fixé et ravy, qu'il ne s'en pouvait jamais oster n'y s'en rassasier; et dire souvent que c'etait la plus belle princesse que nasquit jamais au monde: et tenait le feu roy son frère par trop hereux d'avoir jouy d'une si belle princesse, et qu'il ne debvoit nullement regretter sa mort dans le tumbeau, puisque il avoit possedé en ce monde ceste beante, et son*

plaisir pour si pen d'espace de temps qu'il eust possedée, et que telle jouissance valloit plus que celle de son royaume.—*Dames Illustres.*

96 *Foreign Calendar,* vol. iii. This spiteful remark of Alba gives the measure of sincerity of the new Franco-Spanish alliance, just cemented by the marriage of Philip II with Elizabeth of France. Even to bigoted Alba a heretic England under Elizabeth was better than a Catholic England under French influence.

97 Arran immediately snapped at the bait. He had already found out that Elizabeth had only made a tool of him, and he sent a Captain Forbes hurrying to Anthony of Navarre, with all sorts of pledges and promises. He had been told 'how patent a way God hath made to match him, being heir-apparent, with her that is already in the right of succession.' Knox was a strong supporter of the idea, and, in fact, the match seemed to be that best suited to secure peace for Scotland. It is plain, however, that Mary would never have consented to it, though she was very gracious to Forbes when she saw him, nor was Elizabeth in love with the idea. She knew how weak and unstable Arran was, and that he would be mere clay in the hands of Mary and Lorraine (*Scottish Calendar,* vol. i., Bain). Chatelherault also was against his son's marriage with Mary, whom he deeply distrusted; and Arran himself soon grew alarmed, and went to Randolph full of excuses to be sent to Elizabeth (Randolph to Cecil, *Foreign Calendar,* vol. iv, March 4, 1561).

98 The first proposal of such a marriage was made by Cardinal Lorraine himself, late in December, to Chantonnay (Cardinal de Granvelle's brother, and in after years a leader in the Flemish revolt against the Spaniards, but at this time Spanish ambassador in Paris).—Teulet, *Papiers d'Etat.*

99 *Foreign Calendar,* vol. iii.

100 *Spanish Calendar, Elizabeth,* vol. i., where a full account of this curious intrigue will be found.

101 The Duchess of Ferrara's aid was to be invoked on religious grounds alone.

102 Probably the Archduke Charles, the second son of the Emperor Ferdinand, who was the standing Austro-Spanish pretender to the hand of Elizabeth. For particulars of his wooing see *Courtships of Queen Elizabeth* (Hume).

103 Anthony shortly afterwards sent an envoy, M. de Sault, to see Elizabeth on some mysterious business, probably the marriage referred to, which may have been, as suggested by Mr. Hay Fleming, that of Anthony himself with Mary. If such were the case it gives us one more proof of the King of Navarre's unstable levity. As first prince of the blood, and consort of the strong-minded Jeanne d'Albret, Queen of Navarre, it is difficult

to see how his position could have been improved by a marriage with Mary, and still more difficult to understand how it could have been legally effected.

104 The real reason for the Duchess's visit was to discuss the negotiations proposed by Cardinal Lorraine for Mary's marriage with Don Carlos. (See letter from Catharine to the Bishop of Limoges in Cheruel's *Marie Stuart et Catharine de Medici.*)

105 Cardinal Lorraine's counter-stroke to this suggestion was to bring forward a proposal to marry Margaret, who was only seven years old, to the Prince of Portugal (Du Prat's *Elizabeth de Valois*).

106 The correspondence between Catharine and the French ambassador in Spain is in Cheruel's *Marie Stuart et Catharine de Medici,* and also in Du Prat's *Elizabeth de Valois.*

107 *Scottish Calendar,* Bain, vol. i. The minutes in French of the instructions to be given to Preston of Craigmillar, Ogilvy of Findlater, Lumsden of Blanern, and Leslie of Auchtermuchty, Mary's envoys to Scotland, are printed entire in Labanoff. The documents being purely official and bearing no trace of Mary's personal impress, the somewhat extravagant expressions of her affection for the Queen-Mother, and of sorrow for the loss of her husband, need not be accepted literally. Her autograph letter to Philip II is a much better indication of her real feelings. In it she makes no mention of Catharine, but refers to herself as '*la plus affligée femme qui soit sous le ciel, m'ayant Dieu privée de tout ce qui j'amoyt et tenait cher en ce monde*' (Labanoff, vol. i. p. 91).

108 *Foreign Calendar,* vol. iv. p. 44.

109 Throckmorton says (*Foreign Calendar,* vol. iv. p. 84) that James gave him a full account of what had passed with Mary and the Cardinal, and says that she would not allow her brother to accompany her to Nancy (Lorraine) This aroused his and Throckmorton's suspicions that the Spanish marriage was afoot. Mary, they said, would not ratify the Treaty of Edinburgh until she arrived in Scotland; nor would she marry Arran nor the King of Denmark. She looked no longer towards France, says Throckmorton, but rests her hopes alone upon the King of Spain.

110 Leslie.

111 *Foreign Calendar,* vol. iv. p. 150.

112 Brantome, *Dames Illustres.*

113 *Foreign Calendar,* vol. iv. p. 153.

114 *Foreign Calendar,* vol. iv. p. 187, etc.

115 *Ibid.*

116 *Foreign Calendar,* vol. iv. p. 203.

117 It is evident that Elizabeth's refusal of the safe-conduct was given in the belief that Mary's voyage would be prevented or delayed thereby, and that pressure might thus be brought to bear for the immediate ratification of the Treaty of Edinburgh. When Cecil had become convinced that Mary really intended to sail in any case with or without the permission of the English, then the safe-conduct was granted, although it arrived at Calais after Mary had departed from France. The refusal of the safe-conduct by Elizabeth was resented by Catharine de Medici, as was natural, and both Throckmorton and Lethington doubted the wisdom of offending Mary and her many friends when once she had irrevocably made up her mind to undertake the voyage in any case.

118 The only fairly well-authenticated contemporary portrait of Bothwell known to exist is that which by the kind permission of the owner is reproduced in the present volume. The many descriptions of him, however, when collated one with another, and with the photograph of his skull in my possession, leave no doubt as to his appearance. Mr. Jusseraud's recent letter printed by Mr. Andrew Lang describing the present appearance of Bothwell's mummified corpse affords, moreover, valuable confirmation of the traditional representation of the man, as well as of the portrait referred to.

119 *Scottish State Papers,* Bain, vol. i. p. 540, etc.

120 Randolph to Cecil, 9th August 1561 (*Scottish Calendar*).

121 Lethington to Cecil, 9th and 15th August 1561 (*Scottish Calendar*). The discourtesy referred to was of course the refusal of a safe-conduct by Elizabeth.

122 As a matter of fact, one of the vessels of the convoy was captured by the English on pretence of suspected piracy, and Mary's horses were landed and detained for some weeks, on the pretext that there was no passport for them to go into Scotland.

123 Castelnau de la Mauvissière, who accompanied Mary to Scotland, says that when she landed at Leith, 'receiving no attendance from her subjects, she was one morning taken so extremely ill that, being carried to her palace at Edinburgh, she kept her bed for about twenty days. During her illness most of the nobility came to wait upon her, and, as they paid her all the honours that could be expected, her Majesty, on the other hand, endeavoured to make herself as agreeable as possible' (*Memoirs,* English translation, London, 1724). There must be exaggeration here. Mary only remained in Leith a few hours for breakfast; and before she started for Edinburgh she received visits, amongst many others, from her brothers James and Robert, and from the Duke of Chatelherault and his son Arran. That she was indisposed and low is true, as we

have seen in the text; but she could not have taken to her bed, as Mauvissière says, for twenty days on her arrival, or Randolph would have mentioned the fact.

124 Brantome, *Dames Illustres.*

125 See the divergent accounts given respectively by Brantome and Knox.

126 Randolph to Throckmorton, 26th August (*Scottish Calendar*, vol. i., Bain).

127 Randolph to Throckmorton, 26th August (*Scottish Calendar*, Bain).

128 Randolph, with what appears to have been a great want of tact, gave to Mary Theodore Beza's *Oration*, which she read through; and afterwards he asked Lord James whether the Queen would accept from him a copy of the conclusions arrived at with regard to the Lord's Supper by the great Huguenot convention at Poissy. James undertook to present the book to her. 'She at first doubted the sincerity thereof.' 'She could not reason,' she said, 'but she knew what she ought to believe.' 'The Marquis (*i.e.* her uncle Elbœuf) affirmed that he never thought Christ to be otherwise in the sacrament than as was there written; but yet doubted not but the Mass is good.' This was a bold declaration for a Guise to make, but it shows how far they were prepared to go now that the Spanish match had cooled, in the hope of consolidating Mary's position by obtaining recognition of her presumptive heirship to England.

129 *Scottish Calendar,* vol. i., Bain.

130 Haynes, p. 374.

131 Mary was nearly burnt to death at Stirling at this time by her bed-curtains catching fire while she slept.

132 Randolph to Cecil, 24th September 1561 (*Scottish Calendar,* Bain).

133 See letters from Lethington to Cecil, and from Mary to Elizabeth, in October 1561 and later (*Scottish Calendar,* Bain).

134 The Bailies of Edinburgh, in September, promulgated anew the old edict against the presence in the city of fornicators, drunkards, Mass-mongers and papists. This deeply incensed the Queen, who imprisoned the magistrates, and was herself virulently attacked in consequence.

135 *Foreign Calendar,* 24th September 1561.

136 *Spanish Calendar, Elizabeth,* vol. i. p. 219.

137 *Scottish Calendar,* Bain, vol. i. p. 577.

138 *Scottish Calendar,* Bain, vol, i. p. 576.

139 *Ibid.* p. 603.

140 'For Lord Darnley, to be plain with your honour (writes Randolph to Cecil, 30th

January 1561), I believe that she will never match herself again with any of his age, though no other impediment were.' 'All the practices ever made here with this Queen that ever came to knowledge for the marriage with Lord Darnley, she likes not' (*Scottish Calendar*, Bain, vol. i.). 'She is determined never to match with that race' (*Ibid.*).

141 *Spanish Calendar, Elizabeth,* vol. i. p. 220.

142 *Spanish Calendar, Elizabeth,* vol. i. p. 223.

143 *Ibid.* p. 222.

144 Elizabeth seems to have got wind of the plan about the end of May, after Elbœuf had passed through London. The Spanish ambassador writes in cipher to his King (6th June): 'She (Elizabeth) even went so far as to tell me that the Marquis d'Elbœuf and his servants had publicly stated that his niece would marry our Prince. This was at the time when we had bad news of the health of his Highness, and she used a great many impertinent expressions about it, which I refrain from repeating, but answered as they deserved.' Whoever else may have given Elizabeth a hint of the marriage suggestion, we may be quite sure she told an untruth when she said that it was Elbœuf. (See *Spanish Calendar, Elizabeth,* vol. i.)

145 He had married shortly before the widow of the Laird of Findlater, of whose lands he had the reversion. When he fell in love with Mary and conceived the idea of marrying her, he shut up his wife and claimed the estate for himself.

146 *Scottish Calendar,* Bain, vol. i. p. 651.

147 There seems to be no doubt that the main plot was to murder Murray and perhaps Lethington during their stay in the Gordon country. Buchanan infers that the attempt to capture the Queen was an afterthought conceived on the frustration of the original design.

148 *Spanish Calendar, Elizabeth,* vol. i. p. 307.

149 The Archduke Charles, Duke of Styria, was the third son of the Emperor Ferdinand, and was the Austro-Spanish candidate for Elizabeth's hand. For his long marriage negotiations with her, see *Courtships of Queen Elizabeth.*

150 At this very time Lethington had a young Franco-Scotsman, James Melville, in Austria, sent with Mary's knowledge from France to make inquiries about the Archduke's person and prospects. In Melville's interview with the Archduke Maximilian on the subject, the acting Emperor pretended to be in favour of the match; but Melville ingeniously found out that jealousy would prevent him from helping his brother to a too powerful position. Lethington could not have known this at the time, though he was

quite right in his general conclusion that Charles was useless as a suitor, unless he came with all the power of Spain at his back; and Philip was far too selfish and wary to give that to one of his Austrian cousins whom circumstances had forced to conciliate the German Protestants. (See Melville's *Memoirs.*) However true Melville's intelligence as to the secret dislike of Maximilian to his brother's marriage with Mary may have been, his father Ferdinand had been most anxious for the match. (See *Foreign Calendar, Elizabeth,* vol. vi.)

151 Quadra to Philip, 18th March 1563 (*Spanish Calendar, Elizabeth,* vol. i.).

152 Quadra to Philip, 18th March 1563 (*Spanish Calendar, Elizabeth,* vol. i.).

153 One of Catharine's methods to this end was the industrious promotion by means of her daughter, the wife of Philip II, of the marriage of Don Carlos with her youngest daughter Margaret de Valois, then ten years old.

154 *Spanish Calendar, Elizabeth,* vol. i. p. 314.

155 *Scottish Calendar,* Bain, vol. i. p. 669.

156 *Scottish Calendar,* Bain, vol. i. p. 685.

157 *Scottish Calendar,* Bain, vol. i. p. 884.

158 *Ibid.*

159 He says that the Queen always chose Chastelard to dance with her, frequently leant upon his shoulder, and sometimes kissed him on the neck. He more than hints that Mary's conduct towards him was indecorous, 'more lyke to the bordell than to the comelyness of honest women.'

160 *Spanish Calendar, Elizabeth,* vol. i.

161 Writing at this period (30th January 1563) to the Cardinal Lorraine, Mary asks him to tell the Pope of her 'wretchedness in this miserable country, and her determination if possible to remedy the evils in it, if necessary at the cost of her own life, which she would deem herself happy to sacrifice rather than change her faith, or approve of any of their heresies' (Labanoff, vol. i. p. 176).

162 Randolph to Cecil, 30th December 1562 (*Scottish Calendar,* Bain).

163 Randolph to Cecil, 30th December 1562 (*Scottish Calendar,* Bain).

164 See her fervent letter to this effect, addressed at this period (31st January 1563) to Pope Pius IV (Labanoff, vol. i. p. 177).

165 Randolph, in his letters to Cecil at this period, promptly sounds the alarm about the signs discernible in Scotland of Lethington's sudden sympathy with the Catholics. 'I know not why, but many conceive strangely of him: I would to God he had been

plainer with my Lord Murray; but while absent he never wrote a thing to him seeming to give him credit. The Queen and he so determined before his departure.' He had lately sent the Earl of Eglinton, 'the veriest rebellious papist in the country,' with Mary's commission of justice to punish offences in the country, and had introduced Ruthven, 'whom all men hate,' into Mary's council. The English party in Scotland were therefore already looking upon Lethington as a backslider, though it is difficult to believe that Murray was not secretly a party to his change of front (*Scottish Calendar,* Bain, vol. ii. p. II, etc.).

166 *Spanish Calendar, Elizabeth,* vol. i. p. 332. The Duke of Alba also writes to the Spanish ambassador (16th June) urgently pressing the point of secrecy: 'The whole affair depends upon its being kept absolutely secret until it is settled.'

167 Labanoff, vol. i. p. 296. An apology written by Mary for her marriage with Darnley.

168 Lethington told the Spanish ambassador in London, when explaining the arrest of Hamilton, Archbishop of St. Andrews, for celebrating Mass, that the talk of Cardinal Lorraine's negotiations for the Queen's marriage with the Archduke had alarmed the Protestants, who had thereupon forced Mary to take action against the Catholics. 'The match with the Archduke,' continues the ambassador, 'grows every day more unpopular' (*Spanish Calendar, Elizabeth,* vol. i. p. 337).

169 It will be recollected that in the first days of Mary's widowhood Cardinal Lorraine himself had endeavoured to negotiate a Spanish marriage for her. The circumstances, however, had now changed notably. Philip's attitude during the progress of the religious war which raged in France had convinced Lorraine that the Spanish king did not intend to intervene in favour of the Catholics, or to be drawn into serving any interests other than his own. So long as the Cardinal and his brother thought that the marriage of their niece with Don Carlos would enable them to use the power of Spain for their own benefit in France, they were eager for the match. But Guise was now dead, the 'politicians' paramount, and the lesson of the past two years had taught Lorraine that the marriage of Mary with Carlos would have meant a Spanish domination of Britain, not a Guisan domination of France.

170 The Spanish bishop, who had served as intermediary between Lethington and the English Catholic nobles during the time that the Scottish minister was planning the Catholic Spanish combination, was in great trepidation, now that Lethington had veered again, least he should divulge the whole business to Elizabeth.

171 *Spanish Calendar,* vol. i. p. 346.

172 *Scottish Calendar,* Bain, vol. ii. p. 19.

173 *Scottish Calendar,* Bain, vol. ii. p. 21. Mary had just granted to Lethington the valuable estates of the Abbey of Haddington. This may have influenced him to co-operate in her marriage scheme.

174 *Scottish Calendar,* Bain, vol. ii. p. 21.

175 Still more unlikely is the other explanation venomously suggested by Randolph as the cause of Mary's illness. The Queen's 'potticary' had got 'one of the Quene's maydens, a Frenche woman in credit, and near abowt to her Grace's self, with chylde.' An attempt to avoid the disgrace by drugs had ended disastrously, and both culprits were sent to prison and hanged. 'Whether these things are so heavily taken that they can make her (Mary) so sick, as within 8 days men doubted her life, I know not.'

176 The Duke of Chatelherault, next heir to the Scottish crown after Mary.

177 Granvelle's first communication was sent to Mary in December by means of a Florentine called Angelo, and the Queen's French secretary Raulet was then despatched, ostensibly to see Cardinal Lorraine, but really to arrange with Granvelle, for correspondence. The letters are in Labanoff's *Recueil.*

178 Labanoff, vol. i. p. 214.

179 The English had now evacuated Havre de Grace, and a general peace was concluded in the spring of 1564 between the French and English governments and the Huguenots.

180 One of Randolph's curious inducements to Mary to take a husband was 'that at least she will have compassion on her four Maries, her worthy daughters and mignions, that for her sake have vowed never to marry until she does so.'

181 *Scottish Calendar,* Bain, vol. ii. Cardinal Lorraine's agents were busy now in Scotland, and some artillery and ammunition was sent to Mary from France. The Inch was fortified, and the Scots feared a *coup de main* to force the Mass upon them.

182 *Scottish Calendar,* Bain, vol. ii. p. 58.

183 *Spanish Calendar, Elizabeth,* vol. i. p. 366.

184 Her blandishments on one occasion, at least, took the form, absurd enough in the circumstances, of a hint that Don Carlos should come and marry her! At a great entertainment she gave to Guzman, she asked him if the Spanish prince had grown manly. She was assured that he had, and sighed sentimentally. 'Ah! me! Every one disdains me. I hear that he is to be married to the Queen of Scots.' Guzman earnestly assured her that the Prince's health had been so bad recently that such a thing was quite out of the question, but added that people would gossip about princes. 'That is very true,'

replied the Queen. 'Why, they even said in London the other day that the King was sending an ambassador to treat of the marriage of Don Carlos with *me*!' The hook in the bait was too evident, and nothing came of the hint, for Philip and Catharine were as 'thick as thieves' at the time, and idea of a marriage of Carlos and Mary was no longer being entertained by Philip. (See *Courtships of Queen Elizabeth*.)

185 *Spanish Calendar, Elizabeth*, vol. i. p. 371. Later in the year the Duchess of Arschot wrote to Mary to the same effect, and the answer sent by the Queen of Scots (3rd January 1565) clearly shows her anger at Lorraine's betrayal of her. She begins by saying that she is glad to hear the decision of the King, as now she was in a position to take her own course, without being blamed for hastiness. '*Et quant a ce que á esté asseuré de l'accord entre le fils de l'Empereur et moi, ils sont mal informez, car, fors quelques propos qu'il . . . lus d'un an, qui furent entre le Cardinal de Lorraine, mon oncle, et luy, je n'en ai riens ouy depuis: et je vous asseure que c'est le party á quoy, pour vous parler librement, j'ay le moins pensée . . . pour estre le moins commode pour l'advanchement de mes affaires, tant en ce pays qu'en celuy lá oú je prétend quelque droit. . . . Au reste, je suis bien deliberée de regarder á me resouldre, car mes affaires et mes subjects m'en pressent*' (Labanoff, vol. i. p. 249).

186 In her apologia for having married Darnley (Labanoff, vol. i. p. 296), 1565.

187 Castelnau de la Mauvissière, *Mémoires*.

188 *Ibid.*

189 *Ibid.*

190 The Hamiltons, of course, excluded.

191 *Diary of the Scottish Parliament, Scottish State Papers*, 1564.

192 *Scottish Calendar*, Bain, vol. ii. p. 75.

193 Elizabeth promised him, indeed, that she would make him her intermediary with Mary to propose the Dudley match, but Melville supposed that the influence of the latter caused her only to employ Randolph, her resident agent in Scotland. Elizabeth's real motive in speaking of the matter to Melville in April 1564 was probably only to familiarise Scotsmen with the idea of such a match. (See *Melville Memoirs*.)

194 *Melville Memoirs*.

195 *Ibid.*

196 *Ibid.*

197 *Ibid.*

198 The Queen was to visit Dunbar, and Murray and Lethington were to go hawking over

their estates. Bedford was then to send a message to them asking them to meet him at Berwick to settle some Border questions.

199 In one of Elizabeth's intimate confabulations with Melville she bantered him upon the way in which the Scots were for ever pestering about the succession. Lethington, she said, was the worst of them, for he 'dyd ringe all wayes her knele (knell) in her eares, tawlkynge of nothynge but her succession.' Elizabeth had a shorter way than bantering, when her own subjects ventured too far on the same subject. Cecil wrote a long letter to Murray and Lethington (16th December 1564. *Scottish Calendar,* Bain, vol. ii.), gravely complaining of their insistence in the conference that a recognition to Mary's claims in England should be a condition of her marriage with Leicester, whom Cecil praises to the skies as a perfect character, better than many princes. Murray's and Lethington's reply was equally specious and lacking in sincerity, though both sides continually urged the other to plain dealing.

200 A Catholic named Welch came to see Mary in October, with assurances that all those of his faith in England were in her favour (*Scottish Calendar*).

201 *Scottish Calendar,* vol. ii. p. 94.

202 *Spanish Calendar, Elizabeth,* vol. i. p. 399.

203 *Scottish Calendar,* Bain, vol. ii. p. 99. Randolph throughout appears to have believed in the sincerity of the Leicester negotiation, of which we now know the falsity. On one occasion, at least, it is evident by his letters that Leicester had angrily rebuked him for his over-earnestness in the matter, much to Randolph's surprise.

204 It must not be forgotten that Lennox and his wife enjoyed great estates and revenues granted to them in England by Henry VIII. With the power to confiscate them in Elizabeth's hands, the latter thought she held a pledge for the obedience of the Lennoxes as a last resource, as the Scottish estates, now restored to them, though very extensive, were nothing like so valuable as those in England.

205 Labanoff, vol. i. p. 250.

206 *Scottish Calendar,* Bain, vol. ii. p. 122.

207 Lennox was at his house of Dunkeld at the time.

208 Her apartments at Wemyss are still preserved.

209 *Scottish Calendar,* Bain, vol. ii. p. 128.

210 *Scottish Calendar,* Bain, vol. ii. p. 130, 1st March 1565.

211 *Ibid.*

212 This was Rizzio, who had succeeded Raulet about three weeks previously. As the

dismissal and disgrace of Raulet coincided with that of the Florentine messenger Angelo Menaglio, and with the failure of the negotiations with Flanders for the Spanish match, of which they were the instruments, it is probable that their dismissal was connected either with a suspicion that they had mismanaged the communications or had not been sufficiently reticent about them.

213 On the 15th March he writes that 'Argyle says plainly that he mislikes Darnley's coming; for he says that the affections of women are uncertain. . . . For myself I see no great goodwill borne him (Darnley). Of her Grace's good usage and often talk to him, her countenance and good visage, I think it proceeds rather of her own courteous nature than that anything is meant which some here fear may ensue.'

214 Randolph to Cecil, 17th March 1565 (*Scottish Calendar*, vol. ii.).

215 *Scottish Calendar*, Bain, vol. ii.

216 Castelnau de la Mauvissière, who was present, also gives the idea of the suddenness of Mary's caprice for Darnley, by saying that many people attributed it to 'artificial enchantments.'

217 The letter handed to her by Randolph on the 16th March, and the verbal message that accompanied it, informed Mary definitely that the English queen could not allow the claims of Mary to the succession to be considered or published, 'until we were either married or had fully determined never to marry.'

218 For particulars of this intrigue (February and March 1565), see *Courtships of Queen Elizabeth*.

219 Elizabeth's open approaches to the Catholics and to Spain at the time (spring of 1565), which quite shocked the conscientious Murray and Lethington, also much alarmed Catharine, who courted Elizabeth and Leicester with fulsome amiability, and pushed her son Charles IX's suit, in order to prevent the great danger of an agreement between England and Scotland for religious toleration in conjunction with Spanish or Austrian marriages.

220 Gossips were already talking of this, in conjunction with Elizabeth's even more pronounced philandering with Leicester. Bothwell, who had been a fugitive in England and France since his escape from prison, had just returned (15th March) to Scotland without licence. With characteristic coarseness he said, just before he arrived, 'that both the Queens could not make one honest woman; and as for his own (Queen), if she had taken any one but a cardinal it had been better borne with.' It is fair to say that not one atom of evidence is known to justify the latter vile innuendo, except the

general bad character of Cardinal Lorraine, which surely should not be allowed to weigh against Mary. Randolph describes (*Scottish Calendar,* vol. ii., Bain) a game of skittles that he and Mary Beaton played against the Queen and Darnley at this time (early in April 1565), the latter players losing, Darnley paying the stake, and gave Mary Beaton jewellery worth fifty crowns.

221 Buchanan says that 'there was now much talk abroad of the Queen's marriage with Darnley, and his secret recourse to her, but also of the too great familiarity betwixt her and David Rizzio. Murray, who by his plain downright advice to his sister got nothing but ill will, resolved to leave the court, that so he might not be thought the author of what was acted there.' Buchanan was too much biassed by religion to be accepted unquestionably as trustworthy when he hints at Mary's immorality at this period (3rd April 1565) being the cause of Murray's leaving court. As we have seen, there was ample political and religious reason for Murray's displeasure, and he was no doubt also annoyed at the Queen's imprudently displayed affection for Darnley, and at the growing favour to Rizzio, owing to Mary's new Catholic surroundings. But all these causes existed apart from the suggested immorality of Mary at the time, which was afterwards assumed by Murray, Buchanan, Knox, and the rest of their party for political ends.

222 *Scottish Calendar,* Bain, vol. ii. p. 146.

223 *Ibid.*

224 On his way through London Castelnau was treated by Elizabeth with marked cordiality. In a long conversation with her early in May, she asked if he would be very cross if she married his king. Her only fear was, she said, that she was not worthy of so great a prince, 'as she had nothing to recommend her but a small realm, and her virtue and chastity; for on that point she would not yield to any maiden in the world.'—Castelnau to Catharine (Cheruel).

225 *Spanish Calendar, Elizabeth,* vol. i, p. 423.

226 The general opinion in Scotland at the time was that Elizabeth had deliberately allowed Darnley to go to Scotland for the purpose of promoting his suit for Mary's hand. This was extremely likely to have been the case, the object, however, not being that marriage should result, but that discord, and perhaps discredit, might ensue. Elizabeth and Cecil appear to have supposed that Lennox and his son would never forfeit their great and assured position in England by disobedience.

227 Mary summoned all her Catholic nobles, at the instance of Lennox and Athol, late in

April, to go to Edinburgh and punish the bailies of the town for the ill-treatment of a priest, but she was dissuaded from extreme action.

228 Randolph to Cecil, 29th April 1565 (*Scottish Calendar,* Bain).

229 Randolph to Cecil, 3rd May 1565 (*Scottish Calendar,* Bain).

230 *Ibid.*

231 *Melville Memoirs.*

232 The imprudent new message that Lethington was instructed to give to Elizabeth was that Mary had been beguiled with fair speech too long. She would be fed with yea and nay no longer, but had summoned her parliament, and would follow their advice as to her marriage.

233 It is significant that when she received him later both Murray and Argyle, as well as Chatelherault, were by her side. Lethington's interview with Guzman had probably wrought the change.

234 His advice was taken. On the 4th June the English privy council resolved that Elizabeth should forthwith marry, 'that Lady Lennox should be secluded from intelligence, her husband and son recalled from Scotland, failing which their estates in England be forfeited, Mr. Charles (Stuart), the younger son, being placed where he may be forthcoming, and that some remission of her Majesty's displeasure be showed to Lady Catharine Grey (accounted by the Queen of Scots her competitor) and to the Earl of Hertford.'

235 In one of his letters to Leicester, deploring with crocodile tears Mary's changed demeanour, and even the decay of her beauty, and strongly hinting that she had surrendered herself utterly to Darnley, Randolph says: 'The saying is that surely she is bewitched—the persons are named who are the doers—the tokens, the rings, the bracelets, are found and daily worn that contain sacred mysteries' (*Scottish Calendar,* Bain, vol. ii, p. 172).

236 *Ibid.* There seems to be no doubt that Darnley had already begun to drink more than his weak health or head could stand. His uncontrollable gusts of passion, succeeded by maudlin repentance, were explainable only by madness or drink, and it is certain that he was addicted to the latter.

237 *Spanish Calendar, Elizabeth,* vol. i. p. 433.

238 *Spanish Calendar, Elizabeth,* vol. i. p. 442.

239 *Scottish Calendar,* Bain, vol. ii.

240 Fowler had been Lethington's confidant and assistant. He was now deep in the confidence of Mary.

241 Father Stevenson's *Selections*.

242 Chalmers. The first and second publication appear to have been made at the Canongate Kirk, and the third publication immediately before the ceremony in Holyrood Chapel.

243 Labanoff, etc.

244 Randolph to Leicester (B.M. MSS. *Cotton Caligula*, B. ix. p. 218).

245 See Mary's letter to Paul de Foix, French ambassador in England, 8th November 1565, giving him an account of Murray's revolt and justifying herself for her manner of dealing with it (Labanoff, i. p. 299).

246 Tamworth to Leicester, 10th August 1565 (*Scottish Calendar*, vol. ii.).

247 When Tamworth demanded the passport for his return, the document offered to him was signed by Darnley as King as well as by Mary, and, as Tamworth had been strictly ordered not to recognise the Queen's consort, he refused the safe-conduct and started without it. He was promptly stayed and imprisoned by the Humes on the Border, certainly with Mary's knowledge, since Lord Hume himself was with her at Edinburgh. After much bickering Elizabeth was obliged to instruct Tamworth to accept the passport as offered, and he was thereupon released, the English being obliged to swallow the insult as best they might. Nothing shows better than this the complete and sudden change in the relations between the two queens. As will be seen in the text, however, Mary's triumph was of short duration, though she made the most of it whilst it lasted.

248 Draft taken by Tamworth in Randolph's writing (*Scottish Calendar*, vol. ii.).

249 On the 22nd August the proclamation she had published on her arrival in Scotland was renewed, assuring the subjects that no change should be made in religion, notwithstanding that 'the rebels were trying to cover their rebellion by persuading the good subjects that she and the King were attempting a plain subversion of the estate of religion' (*Register of the Scottish Privy Council*).

250 In her tart conversation with Randolph on the following Wednesday, about Tamworth's arrest on the Border, she stood up stoutly for Darnley's title. 'Well, he is a king now,' she said. 'Yes,' was the reply, 'to those who will acknowledge him to be so, but not to us, for he is an English subject.' 'I know what right he hath,' said Mary, 'and next to myself I am assured the best. We shall not want for friends, the King of France and others who will not see me wronged' (*Scottish Calendar*, vol. ii.).

251 *Scottish Calendar*, vol. ii.

252 Cardinal Pacheco to Philip II, 2nd September 1565 (*Spanish Calendar*).

253 Mary's ambassador in France, Beaton, Archbishop of Glasgow, had accompanied Catharine to Bayonne, and had held friendly conference with the Duke of Alba. This doubly alarmed Elizabeth. See *Spanish Calendar*, vol. i., and Labanoff, vol. i.

254 Labanoff, vol. i.

255 *Spanish Calendar*, vol. i.

256 *Papiers d'Etat relatifs à Ecosse* (Teulet).

257 *Ibid.* Elizabeth was aware that Yaxley had been sent to Spain, and she told de Foix that Mary had only done so to frighten her (*Spanish Calendar*, vol. i.); but she was terribly disturbed at it nevertheless, and Wilson the pirate was encouraged to capture him (*Foreign Calendar*, vol. vii.).

258 Bothwell had hurried back from France at Mary's call, and had only landed, after much danger from English pirates, at Eyemouth on the 19th September, being received graciously at Holyrood on the following day. He was at once restored to his office of lieutenant of the middle marches, and shortly afterwards was appointed a member of the privy council. His bitter enmity to Murray and to England, and the fact that he had fled from Scotland rather than face the foregone conclusion of his condemnation by the latter for his former offence of prison breaking and flight, rendered him an excellent instrument for Mary's purposes at this juncture. He was, moreover, a man of strong purpose, forceful and overbearing, and consequently would naturally appeal to the Queen in her then mood. It need hardly be emphasised that there was no suggestion of love-making between them at this early stage.

259 Randolph to Cecil, 4th October (*Scottish Calendar*, Bain, vol. ii.).

260 Another later cause of quarrel was Mary's pardoning the Hamiltons without Darnley's consent.

261 *Scottish Calendar*, vol. ii.

262 Randolph to Leicester, 18th October (*Scottish Calendar*).

263 Randolph to Cecil, 13th October (*Scottish Calendar*, vol. ii.).

264 Philip to Guzman, 20th October (*Spanish Calendar*, vol. i.).

265 Tytler, Robertson, Froude, and others make the statement apparently on Randolph's hearsay evidence. It was the highest diplomacy for her not to sign the league, whilst keeping its other signatories friendly and in hopes of her doing so. It was Philip's aid she wanted unhampered by the interference of Catharine.

266 *Scottish Calendar*, vol. ii. p. 224.

267 *Spanish Calendar,* vol. i.

268 The same night also the English Council wrote to Sir Thomas Smith, the ambassador in France, instructing him to give their version of the interview with Murray to the French sovereign and his mother. 'Her Majesty spake very roundly to him before the ambassador that, whatsoever the world sayd or reported of hyr, she wold by hyr action lett it appear that she would not, to be prince of a world, maintayn any subject in disobedience against the prince; for besides the offence of hyr conscience, which should condemn hyr, she knew that Almighty God might justly recompense her with the lyke trooble in hyr owne realme' (*Scottish Calendar,* vol. ii. p. 228). The other authorities for this interview are Guzman's account written to Philip, as related to him by the Queen (*Spanish Calendar,* vol. i. p. 502); the *Foreign Calendar,* vol. vii. p. 499; Laing's *Knox,* vol. ii.; and the *Melville Memoirs* (1752), p. 113.

269 Just before his departure from London a week later Murray wrote rather bitterly to Elizabeth wondering how he had deserved 'so hard handling.' 'The more I think hereon it is ever the longer more grievous to me' (*Scottish State Papers,* vol. ii. p. 231).

270 It was at first intended to send Lord Lumley to Mary at this juncture for the purpose of placating the latter. Whilst still complaining of Mary's marriage, etc., Lumley was to assure her that Elizabeth never 'did or meant anything to comfort the lords now in England or any other rebels; and, as for aid of men, ye may precisely bind us that to our knowledge there never entered one man of war into Scotland to aid them. And if it shall be objected that they had aid in money from us, you may say that you are well assured that there was never any money by our order given to any person wherewith any act should be maintained against her.' Lumley was to propose a new friendship and alliance on Mary's confirming the Treaty of 1560, and forgiving Murray and the rebels, Elizabeth offering to 'enquire' into Mary's English claims, to release Lady Lennox, and restore the estates of her husband to him. Elizabeth, however, contented herself with writing to Randolph to a similar effect, as she feared that the proposed embassy might 'rayse hir (Mary's) stomach' overmuch (*Scottish Calendar,* Bain, vol. ii. pp. 229-230).

271 Philip wrote to Cardinal Pacheco to the same effect a few days before, 16th October, telling him to convey it to the Pope, and to ask him also to write to Mary counselling prudence, 'and to be most careful not to let the Queen of England know that anything is being hatched against her during her life' (*Spanish Calendar,* vol. i. p. 490).

272 How deep was the distrust of Catharine and her son on their side at Mary's intrigues with Philip may be seen by a remark quoted by Guzman (24th November), made by a

Scottish envoy passing through London from France. In his interview with the French sovereigns, on behalf of Mary, the former had told him that they were greatly surprised to learn that the King of Spain was disposed to help his mistress secretly; and they appear to have hinted that France was willing to outbid Spain in this respect if Mary wished. She was too wise, however, to fall into the trap, which even her envoy saw and denounced to the Spaniards at once (*Spanish Calendar,* vol. i.).

273 Mary also lodged her claim to the money, and wrote a letter to Northumberland on the subject (11th February 1566, Labanoff, vol. i. p. 321); but although the earl was, to his subsequent ruin, one of her principal supporters in England, and a leader of the Catholic conspiracy in her favour, he made no waiver of his claim for her. The Earl of Bedford, to whom she also wrote on the subject, and the government in London, naturally refused to recognise her claim to funds which they knew were destined to be used against them.

274 The embassy from Elizabeth never went. Sussex and Lumley, who had been designated for it, were both enemies of Leicester and the Puritans, Lumley afterwards being one of the Catholic conspirators with Spain against Elziabeth. The jubilation in Scotland at the proposed embassy and its members probably prevented Elizabeth from sending them. She instructed Randolph (26th November) to say that he had mistaken his instructions, and to take the fault upon himself. Elizabeth, however, offered to send commissioners to meet others to be appointed by Mary.

275 About this time Mary seems to have adopted a new form for signing documents, to some of which she affixed her own name with the word '*Fiat*' after it, omitting Darnley's signature altogether. (See her grant to Hugh Lawder, 26th March 1566, in Dr. Hay Fleming's *Mary Stuart.*) The practice was not, however, invariable, as many documents after this period bear both Mary's and her consort's signatures: that of the Queen first, and usually in similar ink to the body of the document, that of Darnley frequently in different ink, and evidently signed at a subsequent period.

276 Fowler to Lady Lennox (*Hatfield Papers,* vol. i. p. 324; *Scottish Calendar,* vol. ii. p. 247).

277 In Ruthven's relation he makes Darnley complain specially of this night card-playing with Rizzio as one of the reasons for the Italian's murder: 'After supper your Majesty hath a use to sit at the cards with Davie till one or two of the clock after midnight.'

278 Fowler, the Catholic secretary of Darnley, had been sent to England on this business, and had just been captured and condemned to death. Sir Robert Melville, Mary's ambassador, was also, in Randolph's opinion, really in England for the same purpose.

279 Through Lady Murray. See Mary's letters on the subject (Labanoff, vol. i.).

280 He was resisting expulsion as long as he could, and had not yet left Edinburgh on the 25th February.

281 Lethington to Cecil, 9th February 1566 (*Scottish Calendar*, vol. ii.).

282 Tytler

283 6th and 8th March (*Scottish Calendar*, vol. ii.).

284 The Italian secretary was sumptuously attired on the occasion in a 'night-gown of damask, furred, with a satin doublet, and hose of russet velvet, with a jewel about his neck and his plumed cap upon his head.' 'His apparell was very good; as it is said 18 pair of velvet hose: his chamber well furnisshed; armour daggs, pystoletts, harque-busis and 22 swords.'—Bedford and Randolph to the Privy Council (Ellis's *Original Letters*, part 1. vol. ii. p. 218).

285 The principal contemporary authorities for the tragedy are Mary's letter to the Archbishop of Glasgow in Paris, 2nd April 1566 (Labanoff, vol. i. p. 342); Ruthven's narrative (Keith's *Appendix*); the relation sent by Randolph and Bedford, 27th March (Harl. MSS. *Cotton Caligula*, B. x.); letter of Morton and Ruthven to Cecil of same date (*Scottish Calendar*, Bain, vol. ii.); Mary's letter to Catharine and Charles IX (*Venetian Calendar*, vol. vii.), etc.

286 Mary was in great fear of a miscarriage, and sent for a midwife at eight o'clock that night. Darnley said that he overslept himself, and on waking at six o'clock in the morning went to his wife's room, but she refused to receive him as he had not come earlier.

287 Mary asserted that during the Rizzio scene two of the assailants turned their weapons against her, and also that they threatened to cut her into collops and throw the pieces over the wall if she attempted to communicate with the people of Edinburgh.

288 Mary herself says in her letter to Beaton that her death or perpetual captivity was intended, and Blackwood, in his *Life of Mary* (Maitland Club), avers that Murray at this conclave voted for her death.

289 Ruthven's report asserts that when Darnley came down after supper, about six or seven in the evening of the 11th March, to receive from the lords the act of indemnity for the Queen's signature, he asked that the guards might be removed. They replied that if he ordered it, it should be done; but they feared mischief, and he must be responsible for the result, as they thought the Queen would carry him away to Dunbar or inside Edinburgh Castle. Darnley gave his pledge to them, and the lords then went to Morton's house to supper (Keith's *Appendix*).

290 Nau.

291 'He hath declared to us in presence of the lords of our Privy Council his innocence of this last conspiracy: how he never counselled, commanded, consented, assisted, or approved of the same. . . . That at the incitement and persuasion of the late conspirators he, without our advice or knowledge, consented to the bringing forth of England of the Earl of Murray, Glencairn, Rothes, etc. This ye will consider by his declaration, which at his desire hath been published at the market crosses of our realm' (Mary to Archbishop Beaton, Labanoff, vol. i. p. 348). 'Her husband has disclosed all he knew of any man' (Randolph to Cecil, 21st March, *Scottish Calendar,* Bain, vol. ii.).

292 *Lennox MSS.,* Andrew Lang.

293 *Spanish Calendar, Elizabeth,* vol. i. p. 538.

294 How distrustful she was at the time is seen by the characteristic intrigue adopted by her and Cecil of sending the Catholic *agent provocateur,* Ruxbie, as a spy to try to draw Mary into a statement as to her known communications with the English Catholic nobility. Thanks to hot-headed Leslie, the new Bishop of Ross, Mary nearly fell into the trap, but was saved by a warning from her ambassador in London, Sir Robert Melville, who was, however, himself at the time partly sold to England. For the story, see Melville's *Memoirs* and the *Scottish Calendar,* Bain, vol. ii. Another reason for Elizabeth's fear was Mary's active sympathy and co-operation through Argyle with Shan O'Neil's Catholic rising in Ireland. Soon afterwards Murray and Argyle tried to make a bargain with Elizabeth, to the effect that if she would promise to protect the Protestants of Scotland, they (Murray and Argyle) would refrain from affording countenance to O'Neil.

295 Murray was at the same time writing to Elizabeth, begging her, not really unsuccessfully, although apparently so, to shelter and favour in England the fugitive conspirators (Bedford to Cecil, 27th March 1566, Ellis's *Original Letters*). Mary only a few days afterwards wrote to Elizabeth in exactly a contrary sense, begging that Morton should not be allowed sanctuary in England, but be driven back to Scotland. In the same letter she asks the Queen of England to be godmother to her child, and concludes pathetically: '*Excuses moy si jecris si mal, car je suis si grosse, estant en mon septième moys bien auvant*' (4th April 1566—*Scottish Calendar,* Bain, vol. ii.). Elizabeth's pretended expulsion of Morton and others, whilst she winked at their continued stay in England, is another proof of her fear at this period.

296 *Spanish Calendar, Elizabeth,* vol. i. p. 544, and *Scottish Calendar,* Bain, vol. ii. p. 275.

297 *Scottish Calendar,* Bain, vol. ii. p. 276.

298 When Castelnau returned to France he carried a letter from Darnley to Charles IX, protesting his innocence of Rizzio's murder (*Scottish Calendar,* Bain, vol. ii. p. 277).

299 *Lennox Papers,* Andrew Lang; and also Buchanan (1721), p. 5.

300 Labanoff and many other authorities, following Randolph's statement, say that Mary had intended to go to Stirling for her confinement, and that she actually went there for that purpose, but returned to Edinburgh when Darnley joined her at Stirling, it is said to avoid him. That Mary had some intention of going to Stirling is also mentioned by Guzman, but she did not go.

301 Elizabeth in her letter to Mary, ten days previously, had said that she herself was '*grosse du desire*' for the good news of Mary's delivery (*Scottish Calendar,* vol. ii.).

302 It is significant that Melville, when he told Guzman that Mary had asked Elizabeth to be sponsor for the child, and that a same request had been sent to the King of France, said that in order not to arouse suspicion she had refrained from asking the King of Spain to be godfather, as she would like to have done, but had asked the Duke of Savoy, who was connected with Philip, but who would not open the eyes of Elizabeth and Catharine to the close connection between Mary and the King of Spain (*Spanish Calendar, Elizabeth,* vol. i.).

303 How serious was the situation for Elizabeth, and how wide the ramifications of the Catholic intrigue at this time, may be seen by the letter of 5th July from the spy Rogers to Cecil (*Scottish Calendar,* vol. ii.). The Poles had agreed to renounce their claim to the English crown in favour of Mary and her husband, large sums of money were being sent from the Catholics of the north of England to the latter, and armed English Catholics were already creeping into Scotland. A plan was devised for the capture of the Scilly Isles for Mary and her consort, and Darnley was foolish enough openly to boast that he had forty English gentlemen ready to serve him: this in addition to money, arms, and encouraging letters which reached Mary from Spanish agents in Flanders.

304 Whatever Buchanan may mean by Mary's licentious behaviour at Alloa, it is certain that the Queen did not neglect matters of state during the few days she stayed there, as several official documents still extant prove. It was there (28th July), on the advice of her council, that she decided to proceed later in person to Jedburgh, for the purpose of holding an assize, and punishing the riotous borderers, Johnstones, Elliots, Armstrongs, Kers, and the rest of them, who by their forays and feuds had reduced

the neighbourhood to anarchy. It will be seen, therefore, that her journey to Jedburgh was not undertaken suddenly in consequence of Bothwell's wound, as Buchanan and others try to make out.

305 Nau's *Mary Stuart,* p. 30, and Buchanan. On Mary's return from this expedition the new French ambassador in London, La Foret, wrote to Catharine saying that Mary was at Stirling and her husband eight leagues away hunting 'with a very small company, and discontented; which, however, is no new thing or of any importance, for they cannot be together for three days without a riot' (Cheruel).

306 Lethington to Cecil, 20th September (*Foreign Calendar,* vol. viii. p. 131).

307 There is in the *Hatfield Papers,* vol. ii. p. 46, a curious account of this man's career which to some extent confirms Buchanan's statement as to Mary's behaviour at this time. David Chalmers had been educated in France, and was made by Bothwell Provost of Creithtoun, and afterwards Lord of Session, not for his learning, 'but because he had served Bothwell as a bawd and otherwise in his naughty practices. He was a great dealer betwixt the Queen and Bothwell, so, as Mr. David's lodging was chosen as a place meet to exercise their filthiness into, before the King's murder, when as the Queen lay at the Checker House in the Cowgate.' Lennox accused Chalmers of being an accomplice in Darnley's murder.

308 *Foreign Calendar,* vol. viii. p. 128.

309 She gave to Darnley some cloth of gold for a dress, to Murray a green suit, to Argyle red, and to Bothwell blue (*Foreign Calendar,* vol. viii. p. 131).

310 *Ibid.* p. 128.

311 Hosack's quotation of *Book of Articles.*

312 De Croc tells the story, and he says that whilst Mary and the lords were now (October 1566) quite united, they could do nothing with Darnley, who wished to command everything and everybody. No one took any notice of him, says de Croc, and he complained constantly to the latter. At last the Frenchman told him that if he would say what he had to complain of, he would speak to Mary and her council in his favour. 'I want to fill the same position that I did when I was first married,' he replied. 'That is quite impossible,' said de Croc; 'you ought to have kept the place when you had it. You have offended the Queen, and you cannot expect she will give you power again. You ought to think yourself very fortunate that she honours you as she does, treating you as her husband, and providing you and your house with everything' (Labanoff, vol. i. p. 375).

313 The Queen had told Murray about the aid she was receiving from the Pope, and although it is difficult to believe that he would in any case have acquiesced in the establishment of popish predominance in Scotland, he must have been aware of the active negotiations being carried on with the Catholics at this period, the coming and going of papal envoys, the constant messages to Spain and Spanish Flanders, and the close intimacy of all the Scottish envoys to London, even the Melvilles, with the Spanish ambassador there. Even the Scottish Protestants, disgusted at Elizabeth's attitude, appear for a time to have been willing to second Mary's plans, depending doubtless upon her solemn pledge to make no religious changes in her realm.

314 De Croc to Catharine (Labanoff, vol. i. p. 374).

315 Buchanan's *Detection.*

316 Scrope to Cecil, 8th October 1566 (*Foreign Calendar*, vol. viii. p. 137).

317 Mr. Andrew Lang appears to question Bothwell's visit to Jedburgh on the 15th. I know not on what ground, as Sir J. Forster, writing from Berwick on the 15th October, distinctly states that 'Bothwell came *this day* to Jedburgh in a litter'; and writing again on the 23rd, the same officer mentions Bothwell's second visit thus: 'The Earl of Bothwell came to Jedburgh on the 21st in a horse litter.' Bothwell does not appear to have returned to Hermitage after this, and he probably went to visit the Queen when he learned of her serious illness, which appears to have reached a crisis on the 20th or 21st October (*Foreign Calendar*, vol. viii.).

318 On the occasion of her second attack of what may have been some form of hysteria, she was thought actually to have died. Nau, in his account, says that Murray began to seize the plate, jewellery, and other valuables.

319 Melville tells rather an inconsistent story about Mary's horse and herself being viciously attacked by Sir J. Forster's horse at this interview.

320 Lethington wrote to Beaton at the time: 'It is a heartbreak for her to think that he should be her husband, and how to be free of him she sees no way. I see betwixt them no agreement, nor appearance that they will agree thereafter. At least, I am assured that it has been her mind this good while, and it is as I write. How soon, or in what manner it may change, God knows' (Laing's *History of Scotland*).

321 *Diurnal of Occurrents.*

322 Buchanan's *Detection* (1721), p. 13.

323 *Book of Articles* in Hosack.

324 Also in Buchanan's *Detection,* and in Jebb.

325 *Scottish Calendar*, vol. ii. p. 597. It must be recollected that this document was drafted mainly for the purpose of inculpating Murray and Lethington in Darnley's murder, and that every effort was made in it to show that Mary was not a consenting party to any illegal act being committed.

326 According to Lennox's statement there seems to have been another subsequent conference of the lords at Craigmillar on the subject, in which Darnley's death, if he resisted arrest, was agreed upon (Andrew Lang).

327 In answer to this document Murray strenuously denied to Elizabeth that he had ever agreed or subscribed at Craigmillar to any deed for the murder of Darnley, or for any unlawful end, although he says he was earnestly pressed thereto by the Queen's orders. Murray, however, was clever at avoiding personal responsibility.

328 *Foreign Calendar*, vol. viii.

329 *Lennox MSS.*, quoted by Andrew Lang.

330 The statement of Lennox was to the effect that Mary feigned to be angry against the King's tailors, because they had not made such apparel as she had devised for him— perhaps of the gold tissue she had destined for that purpose some time before. She dismissed his guards, and quarrelled when his father sent some of his own men to attend him. During the wrangle Mary said that 'if he were a little daggered, and had bled as much as my Lord Bothwell had lately done, it would make him look the fairer' (*Lennox MSS.*, quoted by Andrew Lang).

331 See many letters from Cecil's spies, Cockburn, Rogers, and others, in *Foreign Calendar*, vol. viii., and Guzman's letters in *Spanish Calendar*. The latter, as well as his colleague in Paris, Francés de Alava, warned Mary of Darnley's plans to outbid her with the Catholic powers; which to some extent she knew by his intercepted letters and by the delation of spies.

332 Appendix to Hay Fleming's *Mary Stuart*.

333 Buchanan's *Detection*. The *Book of Articles* (Hosack) also says in connection with these visits: 'In what order they (*i.e.* Mary and Bothwell) were chambered during their stay in these two houses (*i.e.* Drummond Castle and Tullibardine) many found fault with but dared not reprove. How lascivious also their behaviour was, it was very strange to behold, notwithstanding the news of the King's grievous infirmity, who was departed to Glasgow and there fallen in deadly sickness.' This sickness was suspected at the time to have been caused by poison. It is, of course, not improbable that poison may have been administered, as he was suddenly seized with illness almost immediately after he

left Stirling; but his malady at Glasgow was of a virulent eruptive character, either true smallpox or syphilis. Bedford calls it smallpox, and says that Mary sent her physician to him (*Scottish Calendar,* Bain, vol. ii.).

334 *Lennox MSS.,* quoted by Andrew Lang.

335 Archibald Douglas's letter to Mary during her captivity in England, mentioning this answer to his message (Malcolm Laing's *History of Scotland*).

336 She must have known some time before this indication, even if we admit that she was dense enough at Craigmillar not to understand what Lethington meant; for on the 18th January, the day before Douglas saw her, Guzman in London, writing to his King, says: 'The displeasure of the Queen of Scotland with her husband is carried so far, that she was approached by some who wanted to induce her to allow a plot to be formed against him, which she refused; but she nevertheless shows him no affection. They tell me, even, that she has tried to take away some of his servitors; and for some time past finds him no money for his ordinary expenditure. This is very unfortunate for them both, although it cannot be denied that the King has given grounds for it by what he has done. They ought to come to terms; as if they do not look out for themselves, they are in a bad way' (*Spanish Calendar,* Hume, vol. i. p. 613). This must refer to the period when Darnley was staying at Stirling in December.

337 In illustration of Mary's character, and confirmation of this view, it should be noted that when she discussed with the nobles at Craigmillar their suggestions for ridding her of Darnley, and Lethington gave his sinister hint, the Queen's anxiety was not expressed on account of any suffering or wrong to be done to her husband, but only that no spot should be laid on *her* honour and conscience. She willed the lords to leave things as they were, *not* out of pity to save Darnley from capture or death, but because, whilst the lords thought they were serving her, it 'may possibly turn out to *my* hurt or displeasure' (*Scottish Calendar,* vol. ii. p. 599).

338 Labanoff, vol. i. p. 398.

339 There are many different statements as to the exact dates of Mary's departure from Edinburgh and her arrival in Glasgow. The whole question, as touching the authenticity of the long 'casket letter,' is fully discussed by Andrew Lang, who arrives at the same conclusion as I had already done from separate premises.

340 Crawford's account of the interview as related by Darnley (*Scottish Calendar,* vol. ii. p. 313).

341 The whole subject is exhaustively discussed by Lang, Tytler, etc.

342 The narrative of the crime given here is condensed from the confused, and in many cases contradictory, evidence of Paris (*Papiers d'Etat*, Teulet), Powry, Bowton, Hay of Talla, Nelson, etc.; Buchanan, Keith, and Laing; Drury's Letters, *Foreign Calendar*, vol. viii.; Mary's letter to Beaton on the day after the crime, Labanoff, vol. ii.; the *Lennox Papers*, quoted by Andrew Lang; and the various statements made before the Commission at York, *Scottish Calendar*, Bain, vol. ii.; and *Domestic Calendar*, 1568.

343 We are told that the walls of the chambers and hall were furnished with fine tapestry taken from the Gordons (one of whom, Huntly, was a party to the murder) after their revolt: with velvet cushions, and great velvet chairs, and a fine velvet state bed. In Darnley's room there was a bath by the side of the bed, having, as Nelson, Darnley's valet, says, a door taken from its hinges in the house as its cover.

344 Murray left Edinburgh for St. Andrews on Sunday, 9th February. Paris says that Bothwell told him that Murray would 'neither help nor hinder.' See confession in Teulet's *Papiers d'Etat*.

345 *Lennox Papers*, Lang.

346 Nelson's deposition is the authority for this curious proof of Mary's Scottish economy. Paris also makes her send him on the last night for a valuable fur coverlet that was at Kirk-o'-Field.

347 Labanoff, vol. ii.

348 *Spanish Calendar*, vol. i., Labanoff, vol. vii., and *Venetian Calendar*.

349 Guzman wrote the news of Darnley's death to Philip on the 17th February, two days after he learned it from Cecil, and the first comment that he made was the following: 'In any case (*i.e.* whether Mary be guilty or not), the question of whom she is to marry must be kept in view, for obvious reasons, and when the man she is sending hither (Melville) arrives here, I will endeavour to discover the truth of what has happened, in order to advise your Majesty, and to incline the Queen not to dispose of herself until your Majesty can counsel her on the matter. Of course the French will do ail they can to get her to marry to their liking' (*Spanish Calendar*, Hume, vol. i. p. 618).

350 *Ibid.* p. 620.

351 Huntly and Bothwell remained behind at Holyrood when Mary first went to Seton on the 16th, but they accompanied her when she returned thither a day or two later for a longer stay.

352 Bastien, Joseph Rizzio, and another Italian servant of the Queen, who were said to be implicated in the plot, promptly left Scotland, well rewarded by the Queen; and Sandy

Durham, the groom of the chambers who had led the murderers to Darnley's room on the night of the crime, and had afterwards watched the body, was appointed master of the wardrobe for life to Prince James on the night of Darnley's burial at Holyrood, 15th February (Malcolm Laing, from *Privy Seal Records of Scotland*).

353 Labanoff, vol. ii. p. 17.

354 Their expectations were not disappointed. Before the parliament was dissolved Huntly's confiscated estates were confirmed to him; the grants previously made by Mary to Murray, Morton, Crawford, Rothes, Semple, Herries, and Lethington being also confirmed. Murray had prudently left to travel in France a few days previously.

355 Melville's *Memoirs*.

356 And doubell adulterie has all this land i' shamit.' (*Scottish Calendar, vol. ii. p. 320.*)

357 Buchanan and Robertson's *Inventories*

358 This refers doubtless to his wound on the Border.

359 The rumour had indeed reached as far as London already. Leicester told Guzman, before the 14th April, that a 'divorce was being effected between the Earl of Bothwell and his wife, who is a sister of the Earl of Huntly. . . . When they speak here of Bothwell's divorce, they hint that it is with the object of his marrying the Queen' (*Spanish Calendar,* Hume, vol. i. p. 633). Mary is said to have sent a token and message to Bothwell during the mock-trial (*Foreign Calendar,* vol. viii. p. 230).

360 Herries is said to have signed it, but he came shortly afterwards to Edinburgh, with a sufficient force for his protection, and gravely warned Mary of the evil course she followed.

361 There was produced subsequently, alleged to have been found in the famous casket, an undertaking dated 5th April, a week before Bothwell's mock-trial, in which Mary agreed to marry Bothwell. As, like all the prose writings in the casket, the authenticity of this document has been hotly disputed, I do not wish to produce it in evidence here. There is ample proof without it that Mary's relations with Bothwell before his acquittal, as well as after, were intimate in the extreme; and whether the marriage-contract of the 5th April be genuine or not, it is manifest that if Mary at that date did not contemplate marriage with the earl her conduct was more reprehensible than if she did.

362 *Scottish Calendar,* vol. ii. p. 322.

363 *Ibid.*

364 Melville's *Memoirs.*

365 A curious story is told by Melville of Mary's distrust of Lethington's enmity to Bothwell

shortly before this. It seems that James Melville, shocked at the rumours that were rife of Mary's intention to marry the murderer of her husband, showed her a letter from a Scottish agent in England, expressing indignant grief at the rumour. Mary read the letter without comment, and handed it to Lethington, saying, 'Here is a strange letter that Melville has shown me.' 'What can it mean?' he asked. 'It is a device of your own,' said the Queen, 'tending to wreck the Earl of Bothwell.' When Lethington had read the letter he remonstrated with Melville for showing it to the Queen; 'for so soon as Bothwell gets notice hereof . . . he will cause you to be killed.' Melville fled, though Bothwell, when the Queen told him, hunted for him to kill him. Mary, however, finally made peace, by saying that if Bothwell behaved in that way he would drive all her servants away (Melville's *Memoirs*). Lethington also fled for a time to the safe protection of his friend Athol, after Bothwell's attempt to murder him, Mary ultimately making peace between them also. He was in mortal fear, however, during his stay in Edinburgh Castle with Mary and her new husband in May, and deserted them on the first opportunity.

366 *Scottish Calendar,* Bain, vol. ii. p. 325.

367 *Spanish Calendar, Elizabeth,* Hume, vol. i. p. 638.

368 Guzman to Philip, 17th May 1567 (*Spanish Calendar,* Hume, vol. i. pp. 637, 640).

369 It may be pointed out again in this connection that Mary's essentially selfish character always exacted that, whoever else might be compromised, she should always be protected from the consequences of acts in which she was a consenting party. The crowning instance of this, which does not come within the scope of this book, was her attitude towards the Babington conspirators, though the same tendency is seen throughout the whole of her career.

370 Melville's *Memoirs.*

371 Guzman, writing to Philip on the 21st June 1567, says that Mary was five months pregnant. He appears to have obtained his information from Robert Melville, who left Scotland a fortnight previously. Her marital relations with Darnley must have ceased before the 24th December 1566, the day of his departure from Stirling after the christening of James. Whether Guzman's information was correct or not at the time, no child is known to have been born of Mary that would correspond with his statement. Mary herself told Throckmorton at Lochleven, in the middle of July 1567, that she was then seven weeks pregnant, and it is known that in February 1568 she gave birth to a

girl (Nau says twins) at Lochleven. According to Castelnau's editor, Le Laboreur, the child so born became a nun in the convent of Notre Dame de Soissons.

372 In her message to the court of France by the Bishop of Dunblane after the marriage, Mary excuses herself by saying that, though her captor's methods were somewhat rude, 'his words were gentle, that he would honour and serve us, and nowise offend us; asked pardon of the boldness he had taken . . . constrained by love, the vehemence whereof had made him set apart the reverence he bore us.' After he had urged his suit, Mary says: 'In the end, when we saw no esperance to be rid of him, never man in Scotland making any mind to procure our deliverance . . . we were compelled to mitigate our displeasure, and began to think upon that which he propounded.' In her own apology, in fact, she admits that she was won over by her lover's pleading, his past great services, and the bond he produced signed by the nobles consenting to the marriage (Labanoff, vol. ii. p. 36).

373 Bothwell and his wife, Lady Jane Gordon, were related within the degrees of consanguinity forbidden to husband and wife by the Church, and a papal dispensation was therefore necessary. This had actually been issued by the Archbishop of St. Andrews himself as legate, but he conveniently forgot it.

374 Mary's enemies asserted that she also wished to poison her child; and Drury tells a story of her attempting to do so on her visit to Stirling (*Border Papers*). This, however, seems incredible. Mary had nothing to gain at that time by the death of her child.

375 R. Melville to Cecil, 7th May (*Scottish Calendar*, Bain, vol. ii.).

376 Craig being called before the council for this and reproved, he turned upon Bothwell and accused him of having murdered Darnley, ravished the Queen, and divorced his wife illegally (M'Crie's *Life of Knox*).

377 Drury to Cecil, 5th May 1567 (*Foreign Calendar*).

378 Mary had just created Bothwell Duke of Orkney (12th May).

379 Witchcraft was probably referred to, as Lady Buccleugh was a notoriously reputed witch.

380 Guzman says that Bothwell used to leave Mary for some days each week to stay with his divorced wife.

381 The marriage contract, signed the previous day (Labanoff, vol. ii. p. 23), sets forth at great length the reasons which have moved Mary to consent. The principal is that, 'being a widow, and yet of young flourishing age, and able to procreate and bring forth more children, she had been pressed by her nobles, in writing, to marry the Duke of Orkney rather than a foreigner, and acceded to their petition. In another document

signed the same day the Queen undertakes to refrain for ever from accusing or pro-securing any of the lords for signing the bond (the Ainslie bond) in favour of the marriage with Bothwell.

382 *Foreign Calendar,* 20th May 1567.

383 Tytler and Labanoff, vol. ii. p. 30.

384 Melville's *Memoirs.*

385 Melville says that his speech before the gentlewomen at supper was so filthy that he (Melville) and they left him. The same courtier says: 'He was so beastly and suspicious that he suffered her not to pass over a day in patience.' And Lethington told De Croc that from the day of the marriage there had been no end to Mary's tears and lamentations, for Bothwell 'would not allow her to look at, or be looked upon, by any one, for he knew well that she loved her pleasure' (Teulet, *Papiers d'Etat,* etc.).

386 He even wrote letters in the usual formula, bespeaking favourable dealing, to Queen Elizabeth and Cecil (*Scottish Calendar,* vol. ii. p. 330).

387 As an instance of this jealousy against French intervention in Scotland, Guzman urged Elizabeth repeatedly to get possession of the infant James rather than Catharine should do so. It suited Philip to have even Scotland Protestant rather than French (*Spanish Calendar,* vol. i.).

388 *Foreign Calendar,* vol. viii. p. 249.

389 De Croc to Charles IX, Labanoff, vol. ii. p. 126.

390 The account of Carberry Hill is given on the authority of de Croc's letter to Charles IX, 17th June (Labanoff, vol. vii.); Melville's *Memoirs;* and Drury's letters to Cecil (*Foreign Calendar,* vol. viii.).

391 Keith. See also Melville's *Memoirs.*

392 If this was the original document, it must have been taken from her during her captivity. Drury wrote to Cecil on the 28th October 1567 (*Foreign Calendar,* vol. viii. p. 363) that the bond had been burnt to ashes: 'the same not unknown to the Queen. The part that concerns her has been kept to be shown.' It is certain that Mary's knowledge of the signatures on the bond was a principal reason why Morton and Lethington, at least, were so anxious to prevent her release; and she constantly—though it seems unwisely—threatened them with her knowledge.

393 Melville's *Memoirs.*

394 But Mary appears subsequently to have had an interview with Lethington during her twenty-four hours' imprisonment in Edinburgh, and there are several versions of what

passed. The Queen appears to have refused to abandon Bothwell, and asked to be placed on board a ship with him to drift where the wind might carry them. According to Nau, Mary threatened Lethington, if he went too far, to disclose the fact that he had signed the murder bond, and said that she could hang him. Certainly Lethington was in mortal fear of her, and his strange, and almost incomprehensible, subsequent tergiversation is probably explained by that fact. He was always ready to advocate the worst measures against her, even her secret murder, whilst she was helpless, and to veer round to her favour when she seemed strong. He was her worst enemy after her surrender at Carberry, and yet he died for her when her cause grew hopeful.

395 *Foreign Calendar,* vol. viii. p. 256.

396 This George Dalgleish, with Ormiston, Powry, Hepburn of Bowton, Captain Blackater, and other henchmen of Bothwell, was shortly afterwards hanged for complicity in Darnley's murder. Sir James Balfour, whose share in the tragedy was as active as that of Bothwell himself, remained in high office and honour in Edinburgh at the time; as did another of the actual murderers, Morton's cousin Archibald Douglas, afterwards Scottish ambassador in England, a scoundrel so corrupt as to be almost grotesque. There are great numbers of his letters testifying to this in the *Hatfield Papers* (Hist. MSS. Com.).

397 *Spanish Calendar,* Hume, vol. i. p. 664. Murray in this important interview told the ambassador that Mary was fully cognisant of the intention to murder Darnley; and he made no concealment of his design to undertake the government of the country in consequence of this. Of course, being Murray, he made out that he could not do otherwise even in the interest of the Queen herself, whom he professed a wish to release from captivity. The nobles who had imprisoned her were his own partisans, he said, and held the strongholds, that he was powerless to attack in force. His only chance was to obtain possession of the government by fair means and then act for the best. As usual his 'best' was the best for James Stuart, Earl of Murray.

398 See their letters in the autumn of 1567 (*Foreign Calendar,* vol. viii.).

399 *Spanish Calendar,* Hume, vol. i. p. 663.

400 When Throckmorton was sent to Scotland by Elizabeth in July to remonstrate with the lords, and request them to release Mary on her promise that Darnley's murderers should be punished, Throckmorton wrote to Cecil (*Foreign Calendar,* vol. viii. p. 278) that he was 'sorry to see the Queen's disposition alters not towards the lords, for when all is done it is they who must stand her in more stead than the Queen, her cousin.'

Lethington's clever attempt to force Elizabeth's hand to help the lords by persuading Throckmorton that they were deep in negotiations with the French may be followed in *Foreign Calendar*, vol. viii.

401 *Foreign Calendar*, vol. viii. pp. 264, 268, etc.

402 Throckmorton to Cecil, 14th July (*Foreign Calendar*, vol. viii.).

403 *Ibid.*

404 Throckmorton to Cecil, 14th July (*Foreign Calendar*, vol. viii.).

405 Throckmorton to Cecil, 9th August 1567 (*Foreign Calendar*, vol. viii. p. 309).

406 *Spanish Calendar, Elizabeth,* vol. i., and *Foreign Calendar*, vol. viii.

407 Before Murray arrived Throckmorton reported (14th July): 'The chiefest lords here dare not show the Queen so much lenity as they would, for fear of the rage of the people. The women be most furious and impudent against the Queen, and yet the men be mad enough (*Scottish Calendar*, Bain, vol. ii.). There is no doubt that the agitation against her, especially in the Protestant pulpits, had rendered her extremely unpopular with the common people in Edinburgh, as no doubt it was intended to do by the rebel lords, as it enabled them to shift some of their responsibility on to the populace. The real difficulty to her release, almost on any terms, was, however, the fear of Morton and his party of her vengeance if she were free (*Spanish Calendar*, Hume, vol. i. p. 664). Murray in his two interviews with Mary in August seems to have treated her more as strict father-confessor than as a subject exhorting her to repentance for her crimes, of which he seemed to entertain no doubt' (Keith, p. 445). See also Teulet, *Papiers d'Etat.*

408 *Foreign Calendar*, vol. viii. p. 309.

409 She wrote, for instance, to Sir Robert Melville for a supply of brightcoloured silk, and for materials for embroidery at this time.

410 *Foreign Calendar*, vol. viii. p. 363.

411 *Foreign Calendar*, vol. viii., and *Spanish Calendar,* vol. ii.

412 Drury to Cecil, 20th March 1568 (*Foreign Calendar*, vol. viii.).

413 Only the day before her escape (1st May) she wrote two pathetic letters to Catharine and Elizabeth, praying them to aid her liberation by force, or she would remain a prisoner all her life. To Elizabeth she sent as a token the ring that Randolph had brought her from the English queen: '*Car vous sauey comme mon frère Moray a tout ce que jay.*' She prays passionately that her letters may be burned, and that none may know she has written, or it may cost the bearer his life, and cause her further suffering. To Catharine only she says that all Scotland will rise against Murray and Morton, if it sees that the

French are in earnest. It would not have been wise to tell Elizabeth that; but yet she was much more earnest for Mary's release than Catharine (Labanoff, vol. ii. p. 67).

414 *Spanish Calendar*, Hume, vol. ii. Her clothes, however, were sent to her a few days afterwards from Lochleven. Morton had for some time been trying to raise money in England on the jewels. Riccarton was also despatched from Niddry to capture Dunbar, but failed in the attempt.

415 Labanoff, vol. ii. p. 76.

416 *Spanish Calendar*, vol. ii.

417 *Scottish Calendar*, Bain, vol. ii. p. 409.

418 Knollys and Scrope to the Queen (*Scottish Calendar*, Bain, vol. ii. p. 416).

419 *Spanish Calendar*, Hume, vol. ii. p. 42.

420 He had been dealt with by the Spanish ambassador in Mary's favour at the time of the Darnley marriage (*Spanish Calendar*, Hume, vol. i.), and even before the Conference commenced there had been some talk of his possible marriage with Mary.

421 She doubtless thought that any evidence they produced against her would be exhibited to her, and if this had been done, she had a good retort, at least as against Lethington and Morton, by proving their complicity, as she repeatedly said she could do. This was doubtless the reason why letters were never officially shown to her.

422 *Scottish Calendar*, Bain, vol. ii. p. 526.

423 *Scottish Calendar*, vol. ii. Norfolk to Elizabeth, 11th October 1568, and the same to Pembroke, Leicester, and Cecil, *ibid.*

424 This is James Melville's account. Norfolk on his trial said that it was Lethington who had first made the suggestion to him. The balance of probability is in favour of Melville.

425 The deposition of the Bishop of Ross (*State Trials*).

426 Norfolk's speech (*State Trials*).

427 To prove how unwavering in this hour of distress was Mary's purpose to this end, a few lines of her letter of 24th September 1568 to her schoolfellow Elizabeth, Queen of Spain, may be quoted, in which it will be seen that she is almost willing to rejoice in her exile from Scotland as offering facilities for her projects against the Protestant *régime* in England:—'*Si les roys votre seigneur et frere* (*i.e.* Philip and Charles IX) *estoyent en repos mon desastre servirait a la Chrestiantay, car ma venue en ce pays m'a fait faire aqueintance ici par la quelle j'ay tant apris de l'etat ici que si j'avais tant soit peu d'esperance de secours d'ailleurs je mettrais la religion en su ou je mourais. Tout ce quartier* (*i.e.* the north of England) *ici est entièrement dedié á la foi Catholique, et pour ce respect et du droit*

que j'ai ici, peu de chose apprendrait cette reine à s'entremettre d'ayder aux subjects contre les princes. . . . Dieu merci je pense que j'ay gaigné une bonne parti de cœurs de gens de bien de ce pays depuis ma venue jusqu'à hasader ce qu'ils ont avec moi et pour ma querelle' (Labanoff, vol. ii. p. 186).

428 *Scottish Calendar,* Bain, vol. ii. p. 535.

429 When Leicester understood the real drift of the plan he took fright and told Elizabeth all about it, though she probably knew it already from Cecil's spies. Murray's Apologia for his feigned acceptance of the idea is printed as an Appendix to Robertson, and elsewhere.

430 Labanoff, *Recueil,* vol. ii. p. 344.

431 De Spes to Philip II, 8th January 1569 (*Spanish Calendar,* vol. ii.).

432 *Ibid.*

433 De Spes to Philip, 14th June 1569 (*Spanish Calendar,* vol. ii.).

434 *Spanish Calendar,* Hume, vol. ii.

435 This passage refers to the recent death of the child Lord Dacre, whose great revenues Norfolk enjoyed during his minority. Mary wishes that her own son were in Norfolk's keeping, or else that he were abroad. There is a purposely obscure passage in this letter, which Mary says will be explained verbally by her messenger. She says that the 'physicians write at length. They seem to love you marvellously, and not to mislike me.' I take 'physicians' to mean Alba and the Catholic party in Europe, and that they approved of the proposed marriage.

436 *Spanish Calendar,* Hume, vol. ii., where the ambassador's instructions and his violent letters will be found in full.

437 *Spanish Calendar,* Hume, vol. ii.

438 *Hatfield Papers,* vol. i.

439 Namely, to procure a divorce in Scotland between Mary and Bothwell.

440 In a private letter from La Mothe to Catharine, 1st September, he says that both Mary and Norfolk will be entirely governed by her; and that the duke had solemnly promised this on the honour of his hand; *'et que de sa part, apres la Reine sa maitresse, il démeurera, bien assuré serviteur du Roy et Vostre, tout le temps de sa vie.'* La Mothe calls Norfolk *'ung fort homme de bien, veritable et sécret,'* and begs in his name for six hundred French arquebusiers to occupy Dumbarton. It will be seen by this that Norfolk was indeed all things to all men.

441 *Spanish Calendar,* Hume, vol. ii.

442 La Mothe Fénélon was, indeed, the depositary of the marriage contract, and wrote strongly in favour of it to Catharine and her son. His having done so is a tribute to the clever diplomacy of Mary's English friends, who had convinced him that the Spanish ambassador had not been taken fully into their confidence, but was anxious to interfere in it and gain his King's approval. La Mothe says that the advocates of the marriage were in favour of an immediate consummation of it, in order to place before foreign princes a *fait accompli*. He says that Mary herself not only consented to the match, '*mais bien fort le désirer, comme entrant là en possession de la couronne d'Angleterre, apres sa cousine, vu la bonne part que le dit duc a avec toute la noblesse*' (*Correspondance de La Mothe Fénélon*). Catharine de Medici instructed La Mothe to forward the match in every possible way to prevent Mary from looking solely to Spain.

443 *Spanish Calendar*, Hume, vol. ii. p. 189. When Philip's answer came to the request for his approval of Norfolk's marriage—of course, too late, for the duke was under arrest when it arrived—the tone was very doubtful. 'If the marriage of the Duke of Norfolk with the Queen of Scots is effected in the way and with the objects of which you are informed, there is no doubt that it would be of great importance for the restoration of our true and ancient religion in England, and would console the good Catholics who are now so much oppressed. I desire these objects very warmly, as you know; but they must be very careful how they undertake the business, for if they make a mistake they will all be ruined. You did well in referring them to the Duke of Alba, who will advise them for the best. You will confine yourself to this in accordance with your orders, which you will not exceed.' Philip also expressed doubts of Norfolk's Catholicism.

444 Leicester, so long as he believed that Cecil, Bacon, and their party were to be the only sufferers, was a stout supporter of the plot; indeed the Duke of Norfolk said (*B. M. Harl. MSS.* 6353) that it was Leicester who first proposed it to him. He, with Arundel, Pembroke, and Lumley, signed a letter to Mary (in Haynes, p. 535) asking her to consent to the match, but imposing the condition that no attempt to seize the English crown should be made during the lifetime of Elizabeth. Leicester cannot long have remained ignorant of the fact that the main object was to change the religion of England on the first opportunity; and when he was convinced of this he told the Queen. Camden says, however, that it was some of Elizabeth's ladies that divulged the plot to her at Farnham, but La Mothe Fénélon, the French ambassador, gives a long report to his master (27th July) of Leicester's conversation with the Queen on the subject before Elizabeth started on her progress (*Correspondance de La Mothe Fénélon*).

445 *Hatfield Papers*, vol. i. p. 422.

446 Just before Norfolk's summons to court, de Spes wrote to the King: 'The Duke of Norfolk is here (in London) preparing all his friends. I will advise the Duke of Alba hourly.'

447 De Spes wrote to Philip II on the 14th September: 'A stronger guard has been placed around the Queen of Scots, although I understand that she will nevertheless soon find herself at liberty. All the north is now ready, and only awaits the release of the Queen of Scots. She is anxious to give your Majesty a full account of everything, as events are now coming to a head; but I wait until I see the affair commenced before I write at length. Perhaps God is now opening a wide door which shall lead to the great good of Christendom' (*Spanish Calendar*, vol. ii.). This letter by itself shows how great and imminent was the danger of Elizabeth and her government at the time. On the 30th September de Spes gives another instance of Mary's stout-heartedness. Writing to King Philip, he says: 'Considering the number of Norfolk's friends, I understand he cannot be ruined except by pusillanimity, and the Queen of Scotland has sent to urge him to behave valiantly, and not to fear for his life, which God would protect.'

448 *Spanish Calendar*, Hume, vol. ii. p. 229.

449 Mary wore Norfolk's token till the last hour of her life.

450 Labanoff, vol. iii.

451 15th January 1570 (Labanoff, vol. iii.).

452 She also suggested to the Spaniards, through the Bishop of Ross, that a few determined men might capture her by a *coup de main* and carry her to Spain, where she might organise an invasion of England.

453 Murray had recently been murdered by one of the Hamiltons, to Mary's undisguised delight at first; but her danger was rendered greater than ever when Lennox, the father of Darnley, became ruler of Scotland. His thirst for vengeance upon his daughter-in-law could only be sated by her execution.

454 Melville's *Memoirs*. Elizabeth replied to Dunfermline's doubts on the subject: 'I believed you were a wise man: you would press me to speak what is nowise necessary. You know that, for my honour, I must require pledges; but I think you may judge of yourself what might be best for me.'

455 How strongly this was the case is seen in de Spes's letter to King Philip of 2nd September 1570: 'I am entertaining the Queen of Scots, as your Majesty orders me, with letters praising her constancy and your desires for her liberation. Since the Pope's

bull was published, the Catholic gentlemen . . . are trying more earnestly than ever to shake off the yoke of the heretics, and the Bishop of Ross has come twice with letters of credence from his mistress, to say that the sons of the Earl of Derby, with the Catholic gentry of Lancashire, have determined to rise and seize the person of the Queen of Scots. They tell me that this would be connived at by one of the sons of the Earl of Shrewsbury who guards her, and that they can raise 10,000 foot and 1,000 horse, their only want being a supply of arquebusses, and some small supply of money for the horse. They are against the marriage with Norfolk, as he belongs to the Augsburg Confession, and they want a real Catholic. The Bishop of Ross tells me that Norfolk, either out of timidity or for some other reason, does not wish to leave prison, where he is only guarded by one gentleman. But Montague, Southampton, Lumley, Arundel, and many others will take up arms the moment the Lancastrians rise, as will the Earl of Worcester and his country, and the first thing will be to obtain possession of the Queen of Scots' (*Spanish Calendar,* Hume, vol. ii.).

456 The text of proposed treaty between Elizabeth and Mary is in Labanoff, vol. iii., and also in Haynes.

457 *Spanish Calendar,* vol. ii. p. 300.

458 *Spanish Calendar,* vol. ii. p. 300.

459 Amongst other things Mary, now quite cured of her infatuation for Bothwell, tells the Pope that she was carried away against her will to Dunbar, and violated by Bothwell, who pretended to have obtained a divorce from his wife, and that she was forced by him into a marriage. She begs the Pope to pronounce this union invalid, that she may marry Norfolk.

460 Labanoff, vol. iii.

461 The utter blackness of Norfolk's treason is increased by the solemn pledge he had taken in June 1570 as a condition of his release from custody. 'I do by this writing, signed by my own hand and sealed with my seal, freely, voluntarily, and absolutely grant, promise, and bind myself by the bond of my allegiance to your Majesty, my sovereign lady, never to offend your highness . . . but do utterly renounce and revoke all that which on my part anywise hath passed, with a full intention never to deal in that cause of marriage of the Queen of Scots, nor in any cause belonging to her.' At the very time this pledge was signed, Norfolk and Mary were in full and affectionate correspondence, and continued so afterwards.

462 The whole of the depositions are in *Hatfield Papers*, vol. i., and the circumstances are described in the *Spanish Calendar*, Hume, vol. ii.

463 Curiously enough this sum of money, £600, was received from the French ambassador, so that Mary and Norfolk were deceiving the Spaniards as well as they were others.

464 Wilson reports to Burghley that the bishop said: 'The Queen is not fit for any husband; for she first poisoned her husband the French king; again she hath consented to the murder of her late husband, Lord Darnley; thirdly, she matched with the murderer, and brought him (Darnley) to the field to be murdered; and last of all she pretended marriage with the Duke of Norfolk, with whom she would not long have kept faith, and the Duke would not have had the best days with her.' Well might Wilson add to this: 'Lord! what a people are these, and what a Queen! and what an Ambassador!' It may be safely surmised that, if Leslie really did say what is reported, he must have been crazy with terror at the time (*Hatfield Papers*, vol. i. p. 564).

465 See *State Trials* and letters from Norfolk to Cecil (*Hatfield Papers*, vol. i.).

466 Her agent in Flanders was now Lord Seton, and in March 1572 his confidential papers were seized on his way to Scotland, containing details of the aid that was being prepared by Alba for the liberation and restoration of Mary.

467 A full account of this man and his relations with Mary will be found in my book in Spanish, *Españoles è Ingleses en el Siglo* XVI.

468 Labanoff, vol. iv.

469 Ibid.

470 *Foreign Calendar.*

471 *Spanish Calendar.*

472 *Hatfield Papers*, vol. iii.

473 *Spanish Calendar*, Hume, vol. iii.